TELE-REVOLUTION

Telephone Competition

at the Speed of Light

A History of the Creation of a
Competitive Local Telephone Industry
1984 - 2000

by

Richard G. Tomlinson

First Printing May 2000

This book is available from:

Connecticut Research, Inc.
Box 1379
2906 Main Street
Glastonbury, CT 06033

Manufactured in the United States of America
Printed on 60# acid-free paper

∞

to Judy

TELE - REVOLUTION

Telephone Competition at the Speed of Light

A History of the Creation of a
Competitive Local Telephone Industry
1984 - 2000

Contents

"Don't put all your telecom eggs in one basket"

Marketing Cartoon Used by Teleport Communications Group—1988-1993

PROLOGUE

Successful revolutions leave as a legacy an air of inevitability.

The chaos, doubt and uncertainty that reigned during their creation fade from memory. Events lose their granularity. The possible roles of chance and accident are dismissed. The collective memory embraces an image of smoothly flowing history that seemingly could not have been resisted, diverted nor avoided. Discrete actions of individuals no longer seem so momentous. It becomes difficult to imagine how events might have evolved in any way other than how they actually transpired.

For those who were active participants in the revolution, it will always be quite different. They retain the knowledge of the sense of anxiety and of the reality of the threat of failure and defeat that accompanied those days. Rather than being fore-ordained, eventual outcomes seem more fragile and quixotic and more the product of isolated and sometimes arbitrary decisions and actions by individuals. The motivations of these individuals, as they knew them, were more complex and conflicted than they appear in retrospect. Revolutionary change proceeds unevenly. Virtue didn't always win.

Following the breakup of the AT&T Bell System in 1984, telecommunications in the United States and, ultimately, worldwide was launched on a new path. While this set the stage for the revolution, it was not *the revolution*. That came as the telecommunications industry began an erratic transition from monopoly to competition. In the process, the rules, the technology, the business structures, the markets and the consumers all were changed. State and federal laws were rewritten, and monopoly structures were undermined. A diverse collection of feisty, entrepreneurial competitors arose to challenge the established local telephone companies. Entering the year 2000, these competitors, not one of which existed in 1983, were well on their way to *becoming* the establishment.

This book documents the creation of the competitive local telephone industry and analyzes its history in both its corporate and human dimensions. It seeks to reveal what transpired behind the scenes as well as on the public stage, to illuminate the why and the how and, perhaps, to gain insight into the "what next."

1

1. INTRODUCTION

Since its birth with the first telephone patents in 1876, the telecommunications industry in the United States has largely operated as either a de facto or an ordained monopoly. There was, following the expiration of the original basic Bell patents, a brief period at the turn of the century of multiple, competing telephone companies.[1] However, Theodore Vail, the architect of the AT&T Bell System, in the early part of the 20th century, argued successfully that a regulated monopoly could provide the country with better and cheaper telephone service than either open competition or government ownership.[2,3]

Telephone companies became monopoly franchise holders under the control of state and federal regulators. Congress passed the defining legislation entitled The Communications Act of 1934. The Federal Communications Commission (FCC) was given responsibility for interstate regulation of the industry and the state public utility commissions (PUCs) for intrastate regulation.

Over the years, following a pattern familiar to many industries, advancing technology eroded the ground from under what had previously constituted a "natural monopoly". Microwave and later fiber optic technology made the construction of alternative long distance networks by non-franchise holders economically feasible. In the 1960s, Microwave Communications, Inc. (MCI) launched a 20-year battle which ultimately ended AT&T's monopoly grip on long distance transmission.[4]

By the 1980s AT&T, faced with operating partially in competitive markets and partially in monopoly markets and beset by its third major Sherman Act antitrust suit, suddenly proposed a sweeping, Solomonic solution. It would voluntarily break up the giant Bell System by retaining its competitive long distance and equipment operations and splitting off the local service monopoly operations. On January 8, 1982, the Justice Department and AT&T agreed upon a settlement, and two years later it was implemented. Seven independent Regional Holding Companies were formed to carry on the "natural monopoly" business of local telephone service. Although the technically correct designation for these entities was

3

Regional Holding Company, that designation was rarely used at the working level. Throughout the industry, the seven companies were commonly referred to as the Regional Bell Operating Companies or just the RBOCs. To the popular press, they were simply the"Baby Bells ."

At the time, it seemed impossible that local telephone service could be anything but a monopoly. With millions of miles of installed copper wire linking customers to incumbent telephone company facilities, the creation of an alternative, competitive network appeared impractical.

Furthermore, even if technology should create a practical means to by-pass these "bottle neck" facilities, the incumbent telephone companies looked invulnerable from a business prospective. Collectively in 1984, the U.S. telephone industry had 113 million access lines and $88 billion in revenue.[5] Much of this strength was concentrated in the seven holding companies although there were more than 1,000 small, independent, mostly-rural telephone companies which had never been part of the Bell System.

Divestiture had suddenly created seven of the largest corporations in America, all of similar size and with combined revenues of $58 billion.[6] These massive RBOCs dominated telephone service in their respective regions, particularly in the major cities.

NYNEX from its New York City base controlled New York, five New England States and a small portion of Connecticut. Bell Atlantic from its Philadelphia headquarters served the seven mid-Atlantic states. Ameritech in Chicago had the five Great Lakes states. Atlanta-based BellSouth operated in the nine southern states. Southwestern Bell in St. Louis had operations in Texas and four adjacent states. Pacific Telesis, headquartered in San Francisco, served only California and Nevada. Denver and Minneapolis-centric U S WEST had a sprawling territory covering the fourteen more thinly populated western states.

The richer, more densely populated urban business markets of these RBOCs were the primary targets of initial competition. Led by the formation of the Teleport Communications Group in New York in 1985, a competitive local telecommunications industry arose, grew, spread across the country and changed everything.

By the year 2000 the barriers to competition would be breached in theory, but most Americans would still receive their local telephone service from their traditional phone company. The hand writing, however, would be on the wall; and the revolutionaries would be morphing into the establishment.

But it all began in New York City.

---

[1] See for example, Gerald W. Bock, *"The Telecommunications Industry, The Dynamics of Market Structure,"* (Cambridge, MA, Harvard University Press, 1981) 109-125

[2] In the 1910 AT&T Annual Report Vail both discussed the benefits of regulation and wrote of the necessity for being protected from competition, "If there is to be state control and regulation, there should also be state protection - protection to a corporation striving to serve the whole community ... from aggressive competition which covers only that part which is profitable." This argument against "cream-skimming" would later be routinely raised by telephone companies facing potential competition.

[3] Bock, 158-159

[4] See, for example, Larry Kahaner,*"On The Line, The Men Of MCI - Who Took On AT&T, Risked Everything, And Won!"* (New York: Warner Books, Inc., 1986)

[5] Hyman, Toole & Avellis,"The New Telecommunications Industry: Evolution and Organization .vol. I," (Public Utilities Reports, Inc. and Merrill Lynch, Pierce, Fenner & Smith, 1987) 171

[6] Hyman, Toole & Avellis,*"The New Telecommunications Industry: Evolution and Organization, vol. II, 2nd Edition,"* (Public Utilities Reports, Inc. and Merrill Lynch, Pierce, Fenner & Smith, 1989) 37-61

2. A PORT FOR THE INFORMATION AGE

The Teleport Concept

New York City has always been a port. In the late 1970s, maintaining that role in the Information Age appeared to be in danger. Planners within the Port Authority of New York and New Jersey feared that failure to become a new kind of port—a major information port—would cause the city to lose stature and to fall out of the race into the Information Age.

With more than half the jobs in the city involving information processing and nearly one third of the country's international traffic passing through New York City, communications—the life blood of modern commerce—was considered crucial. But the facilities of the telecommunications gateway to America were faltering under the flood of voice, data and video traffic they were required to carry.

From analog voice calls to digital bit streams, communications traffic growth had been relentless ever since World War II. In every direction, webs of cable, wire, radio, fiber optic and microwave transmission paths converged on New York City. When this great wave of information surged into New York, it often found itself slowed by an aging, copper wire infrastructure that choked it with limited bandwidth, contaminated it with noise and frustrated it with outages. Even the newest technology, communications satellites which used microwave paths beamed overhead, was impeded. Due to dense electromagnetic interference, there were few satellite earth stations in or around Manhattan. Television signals destined for international locations had to first be transmitted on expensive, dedicated private lines all the way to satellite ground stations in West Virginia or Maine.

To the Port Authority, this problem seemed analogous to all the other "port" problems. What New York City lacked was a "window to the satellites" linked to a high-speed network on the ground. What New York needed was a collection of earth stations in a "farm" connected to fiber optic networks running throughout the region … a telecommunications port or "Teleport." "It is like an airport[1]," said Guy Tozzoli, director of the Port Authority's World Trade department. "Every major city needs an airport. Well, this is

7

an airport for communications. We're going to make communications between people easier and cheaper. To take advantage, to do business, we've got to be ready for the future."

The metro area was concerned that it might lose its appeal as a corporate location and that companies might move to remote areas with better satellite facilities. This fear seemed to be confirmed when Citicorp moved its credit card processing operation.[2] The move took 2,000 jobs from Huntington, Long Island in 1981 and relocated them to a satellite-linked location more than half way across the country in Sioux Falls, South Dakota.

The Teleport was envisioned as more than simply earth stations and fiber links. Just as airports are more than runways and aircraft and seaports are more than docks and ships, the Port Authority envisioned a communications-enhanced office park with facilities for data processing, television programming and other broadband services.[3] This state-of-the art communications center would provide as Tozzoli said, "whatever is needed to keep important businesses in the Northeast and to attract others. It will be as secure as a military installation with only one entrance."

The Port Authority Takes Control

Whether the Port Authority's involvement in the Teleport project was within its responsibility was at least open to question. The Port Authority, a for-profit, quasi-governmental agency, had been formed in 1921 to end a century of squabbling between New York and New Jersey over waterway boundaries. Amounting to a third state overlapping the two, its mission was to coordinate, plan and develop "terminal, transportation and other facilities of commerce." The "other facilities" phrase would be used to justify the Teleport project, just as it had been invoked earlier to justify the massive and controversial World Trade Center building project.

The Port Authority was not created with taxing authority but was given control of bridges, tunnels and other transportation facilities and permitted to levy tolls and to develop profit-making, transportation-related enterprises. Without tax revenue nor the right to pledge the states' credit, projects had to be financed by the sale of bonds. As a result the Port Authority sought projects that could show assured profitability in a reasonably short time and resisted calls to invest in the infrastructure of deficit-ridden mass transit.

Its authority to engage in a real estate construction project such as the World Trade Center had been challenged at the time but had been successfully defended in litigation that went all the way to the U.S. Supreme Court. As a part of a political compromise, the Port Authority reluctantly agreed to some involvement in mass transit by taking over and modernizing the decaying, PATH, trans-Hudson, commuter line and to incorporating the subway terminal facilities into the World Trade Center complex.

The Port Authority simply assumed that its mandate would cover the Teleport project and, having won the World Trade Center legal battle, was not seriously challenged. For the Teleport project, the Port Authority turned to the Communications Satellite Corporation (COMSAT) to select the best from among 28 available sites for an earth station satellite farm.[4] COMSAT selected a city-owned, 350-acre location on Staten Island as the best compromise between freedom from electromagnetic interference and proximity to the corporate office buildings in Manhattan. The site, essentially a junk-strewn wetland, was barren and it lacked roads and utilities. COMSAT considered and then declined to enter into a joint venture partnership with the Port Authority to develop the Teleport but indicated its interest in leasing space as a tenant when the facility was completed.

Enter Merrill Lynch And Western Union

Rebuffed by COMSAT, the Port Authority solicited Merrill Lynch, a progressive telecommunications user and Western Union, a venerable telecommunications carrier, to participate in a joint venture to develop the Teleport. Merrill Lynch was rumored to be considering moving some of its data-processing operations to Princeton, New Jersey, if they could be linked to Manhattan via fiber optic cable. Stanley Welland, a strategic technology planning manager at Merrill Lynch, denied the rumor but indicated that his company wanted a role in the rapidly expanding telecommunications world.[5]

Within Merrill Lynch's data processing department, they found enthusiastic support for the venture.[6] Gerald Ely, who had joined Merrill Lynch in 1969 as a 30-year-old project manager, had spent the previous eight years as part of a three-man team designing and developing Merrill Lynch's advanced communications network. High speed local data links and satellite distribution to global branch offices were important components needed to implement the Merrill Lynch network architecture covering its far-flung offices.

Western Union, though in decline, was still a significant telecommunications carrier. As the original domestic satellite carrier with the first Westar launch in 1974, it remained a force in the industry. Westar satellites provided video services primarily for the broadcast and cable television industries and provided bulk transmission for other carriers and corporations transmitting large amounts of data.

Merrill Lynch formed a subsidiary, Merrill Lynch Telecommunications, with Gerald Ely as its Chairman to enter into the joint venture. The Teleport venture was formed between the Port Authority, Merrill Lynch Telecommunications and Western Union Telecommunications. Ownership between Merrill Lynch and Western Union was, after some negotiation, divided 60% and 40%, respectively.[7] The City of New York agreed to spend $15 million on roads and infrastructure and to lease the land to the Port Authority for 40 years.

Rosario P. (Russ) Romanelli, the President of Western Union International, was named President and CEO of Merrill Lynch Telecommunications, reporting to Ely. Romanelli had begun his career as an engineer and attorney and for the previous ten years had served as the President of WUI, the major international telex carrier[8] (Western Union had been forced to divest WUI in 1969).

The Teleport Idea "May Be Valid Only In a Limited Degree"

The Teleport, as initially conceived, was projected to cost about $220 million and take five years to complete.[9] The Staten Island facility would consist of 17 satellite dishes, making it the world's largest satellite cluster. Significant construction would be required as each dish would be shielded by thick earth walls to minimize electromagnetic interference. Thirteen three-story buildings were planned to provide two million square feet of office space for companies using the Teleport facility. The fiber link would begin at the World Trade Center in Manhattan and cross under the Hudson River through the PATH tunnel to the Port Authority terminal in Jersey City. From the Jersey City hub, the fiber would continue south through Bayonne to the Staten Island Teleport, but would also fan out to other corporate concentrations.

Originally it had been hoped that ground breaking for the Teleport could begin in January 1982 with the first leg of the fiber installation to begin the following month. There were repeated delays in obtaining the necessary permits and construction agreements. Ground breaking did not occur until the summer of 1983, and fiber installation began in August 1983. (In fact, final contracts among the four parties to the Teleport project were not signed until June 1984.)

Just as the project was finally getting under way, support from the joint venture partners began to weaken. The brokerage business was in a slump in 1983, reducing Merrill Lynch's profits; and Western Union was entering a period of rapid financial decline in its core business. Enthusiasm for aggressive investment in the Teleport project ebbed.

Throughout 1983 and 1984, Romanelli found himself fighting off criticism and pessimism about the Teleport project. Critics began to challenge the basic concept that communications—satellite or other —were really important factors in corporate location decisions. Even consultants working for the Port Authority concluded that the rationale behind Teleport "may be valid only in a limited degree."[10] A survey of prospective Teleport tenants by A. D. Little found that while communications-related features would influence the decision of corporations to establish operations at the Teleport, cost and geographic factors were much more important drivers at the time.

The Port Authority increased its efforts to sell the Teleport idea and hired sales personnel to call on prospective Teleport tenants. However, by September 1983 only five customers had signed up and two of them—Western Union Telecommunications and Merrill Lynch Telecommunications—were members of the joint venture. Meanwhile private companies had moved more rapidly, erected their own satellite antennas within reach of Manhattan and were operational. These included Atlantic Satellite in Northvale, New Jersey, Hughes Communications in Brooklyn and The Satellite Connection in Carteret, New Jersey.

A new potential impediment to the Teleport project was introduced when New York City's Director of Franchises, Morris Tarshis, asserted that Teleport should be required to obtain a city franchise before running fiber cable within the city limits.[11] Cable television franchisees were required to pay 5% of their gross revenues to the city for the use of city rights-of-way. Tarshis thought that TCG should also pay.

Teleport challenged Tarshis's assertion on the basis of an ancient agreement. They argued that since its Western Union partner had received permission to construct underground cables, without fees, under special state legislation passed in 1848, the current venture should enjoy the same immunity. Cable television operators and other communications providers who were paying franchise fees objected to Teleport's receiving special exemption. After some ne-gotiation, the city entered into an agreement to allow Teleport to pro-ceed without paying a franchise fee, provided it served only business customers and refrained from offering service to residential customers.[12]

Teleport Communications

While the Teleport project struggled to overcome obstacles to its implementation, the precise nature of business to be pursued by the partners, once the facility was complete, had not been defined. The future business entity, Teleport Communications, was incorporated in Delaware in March 1983; and its physical organization began to take shape during the year although its business objectives were still hazy.

Merrill Lynch Telecommunications had always planned to make use of the Teleport to provide satellite communications from New York to Merrill Lynch offices worldwide. One idea was simply for Teleport Communications to sell or lease transport on this network to other companies in New York with similar needs. A business plan was prepared and submitted to the Merrill Lynch financial de-partment. It was reviewed by John Scarpati (later to play a leading role in Teleport Communications) and rejected because the plan showed no significant return on the proposed investment.[13]

Bob Annunziata

Gerald Ely continued to build the Merrill Lynch Telecom organiza-tion and knew that he had to find a "spark plug" to get the operation running. During his tenure in the Merrill Lynch MIS department, Ely had been the customer of an energetic and creative salesman from AT&T. Now Ely turned to this man to drive his organization. Robert Annunziata, AT&T's national account manager for the

Merrill Lynch account, was asked to join the Merrill Lynch Telecom team. Annunziata would ultimately become a central figure not only in the creation and rise of Teleport Communications but also in the formation of the competitive telecommunications industry in the United States.

Annunziata, a Long Island native, had gone to work for AT&T straight out of high school in an entry-level technician's job. Although lacking a college education, he took aggressive advantage of AT&T's extensive employee education opportunities. AT&T offered an array of free courses covering a vast range of technical and business subjects. Bright and ambitious, Annunziata put in a full day's work and then devoured courses at night.

He rose rapidly within AT&T for seventeen years. (The legend at Teleport Communications asserted that Annunziata never worked for anyone at AT&T more than six months before taking over their job.) He ultimately won the prized responsibility of servicing the account of Merrill Lynch, AT&T's fifth or sixth largest customer. But Annunziata was told that without a college degree he would rise no higher in AT&T.[14] The writing was on the wall; and when Merrill Lynch invited Annunziata to leave AT&T and join their in-house telecommunications staff, he readily accepted.

The Annunziata Strategy For Teleport

Annunziata had been on the job only three weeks when on August 23, 1983, he wrote a memorandum to President Romanelli entitled, "Teleport Communications—Main Line of Business." The memo stated:

> Teleport Communications' major business objective
> is to provide transmission access to satellites, inter-
> state carriers and corporate private networks within
> the metropolitan area.[15]

Without arguing the merits of being in the satellite business itself, Annunziata focused on the possibilities presented by the fiber optic network given the pending breakup of AT&T's Bell Telephone System. AT&T had agreed in 1982 to settle the Department of Justice's anti-trust suit against it by divesting itself of its local telephone companies.

On January 1, 1984, that divestiture would be implemented; and AT&T would be only in the long distance telephone business. Interexchange (long distance) carriers like AT&T would have to pay "access charges" to the local telephone companies for carrying the call the "last mile" to the end user. These access charges could amount to 40% of the revenue of the call. Annunziata was keenly aware that the access charges would become a big issue and that Teleport's fiber network could provide a way to by-pass the local phone company and avoid these charges.

> With the breakup of the Bell System there are two major voids in the communications industry that will be business opportunities: local access and full service agent. Teleport Communications will focus on the local access issue ...
>
> The local access service will prove to be profitable and receive much public attention. Today only New York Telephone has a local distribution network in the NY-metropolitan area with a T-1 (*a digital circuit carrying 24 voice channels*) copper system and a fiber optic ring around Manhattan.
>
> There is basically no other local distribution alternative today (cable companies are beginning to expand their services with other than cable programming services). NYT has the basic monopoly on local distribution; they are seeking local access line surcharges to keep residential access services from dramatically increasing. While this is a popular effort for the residential user, business would be encouraged to seek alternatives to reduce major increases in their communications costs.
>
> Teleport Communications will install a fiber optic network in the metropolitan area. Teleport Communications' service is access from a customer's premises to satellite earth stations, interstate carriers or another customer premise, at an attractive rate, less than NYT.[16]

Annunziata laid out the business opportunities in terms of four market segments.

1. Private corporation networks within the metropolitan area.

2. Satellite access for media, communications carriers or private corporations.

3. Teleport industrial park services.

4. Access to interstate carrier offices or (New York Telephone) offices

• Segment 1 and 2 services provide local private network and video/radio access to satellites. This is a basic service and will require Teleport Communications Marketing Account Executives to stimulate the business.

• Segment 3 ... It appears that we need to determine what type of service to provide in the park that will attract the user we want. A clear real estate/communication service has not been developed. Why should data centers move to Staten Island? Why should any corporation move to Staten Island?

• Segment 4 is the most important. While Teleport Communications personnel will be needed for the initial contacts and sales, unlimited re-buy service can be ordered once arrangements are established. Our service will be Metropolitan access for interstate carriers to clients premises or (New York Telephone) central offices.

We can provide express access service from a building directly to a communications carrier central office switch by-passing not only (New York Telephone) cable, but also its central office switch. The interstate carrier could not only provide private line services, but long distance and WATS service as well ... We will be using Merrill Lynch as the test client...

This suggested strategy to commercialize the Teleport network would be debated for several months within Merrill Lynch. However, it was clear that the fiber network would be as important, and possibly more important than the earth stations.

Howard Bruhnke, Fiber Optic Network Builder

Annunziata looked for someone to build the Teleport fiber network. He turned to the person who had installed the New York Telephone company's fiber ring around Manhattan, Howard Bruhnke. Bruhnke had had a distinguished career at New York Telephone and NYNEX spanning 36 years from 1948 to 1984. He introduced the first fiber optic system for New York Telephone in 1979. In fact, it was the first operational fiber optic link in the Bell System.[17] After the breakup of the AT&T Bell System and the formation of NYNEX, he had responsibility for all fiber deployment throughout the New York and New England Telephone areas.

While at NYNEX and New York Telephone, Bruhnke had tried to spread fiber optic expertise within the telephone company. He would send veteran crafts persons to lightwave training classes to learn fiber optic technology. However, to his dismay, after the training was complete, they did not want to work on fiber projects. They would drift back to the old and comfortable way of working with copper technology. By 1982 Bruhnke had gotten fed up and decided that he needed to train only the young engineers who came with "uncluttered minds" and a thirst to work with new technology. He wanted young engineers like Mike Aldridge, freshly graduated from Fairfield University. He found Mike, still looking for a job, coaching Bruhnke's son's summer basketball team and hired him and said, "I'm going to train you to be a lightwave design engineer."

When Annunziata called Howard Bruhnke and said, "How would you like to build a fiber optic ring for us?" Bruhnke promptly re-tired from NYNEX. In August 1984, Bruhnke came on board as Vice President of Engineering for Teleport Communications.[18] Bruhnke played such a key role in creating Teleport that Annunziata often referred to him as a "co-founder." To the Teleport engineers, he became a venerated father figure.

Bruhnke called Mike Aldridge at New York Telephone and said, "I want you to come over here in 30 days." Although his grandfather had been a New York Telephone man for 40 years, Mike did not hesitate. With divestiture, no one knew what would happen next. Some were saying that the traditional telephone companies would just become "wire pullers." Mike figured that since he had no children, he could afford to take a chance on this crazy new company. On Oct. 1, 1994, he started work at Teleport Communications. On his first day on the job he attended a meeting of the staff at the company headquarters on the 26th floor of the World Trade Center. The group was so small that it comfortably fit around one conference table. In a few years he would rise to be the Director of New York Operations for the company.

New Teleport Leadership

In October 1984, the Teleport satellite facility was still not expected to be operational until 1985. After two years of frustrating delays in launching the Teleport project, Romanelli resigned and went off to start a new company, Submarine Lightwave Cable Co., to build a new trans-Atlantic cable.[19] Gerald Ely, to whom he had reported, assumed his duties. The Annunziata plan was adopted.

Teleport Communications entered 1985 with no facilities completed, but with everything in motion. It ended 1985 with the backbone of its 150-mile (miles of cable not route-miles) fiber optic network and four earth stations (three of which it owned) in operation.

The first earth station customer and also first Teleport industrial park tenant was the Catholic Telecommunications Network of America (CTNA) broadcasting five hours of daily programming to 86 affiliates across the country.[20] CTNA went on the air in April 1985.

In June 1985 the earth station in the Teleport facility that was owned and operated by COMSAT International and TRT Communications began providing international service to Europe and the Caribbean. In August, NETCOM signed a contract to route 600 hours a month of programming through the Teleport. Another major video client was Private Satellite Network, a direct broadcast satellite company founded to create private television broadcasting for corporations. The commercial satellite operations at the Teleport facility were well under way.

Using technicians from Western Union, Petrocelli Electric and Harris Corp., Bruhnke drove the fiber network deployment to completion. Along the way his engineers created two new innovations: inner ducting for underground conduit so that half-inch cable could be pulled in a cost-effective manner and aluminum cladding for fiber cable to replace the traditional polyvinyl chloride which produced toxic fumes when burned.

Where possible, the network used Western Union and Port Authority rights-of-way and conduits. The 150-mile fiber network not only linked the Staten Island Teleport to the World Trade Center, it spread throughout Manhattan and into Brooklyn and Queens. It linked Jersey City and Newark and extended south to North Brunswick and Princeton, New Jersey. Thus Teleport's network competed directly for customers served by the operating companies of two RBOCs, NYNEX's New York Telephone and Bell Atlantic's New Jersey Bell.

The High Security, High Reliability, "Self-Healing," Fiber Network

Annunziata understood that the major marketing feature for the Teleport network was that it promised higher quality and higher reliability for broadband data and voice circuits than was available from the RBOCs. To ensure that Teleport could deliver on these promises, the network had to have extraordinary robustness, redundancy, route diversity and physical security. It must be able to survive both internal component failures and major external disasters and traumas.

While the network control center would be developed at the satellite farm on Staten Island, the major network node was located in the heart of Manhattan. The logical centralized and secure placement for this network node in the city was in the bowels of the massive towers of the Port Authority's World Trade Center. Support for the two 110-story towers went down 70 feet to bedrock. In the lowest basement, level six or B-6, Teleport constructed its network node. This well-concealed location appeared to be safe from anything short of a nuclear attack on New York City.

The Teleport network electronics featured new multiplexers (multiplexers combine many digitized voice grade channels into a single bit stream which can be sent over a common shared circuit making more efficient use of the network) from Telco Systems, Inc. of Norwood, MA. These multiplexers were built for high reliability. This included the ability to automatically switch either redundant internal components and/or external fiber paths in the event of an electronic or network failure. With simultaneous transmission for each circuit on two paths, any loss of signal on the primary path caused the multiplexer to switch automatically to the secondary path in about five hundredths of a second. In such an event, even at high data transmission rates, little information would be lost; and the end user might never be aware of the incident. If the two fiber paths were diversely routed, this "self-healing" function could occur even if one fiber cable were completely cut.

Digital Transmission

When digital transmission was introduced into the Bell System, a hierarchy of standardized formats was established. A single analog voice-grade channel, when digitized, requires 64,000 bits per second for transmission and is designated as a DS-0 (Digital Signal - Level Zero). By multiplexing multiple DS-0s onto the same physical circuit, the network capacity can be greatly increased. The first level in the multiplexed hierarchy is called DS-1 (Digital Signal - Level One). A DS-1 carries 24 DS-0s plus some signaling information. Therefore the DS-1 bit rate, 1.544 million bits per second (1.544 Mbps), is slightly greater than 24 times 64,000 bits per second.

A DS-1 signal carried over a copper circuit is called a T-1. T-carrier circuits were first introduced into the AT&T network in 1962, greatly increasing the capacity of the existing wire plant. While these multiplexed signals were originally used only internally within the telephone network, they gradually came to be used for high capacity customer traffic. In 1977, AT&T tariffed a T-1 offering for sale to customers; but the price was high, and there were few buyers.

When Teleport Communications completed its fiber network, it offered transport at DS-1 rates and above. In fact, its first product offering was a DS-3 dedicated, private line transmission between any two locations on its fiber network. DS-3 carries 28 DS-1s (*i.e.*, 672 DS0s) as a 45 Mbps bit stream. This was a service not offered at the time by New York Telephone, the local operating company of the RBOC, NYNEX. Customers who wanted T-3 transmission were required to purchase 28 T-1s, which was the only tariffed offering by New York Telephone.

Teleport Communications had an enormous advantage. A DS-3 circuit from Teleport could be five to ten times less expensive than 28

T-1s from New York Telephone for linking the same end points. In addition, the Teleport fiber circuits came with built-in "self healing" functionality (automatic switching to an alternative circuit in event of failure of the primary circuit) at no extra cost.

NYNEX went to the New York Public Utility Commission in order to stop the Teleport Communications' DS-3 offering. Their claim that Teleport shouldn't be able to do this was quickly turned back by the PUC response of "Yes, they can and you should too."

"Up Your Megabits"

Demand for and acceptance of the Teleport DS-3 offering was very strong. The Teleport fiber network route had been carefully chosen to include the local switch nodes (called "Points of Presence" or "POPs") of the interexchange (long distance) carriers. High reliability, high speed circuits, such as Teleport's fiber-based DS-3, were in great demand by the carriers. Large carriers, like AT&T, which had multiple POPs in the New York area, needed high reliability interconnection between POPs. Smaller carriers needed their POPs connected to those of the larger carriers (such as AT&T, MCI and Sprint) from whom they leased some of their network capacity.

In addition to the higher quality of their self-healing, fiber network and lower prices for equivalent transmission capacity, Teleport could turn up service more rapidly than the New York Telephone Company which could take six to twelve months to fill a T-1 order. Teleport could activate on-net locations within 30 days.

Teleport's first customer went operational on the fiber in April of 1985. Traffic grew rapidly, both from corporate and long distance carrier customers.

At Teleport headquarters, employees plotted the progress on a wall chart with the motto, "Up Your Megabits!" By year end the traffic had reached one thousand Mbps; equivalent to 15,600 voice grade channels.[21]

Isolated Networks Die

While this early rapid growth was satisfying, Annunziata knew that Teleport was serving a limited, niche market that could soon be saturated. Although on a national scale, the local telephone market was a huge market, the market addressable by competitive networks was limited.

The combined revenues of the local telephone companies in the United States for all services in 1984 were $77.6 billion.[22] Of this total, that due to dedicated transport service - the service theoretically addressable by competitive companies - was much smaller: about $3 billion in size.[23] In reality, however, the addressable market for competitive companies was only a fraction of this $3 billion due to the limited reach of their networks.[24]

Teleport's network was an isolated universe, linking only 40 buildings. Traffic could not move between the Teleport network and the ubiquitous networks of New York Telephone and New Jersey Bell. In the telephone company networks the unswitched dedicated transport circuits were frequently routed through the same telephone company central offices which provided switched service. Within the central office facility, this unswitched traffic was concentrated, cross-connected and routed. Without access to these central office points of concentration, there was no convenient way for Teleport to interconnect with this traffic.

If Teleport could only carry traffic between locations physically connected to its own fiber optic network, its future was limited. Extending the fiber network required enormous capital. Construction of the core fiber network could cost $100,000 per mile, and links connecting each new building to the core network could cost $50,000 to $100,000. Furthermore, the cost of adding new customers could be expected to increase as the network expanded from serving the highest density urban centers to reach smaller and/or more dispersed buildings.

The lesson of telecommunications history was that isolated networks ultimately could not survive in competition with a carrier with a ubiquitous network. After all, AT&T had built the Bell network at the turn of the century by refusing to connect local telephone companies to its "Long Lines" until they capitulated and agreed to become members of the Bell System.

When the original Bell patents expired in the mid-1890s, hundreds of new companies entered the telephone business. By 1902 there were 3,000 independent (non-Bell) telephone companies[25]. Isolated networks were a great inconvenience to customers. In many cities, business desks contained multiple telephones and multiple phone directories so that customers connected to the various independent networks could reach each other. Theodore Vail showed the power of interconnection in building the Bell System. By refusing to interconnect the AT&T long distance network with non-Bell local networks, he forced them to join the system or sell out or be squeezed out.

Vail unified the telephone network under the 1908 motto: "One Policy, One System, Universal Service." Ultimately the threat of anti-trust action caused AT&T to stop refusing interconnection to independent telephone companies, but consolidation in the urban areas was essentially already complete.

Teleport wanted access to central offices in order to interconnect its dedicated transport circuits with those of the telephone companies. Annunziata knew that Teleport would not win such interconnection rights without a regulatory fight. He needed a clever, telecommunications-savvy lawyer who could take on the telephone companies and make interconnection happen.

The "Two Bobs"

Following corporate policy, Annunziata filled out a formal requisition for a Vice President of Regulatory and turned it over to the personnel department of Merrill Lynch. The assignment was passed on to the outside head hunter who usually recruited for the semi-executive positions in the Merrill Lynch MIS department.

The head hunter had a problem. His contacts were almost exclusively in the world of IBM computing, not in telecommunications. He called his IBM friends to ask if they could help. He was told that there was a small branch of IBM with its foot in a telecommunications joint venture called Satellite Business Systems (SBS). The venture had failed to live up to expectations and was being disbanded. It was suggested that perhaps some of the lawyers in its associated regulatory department would be available. He might have some luck there.

SBS was a joint venture of COMSAT, Aetna Life and Casualty and IBM. It was formed to provide high speed data transmission via satellite links. In 1982, it had been the first company to launch a commercial satellite from the space shuttle. However, the business demand for massive, long range corporate data transport had been disappointing; and the venture was dissolving.

Interviewing the legal staff of SBS in McLean, VA, the recruiter did not find anyone who was both a suitable prospect and also willing to move to New York. He did, however, receive multiple referrals to a former SBS employee now living in New York. The prospect was a young lawyer, Bob Atkinson, who had formerly worked for SBS as the Counsel for Government and International matters and was now working for RCA Global Communications as the Director of New Services Planning and Development. Atkinson had regulatory, public policy and telecommunications business experience.

Atkinson had a reputation as a mover and a shaker. Early in his career, he had served as Government Relations representative for ITT World Communications and had helped found the Ad Hoc Committee for Competitive Telecommunications (ACCT). ACCT (later CompTel) was a trade association based in Washington, D.C. to promote the development of a competitive long distance telecommunications industry.

Contacting Atkinson, the recruiter quickly explained that the Teleport Communications facility on Staten Island had one international and three domestic earth stations operational and that the job involved being Vice President of Regulatory. Atkinson's response was, "that is not a job since there are no significant regulatory problems remaining for earth stations and international satellite transmission." The recruiter replied that the job related to some new ideas, but that he personally really didn't understand it and that only Bob Annunziata at Teleport could really explain it.

Annunziata's office was on the 27th floor of the World Trade Center. Atkinson decided that since he passed through the World Trade Center every day on the way to his job at RCA, it would not be inconvenient to stop in and, at least, meet Annunziata. The recruiter said, "He gets in early, come by at 8:00 am."

The interview was brief. Annunziata essentially said that Teleport Communications was not really about earth stations and satellites any more. It was the fiber optic network that would form the basis of the future business. He said that the plan was to take on the local telephone company. Did Bob like the challenge? "That," Atkinson responded, "could be interesting. Let's talk."

Annunziata and Atkinson found they shared a common passion for bringing competition to the local telecommunications market. Both were highly self-confident, articulate and aggressive. They had a strong affinity and formed a natural team. This team ultimately had such visibility and impact on the course of competitive telecommunications that they became known throughout the industry simply as, "the two Bobs."

Atkinson missed his first day on the job in October as the World Trade Center was closed due to the threat of hurricane Gloria. When he did report, Annunziata's assignment was succinct: "Establish agreements for interconnection between the Teleport network and those of the telephone companies."

The only problem with the assignment was that no one knew what such an agreement might look like.

Teleport's First Year of Operation: 1985

The year 1985 ended on a triumphant note for Teleport Communications. In November, Gerald Ely was officially announced as the Chairman and CEO of Teleport Communications. Bob Annunziata was named President and COO.[26]

Teleport Communications issued its first year-end report. In the foreword of the report was a joint statement authored by Ely and Annunziata. They were ebullient.[27]

> They said it couldn't be done.
>
> They said it would be impossible to build a regional fiber network in the toughest city in the world.
>
> They said the time had passed for a large satellite communications center in the New York area.
>
> But Teleport Communications achieved the impossible in 1985.
>
> … In one year, we have transformed the communications infrastructure of the New York City and

northern New Jersey region and revolutionized the marketplace for local communications in the area.

… With the ingenuity and commitment of our employees, with the support of our corporate parents and partners, with the approval of governmental regulators and with our understanding of the marketplace, we made remarkable achievements in 1985. We are very proud of our progress in 1985 and look forward to even greater progress in 1986.

Negotiations With New Jersey Bell

The Teleport strategy was to use customer needs to pry concessions from the telephone companies. Discussions with New Jersey Bell were initiated based on a mutual problem the two companies shared in meeting a customer need. Both companies had only limited fiber deployment in 1985 but faced an increasing demand for multiple fiber cables to serve the same locations. Customers with critical communications requirements were becoming concerned over outages due to fiber cable cuts. They wanted more than multiple fibers in the same cable or conduit. They wanted diversely routed back-up fiber.

For instance, New Jersey Bell and Teleport each had roughly parallel single-cable fiber links from Newark/Jersey City to the North Brunswick/Princeton area. Teleport had three customers on this "thin" route and needed to provide them route diversity. Both companies wanted their fiber networks to form closed "rings" so that any location on the ring could be served by two fiber paths transmitting in counter rotation around the ring. With this type of diverse routing, no location could be isolated by a single break in the ring; an arrangement referred to as "self-healing fiber." It was clear that by swapping fibers in each others' cables, a great deal of redundant network construction could be avoided, saving both time and money.

Obviously, to swap fibers, the two networks would have to be interconnected. Since each company utilized different kinds of fiber and electronic multiplexers and regenerators, a mechanism was needed to get one company's type of equipment on the other company's premises so that the swapped fibers could be used. As

Teleport knew it would, this raised the delicate and sensitive issue of central office "collocation" of equipment.

To close the rings, multiplexers in a New Jersey central office would need to interface to both Teleport and New Jersey Bell fiber cables. It was vital to Teleport that these not be just any multiplexers but that they be the Telco Systems multiplexers used throughout their network. Teleport had chosen the Telco Systems multiplexer partly because it had the capability to be remotely monitored and, to some extent, reconfigured, from a central network management center at the Staten Island facility. It was a crucial part of the strategic philosophy of Bob Annunziata that network technology had to leverage the limited Teleport manpower. Howard Bruhnke had implemented this by building a "software driven" network to minimize the number of technicians required in operations.

As the most critical part of the network, telephone companies had always been very protective of their central offices. A central office switch is essentially a software driven computer with over a million lines of code. Telephone companies were about as eager to allow outsiders into their central office buildings as corporations were to allow strangers into their computer centers.

Central office buildings are typically secure facilities with restricted access and house both telephone switches and other electronics. In those central offices which serve as points of concentration for non-switched traffic, "other electronics" might include multiplexers and cross connects to receive, groom and re-route non-switched, dedicated, private line traffic passing through the central office.

The New Jersey Bell's Broad Street central office in Newark was such a point of concentration for non-switched lines. Teleport wanted to place one of its Telco Systems multiplexers in the Broad Street central office in order to provide the interface to its network. Placing "foreign" (non-telephone company) equipment in the central office was referred to as "collocation."

Collocation was not a totally unknown practice. Over the years some telephone companies—although most later denied it—had on occasion allowed important corporate customers to place special equipment in a central office for their own use and convenience even though the network was meant to serve public, not private, needs.

However, Telco Systems' remotely-managed equipment was not on New Jersey Bell's "approved" list of central office equipment. New Jersey Bell, as with most telephone companies, used older multiplexers from AT&T and Northern Telecom that were primarily manually monitored and manually reconfigured.

With an army of technicians on the payroll, New Jersey Bell had no need for the automated features of the newer Telco Systems equipment. New Jersey Bell did not want to train any of its technicians or stock any spare parts for "non-approved" equipment nor would it agree to permit Teleport personnel to enter the central office to service any equipment.

For legal and accounting purposes, New Jersey Bell insisted, that any equipment installed in the central office must carry a New Jersey Bell property tag. New Jersey Bell absolutely would not allow Teleport to own any equipment in the central office.

When Atkinson had joined Teleport in October of 1985, the preliminary technical discussions between New Jersey Bell and Teleport on the engineering aspects of interconnection had already been concluded, but the operational issues of TCG's "collocation" of equipment seemed impossible to resolve.

Atkinson set to work to develop the text of an agreement that would become the Memorandum of Understanding between the two companies. The negotiations would begin with New Jersey Bell and continue through the Fall of 1985 and into the Spring of 1986. Although long, negotiations went surprisingly well through the early months of 1986; and Atkinson found New Jersey Bell more willing to discuss proposed solutions than he had imagined.

The Initial Interconnection Solution: "Virtual Collocation"

The discussions with New Jersey Bell finally led Atkinson to conclude that the telephone company would never agree to allow Teleport to place its equipment in the central office. Therefore he proposed the following "virtual collocation"

> • Teleport would purchase the Telco Systems multiplexers and sell them to New Jersey Bell for one

dollar with the stipulation that, if they were ever removed, Teleport could repurchase them for one dollar.

• Teleport would pay for training of a New Jersey
Bell technician on maintenance of Telco Systems
equipment.

• Teleport would pay for spare parts (mostly cards)
to be stocked in the central office.

• Teleport would remotely monitor the multiplexers
and notify New Jersey Bell if service were required
(*e.g.* to replace a malfunctioning card).

• A New Jersey Bell technician would swap out the
designated card and mail it to Teleport for repair.

These terms and conditions met the New Jersey Bell objections and
were found to be an acceptable way for Teleport to place its multiplexers in New Jersey Bell central offices so that the two companies
could "swap" fiber. Teleport suggested an expansion of the agreement to cover any part of the state of New Jersey. New Jersey Bell
readily agreed to this; and the concept of a 90 fiber-mile "bank" of
fungible, swappable fiber entered negotiation.[28]

The New Jersey Bell Interconnection Agreement

However, attaining "collocation" of its equipment in the New Jersey
Bell CO was only step one on Teleport's agenda. More important
was to get the right to interconnect Teleport's network with the dedicated traffic (mostly T-1) on New Jersey Bell's more extensive fiber
and copper lines. Without such an interface, many potential customer locations were out of reach of the Teleport network.

Therefore, Atkinson also proposed that the Memorandum of
Understanding include the provision that:

• Extra fibers in the Teleport cable, not involved in
the swapping arrangements with New Jersey Bell,
could be used by Teleport for interconnecting to
the New Jersey Bell network.

New Jersey Bell readily agreed that the scope of the Memorandum of Understanding should be expanded to include the interconnection to both companies' tariffed services, recognizing that Teleport would be much more likely to utilize New Jersey Bell's services than vice versa.

On April 14, 1986, New Jersey Bell and Teleport signed the Memorandum of Understanding. From the Teleport perspective, the agreement did not contain everything that might be desired. Whether the total agreement really amounted to a general interconnection agreement or simply to a special purpose, fiber-swap agreement would be debated later.

On December 15, 1986, Teleport signed a Letter of Commitment for specific services under the agreement: (a) 12 fibers into the central office at $1,405 per month and (b) placement of Telco Systems multiplexers—an M90 multiplexer (with two 45 Mbps channels) and a 828M multiplexer (to multiplex one 45 Mbps channel into 28 DS-1 circuits)—in the central office for $645 per month.[29] By Teleport's internal calculations the lease rate for the fiber was "economically comparable" to the costs which Teleport would have incurred had it placed its own fiber cable into the central office. The monthly costs for the multiplexers were taken to represent New Jersey Bell's recovery of power, air conditioning and labor expenses.

In practice, interconnection under this agreement would be somewhat cumbersome since each individual action required that New Jersey Bell file a new modification to the tariff. New Jersey Bell characterized the arrangement as a "facility hub," a characterization which it embodied in the tariffs. On March 29, 1987, the tariff (F.C.C. No. 1) implementing the Letter of Comment was filed with the Federal Communications Commission.[30]

Teleport did not hesitate to hail the agreement as a breakthrough and a model. The "New Jersey Bell agreement" was frequently referenced as the model both for interconnection between telephone companies and their new competitors. It also became the model for later "virtual collocation" agreements for placing the equipment of competitive companies in telephone company central offices.

Atkinson and Teleport had won a tremendous victory. For whatever else it might mean, the agreement established the important precedent that interconnection was physically possible and that it could be accomplished without "harming the network" or imposing unacceptable conditions on the telephone company.

Ironically, the fiber swap that had provided the original rationale for the agreement was never used. By the time the tariff was available, Teleport's three customers on the Newark-North Brunswick route did not require that Teleport provide diverse route protection. Each arranged its own "back up" through the use of private microwave, New Jersey Bell circuits and/or long distance carrier circuits. Shortly, New Jersey Bell enlarged its own fiber network so that "back up" from Teleport was no longer needed to achieve fiber route diversity. Although subsequent discussions were initiated on utilization of the fiber "bank," they never came to fruition.[31]

"Have a Donut ... Drop Dead"

With the New Jersey Bell agreement successfully completed, Atkinson went immediately to negotiate a similar interconnection agreement with New York Telephone, expecting a relatively brief negotiation.

He ran into a stone wall ... or rather a velvet wall. He characterized the reception as, "Glad to see you ... have some coffee ... have a donut ... drop dead." NYNEX was not going to roll over, and their New York Telephone operating company was not going to yield anything to their Teleport competitor without a fight. After eight months of futile attempts at negotiation, Teleport filed a formal complaint with the New York Public Service Commission.[32] Teleport asked that the Commission simply order New York Telephone to interconnect with it.

The Commission preferred to see the parties negotiate an agreement. However, New York was a "bell-weather" state in innovative utility regulation. A proceeding was already underway on telecommunications competition. The Administrative Law Judge added the Teleport interconnection issue to these proceedings. This was the opening round of a battle that would be waged for three years before Teleport won a favorable ruling, and still one more year before the ruling was reduced to acceptable practice.

The "two Bobs" recognized that it would be a long time before a state would be comfortable with what Teleport was trying to do. They decided to adopt a long view strategy with the following tenets:

- Don't be abrasive, but apply steady pressure.
- Take a stance of being educational on the issues.
- Be reasonable and helpful to regulators.
- Be willing to submit to regulation.
- Promote the idea of the validity and desirability of competition over monopoly.
- Use customers to reinforce the need for choice in telecommunications.

Andy Lipman

Other companies were also entering the field of competition with local telephone companies, and Atkinson recognized the need to organize an industry association. Based on his experience with ACCT in the satellite industry, he knew the value of such an organization, particularly when regulatory and legislative issues reached, as they inevitably would, the federal level.

He contacted Andrew D. "Andy" Lipman, a well-known telecommunications lawyer who had worked on the Teleport collocation issues. Lipman and Atkinson would become the two most visible spokesmen for the competitive local telecommunications industry in its fight to gain favorable regulation and, eventually, to see the laws governing telecommunications in the United States rewritten to open the way for competition.

Lipman, a partner in the Washington, D.C. law firm of Pepper, Hamilton & Scheetz, had published books on telecommunication-enhanced real estate and on teleports. A frequent lecturer and industry commentator, he had a high visibility among entrepreneurs interested in starting competitive telecommunications companies.

Lipman actively pursued clients and pushed for the formation of a competitive telecommunications industry on multiple levels. This included ceaseless rounds of speaking at public conferences, publishing articles, helping the formation of companies and agitating for regulatory reform.

Key industry executive, Royce Holland, observed later, "Everywhere behind the scenes in the formation of this industry you can find the hand of Andy Lipman."

ALTs, CAPs, CLECs and ALTS

Many of Lipman's clients and their friends favored the formation of some type of industry-wide advocacy organization. Lipman and Atkinson jointly promoted the idea. Atkinson drew upon his earlier experience in founding a similar organization for the long distance carriers, the Ad Hoc Committee for Competitive Telecommunications (ACCT)

Since the competitive companies were engaged in providing long distance carriers and large corporations with an alternative to the local telephone company for carrying some of their local traffic, they were often referred to as Alternative Local Transport (ALT) companies. This terminology was adapted into the naming of the new organization. In a meeting in Lipman's law office in Washington, DC, the Association of Alternate Local Telecommunications Service Providers (AALTS) was established in 1987.

Shortly after its formation, the founders decided that the word "Alternate" might seem pejorative, as though they were second-class citizens. They felt that the long distance companies which had formed after AT&T had made the mistake of accepting the label "Other Common Carriers" (OCCs) and found themselves constantly living in the shadow of AT&T, "The Common Carrier." AALTS shortened the name to ALTS (Association of Local Telecommunications Services) and was formally incorporated July 30, 1987.[33]

Competitive companies, however, were still referred to as ALTs for many years until the designation,Competitive Access Provider(CAP) was generally adopted. The "CAP" designation came from the fact that most of the dedicated circuits provided by the competitive companies were used to "by pass" the telephone company local network and provide direct access to the networks of long distance carriers. The CAP designation remained in use until competitive companies began offering switched as well as dedicated service. They would look more like traditional telephone companies which are known as Local Exchange Carriers (LECs) in industry jargon. As a result, the CAPs would then become known as Competitive Local Exchange Carriers or CLECs.[34]

As veterans of the conflicts associated with the opening of the telephone equipment, satellite and long distance markets, the founders of ALTS, in a jubilant mode, took as their informal motto, "deja vu and deregulation too." Their formal charter was:

> To establish and maintain a legal and regulatory environment at federal, state and local levels that supports the development of competitive local telecommunications transmission companies and to foster the exchange of ideas between existing and potential local telecommunications transmission companies.[35]

ALTS Membership: 1988

By May of 1988, ALTS made a public appearance to testify at an FCC hearing.[36] The ALTS officers appearing were Bob Atkinson of Teleport as President and Marvin Weatherly of Bay Area Teleport in San Francisco as Vice President. Seven full members and seven associate member companies were acknowledged.

Full membership was reserved for companies that were already operational and actively providing service. Associate members were characterized as companies planning to provide service in the future.

> Full Members of ALTS
> Teleport Communications-New York of Staten Island, NY
> Bay Area Teleport of Alameda, CA
> Institutional Communications Corp. of McLean, VA
> Metropolitan Fiber Systems of Chicago, IL
> Diginet Communications, Inc. of Milwaukee, WI
> Intermedia Communications of Florida in Tampa. FL
> DIGINET of Mercer Island, WA (a microwave-based carrier)

> Associate Members of ALTS
> Teleport Communications-Boston of Staten Island, NY
> Colorado Network, Inc.
> Indiana Digital Access of Indianapolis, IN
> Fiber Optic Corp. of the U.S. of Philadelphia, PA
> Network Communications, Inc. of Houston, TX
> Eastern TeleLogic Corp. of King of Prussia, PA
> Great Lakes Communications of Detroit, MI

For its first few years, ALTS would be run from Atkinson's desk without any dedicated staff support. Mary Rouleau, Assistant General Counsel for Teleport, served as Secretary of ALTS, on an "as required" basis.

Although modest in scale compared to the hundreds of lawyers and lobbyists of the incumbent telephone companies, ALTS did form the basis of a national lobbying platform for the competitive local telecommunications industry. In speaking as the representative of ALTS, Atkinson felt that he had more freedom of action and influence than when he had spoken merely as a representative of a small subsidiary of the Merrill Lynch company.

Pursuing Regulatory Reform

In seeking regulatory reform to open monopoly telecommunications markets to competition, there was the delicate issue of the separate jurisdictions of the state Public Utility Commissions (PUCs) and Federal Communications Commission (FCC). Telecommunications traffic carried within a state (intrastate traffic) was regulated by the PUCs. Interstate traffic was the responsibility of the FCC.

Although, for example, Teleport might be linking to two points on its fiber network that were totally within the State of New York, if one of those points were a long distance carrier's switch and the traffic's destination were out-of-state, it fell within the FCC's regulatory responsibility.

As it happened, long distance carriers were the major initial customers of these fiber networks, and 80% of Teleport's traffic qualified as interstate. Therefore, shortly after filing its complaint on interconnection with the New York Public Service Commission, Teleport filed with the FCC in March 1987. The FCC filing, "Petition for Declaratory Ruling," asked that the FCC require New York Telephone to provide interconnection with Teleport for interstate service.

The state PUCs, which zealously guarded their regulatory domains from federal pre-emption, objected to any action by the FCC on interstate traffic prior to their actions on intrastate traffic. Both the New York PUC and National Association of Regulatory Utility Commissions (NARUC) filed oppositions with the FCC to the

Teleport petition saying essentially, "this is a state issue ... butt the hell out." Teleport was told by the FCC that they had two options. They could wait quietly for FCC action until after the states had dealt with the issue as an intrastate issue, or they could press for a ruling on their FCC petition and be turned down. Teleport chose to wait.

The regulatory maneuvering, particularly interconnection, related to the long term business prospects. In fact, most prospective local telecommunications competitors felt that there was plenty of opportunity without interconnection and did not understand why Teleport was so focused on obtaining interconnection.

Teleport's Second Year: 1986

Teleport's business continued to grow rapidly; by the end of 1986 traffic on the fiber network had more than doubled to a volume of 2,100 Mbps, equivalent to 36,000 voice grade channels. All of the 16 major international and domestic intercity carriers serving New York and New Jersey were now Teleport clients. The Securities Industry Automation Corporation (SIAC), which provided crucial communications links between the stock exchanges and the brokerage community, was an important Teleport customer. Many of the corporate clients were financial services companies in the brokerage and banking industries. Merrill Lynch Chairman, William Schreyer said[37]:

> The financial services industry needs to communicate millions of financial transactions quickly and accurately, every day. Because it is so secure and reliable, Teleport Communications' regional fiber network is ideally suited to meet these needs.

The satellite farm also grew. By the end of 1986 it was serving 25 companies and had signed contracts to bring the number of earth stations to ten by year end 1987.

Not every Teleport initiative was a success. At the Staten Island facility, Teleport had installed a large PBX (Private Branch Exchange) switch similar to that used by many companies to switch voice traffic within their own premises. This switch was offered on a shared basis to any of the tenants in the Staten Island office park. Teleport went to a great deal of effort to get the NYPSC to approve the use of this switch for completing calls between tenants. This allowed, for example, the guard at the security gate to phone any of the tenants in the park without sending the call first to New York Telephone. New York Telephone resisted fiercely because this violated their absolute franchise to handle all local calls.

As it happened the various tenants of the industrial park had very little business in common, and no significant volume of call completion within the PBX switch ever developed. However, the precedent of completing local calls within their own facilities would later be exploited by Teleport in opening the local switched service market.

Teleport's Third Year: 1987

Rapid growth of traffic on the fiber network continued throughout 1987 but at a slightly reduced rate.[38] By year end, traffic volume had increased 80% from 2,100 Megabits to 3,800 Megabits (equivalent to 60,000 voice grade circuits).[39] Teleport Communications advertising placed increasing emphasis on the reliability of the fiber network. It pointed out that for the entire year, the network "availability" averaged 99.99%. That meant that the average circuit in the network, operating 24 hours a day, experienced an outage of only 52.56 minutes for the year. (The "goal" for the equivalent telephone company circuit was 525 minutes of outage per year.)

The bulk of this traffic (70%) was still POP-to-POP interexchange carrier traffic.[40] By meshing traffic from all the long distance carriers serving the New York area, Teleport Communications felt that it was fulfilling its role as a "telecommunications port."

Traffic between customer locations on the network, primarily between the Staten Island satellite facility and locations in Manhattan, accounted for 21% of traffic. Only 9% of the traffic was between interexchange carrier POPs and customer PBXs.[41] However, it was this traffic that brought the greatest protests from the telephone company. Telephone companies told regulators that if "by-passers" were permitted to "cream skim" this long distance access traffic of large corporations, the revenues lost by the telephone companies would force them to increase the local phone rates for small, residential customers. They contended that this, in turn, might jeopardize the societally desirable goal of ubiquitous telephone service ... *i.e.* the goal of Universal Service.

Satellite traffic also continued to grow during 1987. By year end there were 16 earth stations operational at the Staten Island facility. Three of these were owned by Teleport and 13 by various companies leasing space at the satellite farm. Total hours of satellite transmission more than doubled in 1987 to 15,000 hours. Merrill Lynch began construction of a data center in the park that would use the earth stations.

Teleport's organizational structure grew and matured in 1987. Employment reached nearly 100 people, counting long-term contractors. A strategic decision was made that Teleport's future business focus would be fiber-based networks, whether or not they were associated with satellite farms.

Although the rationale for Merrill Lynch to expand its involvement into the broader telecommunications markets beyond the New York area was not clear, support was gained for just such a move, provided joint venture partners could be found. Ely said,

> When we started, our goal was to help Merrill Lynch
> and the City of New York. As we got further into
> it, we became convinced of the utility not only for
> New York, but for other metropolitan areas. We then
> began to look for partners in other cities.[42]

Annunziata was even more outspoken about their aspirations beyond the role of niche player in New York telecommunications.

> We would like to be a national "local distribution
> company." That is, we want to build and operate lo-
> cal or regional communications companies in cities
> throughout the country.[43]

Teleport Communications Group

Teleport Communications Group (TCG) was formed to act as the umbrella organization for a family of Teleport Communications Companies. TCG's mission was to build and operate metropolitan area fiber networks to be built in cities across the U.S. The New York operation became Teleport Communications—New York (TCNY), the first of these entities reporting to TCG. Local companies would seek their own combination of funding, but a major investor in each would be a new subsidiary of Merrill Lynch called Merrill Lynch Teleport Technologies, Inc. (MLTTI).[44]

Teleport Communications - New York sold its three earth stations at the Staten Island facility to IDB Communications Group, Inc. in April 1988.[45] TCNY continued to have responsibility for the overall operation of the industrial park and satellite farm. This included providing back-up power, the shared tenant telephone service and the regional fiber optic distribution network.[46]

TCG planned to launch its multi-city expansion campaign in 1988. The first expansion city was Boston which had many business ties to Teleport's New York customers. As early as October 1987, a joint venture of Merrill Lynch and Fidelity Communications, a subsidiary of Fidelity Investments, Inc., had organized Teleport Communications—Boston and pledged to provide $5 million for a small fiber network in Boston's financial district.[47,48,49]

A race was about to develop between TCG and its major CAP rival, Chicago-based MFS Communications, to establish networks in all the major US cities and become the first local communications competitor with a national presence.

Because CAPs were limited to such a narrow market niche, it was generally thought that only the top 25 largest cities would have enough potential market in POP-to-POP and end-user-to-POP transport to support the entry of a telephone company competitor. The ability of two CAPs to survive in the same market was questionable. While a New York City might provide a healthy market for more than one CAP, it appeared that TCG and the other ALTs would be fighting each other to stake a claim in the major cities across the country by being the first movers and freezing out potential rivals.

Although CAP markets could be expected to gradually expand if interconnection battles were won in more states, the expansion of the market actually occurred in one stroke of luck for the CAPs and misfortune for the telephone companies.

On Mother's Day, May 8, 1988, a disastrous fire in an Illinois Bell Central Office in the Chicago suburb of Hinsdale suddenly changed everything.

Footnotes Chapter 2: A Port For The Information Age

[1] "Teleport on Staten I. Envisioned As City's Link to a Bright Future," *New York Times*, Sept. 10, 1983, A25.

[2] "Business Planners Look To Telecommunications". *New York Times*, May 2, 1983, D1.

[3] "S. I.. Moving Into the Space Age," *New York Times,* June 13, 1982, (VII) R6.

[4] Ibid.

[5] "Staten Island Teleport Is Seen as a Link Future," *New York Times*, Oct. 17, 1982, NJ. 7.

[6] "President Is Leaving Staten Island Teleport," *New York Times*, Oct. 17, 1984.

[7] "Getting Teleport on Track," *New York Times*, July 10, 1984, D1.

[8] Ibid. *New York Times*, Oct. 17, 1984.

[9] "Business Planners Look To Telecommunications," *New York Times*, May 2, 1983, D1.

[10] Ibid.

[11] "Teleport Project Hits Legal Snag," New York Times, May 8. 1983, A30.

[12] "S. I.. Teleport Granted Fee Exemption," *New York Times,* May 12, 1983, B3. Given the criticism of competitive telecommunications companies as "cream skimmers" and particularly the later pressure to force them to offer service to the residential market, it is ironic that the incumbents initially sought to bar them from addressing this specific market.

[13] TCG Interviews.

[14] "Merger Moves Business Services Into The Spotlight," AT&T Press Release, Third And Fourth Quarter 1998 News.

[15] Internal Teleport memo, "Teleport Communications - Main Line of Business," Aug. 23, 1983.

[16] Ibid.

[17] "Testimony of Howard W. Bruhnke," *Ill. C.C. Docket No. 89-0171, Teleport Communications,* July 14, 1989.

[18] Ibid.

[19] See 6 *New York Times*, Oct. 17, 1984.

[20] TCG Annual Report, *"Teleport Communications: 1985,"* New York, NY.

[21] Ibid.

[22] FCC Statistics.

[23] "The ALTS, An Emerging Industry," (Connecticut Research Report, Glastonbury, CT, 1989), 31.

[24] Ibid.

[25] Gerald W. Brock, "The Telecommunications Industry, The Dynamics of Market Structure" (Cambridge, MA: Harvard University Press, , 1981) 112.

[26] "Executive Changes," *New York Times,* Nov. 15, 1985.

[27] TCG Annual Report 1985.

[28] Letter from Bob Atkinson to John Ake, VP, Regulatory, Illinois Bell, Oct. 15, 1990.

[29] Ibid.

[30] A tariff is a publicly filed description of a service offering which details the features, limitations and conditions of the service as well as its pricing. Approval of a tariff requires formal action of the governing regulatory body and is usually a prolonged process. Depending on one's point of view, the primary purpose of a tariff is either (1) to ensure that the identical offering is available to all customers or (2) to limit the liability of the service provider.

[31] Ibid.

[32] State Public Utility Commissions come with a variety of names ... Public Service Commission, Commerce Commission, etc. ... but are generically called Public Utility Commissions or PUCs.

[33] "Local Access Firms Try To Change Image," *Network World,* Sept. 5, 1988, 11.

[34] Competitive companies will be designated as CAPs in the early sections of this book and CLECs in the latter sections.

[35] Ibid.

[36] "Recently-Formed Trade Association Begins Representing LEC Local Facilities Competitors," *Telecommunications Reports*, May 23, 1988.

[37] Quoted in TCG Annual Report, *"Teleport Communications: 1986"* , New York, NY.

[38] TCG Annual Report, *"Teleport Communications 1987 Expanding Frontiers"* , New York, NY.

[39] "The Boom In Teleports," *Teleconnect,* Dec. 1988, 8.

[40] "Teleport Claims Not Much of a Bypasser, Makes Suggestions for Bypass Monitoring," Telecommunications *Reports,* April 18, 1988.

[41] Ibid.

[42] Quoted in "Teleport Communications," *Harvard Business School Case Study N9-189-028,* 1988, 11.

[43] Ibid., 12

[44] "Merrill Lynch Launches Teleport Unit," *Communications Week,* Jan. 4, 1988, 35.

[45] "Teleport Communications Sells Three Remaining Earth Stations to IDB Communications," *Telecommunications Reports,* May 9, 1988.

[46] *Network World,* May 16, 1988, 14.

[47] Application Of Teleport Communications - Boston For A Certificate Of Public Convenience And Necessity, (DPU Case 88-60), March 3, 1988, Exhibit 8.

[48] Ibid.

[49] "Merrill Lynch, Fidelity Affiliates Announce Partnership for Boston Fiber Optic Network," *Telecommunications Reports*, Feb. 29, 1988.

3. A LIGHT IN THE TUNNEL

Secret Tunnels

There are tunnels under the Chicago Loop business district.

Except on rare occasions, the presence of these tunnels has gone unnoticed by Chicagoans. The tunnels gained brief notoriety in 1943 on the CBS radio mystery, "Lights Out," as the mythical home of a giant killer lizard. In 1979 they made a cameo appearance as an escape route in the 1979 Universal Pictures movie, "The Blues Brothers."[1]

The tunnels, however, were originally conceived in the 19th century to bring competitive telecommunications to Chicago. That role was renewed in the 1980s as they became ready-made conduits for the fiber networks of CAPs seeking to serve the Chicago business community.

An Underground Telephone Company

In Chicago in 1898, The Illinois Telephone & Telegraph (IT&T) Company, one of the hundreds of new telephone companies springing up around the turn of the century, proposed to construct and operate an underground telephone system in the heart of the business district.[2] The company proposed to build tunnels under the Loop District, encircled by the Chicago river and to install its switches and wires underground. The company would compete with the existing Chicago Telephone Company, which was the predecessor to the Illinois Bell Telephone Company.

IT&T's stated objectives were to:

> acquire, construct, build, sell, lease and operate plants for the conveyance and transmission of sound and signals by electricity.

They intended to gain market differentiation by installing an ultra-modern, automatic switch that did not need the intervention of a human operator. IT&T was granted the right to construct its system by a city ordinance passed on June 27, 1898.

It is possible that IT&T was a stalking horse for the creation of an underground trolley system. One of the prominent backers of IT&T was Albert G. Wheeler, and his major business activity had been to acquire street trolley franchises for the General Electric Railway Company and to resell them to operating companies such as the Chicago City Railway. There had been litigation by the Chicago City Railway against Wheeler's company, attempting unsuccessfully to prove that it had bribed city alderman to obtain franchises and had forged property owner frontage consent papers.[3]

Tunnel Construction

IT&T, with Wheeler now President, began construction of the tunnel system by sinking a shaft in the rear basement of the Powers & O'Brien saloon, operated by Alderman Johnny Powers. The shaft went down thirty feet where a horizontal tunnel was then constructed, following the alley to the center of LaSalle Street. There the tunnel turned to follow the center line of the street. Miners cut through the blue clay during the night with hand-held knives, and workers constructed wooden forms and poured concrete behind them during the day.

The tunnel was six feet nine inches wide and seven feet six inches high and progressed at twelve-to-sixteen-feet per day. Narrow gauge tracks were laid on the tunnel floor so that small rail cars could be used to remove the excavated clay and dirt. Later construction techniques included increasing the depth to forty feet and using "open trench" construction rather than tunneling.[4]

The "Girl-less, Cuss-less Telephone"

In 1901, IT&T reorganized as the Automatic Electric Company with Wheeler as Secretary-Treasurer.[5] One of Wheeler's associates was involved in telephone equipment development and had contacts at the Strowger Automatic Telephone Company. This equipment manufacturer was founded by Almon B. Strowger, the inventor of the first telephone exchange switch.

Before Strowger's switch, telephone connections were made manually at a plug board by an operator. Strowger, an undertaker in Kansas City, Missouri, reportedly invented his switch because the local operator, the wife of a rival undertaker, was diverting all the business to her husband's company.

Strowger called his automatic switch the "girl-less, cuss-less telephone."[6] The Automatic Electric Company announced that it intended to gain market differentiation by installing an ultra-modern, automatic Strowger switch.[7]

Railway or Telephone Company?

The company decided that it would also use the tunnels for hauling freight but continued to let the city believe that its sole objective was telephone service.[8] Construction was halted briefly in 1902 when the Mayor found out that the company was surreptitiously enlarging the tunnel and planning to haul freight. An accommodation was reached which "legalized" the existing tunnels and amended the franchise to permit construction of a narrow gauge, electric rail system to transport freight, mail and other merchandise.[9] The railway tunnel system eventually covered fifty miles, accessing most of the buildings in the Loop area as well as crossing under the Chicago river to adjacent areas.

The franchise was amended. Telephone operations were relegated to secondary status. However, the company was required to have 20,000 telephone subscribers in five years or forfeit the telephone plant and equipment to the city.[10]

"Chicago's New Modern Automatic Secret Service Telephone Exchange"

Telephone service was inaugurated on Oct. 15, 1903. Company advertising featured the headline, "Chicago's New Modern Automatic Secret Service Telephone Exchange."[11] The word "secret" referred to the fact that the system switched automatically with no local telephone operator involved to eavesdrop.

But superior technology did not win. The Chicago Telephone Company offered not only local service but also access to long distance service through AT&T. Since IT&T was not a Bell company, it could not interconnect with AT&T to provide long distance service. Until 1912, when it worked out an agreement with the Independent Telephone & Telegraph Company for limited long distance service to several counties in Illinois and Indiana, it was a totally isolated island of local service confined to the Loop area.

It operated unprofitably from 1903 to 1917 when the company requested permission to abandon operations. The equipment was acquired by Illinois Bell Telephone which removed it from the tunnels and junked it.

Abandoned Tunnels

The tunnel railway continued to operate until 1959. In the end it was used primarily for hauling coal in and cinders out. Business declined due to competition from trucks and reductions in the use of coal to heat buildings. The rolling stock was removed and the tunnels reverted to city ownership.

The City of Chicago made some attempt to preserve the tunnels for whatever unknown, undefined future need. New building construction was prohibited from damaging or destroying them. This largely succeeded except for the construction of the Eisenhower Expressway in the 1970s when some support pilings were driven through the roofs of the tunnels along the edge of the Loop.

In the 1980s, right-of-way consultants, Bonnie Hendricks and John Miller, looking for a route for a fiber link to the Sprint POP in the Prudential Plaza became aware of the old tunnels. They found them surprisingly intact, although totally without lights and with standing water in some places.

Chicago Fiber Optics, Inc.

Hendricks and Miller realized that the tunnel system was more than a convenient, ready-made conduit for a short fiber link. They saw a potentially profitable opportunity to create a new business by running low-cost, fiber links to every significant office building in the Loop and offering a spectrum of high-speed, digital communications services. Their contact back at Sprint headquarters in Kansas, John Lucas, agreed. Although Lucas' experience was as an attorney, he was excited by the opportunity to create and run a new, fiber-based telecommunications company.

Hendricks and Miller also had contacts in Chicago with political ties. They knew Ken Sain, Deputy Mayor of Chicago, and Howard Carroll, an influential state senator. These two had the right connections to seek a favorable lease agreement from the city to use the tunnels for fiber rights-of-way. They were both willing to be investors in the new company

On May 10, 1984, the group filed incorporation papers in Illinois for the Chicago Fiber Optics, Inc. Lucas, the former General Counsel for Sprint, was designated as President. Sain and Carroll served as Directors.

Lucas began to build the organization. He attended a conference run by the Competitive Telecommunications Associations (CompTel, the successor to ACCT which Bob Atkinson had helped found.) The major purpose of CompTel was to keep small long distance resellers and carriers in the interexchange industry from being crushed by AT&T. It also served as a forum for seminars and discussions among people interested in telecommunications and competitive opportunities.

At the conference, Tricia Breckenridge, the Director of Regulatory Affairs for long distance reseller, Telesphere Corporation, was a speaker. She gave a presentation on how the competitive long distance industry had evolved, how it had matured to a certain level and what the next competitive venue might be.

Later that day Lucas approached Breckenridge to ask if she would consider a new career. He told her that his company was going to build a fiber optic network in abandoned coal tunnels under the Loop in Chicago and to compete against the local telephone company, Illinois Bell Telephone.

The following week Tricia was invited to meet with the investor group: Bonnie Hendricks, John Miller, Ken Sain, Howard Carroll and John Lucas. They offered her the opportunity to become a founder/director/employee and to pitch the business plan of attacking Illinois Bell to prospective backers. In addition to Breckenridge, the Lucas operating team consisted of Jack Rabin (Treasurer), Carol Barrett (Sales) and David Goggin (Engineering).

"City Leases Tunnels at Basement Prices"

Sain and Carroll, partners in the law firm of Carroll, Sain and Epstein, Ltd., were active in the Chicago Democratic Party. Sain had served as Deputy Mayor under both Richard J. Daly and Michael Bilandic. Sain introduced a proposal to the City Council to lease several miles of the unused tunnel right-of-way to Chicago Fiber Optic, Inc.(CFO). On Oct. 17, 1984, an ordinance was passed which would allow CFO to pay an annual rental fee of a nominal $1 per foot.

CFO engaged the Goddard Group of Bethesda, Maryland to conduct a survey to determine the potential market for bypass in the Loop. The survey indicated the possibility of 125,000 voice grade equivalent circuits. In November 1984, CFO announced its plans to build a 59-mile fiber network.[12]

Dennis Goddard, President of the Goddard Group, stated that the network should be operational by year end 1985, although he admitted that the project was still looking for funding.[13]

In December, he indicated that the first phase of the construction would be a six mile network linking 21 buildings and could be operational by mid-1985. However, he indicated that completion of funding, which was expected to include a 25% interest from North American Satellite Systems, could hold up the project.[14]

Obtaining funding for the CFO network proved elusive. In May 1985, still without funding, CFO announced its intention to build a more modest, 3.4 mile network at a projected cost of $3 million.[15] At the $1 per foot lease rate, CFO would pay an annual rental of $17,952 to the City for the new network. However, that same month the Chicago Tribune published an investigative report entitled, "City Leases Tunnels at Basement Prices," attacking the tunnel lease agreement as a "sweetheart" deal.[16]

CFO was forced to agree to a higher lease rate.[17] Ultimately, on March 12, 1986, the City rescinded the original ordinance and the next day approved a new one.[18] The new lease rate would be computed on the basis of both linear feet and circuit capacity ($0.185 per DS-3-ft) or a minimum annual charge of $309,000.

FOCUS

In May 1985, CFO projected that its 3.4 mile network would be finished by the end of the year 1985. Once more this goal was premature due to lack of funding. Although it lacked funding, CFO had plenty of ambition. In October of 1985, CFO announced that it was forming a holding company, Fiber Optic Corporation of the

United States (FOCUS), to build fiber networks in multiple cities across the country.[19] Meanwhile the company continued to struggle to find construction funding.

Illinois Bell Responds

Possible competition from tiny Chicago Fiber Optic, Inc. did not escape the notice of Illinois Bell Telephone. This was the second time the tunnels might provide a launching pad for telecommunications competition, and the incumbent telephone company was not going to wait around to see whether it would be successful.

The city ordinance to lease the tunnel was passed on October 16, 1984; and on November 30, 1984, Illinois Bell responded by filing a tariff with the Illinois Commerce Commission for "Novalink," a special fiber optic offering available only in the Loop district.[20] As a limited, local transport offering that did not link to long distance carriers, Novalink did not have much market impact. It did, however, signal that Illinois Bell would respond vigorously to any competitors entering its turf.

James Q. Crowe

James Q. Crowe began his career as an engineer for Morrison-Knudsen, a construction and engineering company in Boise, Idaho. At Morrison-Knudsen he became a Group Vice President with responsibility for business in the electric power market. Many of the projects involved the construction of generation facilities for Independent Power Producers (IPPs).

These very entrepreneurial projects were spawned by the Public Utility Regulatory Practices Act (PURPA), enacted in 1978. Under PURPA, which was a move toward deregulation, electric utilities were required to purchase some of their electric power from IPPs.

Morrison-Knudsen was also involved in installing fiber systems for telecommunications carriers. The long haul fiber business peaked around 1985 with the completion of the major transcontinental networks. The next proposed national network was Fibertrak, a joint venture of Southern Pacific Railroad and Norfolk Southern Corp.

Fibertrak was intended as a carrier's carrier provider of wholesale transmission. Morrison-Knudsen won the contract to be system integrator, but the project never went forward. There was talk of a "fiber glut." The railroads grew cautious. They insisted that Fibertrak must sign-up customers before funding would be provided.[21] Customers, however, were unwilling to commit until the network was built.

By late 1985, the project died.

In 1986 Crowe left Morrison-Knudsen and went to Peter Kiewit Sons' Company (PKS) He was still intrigued by the fiber network construction potential. He also saw strong analogies to the entrepreneurs in the Independent Power Business and those attempting to start CAPs.

IPP entrepreneurs typically started with nothing, got a long-term contract to supply power to a utility, lined up a fuel source and finally went for funding. Then they turned to companies like Morrison-Knudsen or PKS to build the generating facility and sometimes to provide funding to the principals.

The CAP business might be a little different from the IPP business, but the concept of dealing with customers who start with a dream and no money was not unfamiliar to anyone who had been an IPP system developer.

Peter Kiewit Sons': A Gung-Ho Private Company

Peter Kiewit Sons' Co. (PKS) of Omaha, Nebraska was originally founded in 1884 by a Dutch immigrant brick maker. It soon expanded into a very successful construction company. The founder's son, Peter Kiewit Jr., took over in 1931 and ran the company until his death in 1979. He was considered a tough but resourceful, successful and venerated leader.

The company developed a gung-ho culture in which salaried employees worked six-day weeks, over-weight employees received mandatory reducing trips to the "fat farm" and high-performing employees were rewarded by being allowed to buy stock in the company.[22] Although not a public company, stock in PKS was widely held by the employees.

Walter K. Scott, an Omaha-born engineer, who had worked for PKS since his summer vacations in high school and college, took over from Peter Kiewit Jr. in 1979. The hand-off from the plain-spoken Peter Kiewit was characteristic. He called Scott from his hospital room shortly before his death and said, "Walter, this is Pete. My time is short. I've tried to show or tell you everything I know. Good luck to you."[23] Before Scott could reply, he hung up.

Scott relaxed the Calvinistic employee guidelines slightly. Salaried employees no longer had to work Saturday afternoons, and the cafeteria was permitted to serve desserts. However, the company retained its hard-charging, work-focused, employee-owned culture and maintained its rapid growth.

Shares were divided into C class and D class. Only active employees could own hold the C stock, which represented ownership in the core construction and mining operations. Upon retirement, employees could cash out their shares at book value or swap their shares for D class shares. The D class shares represented ownership in the PKS diversified operations and largely benefited from Scott's investment and acquisition acumen. (Over a five year period from 1991 to 1996, the Class C shares would rise 268% and the Class D shares 351%.)[24]

Legendary investment guru, Warren Buffett, a close friend of Scott's since boyhood said, "Walter Scott presides over the ultimate meritocracy in American business."[25] Buffett described Scott's business acumen as "sensational."[26]

By the time of its involvement with CFO, PKS had grown into the 10th largest privately owned company in the United States. With involvement in construction (Alaska pipeline), coal mining and packaging (Continental Can), it had revenues approaching $5 billion.

At PKS, Crowe was put in charge of Southern Electric Contractors (SEC), an electrical contracting group within the construction operation. SEC was a large organization that had traditionally carried out "cost plus fee" contracts with government entities or other substantial customers. It had just finished an eight year construction project at Prudhoe Bay, Alaska and was hungry for new projects.

A small part of their business involved fiber optics. SEC had installed about 6,000 miles of fiber, working on the installation of national fiber networks for AT&T, Sprint, MCI and LightNet (a project of Southern New England Telephone and the CSX railroad).

More of the profitable fiber projects would have been welcome, but it appeared that, after the demise of Fibertrak, there might never be another major, long-haul fiber build. Southern Electric Contractors could not live on building small, local fiber projects such as CAP network builds. It was too large, with too much overhead.

Kiewit Telecommunications Services

However, within SEC Crowe found a sub-unit of the right size. Kiewit Telecommunications Services (KTS) had been formed specifically to do fiber splicing and testing. KTS was a high margin operation. Fiber splicing, as opposed to fiber cable pulling, was a skilled task and could bring $150 for a single splice. On its own, Kiewit Telecom could be profitable on small fiber jobs such as CAP networks.

Since PKS traditionally obtained business by bidding on projects, they had no sales and marketing departments. Crowe told Ron Vidal who was responsible for KTS operations that he was designating him, "National Sales Manager." Not only was he the national sales manager for KTS, he was, in fact, the only sales manager in the company. His mission would be to go out and find CAP projects and win them.

Vidal had been buying splice cases from AT&T Network Systems, the equipment division of AT&T. Through his AT&T account contact, Frank Kurtz, he proposed that the two companies jointly approach CAPs as a team, offering an integrated package of network construction, equipment and system integration.

The first major opportunity came looking for KTS in the form of a self-styled broker, who brought them the opportunity to bid on a CAP network construction job in exchange for a $50,000 finder's fee. The CAP was Chicago Fiber Optic Inc.

"The Money In The Glass Box"

John Lucas was delighted with the arrival of the Kiewit/AT&T team, which clearly had the skills to build the CFO network. In March 1986 he announced that this team had begun to construct the CFO network. Once more the announcement was premature. It would take another year before funding and a construction contract was in place.

Lucas was aware that Rod Hackman and John Baring at Kidder-Peabody had found financing for the Institutional Communications Company (ICC) in Washington, DC. He contacted Hackman in 1986 to see if he could help Chicago Fiber Optic. When Hackman and Baring reviewed the CFO business plan they found that they were in very strong disagreement with the proposed strategy.

Hackman and Baring thought that a tandem switch[27] should be included in the network, as it was in Institutional Communications Company's network, to allow customers to switch their traffic among multiple long distance providers. Lucas and Breckenridge disagreed. They argued that the presence of such a switch would alienate the long distance carriers, which were CFO's best potential customers. Hackman was not convinced but finally decided to proceed with promoting the venture, sans switch.

Hackman shopped the deal and brought in new equity investors, real estate developers, Howard Gimbel and Arthur Brantman as well as David Husman, who was associated with the large real estate operations of Jerry Wexler. Husman became Chairman of the Board of Directors of CFO. Gimbel and Brantman became Treasurer and Secretary, respectively.

To finance the construction, Hackman and Baring were able to interest the Barclay Bank, using the same appeal that had won support for the Institutional Communications Co. network in Washington, D.C., namely, that the network represented a durable asset. However, unlike CIT Financial in Washington, the Barclay Bank believed that the network only took on value when it was completely finished and had essentially no value in the partially constructed phase. The bank agreed to provide $11.8 million for construction of the network but would not agree to release the money until the network was complete and in turn-key operation.

This issue was debated and the bank finally settled on a market acceptance test stipulation. If CFO could show firm customer orders of $2 million or letters of intent of $3 million, the bank would release the funding. It appeared to be a "Catch 22" since most customers would not sign up without evidence that the network was being constructed. CFO needed the money to get a contractor to start work. The issue did not appear resolvable, but CFO had no alternative but to try.

The CFO investors contacted Crowe and offered KTS a "no lose" proposition. They told him that they were willing to issue him a Letter of Credit for $2 million if he would begin construction of the network. If the bank financing came through, he would be paid from the bank funds. But if the construction cost reached $2 million without the Barclay Bank having released the money, he could stop work and cash in the Letter of Credit.

Crowe agreed, but said that he would keep accurate records of his expenditures and, if they reached $1,999,999, construction would stop. At Kiewit Telecommunications Services, the arrangement was referred to as "the money in the glass box" as in "Break glass in event of emergency."

Up To The Brink

Make-ready construction activity in the tunnels began. The tunnel entrances were eclectic and largely forgotten. In a sub-basement of the Marshall Field's department store, a tunnel opening was closed off from a working area by a wire mesh screen. Store personnel had learned to ignore the black void on the other side of the wire. Suddenly they were startled by voices and lights as construction workers with miners' lamps on their helmets suddenly appeared out of the dark on the other side of the long-ignored screen.

In the Insurance Exchange building, where one of the two network control nodes would be built, access to the tunnel required laying flat on your belly and sliding sideways through a slit in the wall. Other entrances involved only rolling aside a metal fire door in a basement boiler room and walking in.

The construction activity was intentionally made conspicuous. With Kiewit trucks in the streets and construction bustle underway, it was believed that potential customers would be more receptive to the CFO pending services. Firm commitments, however, still proved difficult to obtain. As construction costs approached the $2 million threshold, it did not look as though CFO would be able to meet the market acceptance test in time.

AT&T Will Do Whatever It Takes For CFO To Succeed

Kiewit Telecom and their AT&T Network Systems working partner met with representatives of the Barclay Bank. In addition to AT&T Network Systems, a representative of AT&T Communications also attended the meeting. During the meeting the new player from AT&T assured the bank officials that AT&T Communications would definitely buy circuits from CFO. Then he astonished the Kiewit Telecom/AT&T Network Systems team by unexpectedly promising that AT&T Communications would provide whatever level of business was necessary to ensure that the CFO was financially viable.

The team doubted that such a sweeping commitment had actually been authorized at higher levels in AT&T. The role of these verbal assurances, which never became reality, is uncertain. But, for whatever reason, the bank relented on the requirement for firm orders and released the $11.8 million funding.

The Kiewit construction spending had come within $2,000 of the $2 million stop limit. The CFO team convened in a local bar to celebrate. After a nearly three-year struggle, they now had an approved business plan and the funding to execute it.

Finally Building The CFO Network

On March 17, 1987, a year after negotiations between CFO and Kiewit had begun, a Notice to Proceed with construction was issued. A 3.4 mile, four inch diameter conduit system was run along the roof of the tunnel. Three one inch diameter plastic interducts were installed inside the conduit and 5.6 miles of fiber cable were pulled through the interducts. Each of these backbone cables contained 72 fibers. At junction boxes along the route, lateral cables containing 12 fibers were run from the backbone cable to interface electronics in the buildings.

There was no standard way of obtaining access to each building. Building access might be obtained through a sub-basement entrance by unblocking an old coal chute or by boring a new hole through the tunnel wall. The electronics, which consisted of self-healing, dual multiplexers from AT&T Network Systems, were installed in the telephone equipment closets in the building.

These closets were reached by communications ducts running vertically through the building and usually were high in the building, for example on the 40th floor. This would turn out to be fortunate when the tunnels later flooded.

The network was built to be durable and have a high survivability. In addition to redundant, diversely-routed fiber in protective steel conduits, the network had both a primary and back-up control center. The network architecture was a double star with fiber cables converging on the dual control centers: one at the Insurance Exchange building and one at the Prudential Plaza.

Reorganizing CFO

Meanwhile, there were changes in the CFO organization. The investors were exasperated with the company's slow pace of development. In April Lucas revealed that CFO had, in fact, no firm customer commitments. The investors brought in Anthony J. (Tony) Pompliano, ostensibly to review the project but in reality to replace Lucas. Pompliano had served as Vice President of MCI's Midwest operations and had 26 years of telecommunications experience.

Pompliano began bringing his own team of experienced people into CFO. This included: Allen Barry Jr., formerly a division manager of AT&T, George Tronsrue III and Judith Riley, formerly with MCI, and William Sumner, formerly Director of Operations for LDX Net. There was constant arguing between Pompliano and Lucas.

In July, Lucas announced that the company had begun development of Philadelphia Fiber Optic (PFO) under the holding company structured earlier, FOCUS.[28] It was expected that both PFO and CFO, as well as future expansion city networks, would operate under the "umbrella" of FOCUS. FOCUS, under Dan Goggin as COO, intended to provide management services for the multiple companies under it.

Completion of the CFO network was forecast for September. PFO network construction was projected to begin in the first quarter of 1988 with Goggin serving as General Manager and acting President.[29]

Shortly after, Lucas, Breckenridge, Barrett, Goggin and Jack Rabin jointly approached the CFO investors and asked for a financial settlement which was granted. The Lucas group retained FOCUS and left CFO to pursue the development of CAP networks under the FOCUS holding company structure.

On Aug. 26, 1987, Tony Pompliano was named CEO and President of CFO.[30]

Kiewit Communications Company, Inc.

Finding suitable CAP projects for KTS to build was proving difficult. Crowe and Vidal began to develop a different plan. Based on what they had learned about the CAP industry, they felt that there was a reasonable chance that AT&T would eventually buy a multicity chain of fiber networks once they were constructed. They decided to ask PKS to invest some money in market development.

This was an unprecedented thing to do. PKS was a very disciplined company. In a Kiewit company, there were no coffee breaks. The coffee wagon would arrive at your location on schedule, and you could buy coffee and take it to your desk. Coffee makers or hot plates found in your work area would be confiscated, and you would be fined. Everyone was expected to concern themselves only with their specifically defined duties.

Operations personnel did not traditionally make suggestions to the senior management at PKS about how to invest corporate money. Nevertheless, Jim Crowe asked for and received an appointment on the calendar of Walter Scott, the CEO of PKS. The meeting was scheduled for Saturday on the 10th floor of the Kiewit Tower in Omaha. Crowe was accompanied to the meeting by a small group including Ron Vidal and Terry Ferguson, a construction lawyer. Crowe expected that his presentation would last 30 to 40 minutes. He anticipated that he would then be in for a question and answer grilling from Scott's senior lieutenants, Bill Grewcock and Charlie Campbell.

It was Crowe's intention to ask for $300,000 to $400,000 to:

> (1) study the market
> (2) figure out how to get rights-of-way.

At the end of the presentation, Grewcock asked what made Crowe think that he could acquire rights-of-way. Before Crowe could reply, Scott answered the question himself. He said that there were lots of sources including utilities, subways, etc. Campbell asked what made Crowe think he could build these fiber systems cost effectively. Again, Scott jumped in with the answer. He said, "They've already done it in Chicago."

It was clear that Scott had already decided that the construction of these fiber networks was an interesting business opportunity. Further selling by Crowe and his group was unnecessary. They stopped talking. The money was approved. Kiewit Communications Company, Inc. was launched.

The $80 Million Plan

Jim Crowe called Andy Lipman. Lipman had already done regulatory work for pioneering competitive companies: Institutional Communications Company in Washington and Teleport Communications Group in New York.

In one month, Lipman and his firm carried out a 55-city study for Crowe. This was a massive study of state regulations, rights-of-way, utilities and regulatory climate. The study was contained in four or five volumes. It scored and ranked the cities in terms of relative attractiveness from both a right-of-way and regulatory perspective. The three top-ranked cities were: Baltimore, Philadelphia and Minneapolis. At Lipman's suggestion, the San Francisco Consulting Group was engaged to do a market study. They examined the size of the potential market for CAP services in five cities: Boston, New York, Detroit, San Francisco and Los Angeles.

Crowe and Vidal developed a business plan to build small, central networks in ten cities at a projected total cost of approximately $80 million. They saw these network builds as simply speculative construction opportunities. It appeared possible to invest about $80 million of Kiewit's money in network construction and then sell the networks to AT&T for a nice profit of around $200 million.

Royce Holland

Crowe knew that he would need to develop the Kiewit Communications Company to carry out this plan. He had remained in touch with Royce Holland, a former colleague at Morrison-Knudsen. Royce had also left Morrison-Knudsen and was now at Energy Factors, a San Diego company in the IPP business.

Holland was interested in Crowe's plans to build CAP networks but had no background in telecommunications. He read the CFO business plan and two books on the history of telecommunications which fired his imagination; *The Deal of the Century—The Breakup of AT&T* and *On the Line—the Men of MCI Who Took on AT&T, Risked Everything and Won* [31],[32].

The Deal of the Century, by Steve Coll, a former Washington Post staff writer, provided a great insight into the dynamics of the telephone industry. The reality of a continual societal, legislative and judicial pressure toward a competitive telecommunications industry was clear.

The resulting, sometimes erratic, cracking and shifting of telecommunications business entities and markets under these stresses and strains began to make sense. *On the Line,* by Larry Kahaner, a founder of an industry newsletter, *Telecommunications Reports,* gave a sense of both the personal risk and personal triumph of successfully taking on an entrenched monopoly.

Holland dug into an analysis of the ten-city plan that Crowe and Vidal had prepared. Even though PKS had not yet given its approval and support to the plan, Holland was excited by the vision. He decided to join Crowe's organization in the hope that Kiewit support for the venture would be forthcoming. However, a major snag appeared immediately.

The "Oliver North" Memo

Walter Scott's operating motto for successful project management was: "Cover your downside and the upside will take care of itself."[33] In considering the construction of local fiber networks, the downside protection was that the physical facility, once completed, always had an intrinsic value to long distance carriers seeking to avoid the onerous access charges levied by local telephone companies. The largest long distance company, and presumably most likely buyer of these networks, was AT&T.

Suddenly AT&T seemed to remove itself from the list of potential network buyers. Not only did it look as though AT&T would not be a candidate to buy the networks but also might not even be a customer to buy service from any such networks.

The bad news came in a letter in mid-1987 from AT&T CEO Jim Olson to Congressman John Dingell, Chairman of the House Commerce Committee. The letter seemed to promise that AT&T would not seek to bypass the local telephone networks of the RBOCs. Olson said that AT&T policy was to "always include local telephone company access when designing private networks."[34]

The letter had actually been ghost-written for Olson's signature by John Zeglis, AT&T's corporate attorney, and his staff. Zeglis (later to become President of AT&T) had played a major role in devising AT&T's strategy of self-imposed divestiture leading to the agreement ending the Department of Justice's antitrust case against AT&T.

The divestiture settlement had been attacked with a vengeance by AT&T's most daunting nemesis in Congress, Tim Wirth of Colorado.[35] In March 1982, Congressman Wirth had introduced legislation (H.R. 5158) that, among other things, would bar AT&T from bypassing the local RBOC networks for five years. While this effort failed, there was continuing discussion that the RBOCs needed to be protected from any loss of access revenue and also from competition, particularly from their former parent, AT&T. Otherwise, it was feared, the RBOCs would not be financially healthy; and the United States would no longer enjoy low residential telephone rates.

There could not have been a sharper divergence of view. Certain Congressmen such as Wirth and Dingell saw the RBOC control of the "last mile" as a benevolent monopoly extracting a toll from the business-dominated, long distance market to subsidize low-cost, local phone service for the common man. Potential competitors saw the RBOC monopoly as a choke hold, frustrating competition and artificially denying consumers the benefits of innovation, choice and lower prices that flow from a healthy, free market.

AT&T's legal and regulatory experts, apparently concerned about heading off possible new restrictive legislation, devised the letter. The Olson letter pledged that AT&T would not bypass the RBOC networks except in the case where comparable RBOC facilities were not available. Olson's explanation of his company's policy was interpreted by FCC Chairman Dennis Patrick to mean that AT&T "comes first to the local company" to meet AT&T's needs for local exchange access.[36]

The Olson letter had been prepared by John Zeglis and the legal/regulatory team without consultation with the AT&T operating groups. This lack of consultation reflected the internal conflicts that were then current inside the AT&T organization.

AT&T's marketing group was furious. They were pursuing deals with customers that incorporated the assumption of the use of low-cost CAP access. AT&T's Access Group had many access agreements with CFO and other CAPs. They also had active negotiations for more in process. As a result, these groups had been blindsided and were dumbfounded.

However, the network equipment sales group, AT&T Network Systems, whose major customers were the RBOCs, did not want AT&T to irritate their best customers and were pleased to side with the Zeglis group. AT&T became two warring camps.

The Chairman Disavows All Knowledge Of Your Actions

Those responsible for developing network access asked how they should now proceed. Frank Blount, President of the Network Operations Group, referred to the Olson/Zieglis letter ruefully as the "Oliver North Memo." The country was then in the midst of the Iran/Contra Affair in which it was alleged that Colonel North was directed to undertake missions which, if they became public, the Reagan administration would deny they ever knew existed. Access arrangements and negotiations with CAPs continued under the implied threat that, if they became public, the AT&T policy might be: "The Chairman Disavows All Knowledge Of Your Actions."[37]

TCG, having extensive experience with AT&T's bureaucratic complexities, was not disturbed by the Olson letter. They focused on the "out" clause which indicated that AT&T would use CAP circuits if the RBOCs didn't have a "comparable" offering. At Kiewit, the letter was given a more literal reading and more credence.

It was immediately assumed by Crowe and his associates that it would no longer be possible to present a case to the PKS Board for an $80 million speculative network build based on the idea that AT&T would first patronize and then, eventually, buy the networks.

Looking For Plan B

Kiewit continued to propose building turn-key networks for emerging CAPs including Richard Kolsby and Barbara Samson's Intermedia Communications in Florida, Scott Yeager's Network Communications in Houston, Gary Lasher's Eastern TeleLogic in Philadelphia, Cliff Arellano's Indiana Digital Access in Indianapolis and dozens of others. There were few takers. Creating a business based on building fiber networks for emerging CAPs was turning out to be a tough row to hoe. Crowe and Holland still wanted to launch a Kiewit-backed, proactive build of fiber networks in the major cities without waiting for someone to start an CAP in each one. They needed to come up with a plan that could win backing from the Kiewit board.

Rebuffed By TCG

One obvious short coming of any multi-city roll-out was the lack, within Kiewit, of the telecommunications experience needed to operate and run the networks once they were completed. Crowe and Holland decided that before they could propose a plan that would get support, they needed to line up a partner who could supply the telecommunications expertise in general and the CAP expertise, specifically. The obvious choice would seem to be TCG.

In the Fall of 1987 Crowe and Holland went to TCG to meet with the "two Bobs," Annunziata and Atkinson. They did not get a warm reception. The Kiewit group appeared to TCG to offer little more than "wire pulling" expertise. TCG had its own dreams of national expansion and felt they didn't feel they needed anyone to help build their networks. TCG definitely didn't want Kiewit to become its partner and possibly carry off the fruits of TCG's hard-won experience.

Revenue, At Last

Back in Chicago, CFO was now making progress and, for once, was developing ahead of schedule. On Oct. 12, 1987, with the network nearly ready to carry its first customer, CFO held an official "ground breaking ceremony" at the Palmer House.[38] Mayor Harold Washington and members of the City Council were in attendance to denote the significance of the event.[39] CFO President and CEO, Tony Pompliano, gave a speech praising both Kiewit and the City for their work and support in bringing the project to a reality.

CFO ran ads stating that they were so confident that customers would be pleased with their DS-1 and DS-3 service quality that new installations would have a 120-day cancellation option with no penalty.[40] By October 15, 1987, the first seven buildings were on-line. Pompliano announced that the first DS-1 customer, Contel ASC, had been activated and that their first DS-3 customer, Allnet-Lexitel, would be operational shortly.

By December of 1987, the network was complete with all thirty buildings in the contract operational well ahead of the March 1988 scheduled date[41]. Revenue for 1988 was just shy of one million dollars ($903,735), although the company was not profitable. The operating loss was $2.4 million, and the accumulated debt was $6.8 million for the year.[42] Long term debt stood at $18.4 million.

Metropolitan Fiber Systems, Inc. And The $18 Million Plan

As the Chicago network had neared completion, at last, the CFO backers were invigorated and entertained dreams of expansion, as in the Lucas days. President Pompliano announced that CFO would be expanding into, perhaps, as many as seven new cities. The first expansion city would be Philadelphia, apparently in direct competition with FOCUS and its Philadelphia Fiber Optic network.[43]

Crowe began discussions with the CFO investor group about joining forces for a nationwide rollout. In place of the now abandoned $80 million plan, he proposed a more modest project consisting of three city networks for $18 million, if CFO would provide $9 million and Kiewit would provide the other $9 million.

The investors agreed and on January 21, 1988, a letter of intent was signed by the parties to create the new company.[44] The name of the new company would be, Metropolitan Fiber Systems, Inc. (MFS). Tony Pompliano, the CEO of the newly formed MFS, announced that the expansion into Philadelphia would become the first project under the MFS banner.[45] Thus Philadelphia, a modest-sized market in terms of dedicated, fiber transport, was now the target for network construction by three rival CAPs: Eastern TeleLogic, Philadelphia Fiber Optic and MFS.

MFS CEO Pompliano was ecstatic about the new organization and the support from Kiewit. He told reporters, "We're extremely excited about this, needless to say. MFS is a perfect marriage between Kiewit, an organization that has put networks together in the past, and the strong management team here at CFO."[46]

Jim Crowe, the President of Kiewit Communications, was equally enthusiastic. "Kiewit had been interested in the whole telecommunications market and had spent time analyzing this....Because we're looking internally for our financing, we won't be subject to anyone's restrictions, and through MFS, we're ... going to go forward with this rapidly ... Even though it's a 100-year-old business, it's as if it started yesterday. There are opportunities every time you look around."[47]

Rolling Out Expansion Cities

In the earlier studies with Lipman, Kiewit Communications had selected Philadelphia, Boston and Minneapolis as the first three cities that should be targeted. Now it was time to re-evaluate.

Philadelphia was obviously still the first city, since CFO had already begun preliminary development there. The people who had begun the work, however, were now at Philadelphia Fiber Optic and had become the competition for fiber rights-of-way. In the new effort, Royce Holland took on the role of chief right-of-way negotiator for MFS in Philadelphia. Showing an aptitude for the business, he obtained rights-of-way from the local rapid transit system and from Philadelphia Electric, the local electric utility. As a result the MFS network moved ahead quickly and was not slowed by competition with the Lucas group.

In Baltimore, the local utility, Baltimore Gas & Electric, was interested in a joint venture with MFS and had conduit and right-of-way in-place that could be used for rapid fiber deployment. Because of these favorable conditions, Baltimore was substituted for Boston in MFS' roll-out schedule.

In Minneapolis, Northern States Power, was also interested in the potential of fiber-based opportunities in local telecommunications. Northern States Power had available space in its conduit system for immediate fiber cable placement. The Minneapolis network build also proceeded rapidly.

Illinois Bell's "Fiber Hub"

In Chicago, Illinois Bell continued to counter-attack even the hint of potential competition. On August 12, 1987, Illinois Bell dropped the monthly price for a DS-1 circuit from $528.75 to $478.05, nearly matching CFO's $400. In addition to price reductions for DS-1s, Illinois Bell focused marketing efforts on the long distance carriers, offering special attention and faster installation intervals for dedicated circuits in the Loop area.

Chicago was not only a rail hub, it was also a network hub. Many long distance carrier networks converged on Chicago. These networks often needed to be linked to exchange traffic since most of the small carriers leased some or all of their capacity from the larger carriers. The rapid growth in business by the small carriers resulted in an increasingly attractive local market for high-speed digital links (multiple DS-1s and DS-3s) in downtown Chicago.

Illinois Bell moved to preempt this market from CAP competitors by developing a "Fiber Hub" facility for Interexchange Carriers in its key Wabash central office. The Hub provided flexible and convenient high speed cross connection among carriers and was manned with trained technicians 24 hours a day.[48] The Hub went into operation in April 1987.[49] By August eighteen carriers were using the Hub; and by the time the CFO network was ready for business, the Illinois Bell Wabash Fiber Hub was already serving twenty-three long distance carriers.[50] The Illinois Bell market position, particularly with the carrier market, looked formidable and relatively immune to CAP competitive challenge. The Fiber Hub provided everything—everything except diversity. Soon diversity would assume unprecedented importance.

MFS' National Expansion

As MFS began its national roll-out, it still viewed itself as engaged in a limited construction project. These fiber networks constituted a speculative construction effort and were being built to be sold. In

February, CEO Tony Pompliano had anticipated that MFS would be operational in four cities—Chicago, Philadelphia, Baltimore and Minneapolis—by year end 1988.[51]

However, as MFS experienced increasing success in the operation of its networks, the company's management and owners began to become more committed to staying in the telecommunications business. In May 1988, the "Hinsdale Incident"—a disastrous fire in a key Illinois Bell central office—suddenly created an dramatically increased demand for competitive, alternative networks like those of MFS.

Energized by this new opportunity, MFS devoted more resources to a national expansion. In November 1988 Pompliano announced MFS' commitment to a fifth city network to be built in Boston and also unveiled a greatly enhanced expansion program which anticipated that ten additional networks would be launched during 1989.[52,53]

Footnotes Chapter 3: A Light In The Tunnel

[1] Bruce Moffat, *"Forty Feet Below - The Story of Chicago's Tunnels,"* (Glendale, CA, Interurban Press, 1982), 48-49.

[2] Ibid. , 7.

[3] Ibid., 7-8.

[4] Ibid., 9.

[5] Ibid., 8.

[6] Leonard S. Hyman, Richard C. Toole and Rosemary M. Avellis, "The New Telecommunications Industry: Evolution and Organization," (Public Utilities Reports, Inc. and Merrill Lynch, Pierce, Fenner & Smith, Inc., 1987), 36.

[7] Bruce Moffat, 8.

[8] Ibid., 11-12.

[9] Ibid., 13.

[10] Ibid., 39.

[11] Ibid., 40.

[12] "16 Tons of Underground Words," *MIS Week*, Nov. 21, 1984, 20.

[13] "And Chicago Fiber Optics Corporation Would Offer Downtown Chicago Bypass," *Fiber/Laser News*, Nov. 23, 1984.

[14] "Illinois Bell Will Have Fiber Optic Competitor for Chicago Market," *Telephone News,* Dec. 10, 1984.

[15] "Digital Fiber-Optic Network to be Developed for Chicago's Loop Area," *Communications News,* May 1985, 11.

[16] "City Leases Tunnels At Basement Prices," *Chicago Tribune,* March 10, 1985, Sect. 1, 1.

[17] "Chicago Fiber Optic Tentatively Agrees To Pay City Sharply Increased Fees...," *Chicago Tribune,* Dec. 3, 1985, Sec. 2,1.

[18] "Council Approves Telecommunications Tunnel Lease," *Chicago Tribune,* March 13, 1986.

[19] "Chicago Fiber Optic Forms Holding Co. Called Fiber Optic Corp. of the United States ...," *Chicago Tribune,* Oct. 4, 1985, Sec. 3, 2.

[20] Illinois Bell, ICC 5.

[21] "Whither Fibertrak: The Venture Stumbles, But Will It Fall ?", *Fiber Optic News,* Aug. 5, 1985.

[22] "The Other Man From Omaha," *Barons,* June 17, 1996, 30.

[23] Ibid. , 33.

[24] Ibid. , 30.

[25] Ibid. , 30.

[26] Ibid. , 33.

[27] A tandem or Class 4 switch switches traffic between switches. For example, it can switch traffic between the Class 5 switch in a local central office and the switch in a long distance carrier's Point of Presence or it can switch traffic

between two Class 5 switches. It cannot switch local telephone calls directly to end users.

[28] "Philadelphia Fiber Optic Corp. Gets Under Way," *Fiber Optic News,* July 27, 1987.

[29] "Letters Of Intent For Services Signed," *Fiber Optic News,* July 27, 1987.

[30] "Chicago Fiber Optic Announces Management Changes," *PR Newswire,* Chicago, Aug.. 26, 1987.

[31] Steve Coll, *"The Deal of The Century, The Breakup of AT&T,"* (New York: Atheneum, 1986).

[32] Larry Kahaner, *"On The Line - the Men of MCI Who Took On AT&T, Risked Everything and Won,"* (New York: Warner Books, 1986).

[33] "We Kind of Focus on Our Mistakes," *Forbes,* Oct. 24, 1994, 164.

[34] Letter from AT&T CEO James E. Olson to Congressman John Dingell. See, for example, ref. 35.

[35] Steve Coll, 353.

[36] "Switched Access Competition In U.S. Telephony: Evidence and Interpretation," *Review of Business,* Spring 1989, v10, n4, 19.

[37] This internal conflict was never really resolved. Ironically, when a meeting was later held on April 18, 1988, specifically to resolve the feud, Olson, who was apparently recovering at home from cancer surgery, unexpectedly died that very morning. The meeting dissolved into a discussion of succession issues, and the bypass disagreement was never addressed.

[38] "Chicago Fiber Optic Corp. Announces Ground Breaking Ceremony," CFO Press Release, Oct. 12, 1987.

[39] "No End to Light In the Tunnels - City's Fiber Optic Network Is Underway Underground," *Chicago Tribune, Oct. 14, 1987.*

[40] Advertisement in Crains Chicago Business, Oct. 5, 1987.

[41] "Chicago Fiber Optic Announces Completion of Construction Project and Name Change for Company," *PR Newswire,* March 29, 1988.

[42] Chicago Fiber Optic Corporation d/b/a Metropolitan Fiber Systems of Chicago, Inc., Financial Statements for Year Ended December 31, 1989, April 20, 1990.

[43] "Chicago Fiber Expands Markets, Shifts Management," *Fiber Optic News,* Sept. 14, 1987.

[44] "The Majority Owners of Chicago Fiber Optic Corporation Announces Letter of Intent With Kiewit Communications Company, Inc.," *PR Newswire,* Jan. 27, 1988.

[45] Ibid.

[46] "Chicago Fiber Optic and Kiewit Communications Form Metropolitan Fiber Systems," *Fiber Optic News,* Feb. 8, 1988.

[47] Ibid.

[48] Fiber Hub Service, Ameritech Access Services Brochure, April 1988.

[49] Illinois Bell.

[50] "Illinois Bell Snags AT&T for Fiber Hub," *BOC Week,* Aug. 10, 1987.

[51] "Chicago Fiber Optic and Kiewit Communications Form Metropolitan Fiber Systems," *Fiber Optic News,* Feb. 8, 1988.

[52] " MFS Adds New Alternative Networks -- Sees Opportunity in Telecom's Last Frontier," *Fiber Optic News,* Nov. 14, 1988.

[53] "Metropolitan Fiber Systems, Inc. (MFS) Comes Out Of The Closet," *Fiber Optic Weekly Update,* v8, No. 44, November 4, 1988, 1.

4. THE HINSDALE INCIDENT

The Central Office: The Network Nerve Center

The nerve center and the center of intelligence of a telephone network is in its central offices.

The central office (CO) facility is a wire center facility that usually houses one or more large telephone switches as well as other network electronics. A central office telephone switch is a sophisticated, computerized device. It consists of multiple modules—a computer module, driven by software containing over one million lines of code, an expandable memory module, a line module which connects to user phone lines, a trunk module which connects to other switches and a switching module which makes the required physical connections to complete a call. Some central offices are also points of concentration for non-switched circuits which, increasingly, are fiber optic. The central offices houses the digital electronics associated these dedicated circuits.

Copper wires provide a metal path from the homes and offices served by a given central office to the line-side of the switch. This line-side circuit is more commonly called "the local loop." The line module contains integrated circuit cards which are the electronic interfaces to each local loop. A single "shelf" typically contains cards supporting 2,000 lines. By adding shelves (and memory) a single switch can be expanded to support as many as 100,000 lines. (However, of the 15,000 central office switches installed in the United States, the average switch has fewer than 1,000 active lines.) Similarly, the trunk modules on the network side of the switch contain an expandable number of trunk cards. Trunk circuits provide connection to other local and long distance carrier switches.

The central office also contains a bank of batteries to supply low voltage, direct current through the copper lines to the telephones for ringing and control functions. This is why traditional telephones work even in a power outage.

Central office switches and electronics typically run on direct current (DC) rather than alternating current (AC) power. Commercial AC power is converted to DC in the central office by rectifier banks. This primary power source is backed up by a secondary power source from diesel-driven generators maintained in the central office in the event commercial power is lost. Finally, should auxiliary generator power fail, the switch and CO equipment can be run for several hours by using the DC power from the battery banks.

Central offices are neatly maintained, and craft work is performed by technicians following meticulous "Bell System Practices." The thousands of wires converging on the switch are carried in bundles of cables on overhead cable trays. The electronics are lined up in equipment racks or "bays."

The building is usually clean, secure, sometimes windowless and always air conditioned. The equipment is monitored from one or more network control centers and the building contains fire, smoke and intrusion detection. The facility is carefully maintained, but not all central offices contain office space and may not be routinely occupied by staff.

Cable Mining at Hinsdale

The Illinois Bell Telephone Company is one of the five operating companies (along with Michigan Bell, Ohio Bell, Indiana Bell and Wisconsin Bell) which, at divestiture, constituted the Chicago-based Regional Bell Operating Company, Ameritech.

In the Spring of 1988, Illinois Bell hired Garrett and West;, a Knoxville, Tennessee-based electrical contractor, to carry out a routine house-keeping chore called "cable mining" in some of its central offices.[1] In the "cable mining" operations, cabling is consolidated, excess and unused cable is removed and, if required, new cable added.

In 1988 Illinois Bell had over 340 central offices; 30 in the Chicago suburbs alone. For periods in February, March and April of 1988, the Garrett and West Company cable mining project reached Illinois Bell's Hinsdale Central office. The town of Hinsdale is in the western suburbs of Chicago, twelve miles south of O'Hare International Airport and about twenty miles west of downtown Chicago.

The Hinsdale central office was one of the three largest COs in Illinois Bell. It housed an 1AESS switch (manufactured by AT&T's equipment division, now Lucent Technologies), an analog but computer controlled switch, then the most commonly deployed switch in the United States.

The office served 42,000 lines of local service, mostly in the residential communities of Hinsdale, Clarendon Hills, Willowbrook, Burr Ridge, Darien, Oak Brook, Westmont and southern DuPage county.[2] There were also 118,000 trunk circuits and 13,000 dedicated or "special" circuits and their associated electronics in this CO.[3]

During the Spring cable mining work in the Hinsdale CO, an Illinois Bell technician reported he thought he had heard arcing and had seen sparks fall.[4] He was told by a Garrett and West employee that a power cable, in the same tray with the telephone cables, had been damaged but also that it had subsequently been repaired.

The Hinsdale CO is a two-story building with fourteen-foot high ceilings. The cable racks run high overhead and the cables in the trays are not easily viewed.

Mother's Day: The Busiest Calling Day Of The Year

Mother's Day Sunday usually has the greatest peak calling volume of the year for long distance companies. Mother's Day May 8, 1988, was no different; and traffic through the Hinsdale office was very high.[5]

In the afternoon of that day, a line of strong thunderstorms rolled through the western suburbs of Chicago; and lightning strikes caused some local power outages. On the first floor of the Hinsdale CO, high up in a cable tray some cables shifted.[6] It was never determined exactly why. It may have been due to a temperature change. It may have been a vibration. It may have been due to surges related to the power outages. The damaged power cable rubbed against the metal sheath of an armored cable. The repair, assuming it had been made, was insufficient. There was a spark. The cable insulation began to smolder.

Probably A False Alarm

The Hinsdale office was unoccupied over the weekend but it was being monitored from two network control centers—one in nearby Chicago and one 200 miles away in Springfield, Illinois. The

Springfield Division Alarm Reporting Center (DARC) received a power outage alarm for the Hinsdale central office at 3:50 PM in the afternoon. The power outage alarm was accompanied by a fire detection alarm. The power system in the central office switched over smoothly from commercial power to diesel power and, in the process, the fire alarm cleared itself.[7]

The Hinsdale CO was equipped with two diesel back-up generators. Shortly, the diesel power failed and again the DARC received both a power outage and a fire detection alarm. The system in the central office switched smoothly from the failed diesel system to the battery back-up system, and again the fire alarms cleared. At 4:20 PM an isolated fire alarm signal came in, but the DARC operator thought it was probably a false signal related to the earlier power outages and the sequence of back-up system switching.[8]

Illinois Bell had not had a central office fire in 42 years.[9] It was difficult to believe that one might be happening now. Rather than calling the Hinsdale Fire Department as operating procedures required, the DARC operator in Springfield called his duty supervisor for instructions.

Meanwhile, the Chicago network center had also observed the power outages and the back-up system activations and began to dispatch a local technician to physically check the central office facility. Growing increasingly concerned, the Springfield supervisor attempted to call the Hinsdale Fire Department at 4:30, but found that it was impossible. By then all the phone lines serving Hinsdale were dead.[10]

Arriving at the Hinsdale central office, the Illinois Bell technician found the scene quiet with the building apparently secure and unharmed.[11] But, upon opening the door he was greeted by thick, black, acrid smoke billowing from burning polyvinyl chloride insulation on the cables in the trays overhead. He attempted to call in the alarm, but no phones in the facility were operational.[12]

He ran to the nearby highway and flagged down a motorist. The motorist called the police on his cell phone. At 4:58, a controversial 38 minutes after the first alarm came into the Springfield DARC, the Hinsdale Fire Dept. was alerted to the fire.[13]

The Fire Kept Re-Igniting

At first, it looked like a simple fire to extinguish. The firemen found the fire extended along the cable tray for only about six feet. Melting insulation dripping down and corrosive gases from the polyvinyl chloride were the only hazards. Spraying the burning cable with water knocked down the flames but, surprisingly, the fire kept re-igniting. It seemed to be fed by on-going electrical discharges.[14]

Even with the circuit breakers open to the commercial power system and with the two diesel generators turned off, the fire persisted. The fire was being re-ignited by electrical arcing fed by the batteries. There was no convenient way to quickly disconnect the hard-wired batteries.[15]

Only by manually pulling all the fuses, one-by-one from the battery banks could the fire finally be extinguished. At 7:15, the fire was out for good.[16]

No Quick Fix

The outage impact was widespread. In addition to 35,000 local phone customers who lost service, both O'Hare and Midway Airports lost critical communications lines to the FAA, 911 service was interrupted and hundreds of thousands of long distance calls on circuits routed through the Hinsdale CO were blocked.[17]

Within hours AT&T and MCI rushed to install temporary microwave dishes on the roofs of nearby buildings to bypass the Hinsdale CO and to restore service to major business customers. Where a line-of-sight path was available from a building rooftop to one of the long distance carrier's POPs, the simple use of a $60,000 dish the size of a garbage can lid provided a direct link to the long distance carrier, completely bypassing the Illinois Bell network. Over the next few days AT&T installed this service for 25 corporate customers and MCI for six.[18]

Illinois Bell technicians worked through the night to install ten emergency lines linking local fire and police stations to other Illinois Bell central offices and set up a phone facility outside the Hinsdale office. By the end of the second day, 55 lines had been installed at businesses and schools in the area for calls to emergency agencies.[19] For most of the residential and small business customers, however, there would be no quick fix.[20]

The initial assessment of the damaged Hinsdale central office was promising. The heavy smoke damage was confined primarily to the first floor area. A lower level and the second floor showed little obvious impact. The 1AESS switch's computer module was not damaged, and the database software was intact.

An army of Illinois Bell Technicians descended on the facility and began re-routing lines and putting the switch back into operation. By Wednesday, May 11th, however, a team of experts from Bellcore, the RBOC national research organization, delivered grim news.

Replacing A Mortally Damaged Switch

The switch would have to be replaced. Acid formed by the interaction of toxic fumes and water was destroying the integrated circuits inside the switch. Not even replacing all the line and trunk cards could control the advancing corrosion. The switch was mortally damaged.[21]

While work continued on the crippled 1AESS switch, turning up 3,000 lines per day, Illinois Bell decided that they would have to install a replacement switch, an advanced, digital 5ESS on the second floor. On May 15th, they ordered the switch from AT&T Network Systems. It was anticipated that the switch would be in service by June 1st, but that customer service would not be completely restored until mid-June.[22]

Fortunately, a completed switch that was ready for shipment was able to be diverted to Hinsdale.[23] The next day the modular components began arriving, along with AT&T installation technicians. With crews working around the clock in 12 hour shifts, the major components were in place by May 16th; and line side connections were begun.

It was an unprecedented event. Central office switch installations normally take months of planning, followed by months of work to complete and a long period of testing before being placed on line.

Many of the fiber trunk lines utilized Northern Telecom electronics. Northern Telecom sent in 41 installers and brought fiber terminal equipment in from as far away as the U.K. By Monday, May 16, 1988, most of the 118,000 trunks were back in service. AT&T brought in digital cross connects and T-1 multiplexers, working toward a May 21st goal for restoring the 13,000 dedicated circuits.

Spokesmen for AT&T and Northern Telecom called the damage caused by the fire, "the worst since a 1974 blaze knocked out the large 2nd Avenue central office in New York City."[24]

Technicians were jammed shoulder to shoulder, limited by the physical space around the equipment to about two hundred workers at a time. Four television sets were set up at convenient spots within the Hinsdale central office. On the screen was the latest status news under the heading: "Cutover/Cutback Execution Status." On May 30, 1988, it flashed the welcome news. "Migration Complete." Two hundred workers burst into spontaneous cheering.[25]

Within twenty-two days they had installed sixty bays of complex equipment and 180,000 circuits. Along the way they had carried out the fastest central office switch installation ever, and they had done it on the newest, most advanced digital switch on the market.

Meanwhile, they had also maintained some minimum level of service on the damaged switch and translated the database to the new switch. They had re-wired, loaded and cut-over a complete new switch. They had carried out what was normally a fifty-week task in just one day over three weeks and they were jubilant.

Customers Were Less Inclined To Celebrate The Record Achievement

Ameritech Chairman, William Weiss, issued a statement on June 6, 1988, that said:

> Hinsdale will be regarded as a watershed event in the history of telecommunications in this country. You may be sure we will share what we learn with the entire industry.[26]

Customers were less inclined to celebrate the record achievement. In the second day of the outage, the Illinois State Attorney General,

Neil Hartigan, called for the Illinois Commerce Commission to investigate the circumstances surrounding the fire and to determine the extent of customers' losses.[27] Hartigan suggested that Illinois Bell should establish a multi-million dollar special fund to compensate businesses for their lost revenues.[28]

Even while the restoration had been in process, speculation had begun about whether the public telephone network had built-in vulnerabilities due to the concentration of traffic in certain switches or over certain fiber routes. Illinois Bell Vice President of Operations, James A. Eibel, noted that the company had engineered the network with redundant primary and back-up fiber for higher reliability. "Unfortunately," he noted, "both fibers went through the same switching center and both were destroyed."[29] The Chief Engineer for the Illinois Commerce Commission, Jerry Hoppe, responding to a reporter's query on this issue, said, "There are certain advantages of scale, but there obviously is a disadvantage when you put all your eggs in one basket."[30]

Acting on the complaint from the Attorney General, the Illinois Commerce Commission began an extensive investigation. The probe began with a public hearing and continued with detailed investigations. Smaller telecom-intensive businesses had been particularly hard hit. Two travel agencies claimed losses of $250,000 and $350,000, respectively. A catering company claimed losses of $200,000. Two construction companies, two marketing firms, an accounting agency, a manufacturer and a commodities broker filed suits against Illinois Bell. Blue Angel International Travel of Naperville, Illinois filed a class-action suit on behalf of travel agents and others. The catering company and two individuals also filed a class-action suit.[31]

Illinois Bell defended itself by pointing out that under Illinois state law it was not required to compensate customers for business revenue lost during the outage. Illinois Bell noted that Illinois Commerce Commission rules limited its liability to a billing credit for the time service was interrupted plus an equal amount. Therefore, a customer with a usual $20 monthly bill, who was out of service for two weeks, would receive a $10 credit plus another $10.[32] Under no circumstances, however, was the company willing to pay for contingent liability or other damages.

A spokeswoman for Illinois Bell said, "The law limits Illinois Bell's liability for obvious reasons. This helps keep rates down and service affordable." Litigants and the Attorney General argued that the law was not meant to shield the company from the results of negligent actions. The Courts agreed with Illinois Bell and dismissed the suits.

Focus On the Heroic Efforts: "The Hinsdale Challenge"

Illinois Bell continued to try to focus attention on the heroic efforts of the technicians who restored the Hinsdale central office with un-precedented speed. Ameritech, the RBOC parent of Illinois Bell, undertook a campaign to emphasize the value of the "lessons-learned" about protecting the central office from disaster.

A letter was issued by Ameritech Bell Group President, Ormand J. Wade:

> An open letter to the telecommunications industry:
>
> The May 8, 1988, fire at a major fiber switching hub in Hinsdale, Illinois, underscored once again the critical role the telecommunications industry plays in the nation's welfare.
>
> In April, 1989, Ameritech will share information gained from its Hinsdale experience at a national in-dustry Forum entitled, "The Hinsdale Challenge."
>
> "The Hinsdale Challenge" embodies Ameritech's commitment to the telecommunications industry. We invite our colleagues in the network, operations and engineering areas to join us on either day of the Forum's two-day run in Chicago and learn from our experience as we head into a strengthened future for our customers, our networks and our companies.

On April 10 and 11, 1989, Ameritech ran two sessions of the semi-nar entitled, "The Hinsdale Challenge."

The President and CEO of Ameritech Services, Bruce DeMaeyer, served as moderator for the seminar. In a flyer advertising the seminar he wrote:[33]

The May 8, 1988, Hinsdale, Illinois central office fire provided the industry's first real-life example of the damage fire can do to an electronic office which includes a major fiber hub—as well as real-life experience in what is required for successful service reconstruction and restoral.

"The Hinsdale Challenge" is an opportunity for operations, network and engineering leaders to learn and grow from our experience. At this Forum, you will hear from Ameritech and Bellcore experts on key issues related to service restoration and recovery, and about potential alternatives developed by Ameritech to protect service continuity.

Ameritech Services—the planning company for the five Ameritech operating companies—is proud to host "The Hinsdale Challenge" as part of Ameritech's commitment to the telecommunications industry.

Ameritech clearly failed to appreciate the depth of customers' anger over the Hinsdale Incident and its aftermath. One respected telecommunications expert wrote that, "Asking people to pay $185 to come to a seminar and listen to how you screwed up is the height of arrogance."

A Windfall For CAPs

For the CAPs, Illinois Bell's misfortune was a windfall which they seized with relish. Their sales and marketing pitch changed immediately. The week before Hinsdale the marketing presentation of a typical CAP was: "We offer high-tech fiber optic service at a lower cost than the telephone company, and we offer a diverse routing capability."

After Hinsdale the presentation was: "We offer route diversity so that your telecommunications traffic will never suffer a "Hinsdale" disaster; and we will provide all this on state-of-the-art, self-healing fiber networks for less than the telephone company."

AT&T, still a major RBOC equipment supplier, took a low-key approach to its criticism of Illinois Bell. AT&T's Director of Network Operations, Joe Nacchio, was quoted in the Wall Street Journal as saying, "I think that the big users have a lot of risk with a network that funnels calls through choke points."[34] MFS was unrestrained in blasting Illinois Bell and pointing out that, "The fire illustrates the vulnerability of the Illinois Bell network to disruption from natural disasters, terrorism, arson, vandalism and other causes."

Bob Atkinson, speaking both for TCG and as President of ALTS, wrote a commentary piece for the August 8, 1988, publication of *Communications Week*, entitled, "Where The Blazes Is Security— To Avoid The Burning Bottleneck Users Must Seek Alternatives."[35] He addressed policy makers as well as consumers by saying:

> The Hinsdale fire was a watershed event that will reshape the way we look at local telecommunications for years to come.
>
> ... Businesses ... lost millions of dollars of sales and the disaster wreaked havoc on long distance networks. It was a catastrophe of such magnitude largely because the local exchange company had a monopoly ...
>
> No telecommunications user can afford to place all its eggs in one basket; what's needed is an alternative to the telephone company for local telecommunications.
>
> There is a solution.
>
> The answer: local competition
>
> Telephone company networks and alternative local networks should be interconnected so that each backs up the other...if alternative local networks are interconnected to the local telephone networks at several central offices, a diverse local public network would exist without the needless expenditure of billions of rate payer dollars.

By not actively promoting local competition, public policy makers are ignoring their mandate, putting an Information Age economy dangerously at risk. They are fiddling while the bottleneck burns.

"Don't Put All Your Telecom Eggs in One Basket"

All the CAPs, but particularly Teleport, used the Hinsdale event to vigorously attack the RBOCs. Teleport consistently pursued what it saw as its mission to break the monopoly hold of telephone companies on local telecommunications with missionary zeal. This included a full court press to control the words and images of the discussion as well as the substance.

In a speech on the value of an alternative network, TCG CEO Annunziata had said,

> New York City businesses will no longer have to put all their telecommunications eggs in one basket, a fact that will improve the city's business climate.[36]

That comment was now translated into an image which was made the centerpiece of a marketing campaign. Teleport developed a cartoon of an upside-down bell spilling its cargo of eggs. The symbol along with the slogan, "Don't Put All Your Telecom Eggs in One Basket," was used on TCG stationery, fax cover sheets and in Teleport's 1988 Annual Report.[37]

Teleport's taunting produced no response from the RBOCs until 1990.[38]

Selling "Brand X" To Corporations

While to some in the traditionally staid telecommunications industry, the CAP rhetoric on network vulnerability seemed overheated. However, it quickly became apparent that the Hinsdale Incident had "legs." Market surveys showed that nearly 40% of small businesses felt they were trapped in the grip of an insensitive and uncaring telephone monopoly. This key customer base was more than willing and ready for a change.

Large businesses, which received more marketing attention from RBOCs, felt less alienated but also, generally, had more financial risk from a communications outage. They, however, took a greater interest in the opportunity to diversify and thus increase the reliability of their networks by buying some circuits from the CAPs.

In marketing to businesses, CAPs had traditionally been dealing with the telecommunications managers. Only the telecommunications managers in companies with a high revenue dependence on communications (*e.g.*, a financial services company) carried significant stature within their corporate structures. Most telecommunications managers did not fall into this category.

Without internal standing in their own corporations, telecommunications managers had little to gain and everything to lose by making an error in choosing telecommunications services. They were characteristically risk-averse and not likely to be an "early adopter" for a new carrier. A decision to buy service from a "Brand X" CAP was difficult for a low-ranking corporate employee to make.

After the Hinsdale Incident, ensuring that corporate communications were diversified and insulated from a single network failure was a subject that now could engage the interest of the senior corporate officers. CAPs found that they were now marketing to higher-level officers or dealing with newly emboldened telecommunications managers willing to buy their services.

Who's To Blame?

On March 10, 1989, nearly a year after the fire, the results of the investigation of the fire by the Illinois Commerce Commission, the Office of the State Fire Marshal and the Emergency Services & Disaster Agency were released at a press conference in Chicago.

A voluminous analysis by Forensic Technologies International, a Maryland-based consulting company hired by the Illinois Commerce Commission, dissected the probable origin and pathology of the fire. It ruled out arson and concluded that the fire was accidental.[39] It identified the probable cause as an electrical arc between a damaged power cable and the metallic sheath of an armored communications cable in the same cable tray.[40]

The State Fire Marshal noted that the report found that, "The smoke/fire detection system was adequate, but company procedures were not followed completely, leading to an excessive delay in the notification of the fire department ... cable tray loading was excessive in some areas, and the procedure to cut the power was too complex."[41],[42]

In general, the report was as benign as Ameritech could have hoped for. It was generally conceded that a more sophisticated fire suppression system using Halon gas (as in most computer rooms) would not have been effective in smothering a fire fourteen feet overhead as the heavy, inert gas sinks to the floor. It was also not clearly determined whether a more timely notification of the fire department could have significantly limited the damage.[43]

Some media reports blasted Ameritech with headlines like, "Hinsdale Fire Report Faults Bell"[44] and "ICC Report Faults BOC In Hinsdale Fire"[45]   Others were relatively mild, placing the blame more vaguely as in "Procedures Blamed In Hinsdale Fire."[46]

Attorney General Hartigan, however, was satisfied that the report established that Illinois Bell had been negligent. Despite the earlier dismissal by the Illinois Circuit Court of the class-action suit against Illinois Bell he believed that the report "confirms that the company's emergency procedures were inadequate," that the company's liability had been established and that it should now provide compensation.[47]

In the end, the Attorney General's statement produced no action.[48]

Network Diversity: Not Just "Nice To Have," An Absolute Requirement

For long distance carriers, who were already the major CAP customers, the lesson from the Hinsdale Incident was that route diversity was an absolute requirement. Convenient telephone facilities like the Wabash Fiber Hub available from Illinois Bell could not displace the need for network, and hence, carrier diversity. After Hinsdale it was clear, if it not been before, that long distance carriers must give enough of their business to CAPs so that there was at least one viable alternative to the local telephone network in each major market.

Giving a portion of their business to CAPs also produced other benefits for the long distance carriers. Beyond providing a source of network diversity, the presence of a CAP could also serve as a lever on the telephone company to induce better, more responsive service, faster provisioning and lower prices. The most profound impact of the Hinsdale Incident, however, was on regulators and legislators. Network diversity was not just "nice to have." For telecommunications -intensive corporations and for long distance carriers, it was a basic requirement.[49] Once the economic aspects of telecommunications services were understood by policy-makers, the path for policy evolution was set. This path would lead to one end: a concerted drive for competition in local telecommunications markets.

Aftermath

Ameritech had ample time to anticipate the findings of the Illinois Commerce Commission investigation and was prepared to minimize the damage from the report findings. Simultaneously with the release of the report, Ameritech announced its own press conference.[50] At the press conference they unveiled the "Ameritech Network Protection Plan."[51]

Under the plan, Illinois Bell proposed, among other actions, to spend $80 million over five years to provide the entire Chicago area with protection against network failure. The plan incorporated redundant and diverse fiber network paths and other protections designed to automatically maintain communications in the event of a fire.[52,53] Ameritech said that although it was initially deploying the "Ameritech Network Protection Plan" to Chicago, it would create similar programs for use in major cities in the other Ameritech states.[54] It was too little, too late to stop the budding competitors, the CAPs. They would never go away now. The value of alternative networks had become clear. Customers felt that Illinois Bell had abandoned them and ducked their responsibilities by hiding behind "legalisms." The public interest benefits of opening the local to CAP competitors and the case for mandating network interconnection of CAP and RBOC networks were now apparent and compelling.

One by one leading state PUCs, like those in Illinois and New York, would move in the direction of mandated interconnection and opening the local telecommunications markets to competition. After several states had taken action, the FCC proposed similar rules to encourage interconnection and competition on a national scale. Ultimately, the Congress would bring these all together in the Telecommunications Act of 1996.

Footnotes Chapter 4: The Hinsdale Incident

[1] "Hinsdale Aftermath: COs At Risk," *Telephony,* March 20, 1989, 22.

[2] Ibid. , 21-22.

[3] "ICC Report Faults BOC In Hinsdale Fire," *BOC Week,* March 13, 1989.

[4] Hinsdale Aftermath, 22.

[5] "Mother's Day CO Fire Produces Ill. Bell's Worst Service Outage," *Telephony,* May 16, 1988, 8.

[6] Hinsdale Aftermath, 21.

[7] Ibid. , 22.

[8] Ibid. , 22.

[9] "Extraordinary In Every Way," Letter to the Editor, William Hensley, VP Illinois Bell, *Telephony,* June 20, 1988, 29.

[10] Hinsdale Aftermath, 22.

[11] WLS-TV, May 9, 1988.

[12] Ibid. , 22.

[13] Ibid. , 22.

[14] Ibid. , 24.

[15] Ibid. , 24.

[16] "Final Report Says Hinsdale Fire Caused By Electrical Fault; Recommends Fire Prevention Procedures For Illinois Bell, Including New Office Of Fire Protection And Investigation," *Telecommunications Reports,* March 13, 1989.

[17] "Fire Causes Airport Delays," *New York Times,* May 10, 1988, D24.

[18] "MCI, AT&T Acted To Plug In Business of Midwest Clients," *Wall Street Journal,* June 6, 1988.

[19] "Extraordinary In Every Way," Letter from William Hensley, VP Illinois Bell, *Telephony,* June 20, 1988, 29.

[20] "West Of Chicago Waiting For Dial Tone," *New York Times,* May 20, A1 (A12).

[21] "Mother's Day CO Fire Produces Ill. Bell's Worst Service Outage," *Telephony,* May 16, 1988, 8.

[22] "Illinois Bell Speeds Recovery," *Telephony,* am report, June 6, 1988.

[23] "At Last, Good News for IBT," *Telephony,* am report, May 23, 1988.

[24] "Mother's Day CO Fire Produces Ill. Bell's Worst Service Outage," *Telephony,* May 16, 1988, 9.

[25] *The Naperville Sun,* May 30, 1988.

[26] Quoted in "The Hinsdale Challenge" flyer.

[27] "Procedure Blamed In Hinsdale Fire," *Computerworld,* March 20, 1989, 120.

[28] "Fire Liability Issue Looming for Illinois Bell," *Telephony,* May 23, 1988, 9.

[29] "Phone System Feared Vulnerable To Wider Disruptions Of Services," *New York Times,* May 26, 1988, A1 (D8).

[30] Ibid.

31 "Citing Negligence, Users File Suits Against Ill Bell," *Network World,* June 6, 1988, 1.

32 "ICC Report Faults BOC In Hinsdale Fire," *BOC Week,* March 13, 1989.

33 "The Hinsdale Challenge," seminar advertising flyer issued by Ameritech.

34 "MCI, AT&T Acted To Plug In Business of Midwest Clients," *Wall Street Journal,* June 6, 1988.

35 "Where The Blazes Is Security? - To Avoid The Burning Bottleneck, Users Must Seek Alternatives," *Communications Week,* August 8, 1988, 208.

36 Teleport Report, Spring 1989, No. 7, 4.

37 Teleport Communications Group 1988 Annual Report, 5.

38 "Actually, It's Pretty Hard to Put Eggs in the Right-Side-Up One," *Wall Street Journal*, March 13, 1990, B3.

39 Hinsdale Fire Report Faults Bell," *State Telephone Regulation Report,* March 23, 1989.

40 "Final Report Says Hinsdale Fire Caused By Electrical Fault; Recommends Fire Prevention Procedures For Illinois Bell, Including New Office Of Fire Protection And Investigation," *Telecommunications Reports,* March 13, 1989.

41 Hinsdale Fire Report Faults Bell," *State Telephone Regulation Report,* March 23, 1989.

42 "ICC Report Faults BOC In Hinsdale Fire," *BOC Week,* March 13, 1989.

43 "Hinsdale's Aftermath: COs At Risk," 25.

44 *State Telephone Regulation Report,* March 23, 1989.

45 *BOC Week,* March 13, 1989.

46 *Computerworld,* March 20, 1989.

47 Ibid.

48 There was considerable editorial criticism in Chicago papers of Hartigan's decision not to refile an action. After Hartigan was defeated in a run for Governor of Illinois in 1992, he became a highly-paid outside attorney for Illinois Bell.

49 "The Phoenix Factor - Will Wall Street Survive Computer Disasters," *Wall Street Computer Review,* August 1989, 26.

50 *Communications Daily,* March 9, 1989.

51 "Illinois Bell To Install New Fiber Network As Part Of Disaster Plan,"*Data Channels,* March 22, 1989.

52 Ibid.

53 "Illinois Bell To Implement New Network Protection Plan, In Wake of Hinsdale Fire," *Telecommunications Reports,* March 20, 1989.

54 "Hinsdale Fire Report Faults Bell," *State Telephone Regulation Report,* March 23, 1989.

5. THE PIONEERS

A Handful of Players

Few CAPs existed to take advantage of the demand for diverse networks sparked by the Hinsdale fire of May 1988. There was, however, a handful of other CAP companies in existence, in addition to Teleport Communications Group (TCG) and Chicago Fiber Optic/MFS. These pioneers included Institutional Communications Co., Bay Area Teleport and PSO/MetroLink, all of which had local fiber optic networks operational prior to year end 1987.

During 1988, three fiber networks came into operation. The largest of these new CAP companies was Intermedia Communications of Florida, which was owned by private investors and venture capitalists. The other networks, Indiana Digital Access in Indianapolis, Indiana and Kansas City FiberNet in Kansas City, Missouri, were owned or controlled by cable television conglomerate, Time Warner. However, the Indiana network was created because of the persistent efforts of a single entrepreneur and minority owner.

The only CAP that had clearly established itself by 1988 was Teleport Communications Group. TCG's New York network had successfully passed the start-up stage, and the company had firmly established operations with 170 buildings on-net and 110,000 voice grade equivalent circuits in service. TCG had the largest CAP revenue for 1988, an estimated $11 million, and was growing at 100% per year.

Institutional Communications Co. (ICC) of Washington, D.C., was second to TCG in size, and had 1988 revenue of $3.4 million.[1] The company, however, was in shaky condition. ICC had expanded rapidly on limited capital. It was not experiencing TCG's success nor growth rate. It could not service its debt load and was desperately in need of a financial infusion.

Chicago Fiber Optic's revenue was $0.9 million for 1988, its first full year of operation. The Metropolitan Fiber System/Chicago Fiber Optic joint venture was poised to launch a national roll-out of urban networks. Networks were under construction in Philadelphia and Baltimore.[2]

The Pioneers
Local Fiber CAP Companies Operational
By Year End 1988

Company	Network Location	Operational
Teleport Communications Group	New York, NY	1985
Institutional Communications Co.	Washington, D.C.	1986
Bay Area Teleport	San Francisco, CA	1986
PSO/MetroLink	Tulsa, OK	1986
Chicago Fiber Optic Co./MFS	Chicago, IL	1987
Intermedia Commun. of Florida	Orlando, FL	1988
Indiana Digital Access	Indianapolis, IN	1988
Kansas City FiberNet	Kansas City, MO	1988

There were a few other companies that, while technically not operating local fiber networks, considered themselves as members of the CAP industry and joined ALTS.

Other CAP-Like Companies Operational
By Year End 1988

Company	Network Location	Operational
Diginet Communications	Milwaukee/Chicago	1985
DigiNet	Northwest	1987
LOCATE	New York	1981

Although listed as a full member of the ALTS industry association, Diginet Communications was, in 1988, a long-haul fiber carrier, providing service between Milwaukee, Wisconsin and Chicago, Illinois.[3] It would later create local fiber networks in both cities and operate as a combination CAP and long-haul transport provider.

Diginet of Mercer Island, Washington was owned by Northwest Energy Company, a subsidiary of Williams Communications of Tulsa, OK which also owned Williams Telecommunications, a fiber-based, national interexchange carrier.[4] Although DigiNet was a full member of the ALTS industry association, it really was a provider of long-haul digital transport throughout the Northwest and not a local carrier.[5]

LOCATE (Local Area Telecommunications, Inc.) was a microwave-based carrier that was founded in 1981. By 1988 it had built point-to-point digital links in many cities. In New York City, it created something that looked more like a local network. Using a web of digital microwave paths it linked a cluster of high-rise buildings in Manhattan. LOCATE became a very active member of the industry association, ALTS.

*****

I. Institutional Communications Co.

Starting With Only A Dream

The second largest CAP in 1988 (behind TCG) was Institutional Communications Company (ICC) of Washington, D.C.; but it was struggling. Unlike TCG with backing from Merrill Lynch and MFS with backing from the Peter Kiewit Sons' Company, ICC did not have the deep pockets of a corporate parent. ICC started only with a dream.

The Institutional Communications Company had gotten off to an early, but slow start. It had been incorporated in Maryland on November 17, 1980, by G. Scott Brodey, Sr. and Robert J. Sankey. ICC was conceived as a company that would provide regional transport for cable television in the Washington, D.C. metro area. It received an FCC license in 1983 to install and operate, on an interstate basis, fiber optic and coaxial facilities and to resell the services to other carriers.[6] However, the company remained in a conceptual and planning stage until 1985.

The 46-year-old Brodey came from a diverse communications background. He had worked for the telephone company in Philadelphia for eight years, MCI for four years and the satellite division of RCA for four years. At RCA Global Communications, he was the Vice President for Sales and Marketing. He also served for four years as the President of LIN Communications, a cellular subsidiary of LIN Broadcasting. Sankey was an electrical engineer who had worked 21 years for Raytheon and later owned his own business in Washington, D.C.

Seeing that the demand for a fiber-based, private line, telecommunications transport company was growing, Sankey suggested that ICC change its strategic focus from the cable industry to telecommunications. In April 1985, encouraged by the expanding telecommunications opportunities, Brodey began working full time at establishing ICC as a CAP company.[7] By July 1985, Brodey announced that site engineering had begun on a $32 million, 128-mile fiber network reaching from Washington, D.C. to Baltimore, Maryland. He hoped to begin actual construction of the network by year-end 1985.[8]

Three ICC service offerings were proposed: (1) raw (unlit) fiber capacity for long distance carriers; (2) dedicated transport at DS-1 and DS-3 rates; and (3) switched service.[9] The switched service was only to provide switched access for long distance service not for local service. The network would include a tandem switch (a tandem switch connects to other switches and not to end users) to direct switched long distance calls from customers' PBXs to the POPs of various interexchange carriers.

Looking For Funding

However, the project could not be launched, as planned, because ICC had not been able to secure the necessary funding. Nevertheless, Brodey remained optimistic. Brash and confident with a booming voice, Brodey became a familiar figure and frequent speaker at telecommunications conferences, presenting his fiber network plans and looking for investors interested in backing them. His plans envisioned networking hundreds of buildings in the surrounding Washington, D.C. metro area, including the nearby Maryland and Virginia suburbs.

Required capital for some of these projects was estimated at $50 to $60 million. This was an unprecedented level of investment for a start-up competitive company, and critics said the plans were too grandiose. There was no doubt, however, that Brodey's boldness fired the imaginations of his audiences. Many found Brodey's presentations exciting; and several who listened to him would ultimately enter the CAP business themselves inspired, at least in part, by Brodey's compelling vision.

Looking To Invest

Rod Hackman was a graduate of the United States Naval Academy. Although his formal education was not technical, he found he had a natural affinity for dealing with technology issues. During his active duty service in the Navy, he worked in operations and maintenance, including the supervision of nuclear reactors. After his naval service, he attended Cornell University and graduated with an MBA in finance.

Hackman worked for a while as a consultant in the power generation industry, then in the merger and acquisition department of the Bendix Corp. and then in investment banking for Kidder Peabody. Because of his familiarity with the regulated electric and gas industries, Rod worked in the group dealing with utilities. However, their work focused primarily on research and development projects; and such abstract activities did not interest him.

Kidder Peabody was not among the leading investment bankers and was struggling to compete for business with firms like Merrill Lynch, Goldman-Sachs and Morgan-Stanley. Against these established firms, Kidder Peabody was not on the radar screen of large corporations.

With the pending break-up of the AT&T Bell System, Kidder Peabody hoped to win business from some of the newly created Regional Bell Companies (RBOCs). Despite being fragments of the former AT&T Bell System, each of the individual RBOCs was a large, multi-billion dollar company. It was presumed that these newly minted entities did not have established relationships with investment bankers and might be addressable.

A new group was formed within Kidder Peabody to address opportunities in the post-divestiture telecommunications world. Volunteers were solicited from among the Kidder Peabody utility group. Hackman signed up. Hackman and John Baring were made co-heads of the Kidder Peabody Telecommunications Group. The Telecommunications Group's task of winning RBOC business proved frustrating. The larger investment bankers, particularly Merrill Lynch, focused successfully on establishing themselves with the RBOCs.

Hackman began to read and study the dynamics of the post-divestiture telephone industry. He found the fees charged to the long distance carriers by the telephone companies for access to their local networks for completing a call particularly interesting. These "access fees" for transporting the call over the "last-mile-bottle-neck" facilities of the local telephone company were priced well above actual cost. The economic incentive for bypassing the local carrier's network by using private microwave or fiber links was compelling.

It seemed reasonable to Hackman that companies would form to exploit these new opportunities. Hackman reasoned that if the RBOCs were not readily available as customers of Kidder Peabody's investment banking services, maybe there were small, competitive companies—who specialized in bypassing RBOCs— that needed an investment banker. Hackman went looking for such competitive companies in which to invest. The search was disappointing. Except for TCG, Hackman found no competitive local companies in operation. Since TCG was a subsidiary of financial services giant, Merrill Lynch, there was no opportunity for Kidder Peabody to get involved. Hackman kept looking, reading and attending conferences.

At a conference in 1985, Hackman heard Brodey give his pitch.

The Network: A Durable Asset?

Hackman engaged with Brodey to raise the money which ICC needed to execute its plan. Brodey had raised only a little seed money from some real estate investors. The tiny company still consisted of Brodey, a secretary and, on a part-time basis, Sankey.

Hackman and Baring went over the ICC business plan. They judged it to be long on hype and short on facts. There was very little quantitative information in the plan, but this was not easily remedied. Definitive financial and market data were hard to come by. Although the Bell companies reported revenue by category, it was not sufficiently detailed to determine how much revenue was "addressable" by a small, competitive fiber network. Hackman did his best to get better numbers and more defensible projections. He also scrubbed the business plan to minimize the required capital. The "scrubbed" plan called for $20 million to build the network and to provide the initial operating capital. Hackman shopped the plan simultaneously to banks, finance companies and venture capitalists.

The opportunity that was presented to potential backers was based on both cash flow and asset value. Although firm cash flow numbers were not documented, the *prospect* of positive cash flow seemed plausible because the telecommunications markets were so huge. For 1985, the total operating revenues for the 57 largest telephone companies reporting to the FCC was $89.4 billion.[10] Only a small market penetration would be required to produce very large revenue streams for new competitors like ICC.

Beyond the cash flow argument, there was the concept of durable asset value. It was posited that once a network were constructed, it would have lasting value and could be sold profitably even if the original business operators failed ... that is, that the value of the assets in the ground exceeded the cost to duplicate them. Although there was no franchise or exclusivity and anyone could, in theory, duplicate the network, it was asserted that "first-mover" positioning created a permanent advantage. By deploying the fiber, constructing the network, and particularly by negotiating access and constructing entrance facilities to the buildings along the network, the network operator created a "de facto franchise" based on "squatters' rights."

Some banks found these arguments persuasive. The CIT Financial Group of Manufacturers Hanover Bank agreed to lend ICC $17.4 million in construction loan financing. The remainder of the funding was raised from venture capitalist investors. The initial venture capital backer was Regional Financial Enterprises, Inc. (RFE) of New Caanan, Connecticut, which purchased a 20% equity interest in ICC.[11] Other investors owned 30% of the equity, while Brodey and Sankey held 50%.

Construction Of ICC's Washington Metro-Area Network

ICC began construction of its network using a team composed of construction company, Morrison-Knudsen, and telephone equipment maker, Northern Telecom. From its network control center in McLean, VA, the ICC network reached west to Dulles International Airport, north to Rockville, MD, to the eastern boundary of Washington, D.C. and south to Arlington, VA. This initial $20-million network covered 77 miles and connected 58 buildings and was completed in June 1986. The network electronics were primarily from Northern Telecom, and the network included a Northern Telecom DMS 250C tandem switch. Much of the network consisted of fiber cables which were in the underground conduits of the Chesapeake and Potomac Telephone Co., an operating company of the RBOC, Bell Atlantic. ICC had begun life as a cable television-related company. It was not unusual for the telephone company to lease conduit and pole space to cable companies.

Although a C&P spokesperson acknowledged that ICC, no longer intending to be a cable company, might become a significant telephone competitor, ICC was able to continue purchasing conduit space based on the existing tariff. C&P did, however, move to counter potential competition from ICC by dropping rates for its dedicated private line offering by 17% and by increasing deployment of its own fiber.

Addressing The Markets

With the DMS 250C linked to 19 interexchange carriers, ICC was able to buy long distance service at bulk discounts and resell at retail to customers on its network. This process, however, produced some difficulties. On the one hand, ICC got about 60% of its business by selling dedicated transport between large customer locations and the long distance carriers switch or "point of presence" (POP). These circuits were most often purchased by the long distance carriers themselves, acting as agent for the customer. On the other hand, ICC sales personnel were entering these same buildings and attempting to sell their discounted long distance service directly to the same customers. Interexchange carriers expressed their annoyance for this practice to ICC and threatened to limit their use of ICC dedicated transport.

ICC did stumble upon one lucrative market not contemplated in the original business plan. Certain federal government agencies, particularly those engaged in secretive operations, were instantly attracted to the presence of highly secure, fiber optic links between their buildings.

ICC did not attempt to pre-market to prospective on-net buildings, but rather linked buildings to the network on a speculative basis, making a conjecture as to which buildings contained future customers. Gaining access to buildings and building risers could involve extended negotiations with building owners, and constructing entrance facilities could be expensive at $50,000 to $100,000 per building.

Growing The Network

By the end of 1986, ICC reported that it was providing services to long distance carriers and federal government agencies in the Washington, D.C. area through its network's 22 hub locations.[12]

ICC network expansion reached 112 miles and 105 buildings by July 1987. Chief Operating Officer, Sankey, said that the company had run fiber spurs into 22 specific business parks.[13] He stated that the core network fiber passed within 2,000 feet of most of its potential customers.

The company was confident that expansion would continue with 250 buildings expected to be on-line by year-end 1987. ICC forecast that ultimately, by the end of 1989, it would have a 250-mile network with 600 buildings on-line.[14]

Not only did ICC intend to grow its Washington, D.C. network, it planned to have operations in other major cities. A $35-million network to Baltimore was announced. ICC revealed that it owned 26% of Eastern TeleLogic which was building a fiber network in Philadelphia.[15] Eastern TeleLogic President, Gary Lasher, was also an ICC Director.[16]

Sales for the second quarter of 1987 were only $478,000, and the operating loss was $2.4 million.[17] Nevertheless, in the July forecast, Brodey projected that the 1987 revenue would run around $6 million to $10 million and that the company would attain profitability in the third quarter of 1987. He maintained this confident position even while acknowledging that the company was laying off some sales personnel due to a cash crunch.[18]

But the company lagged behind the forecasts and ultimately struggled to sales for 1987 of just over $5 million.[19]

We Guessed Wrong

By July 1988, after another year of operation, the network reached 135 miles and 120 buildings. With network build-out costs continuing, ICC was running out of money. ICC announced that it was scrapping its expansion plans.[20]

Brodey shocked an audience at a telecommunications conference by frankly stating that ICC had guessed wrong about many of the on-line buildings on its fiber network. The fiber had been extended to these buildings on speculation; and now it was discovered that the real business often lay in other, near-by, buildings. ICC would need significantly more capital to connect buildings where real revenue potential had been identified.

ICC Reorganized

In March 1988, the investors regrouped, forming a new entity, ICC Telecommunications, Inc. In August 1988, a new ICC President, Gordan (Don) Hutchins, was installed. ICC Telecommunications, Inc. was incorporated in Delaware in March 27, 1989, and acquired sole ownership of ICC in July 1989. In the new company, RFE owned 24% of the equity, the Union Pacific Credit Corp. owned 28%, the Bender Group, representing a group of investors, owned 34% and miscellaneous outside investors owned 14%.

Don Hutchins had an extensive telecommunications background, including working for AT&T and MCI. He was a founder of LDX NET, a long-haul, intercity fiber optic network and served variously as COO and CEO. In 1987 he had helped orchestrate the merger of LDX NET and WilTel to create Williams Telecommunications Group and had served as Senior Vice President of Sales and Marketing of the combined company until early 1988.

Although switched services contributed approximately half of ICC's revenue, the company decided to sell this part of its business in March 1989. ICC sold off its switched customer base to the SouthernNet subsidiary of Telecom*USA. Telecom*USA, at that time the fourth largest long distance carrier, was later acquired by MCI. In addition to raising $2.2 million in much needed cash, Hutchins explained the secondary reason for the sale of long distance business by saying, "There were certainly suggestions from some of the major carriers that they would like us better if we got out ..."[21,22] At a June conference, ICC President Hutchins presented the Corporate Objectives for ICC. Objective number one was simply: "Survive."[23]

The company continued to struggle, and the Board of Directors took over the operation of the company. Board Chairman, Frank Ikard, a lawyer and onetime judge with experience in Washington D.C. political circles, became ICC's third President.[24] In July 1989 long-time Director, Jeffrey J. Milton, an attorney and ICC's outside legal counsel from the Washington law firm of Laxalt, Washington, Perito and Dubuc took over as the fourth President of ICC.[25]

The company attempted to reorganize its finances, raising $18 million in new funding and credit lines in 1989. Northern Telecom, its major supplier, provided a $7.4 million line of credit to buy equipment for upgrade and expansion of the network. However, the company's financial position remained precarious; and operating losses mounted.

Becoming Legal

ICC came under pressure for failure to apply for certification from the public utility commissions of the states in which it operated. ICC had not done so because it believed that it hauled only interstate traffic that was under the jurisdiction of the FCC. However, it was alleged that some of its traffic, particularly in the Washington, D.C. portion of its network was, in fact, intrastate. Somewhat belatedly on October 10, 1989, ICC requested a Certificate of Public Convenience and Necessity to provide dedicated intrastate private-line services in the District of Columbia. This tardy application resulted in a difficult process for ICC as it faced hearings before an irate Public Service Commission for the District of Columbia.

ICC was cautioned by the D.C. Public Service Commission that it should not expect the Commission to act favorably upon its request "simply because it was currently operating within the District of Columbia." It noted that, "ICC's substantial investment for its intra-District of Columbia services was made at its own risk, without appropriate regulatory approvals."[26]

Since MFS and TCG had also filed for such a Certificate, the cases were consolidated into one. With three companies proposing to offer the same service in competition with C&P, the Commission was eager to inquire into the possible impact on telephone rate payers in the District. The District hearing also became a battle ground for the struggle between MFS and TCG in their race to become the dominant national CAP. MFS introduced the issue of ICC's membership in a national marketing consortium with TCG called NatMet. MFS suggested that such membership might create problems that the Commission should investigate. The Commission was not enthusiastic about the relevance. Ultimately, the Commission granted certification to all three companies in 1990.

ICC requested that the Commission make its certificate of authority retroactive in order to allow it to execute a $12 million loan with Northern Telecom Finance Co. and restructure approximately $22 million with the CIT Group Equipment Financing, Inc.[27] The

Commission granted the request but instituted a "quarterly financial review of ICC's operations until ICC can produce positive income from continuing operations and maintain such performance for four consecutive operating periods."[28]

MFS Communications Acquires ICC

ICC attempted to continue growing its network. In September 1990 it announced a three-phase expansion plan, totaling 80 miles. Phase 1 was a $5 million network expansion into northern Virginia to be completed by February 1991. Phase II and phase III, scheduled for July 1991 and January 1992, respectively, would complete loops from downtown Washington into Virginia and in Maryland.

By the Fall of 1991 the network had grown to 200 miles and accessed 550 buildings, but ICC continued to lose money and was unable to gain its footing as an on-going, viable business. Discouraged creditors of ICC shopped the company to TCG, MFS and other prospective buyers.

In August 1991, MFS announced that it had agreed to acquire controlling interest in ICC from Northern Telecom Finance Corp. and CIT/Equipment Financing, Inc.[29] In October 1991 MFS Communications bought 85% of the stock for $41.2 million in cash.[30] The CIT Group/Equipment Financing retained a 15% minority share.[31] The minority stockholders were given the future right to "put" their stock to MFS beginning in 1996.

The ICC network began immediately to benefit MFS. For the last quarter of 1991, it contributed $3 million to MFS' gross revenues.[32] In this sense, the ICC transaction confirmed the hypothesis that an established network represented a durable asset and a "de facto" franchise. As operation of the Washington D.C. network went on to become one of MFS' most productive, it gave credence to the theory that a CAP, if forced out of business, only gave birth to a new CAP with a lower cost base.

The Bloom Is Off The Rose

Nevertheless, it had also become clear that simply putting fiber in the ground and challenging the local telephone company was not a guaranteed route to riches. While the debt holders eventually saw their investments in ICC yield a profit, the venture capital investors had been wiped out in the restructuring. The financial hardships of ICC had a sobering effect on the willingness of investors to back CAPs and other start-up competitive telecommunications companies.

Hackman and Baring had been able to find financing for ICC in 1985, Chicago Fiber Optics:financing in 1986 and Eastern TeleLogic in 1987; but the financial struggles of ICC were making fund raising for CAPs an increasingly difficult task.

Hackman warned a CAP audience in a 1989 conference that, "The bloom is off the rose as far as venture capitalists are concerned. Revenue has not ramped up as fast as planned. Incremental capital for growth was greater than imagined. Payback has stretched from the 3-5 year range to the 4-7 year range. That is too great. Venture capitalists have more interesting opportunities for placing their money."[33]

When Hackman attempted to establish a CAP operation in New York City, his fears about the impact of the ICC story came true. Organization of the new company floundered when venture capital investors became unwilling to provide funding due to concerns over fate of venture capitalists involved with ICC.

*****

II. Bay Area Teleport

Telecommunications-Enhanced Real Estate

New York City was not the only urban center that saw the allure of space age technology in the form of satellites to leverage a new economic boom. Two of the fashionable ideas of the early 1980s were satellite earth stations - Teleports- and telecommunications-enhanced real estate.

Bay Area Teleport was formed in the San Francisco area with the idea of marrying these two concepts to create unique value. Unlike Teleport Communications in New York, Bay Area Teleport did not have the benefit of any local government or quasi-governmental agencies to aid in its launch.

To some, telecommunications-enhanced real estate simply meant shared tenant service - corporate tenants in a large building sharing a PBX switch and other telephone services. Bay Area Teleport was conceived on a grander scale. Namely, commercial buildings tied together with a regional, digital, microwave network and linked directly to a Teleport for earth station access.

A partnership was formed in June 1984 between real estate development company, Doric Development;, Inc. of Alameda, California and Pacific Telecom.[34] Pacific Telecom was the telecommunications subsidiary of electric power company Pacific Light & Power. The network was initially based on digital microwave, but by 1988 included a significant amount of fiber.

The network became operational in 1986 and was gradually expanded until it linked 20 cities and the Niles Canyon earth station complex at Fremont, California. In 1987 Bay Area Teleport began to add fiber transport to its network. John Ayers was installed as President and CEO in 1987.[35] Ayers had a background that included ten years with AT&T and several stints with Alaska long distance carrier, Alascom, Inc.

A Modest Reception

The project had envisioned corporate end users as the major customer group. The use of the network to provide low cost DS-1 private line transport to the earth stations and other on-net locations, or to access long distance carrier POPs, was expected to predominate. The company found its acceptance among corporate telecommunications managers to be weak. Without credibility as an established telecommunications supplier and lacking back-office systems and processes, the sales cycle was long. Revenue was modest. For 1987, revenue was $1.8 million and for 1988 it was $2.5 million.

Other CAPs - MFS, Teleport and Diginet - all expressed their intention to build fiber networks in San Franciso. In response to the competitive threat from Bay Area Teleport and the potential entry of these other CAPs, Pacific Bell suddenly slashed its monthly rates for short-distance DS-1 circuits by 70% in 1989. For 1989, Bay Area Teleport's revenue reached $4.4 million, but its losses for the year were $5.4 million.

Late in 1990, Michael Rosenquist, a Bay Area Teleport employee since 1987, took over as President. Rosenquist had served in various finance-related positions and was focused on achieving a positive cash flow. By year end the company was slightly cash flow positive, for the first time, on revenue of $5.5 million, but still lost money.[36]

Giving Up On Telecommunications-Enhanced Real Estate

By 1991, Bay Area Teleport had invested $18 million in its network which included 300 miles of fiber, reached 22 cities and linked 18 carrier POPs. The network reached north to Santa Rosa, northeast to Sacramento, south from San Francisco to Sunnyvale and south from Oakland to San Jose and Santa Cruz.

Pacific Bell's rate reductions had cooled corporate customers' demand but not that from carriers. In the post-Hinsdale era, carrier demand for DS-1 and DS-3 circuits providing diverse inter-connections between area POPs was strong.

With most of Bay Area Teleport's revenue coming from carriers rather than end users, it seemed that the concept of "telecommunications-enhanced" real estate had not panned out and was abandoned. Revenue reached $8 million in 1991, and operating cash flow was a positive $1.9 million; but the company was still losing money on the bottom line.

Operating As a "Carrier's Carrier"

With the real estate angle discredited, Doric Development's involvement in the business no longer made sense. The joint venture partnership was dissolved, and Pacific Telecom became the sole owner of Bay Area Teleport. Pacific Telecom formed PTI Harbor Bay, Inc., consisting of two subsidiaries, Bay Area Teleport and UpSouth Corp. (which provided television transmission via satellites). Pacific Telecom did not find these businesses attractive, and was actively looking for a buyer.[37] An offering memorandum was drawn up and circulated to CAPs and other prospective buyers.

In 1992, the revenue for BAT increased to $10.2 million and was highly dependent on the long distance companies. As the major BAT customers, MCI accounted for 24% of 1992 revenue and 8% came from AT&T.[38] As the business had evolved, Bay Area Teleport now considered itself more of a "carrier's carrier" than a CAP. As such, Bay Area Teleport was viewed by other CAPs, like MFS and TCG, entering the San Franciso area not as competitors but as customers for its long-haul fiber network.

Entering 1993, no buyer for BAT had been found; and the year was proving difficult. A large customer declared bankruptcy in August, and private-line sales declined for the first time. Faced with an operating loss of $2.2 million on revenue of $9.8 million, Pacific Telecom sold the Niles Canyon earth station complex for $4.5 million in stock to IDB Communications, the same company that had earlier purchased TCG's Staten Island earth stations.

Bay Area Teleportdid not survive as an independent entity. The PTI Harbor Bay, Inc. holding company and its subsidiaries, Bay Area Teleport and UpSouth Corp. were sold by Pacific Telecom to Denver-based CAP, IntelCom Group, in November 1993 for $200,000 in cash and approximately 1.1 million shares of stock.

*****

III. PSO/MetroLink

Electric Utilities Have The Right Infrastructure

Electric utilities have always been viewed as logical candidates for expansion into telecommunications ventures. They possess or have access to rights-of-way, such as conduits, poles and towers, which are attractive for fiber deployment. They have existing infrastructure facilities such as manholes in the street and entrance facilities into buildings. Furthermore, utilities use communications in their core operations and often operate their own microwave and fiber systems.

The potential of these assets for expansion into telecommunications was not lost on the electric utilities. Early in the 1980s, Minnesota Power replaced one of the wires in a high-voltage transmission system with a composite fiber-optic, conductor-cable to provide a communication link to a remote hydro-electric station. On August 7, 1983, John Carlson, a manager of system telecommunications for Minnesota Power presented the idea of a regional fiber-optic network routed along power transmission lines to a gathering of Wisconsin utilities.[39]

This ultimately led to the formation of a partnership among the telecommunications subsidiaries of five utilities to build a fiber network. Wisconsin Power & Light;, Madison, Wisconsin Public Service, Green Bay, Madison Gas & Electric, Madison, Dairyland Power Cooperative, La Crosse and Minnesota Power & Light, Duluth formed NorLight, on September 27, 1985.[40]

In building its network, NorLight, used the static or ground-wire cable which is strung above the power cables on a high voltage transmission for protection. The ground-wire cable was replaced with a composite conducting cable with twelve optic fibers embedded in it.[41] The deployment of composite ground wire containing fiber cables became standard operating procedure for most electric utilities in future high voltage transmission line construction.

While state regulators did not object to utilities developing communications systems for their own use, they did resist the use of those facilities to enter telecommunications as a line of business. The NorLight project was delayed for two years while the PUC wrestled with the issue of the proper compensation the regulated entities should receive in exchange for the use of their rights-of-way for a commercial telecommunications business.

Creating PSO/MetroLink

Public Service of Oklahoma, an electric utility in Tulsa, developed an internal communications network for the company using fiber optics and digital microwaves in order to satisfy its need for high-reliability service.[42] Construction was begun in 1984. The network used the company's rights-of-way, placing fiber cables in an underground duct system in downtown Tulsa and on utility poles throughout the city.[43]

The network was named PSO/MetroLink, but it was not an independent entity. It operated as a department within the utility. In 1986, PSO/MetroLink provided dedicated transport for its first commercial customer and applied to the Federal Communications Commission for private carrier status.[44]

The local Regional Bell Operating Company, Southwestern Bell Telephone (later renamed SBC Corporation), opposed the application on the grounds that PSO/MetroLink was really providing local private line service and should be regulated as a common carrier by the state public utility commission. Hearings were held, and the FCC ruled that the traffic carried by PSO/MetroLink, while physically local, was not local in terms of its destination. The FCC ruled that it, and not the state PUC, therefore had jurisdiction. Further, the FCC classified the operation as a private carrier and, thus, under its rules, would be unregulated.

Regulatory Friction

Oklahoma state regulators, as well as state regulators elsewhere, were aware of the issues raised by the NorLight project and were generally not pleased with the attempts of utilities to use their rights-of-way for telecommunications ventures. Nevertheless, Oklahoma did not challenge the FCC PSO/MetroLink was, grudgingly, allowed to operate.

Central & Southwest Corp., the holding company that owned Public Service of Oklahoma, decided to build a second fiber network, DFW MetroLink, in the Dallas - Fort Worth area on the rights-of-way of its subsidiary, Texas Utilities. The Texas PUC resisted and expressed concern about regulating Central & Southwest as both an electric utility and a telecommunications company.[45]

There was a general awareness in the electric industry that its core business would face deregulation sometime in the future. Utility executives did not want this event to happen any sooner than necessary. This translated into some reluctance to pursue commercial telecommunications ventures due to a concern that utility involvement might hasten the advent of electric deregulation.

Moving Into The Background

In 1989 Central & Southwest concluded that its wisest course was to sell both PSO/MetroLink and the nascent DFW MetroLink. A small company, Columbine Telenet, agreed to buy both companies but was unable to raise the funding.

Central & Southwest spun off DFW MetroLink as an independent company. DFW MetroLink tried to complete the construction of the Dallas-Fort Worth network but failed, declaring Chapter 7 bankruptcy on Feb. 13, 1991.[46] The network assets were acquired by TCG in June 1991.[47] Central & Southwest continued to operate PSO/MetroLink until was acquired by Brooks Fiber Properties, Inc. in April 1995.[48]

While many utilities formed telecommunications subsidiaries, most eventually withdrew from direct responsibility for operations of telecommunications businesses. Leasing fiber, conduit, towers and rights-of-way or assuming a passive partner role in joint ventures with CAPs and other telecommunications companies seemed to be a more compatible role for utilities for both regulatory and corporate culture reasons.[49]

Footnotes Chapter 5: The Pioneers

[1] Dun & Bradstreet, Dun's Financial Records Plus, Dec. 1989, DN = 60-676-8323.

[2] Prospectus for MFS Communications, Salomon Brothers Inc., Bear, Stearns & Co. Inc., May 19, 1993, 17.

[3] "Recently-Formed Trade Association Begins Representing LEC Local Facilities Competitors," *Telecommunications Reports,* May 23, 1988.

[4] Dun & Bradstreet, Dun's Market Identifiers, Dec. 1990, DN = 19-456-9125.

[5] "Recently-Formed Trade Association Begins Representing LEC Local Facilities Competitors," *Telecommunications Reports,* May 23, 1988.

[6] "Application Of The Institutional Communications Company For A Certificate Of Public Convenience And Necessity," Public Service Commission Of The District Of Columbia, Case No. 867, Oct. 3, 1989, 2.

[7] Dun & Bradstreet, Dun's Financial Records Plus, May 1989, DN = 12-230-3779.

[8] "Start-up Plans 128-Mile Fiber System," *MIS Week,* July 3, 1985, 29.

[9] Ibid.

[10] "Statistics of Communications Common Carriers," FCC, 1990-91 Edition, 236.

[11] RFE would later also invest in ICC Director Gary Lasher's CAP, Eastern TeleLogic Company in Philadelphia.

[12] "Institutional Communications Markets Services To Long-Distance Companies," *Fiber Optic News,* Dec. 8, 1986, 5.

[13] "Local Loop Applications," *Telephone News,* July 6, 1987.

[14] "Firm Competes With C&P For Local Business," *Washington Post,* July 13, 1987, 1.

[15] Ibid.

[16] D & B - Million Dollar Directory, Institutional Communications, Co., DN = 12-230-3779, June, 1989.

[17] Ibid.

[18] "Firm Competes With C&P For Local Business," *Washington Post,* July 13, 1987, 1.

[19] D & B - Million Dollar Directory, Institutional Communications, Co., DN = 12-230-3779, Sept., 1988.

[20] "Firm Scraps Plan To Add Phone Link," *Baltimore Sun,* July 9, 1988, B15.

[21] The Rise of the MAN Handlers," *Data Communications,* October 1989, 67.

[22] "ICC Divests Long-Distance Interest to Focus On Metro Area Network, Local Side of Business," *The Long Distance Letter,* April 1989.

[23] The Sixth Annual Conference on LOCAL EXCHANGE COMPETITION: The Emerging Reality, June 8-9, 1989, Crystal City Marriott, Arlington, VA.

[24] "The Rise of the MAN Handlers," *Data Communications,* October 1989, 68.

[25] *1991 Alternate Local Transport... a Total Industry Report* (Glastonbury, CT, Connecticut Research Report, Feb. 1991), 87.

[26] Formal Case No. 892, In The Matter of the Applications for a Certificate of Public Convenience and Necessity of Teleport Communications Washington, D.C., Inc. and The Institutional Communications Co., Jan. 23, 1990, 9, footnote 10.

[27] *Telecommunications Reports,* Sept. 3, 1990.

[28] *Telecommunications Reports,* Dec. 24, 1990.

[29] "Metropolitan Fiber Systems Acquires Controlling Interest In Institutional Communications Co.," *MFS Press Release,* Aug. 26, 1991.

[30] Prospectus for MFS Communications, Salomon Brothers Inc., Bear, Stearns & Co. Inc., May 19, 1993, F-10.

[31] "Metropolitan Fiber Systems Completes Acquisition of Institutional Communications Co.," *MFS Press Release,* Oct. 22 , 1991.

[32] Prospectus for MFS Communications, Salomon Brothers Inc., Bear, Stearns & Co. Inc., May 19, 1993, , 23.

[33] The 6th Annual Local Exchange Area Competition: The Emerging Reality, Phillips Publishing, Inc. and Andrew D. Lipman, Partner, Swidler & Berlin, Washington, D.C., June 8-9, 1989

[34] D&B - Duns Financial Records, Sept. 1989, DN = 14-471-3203.

[35] Ibid.

[36] ALTS Spring Conference, May 1991.

[37] *Communications Week,* July, 1991.

[38] Independent Auditors Report, Deloitte & Touche, in IntelCom Group Prospectus, May 6, 1994, Paine Webber, C.J. Lawrence/Deutsche Bank, Hanifen, Imhoff, F-45.

[39] "Fiber Optics Brightens 1980 Communications Picture and Creates NorLight," *Transmission & Distribution,* January 1990, 46.

[40] Ibid.

[41] " 'Old Timer' James Rice Brings Energy, Enthusiasm to NorLight," *The Business Journal - Milwaukee,* March 31, 1986, v3, n24, Sect. 1, 10.

[42] *1991 Alternate Local Transport ... a Total Industry Report,"* (Glastonbury, CT: Connecticut Research Report, Feb. 1991), 134.

[43] *"1993 Local Telecommunications Competition ... the ALT Report,"* (Glastonbury, CT: Connecticut Research, 1993) VII-77A.

[44] Ibid.

[45] *"1991 Alternate Local Transport ... a Total Industry Report,"* (Glastonbury, CT: Connecticut Research Report, Feb. 1991), 134.

[46] *"1991 Alternate Local Transport ... a Total Industry Report,"* (Glastonbury, CT: Connecticut Research Report, Feb. 1991), 98.

[47] "Teleport Communications To Purchase Dallas Assets Of DFW/MetroLink; Enhance Telecommunications For Business Community; Strengthen Dallas Economy," TCG Press Release, June 19, 1991.

[48] "New In The Loop," *Local Telecom Competition News,* April 12, 1995.

[49] "Fiber Deployment Update - End of Year 1989," Jonathan M. Kraushaar, Industry Analysis Division, Common Carrier Bureau, FCC, Feb. 28, 1990, 9-12.

6. ENTREPRENEURS

I. The Founders Of Intertel Communications

Teleports In Denver

Denver benefits from being centrally located in the United States and having spectacular mountain scenery. Many corporations have established their national headquarters there, and Denver has particularly become a center of cable and telecommunications activity.

The "Mile High City" is on the 105th meridian; and local boosters liked to point out that an earth station placed here could, with a single satellite hop, reach any point in the United States as well as South America and Canada for communications. Of potentially greater importance, Denver is equidistant between Munich and Tokyo, with a direct line of view to every satellite in orbit over both the Atlantic and Pacific oceans. Therefore, unlike coastal teleports in New York or San Francisco, a teleport in Denver could communicate with either Europe or Asia without multiple earth-to-satellite hops and their associated costs and transmission time delays.

Taking advantage of this unique location, NASA built a satellite uplink facility in Morrison, Colorado, just west of Denver, in 1973.[1] At the time, it was the first non-military uplink in the country and was used primarily for experimental projects until December 1986 when the facility was sold and converted to commercial use.[2]

Teleport Denver: Better Than A Car Wash

At nearly the same time a rival teleport company, Teleport Denver, Inc., was formed to fully exploit both domestic and international opportunities.[3] Teleport Denver intended to broadcast television signals worldwide from Denver while simultaneously sending, receiving and distributing electronic data from every bank and brokerage firm in the metropolitan Denver area. The development was led by Sattime, Inc. of Aspen, Colorado, a broker of satellite time and transmission facilities.[4]

The Denver economy in 1986 was experiencing a recession. Asked about his company's decision to build a teleport, Sattime President Andre Schwegler gave the usual response. He pointed out that satellites were the gateways to the new information age and therefore attractive investments. "Besides," he said, "the teleport is one of the few things you can build in Denver right now that will make money. Unless you want to build a car wash."[5]

Teleport Denver selected ex-U S WEST executive George Bruno as its President and CEO. Bruno had 25 years of experience in tele-communications extending from AT&T to U S WEST's Operating Company, Mountain Bell Telephone. Very involved in the pro-motion of Colorado, Bruno saw the teleport as an opportunity to enhance the State's economic development, as the TCG teleport was doing for New York.[6] Teleport Denver intended to have twelve dishes operational in two years and to beam directly via one satellite hop to Europe, Asia, Africa and South America.[7]

Canuck Resources: Out Of Canada

In the late 1980s, satellites were still the glamour technology of leading edge communications and, as such, attracted high-risk capital and visionaries. In August of 1986, Canuck Resources Corp. of British Columbia, a company controlled by Canadian entrepreneur, William Becker, acquired a 50% interest in the Teleport Denver project for $2 million.[8]

In 1986, when Becker decided to invest in Teleport Denver, there were nearly 20 teleports in operation worldwide, including the TCG teleport facility on Staten Island. However, most teleports served major financial centers like New York and Los Angeles; and it required an entrepreneur's risk tolerance to build an early teleport in Denver.

By August 1986, the venture had raised the $5 million[9] needed for its phase one earth station build-out.[10] The Teleport Denver facility, built in the Meridian Office Park near the Denver Technology Center, began operation in early 1987 with four dish antennas.

Although its target was international communications, Teleport Denver's first job was more domestic. In 1987, Teleport Denver announced that it was working with Becker Oil and Gas, Ltd. of Vancouver, British Columbia, Canada, a subsidiary of Canuck

Resources, to create a shared hub to monitor gas and oil wells in the United States and Canada.[11] Since the Becker interests had ownership positions in no more than a handful of gas and oil wells, the announcement apparently referred to the future potential of Nova-Net Communications, an early pioneer in Very Small Aperture Terminals (VSATs) which began serving major oil companies in 1986. Teleport Denver had only meager revenues of $25,172 in 1988. A shared VSAT hub-station agreement was not negotiated until 1989. Nova-Net Communications was later acquired by Becker interests.

W.W. "Bill" Becker, Entrepreneur

W.W. "Bill" Becker was an entrepreneur from an early age[12]. Born in the rural town of Allx and educated at Tomahawk in Alberta, Canada, he worked in the rough, tough oil fields. He formed his first company, Tomahawk Well Servicing, Ltd., in 1957 at age 28. In 1970 Becker entered real estate, developing Sir William Place, a residential and business complex with a sixteen-story tower, in Edmonton, Alberta. He went on to develop over 2,000 units of residential, commercial and warehouse projects in Canada and Hawaii.

In 1971 he founded Northern Cablevision, Ltd. to provide cable service in Edmonton and, eventually, in 25 Canadian cities. In 1972, he launched a waste container company, Waste Removal, Ltd., in Edmonton. In 1975 he founded W.W. Becker Oil & Gas, Ltd., for exploration and discovery of natural gas and petroleum. In 1978 he started a second exploration company, Becker Oil & Gas, Inc. in Colorado.[13]

He founded Canuck Petroleum Corporation on June 5, 1981, re-named it Canuck Resources Corporation on April 21, 1983, and took it public on the Vancouver Stock Exchange in 1984. The IPO sold 300,000 units (consisting of one share of stock and two war-rants) at $0.60 per unit. The company was classified as a "Venture" company, a development stage designation by the Vancouver Stock Exchange. It would not attain reclassification as an industrial/ commercial enterprise until 1990. In 1984 the stock began trading in the United States on the Over The Counter Market (OTC) in the "Pink Sheets" pursuant to an exception from Section 12(g) of the 1934 Securities Act.

On March 5, 1987, Canuck Resources acquired 96% of Becker Oil & Gas, Ltd. and 87% of W.W. Becker Oil & Gas, Ltd. mostly Becker Oil and Gasin exchange for stock in a reverse takeover. The stock of Canuck Resources was very volatile in 1987, going from a low of 99¢ to a high of $7.75 before plunging in the stock market crash of October 1987.[14]

The company struggled and did not grow. Gross revenues went from $C 292,000 in fiscal year 1987 to $C 268,000 in fiscal year 1990, with most of the revenue (68%) coming from gas sales.[15] Canuck Resources raised more equity capital with two private placements in 1988.

This Is Like The Cable Opportunity: Be In There First

Canuck Resources continued to increase its investment in satellite technology. In 1989, it increased its ownership of Teleport Denver to 54% and in 1990 to 94%.[16] By this time, two lessons were obvious. First, TCG's strategy in New York, shifting its focus from earth stations to the fiber network feeding the teleport to fiber networks in general, was clearly succeeding. Second, TCG and MFS were racing to be first to stake their claim with fiber networks in as many major cities as possible.

From his prior experience in the cable industry, Becker thought he could see what was happening; and he was eager to join in. He said, "If you go back to the cable companies, when they were expanding across the country, there was an opportunity to pick up cities, be in there first. This is like the cable opportunity."[17]

Canuck Resources Becomes Intertel Communications

The year 1990 was the year that Becker tried to make a major push to turn Canuck Resources into a telecommunications company. With completion of a transaction to gain 94% control of Teleport Denver in September 1990, application was made to the Vancouver Stock Exchange to change the name of Canuck Resources to Intertel which stood for INTERnational TELeport Communications.[18,19]

A fiber optic Denver network was designed and a construction loan sought. In December 1990, Intertel announced that it had negotiated an $18 million loan with Communications Credit Corporation, a financial subsidiary of telecommunications equipment manufacturer,

Northern Telecom.[20],[21] Funding from the loan could be taken down as needed to finance network construction and required that 68% of the funds be used to buy equipment and services from Northern Telecom, Inc.

The announcement also indicated that while Intertel would continue to provide satellite services and to operate gas and oil properties, its main business, through the Teleport Denver subsidiary, would be the installation and operation of self-healing fiber networks for alternate access.

The Communications Credit Corporation loan agreement also required that most of the company's debt be eliminated by Jan. 31, 1990. This was accomplished by converting $5.6 million of debt (mostly with Becker affiliated companies) into equity and by an infusion of $3 million in cash for stock by The Becker Group.

Stock Promotion

Intertel Communications, Inc. tried to raise its visibility. It hired an investor relations firm that put out press releases emphasizing Intertel's position that it was the only publicly-held access company. Privately, this promotion caused a great deal of concern among CAP companies. They were hoping that they could eventually tap the equity markets for the capital needed to grow their networks but felt that they needed to establish themselves more substantially first.

Their concern centered on Intertel's fragile finances and its origins in the Vancouver Stock Market. Historically this market had been associated with highly speculative oil and gas "penny stocks" of questionable value. In some U.S. financial circles, "Vancouver Exchange stock" suggested low-quality as well as the possibility of stock manipulation and fraud. If Intertel stock should falter or be tainted by scandal, the CAP companies feared that financial markets would never be receptive to future Initial Public Offerings from them. On the other hand, they did not want to speak openly of their fears and focus unnecessary attention on the issue.

On November 30, 1990, there were 37,087,681 shares of Intertel stock issued with 25 million held by management and 12 million in the hands of the general public. The stock was trading under the symbol IRT at $0.85 per share on the Vancouver Exchange and in the U.S. through the Over-The-Counter "Pink Sheets." In February

1991, Intertel filed a form 20-F registration statement for foreign securities with the Security and Exchange Commission and prepared to apply for formal listing on the NASDAQ stock exchange in the United States.

Growing The Denver Network

Intertel pushed ahead with its fiber network deployment, spending $7.5 million on fiber cable and equipment. In March 1991, Intertel completed construction for an 11.5 mile "self-healing" fiber ring in the Denver Tech Center and Greenwood Village business parks in the Denver suburb of Englewood. Together with its fiber construction in the Denver Tech Center and the Greenwood Village and its leased fiber link from Meridian Park to downtown Denver, Intertel had 44 miles of fiber in operation by June 1991 and earned its first revenue from CAP services in July 1991.

Even before its Denver network construction was complete, Intertel announced, despite its fragile finances, plans to expand network operations to five other cities. Intertel began what would be an ongoing marathon quest for expansion capital. Becker stated, "We have also begun discussions with several investment banking firms to find ways to expand our capital base for this kind of focused expansion."

John Evans, Activist Investor

John Evans graduated from McMaster University in Hamilton, Ontario, Canada with a Bachelors of Commerce degree. He worked for six years for the public accounting firm of Coopers & Lybrand in Toronto and received his Chartered Accountancy in 1981. Evans also had five years of experience in strategic financial planning, analysis and budgeting in the telecommunications industry with Northern Telecom.

Evans was an aggressive investor in Canuck Resources and eventually had two thirds of his net worth invested in the company. Despite the stock market crash of 1987 and the slow development of Canuck Resources, he continued to invest, as the company pursued its transformation into Intertel Communications.

He was, however, a vocal shareholder, calling Board members and Becker to discuss the company's slow progress. It had been almost five years since Canuck Resources first began its entry into telecommunications by investing in Teleport Denver. The revenue from communications declined and for the quarter ended March 31, 1991, were less than $5,000.[22]

Becker himself, who had been the primary source of funding for Canuck Resources and Intertel Communications, had nearly 80% of his net worth tied up in the company and had empathy for Evans' critical comments.

In July 1991, Becker invited Evans to come to Denver and tour the Intertel operations. Evans arrived on Friday and stayed until Sunday, discussing the corporate strategy with Becker. At the conclusion of their discussions Becker offered him the position of Chief Financial Officer, and Evans accepted. Two weeks later Evans came to Denver and began work, not seeing his family again for three months.

Evans found Intertel's financial records and financial operations in disarray. On his second day as CFO, he was confronted by IRS agents and had to scramble to cover unpaid payroll taxes in order to avoid an immediate shut down of the company.

Also, the outside auditing firm, KPMG, was also having difficulties of its own. It had taken them six months (until March 1991) to complete the audit for the fiscal year which had ended back on September 30, 1990. Among other issues, $3 million of Becker's contributions to fund the company could not be identified in the current corporate financial records.

Evans first cleared the issues with the IRS and then set to work on the financial records. By consolidating the accounts in Canada and United States he was able reconstruct the balance sheet and to identify the missing equity. With the financial records in order, the audit was successfully completed.[23]

Progress & Public Acceptance

Having cleared up its bookkeeping woes, Intertel began to make progress on its facilities front. Intertel completed the construction of a 115-mile backbone fiber network in Denver and acquired an operating 8.5-mile fiber loop serving a suburban business park. Aided by the contribution from the newly operational fiber network, communications-related revenue for the quarter ending March 31, 1992, inched up to $532,184   versus a nearly invisible $4,932 for the same quarter in 1991.

Intertel began to take on a more formal and recognizable corporate structure. As TCG had done earlier, Intertel realized that success would require winning on multiple fronts, including public relations. A full time Director of Public Relations was hired, and a publicity campaign was pursued to raise public awareness of the Company and to develop its corporate image.

With its financial house in order and revenues ramping up, Intertel Communications was able to qualify for formal listing on a U.S. stock exchange. The listing was not, as expected, on the NASDAQ, but rather on the American Stock Exchange (AMEX). The American Stock Exchange had created a new category for young, growth companies called, "Emerging Companies Marketplace."[24]

American Stock Exchange Chairman James Joyce said of companies that qualify for "Emerging Companies Marketplace" listing, "Just the fact that these companies met the ECM numerical criteria did not, by any means, guarantee them an ECM listing. They also had to go through a qualitative screening process by a blue-ribbon committee that evaluated the company's long-term growth potential and investor interest."[25]

Intertel Communications, Inc. began trading on the American Stock Exchange on March 18, 1992, under the ticker symbol, "ITR.EC." Its acceptance on a major U.S. stock exchange gave status both to Intertel and to the CAP industry as a whole.

The CAP industry breathed a collective sigh of relief. Bob Atkinson of Teleport Communications Group was quoted as saying, "Intertel's ability to become listed on the AMEX is good news for users and carriers because it shows that investors may be starting to recognize the value of this industry."[26]

Beefing Up Revenues

As MFS Communications had done in folding the MFS Network Technologies network construction group into its telecommunications company, Intertel beefed up its "telecommunications revenues" by adding a network development and systems integration company.

On May 1, 1992, Intertel bought a 51% ownership interest in Englewood, Colorado based Fiber Optics Technologies, Inc. (FOTI) for $1.6 million.[27]

Fiber Optic Technologies, Inc. was involved in designing, building and maintenance of fiber optic, wireline and microwave networks, but its focus was on turnkey fiber optic systems. The Company also functioned as a system integrator. FOTI's CEO Keith Burge said, "We've taken a white-collar approach to what is typically a blue-collar industry. We provide more than a network cable plant. We implement communications solutions for businesses."[28]

With widespread western operations and offices in San Francisco, Seattle, Portland, Salt Lake City, Los Angeles, Houston and Dallas, Fiber Optic Technologies, Inc. had a dramatic impact on Intertel's financial results. With only five months of operation in 1992, this "Network Services" revenue accounted for 62% of Intertel's total $12.4 million revenue for the year.

Despite an aggressive program of network acquisition and expansion, revenue from CAP-type telecommunications services would trail those of Network Services as the dominant source of Intertel Communication's revenues until 1996.

However, Intertel Communications was now more established than most players in the young competitive industry. The company would eventually change its name once again. This time, Intertel Communications would become, ICG Communications. As ICG Communications, it would grow into one of the largest companies in the competitive telecommunications industry

****

II. The Founders of Intermedia Communications of Florida

A Timely Beginning

One of the new CAP networks poised to take advantage of the enhanced market opportunities in the aftermath of the 1988 Hinsdale incident was Intermedia Communications of Florida. The company, founded by Richard Kolsby and Barbara Samson, signed up its first customer, a long distance carrier in Orlando, Florida, in June 1988, one month after the Hinsdale fire. Service installation was completed August 1, 1988.[29]

Unlike TCG and MFS, Intermedia Communications had no "deep pockets" parent. The Company was the brain child of two young entrepreneurs who scrambled to find the money to build the network.

Richard Kolsby

Richard Kolsby, following graduation from Rollins College in Winter Park, Florida, did not find a job that utilized his degree in chemistry; instead he went to work for a tiny, independent telephone company, Winter Park Telephone. He learned, on the job, to be a telephone engineer.

Digital T-carrier transmission and digital microwave links were just emerging, and Kolsby loved to work with new technology. This digital work eventually led to his involvement in fiber optic systems. He rose to become Director of Transmission Engineering for Winter Park Telephone.

In 1980, Winter Park Telephone was acquired by United Telephone, which owned small telephone operations across the country. As a part of United Telephone of Florida, Kolsby began to work in planning, first network planning and then business planning. For a United Telephone planning exercise, a task force was formed to study the possible impact of fiber optic links being used to bypass the telephone company's network.

Due to his familiarity with the technology, it was Kolsby's job to calculate the costs of installing fiber systems, as well as determining the economic impact of fiber-based bypass on the telephone company. He concluded that such bypass was both feasible and potentially profitable for the entity providing the bypass service. While he found this intriguing, he did not immediately recognize a way to act on his conclusions.

As the January 1, 1984, AT&T divestiture approached, independent telephone companies, as well as RBOCs, were stirred by the potential changes in the newly reorganized telecommunications industry. Kolsby was freshly divorced and felt empowered to strike out on his own, leave his current employer and create a new life and his own opportunity.

He established a consulting company which he dubbed Intermedia Consulting. Kolsby's first consulting job was for a Jacksonville-based, long distance reseller, Americall. He created a plan for them, predicated on leasing a state-wide fiber network from Lightnet. Lightnet (later acquired by WilTel) was an ambitious project by Connecticut-based, Southern New England Telephone of Connecticut to create a national fiber network.

Americall did not implement the plan. However, Kolsby thought that it could succeed and found a backer. Bill Erdman, an ex-IBM salesman and owner of several small companies, agreed to invest $1 million in the venture. The partners named the company, Florida Digital Network, and created a facilities-based long distance company. They leased fiber from Lightnet and linked Jacksonville, Miami, Tampa and Orlando. They also installed their own Stromberg-Carlson tandem switch.

Florida Digital Network became involved in a project which re-awakened Kolsby's interest in the attractive economics of bypass. The project, for an Orlando real-estate developer, was to link his multi-tenant office building to Florida Digital network's tandem switch by a fiber cable and to sell long distance service to the tenants. But before the project was complete, the real-estate company was in trouble and soon so was Florida Digital Network. Florida Digital Network ramped up to $6 million in revenue by 1986 but had cash flow problems. Kolsby and Erdman quarreled, and Kolsby found himself out on the street.[30] .

Kolsby went back to consulting and took on a job for another long distance reseller. American Pioneer Telephone (Execulines of

Florida) in Orlando wanted to install a small fiber link. While working on this small job he met a young woman who was a sales-person for American Pioneer. She was not happy in sales.

After work, they met and they talked about business opportunities. Kolsby told her about the bypass plans he had worked on at Florida Digital Network. He thought that if he could only get some money, he could create a viable business. She said she could get money.

Barbara Samson

Articulate, poised and photogenic, Barbara Samson seemed well suited for her chosen career path of television news reporter. She graduated from the University of Florida with a B.S. in Telecommunications and from University of South Florida with an M.B.A. in 1983. She went to work doing broadcast journalism for the ABC television affiliate in Gainesville, Florida.

However, starting in a $10,000-a-year job and being stuck in a dingy basement doing research did not seem very appealing. Samson reasoned that to become a famous national TV newswoman - the next "Barbara Walters" - she would have to labor for years under someone else's direction.[31] She was too independent for that. She wanted to be in charge and to run her own business.

Samson left the television station and took a job re-selling long distance service to corporations for American Pioneer Telephone. Samson did not enjoy the job but nevertheless was successful at it. She described the secret of her success as: "You have to give people something to remember you by. For some people, it's their accent or style of dress. For me, it's a style of dress."[32]

The customers clearly liked Samson, and her boss at American Pioneer asked her to use her contacts to learn more about what kinds of telecommunications services corporations really needed. What she found was that they had dozens of acceptable alternatives for long distance service but really wanted good local service and access to long distance carriers.[33]

I Need Your Help

Richard Kolsby's business plans for a fiber-based bypass network fit perfectly with Samson's knowledge of unmet customer needs.

They also shared a desire to create their own business. Samson suggested to Kolsby that they might be able to launch the business on money from a trust fund administered by her mother.

Kolsby and Samson went to Tampa and presented their plans for their endeavor, which they called Intermedia Communications, to Samson's mother and her accountant. She agreed to provide the venture with seed money of $50,000 from a trust fund left to Barbara by her father.[34] The company was organized September 25, 1986, in St. Petersburg, Florida.

Samson called Scott Brodey at Institutional Communications Co., one of the few CAPs in actual operation, and sought his advice on entering the business. Brodey said that he was not interested in helping Intermedia. Samson would not accept "no" for an answer. She asked him pointedly, "Do you have a daughter?"[35] Brodey did have a daughter of nearly the same age. "If you weren't here and she needed someone to help her, would you want her to have someone to go to?" Samson asked. Brodey said he would. "Well," she said, "my father died a few years ago and I need your help." [36] Brodey agreed to give guidance to her new company and to serve on its Board of Directors. He called her every day at 5:30 a.m. with advice and then again at 5:30 p.m. to make sure the advice had been put to work.[37]

Kolsby and Samson made several trips to Washington, D.C. to visit Brodey. They found him working in his network control node which was a damp room housed under a parking garage. Kolsby's assessment of Brodey was, "He was very helpful. Of course, he is a character and you had to filter out a certain amount of bullshit; but we ended up getting good information from him. He was very encouraging."

Find A CEO And Get Some Real Money

In February, 1987, Kolsby and Samson hired William J. Miller, another former American Pioneer employee, as Vice President of Operations. Miller had a background in telephone engineering at Contel Executone and ITT Puerto Rico Telephone and developed the cost studies for the Intermedia business plan. The Company was beginning to become more than just an idea shared by the two founders.

Throughout 1987, as the Company formed and created its business plan, Kolsby and Samson made periodic visits to Barbara's mother for more funds; and when they had reached a level of $500,000, she put her foot down. She suggested that Intermedia needed to hire a full-time CEO and go after significant investor backing, if it were going to succeed.

Several CEO candidates were interviewed, including Gary Lasher, then Executive Vice President and Chief Operating Officer of Public Satellite Network in New York. Recruiting Lasher, who was a Director of Brodey's ICC, would have been a great coup for the little start-up. But Lasher, who would become a major figure in the CAP industry, preferred to run his own show and would soon become President and CEO of Eastern TeleLogic in Philadelphia.

By offering the combined posts of President, CEO and Chairman, Intermedia was able to attract Robert F. Benton, Bill Miller's former boss at Contel. Benton took on these duties at Intermedia in June 1987. The fifty-seven year-old Benton was in semi-retirement after a long and successful career in telecommunications. He had recently owned, operated and sold several start-up telecommunications companies, including a telephone equipment sales company, a telecommunications services company and a long-distance resale company. During his earlier career at Contel, he had served as Vice President, Telecommunications Services Group from 1979 to 1982.

The company changed its name from "Intermedia Communications, Inc.", which had been the name of Kolsby's consulting company to "Intermedia Communications of Florida, Inc." and re-incorporated in Delaware, November 9, 1987.

Benton's background also included experience in finance, having served as Vice President of Finance for a Midwest utility and Manager of Financial Planning at ITT's headquarters in New York. He began to exercise his contacts from the financial world to introduce Intermedia to venture capital firms. John C. Baker of Patricof & Co. Ventures of New York developed an interest in Intermedia and led a group of venture capital firms to back the tiny company. By March 1988 the venture capitalists, including The Vista Group of New Canaan, Connecticut, Morgan Holland Ventures of Boston and MBW Venture Partners of Morristown, New Jersey, had raised $5.2 million in private placement money.[38]

Building The Intermedia Network

With its initial venture capital funding in place, Intermedia was able to sign-up with a contractor to begin construction of its network in February 1988. Kiewit Telecom and other contractors had been actively soliciting Intermedia's business; but the Company selected a proposal from a local contractor, Commercial Systems Integration (CIS).[39] This was the first CAP network project for CIS which was a unit of aerospace giant, Martin Marietta.

The contract included designing, building and maintaining a three-mile fiber ring in downtown Orlando. In the first phase, this ring linked long distance carriers' points-of-presence (POPs) and provided POP-to-POP transport. Construction of the Orlando ring was completed in May 1988 just in time to take advantage of the enhanced awareness of the need for diversity produced by the Hinsdale incident in Illinois.[40] One month after the fire in Illinois, Intermedia used the argument of the need for diversity and signed up its first long distance carrier customer in Orlando.

Intermedia's strategy involved a phased roll-out of its network. In phase one a "carrier ring" linking the POPs around the city was constructed. In phase two a larger, "backbone ring" reaching the major building complexes and linking to the "carrier ring" was constructed. Lastly, "distribution rings" were built from hub locations on the "distribution ring" into those surrounding areas that had a high density of commercial buildings.

After Orlando, Intermedia constructed a network in Tampa. To facilitate network installation, Intermedia signed a contract with the Tampa Electric Company to engineer and construct a network using its rights-of-way. Phase one of the Tampa network was quickly made operational by November 1988.

Financial Struggle

Intermedia's revenue for 1988 was still small ($67,000), and losses mounted to nearly million dollars.[41] Only eighteen miles of network had been constructed, and heavy capital expenditures lay ahead to carry out Intermedia's business plan.[42]

Intermedia tried to minimize the capital required for network expansion by leasing rather than owning fiber and conduit. An abandoned water main system in downtown Orlando was leased from the Orlando Utilities Commission. A dark (unlit) fiber ring outside downtown Orlando was leased from American Digital Communications, and a pole attachment agreement with Florida Power and Light was used to cover the rest of the city. In Tampa, the network relied upon both owned and leased fiber cable on the utility poles and in the underground electrical conduits of the Tampa Electric Company[43] However, leasing options were not universally available.

Intermedia also tried to pre-sell customers prior to completion of the networks, but found customers reluctant to commit to non-existent facilities. The necessity of constructing network infrastructure in advance of significant customer orders meant that Intermedia expended a great deal of capital before seeing any revenue.

The difficulty of raising the needed capital was increased by the fear of competitive responses from the incumbent telephone companies which might make the business case for Intermedia less attractive. Some competitive response did occur. Orlando was served by Southern Bell (an operating company of RBOC, BellSouth). Telephone company tariffs for DS-1 circuits were mileage dependent, and BellSouth's rates started in the $900 per month range for the first mile. Intermedia's business plan was originally based on pricing its competitive DS-1 service at $650 per month.[44] By year end 1988 Southern Bell dropped its short-haul DS-1 rate by 54%.[45] Pricing pressure continued; and Intermedia sometimes found itself selling its DS-1 service as low as $300 per month, stretching its projected "break-even" point several years into the future.[46]

Despite these less favorable business conditions, Intermedia was still able to find new investors. In July 1989, Intermedia raised $10 million in new private equity and debt from New York Life Insurance Co. By year end, with 77 network miles operational, Intermedia's revenue climbed to $781,000; but losses increased to $1,283,000. Intermedia needed much more capital to continue expanding and to reach viability.

We Mutually Decided We Hated Each Other

As the company grew, Kolsby was increasingly unhappy. He was a natural entrepreneur and free spirit who didn't care for dealing with reports and endless meetings. He asked Benton to release him from day-to-day operations. Rather than being Vice President of Planning, he wanted to operate as a consultant outside the corporate structure. Working in this mode, Kolsby developed the expansion plans for new networks in Miami and Jacksonville. Once these plans were complete, relations between Kolsby and Benton deteriorated. One day, according to Kolsby, "We went out to lunch together and mutually decided we hated each other."

Although the various venture capital contributions had steadily decreased Kolsby's equity position in Intermedia, he still held 1.2% of the stock.[47]   However, there was a stipulation that Kolsby would lose his rights to this stock if he should leave the company. Benton agreed to wave the stipulation if Kolsby would please just leave. The Intermedia Board later balked at affirming this deal and asserted that Benton was never authorized to make such an offer. However, under threat of litigation, they finally ratified the transaction.

Metrex Corporation

Kolsby left Intermedia in 1989 to found a new CAP, Metrex Corporation, in Atlanta, Georgia. Kolsby's partners in Metrex were cellular entrepreneurs, Chris Blaine and Tom Body. These partners had done well in cashing in their cellular franchise and were eager to do the same with Metrex by finding a buyer for as soon as the network was operational.

Discussions were held with several CAPs about buying Metrex. Despite the bad blood during his departure, Kolsby really wanted to help Intermedia. He thought that it would be good for Intermedia to buy the Metrex network in Atlanta and become a multi-state CAP. But Intermedia did not buy Metrex. Both Teleport Communications and MFS Communications made offers. The MFS offer was accepted. Kolsby was retained as President of MFS Atlanta and, to his relief, he had a dependable salary for the first time in years. However, he also found that he was now an executive in a disciplined company - a role he did not enjoy.

Kolsby would ultimately found a total of four CAP companies— Intermedia Communications, Metrex in 1989, Metro Access Networks in 1993, and a new company re-using the old Florida Digital Network name in 1998.

ALTS Spokeswoman

Back at Intermedia Communications, the company's growth accelerated. As one of the few CAPs actually operational at the time of
the Hinsdale incident, it attracted attention and mention in national
news stories. Barbara Samson quickly became one of the most
visible figures in the industry, both as spokesperson for Intermedia
and, on a larger scale, for the industry. Active in ALTS, the industry association, she served two terms as its Chairman.

While the attention was useful to the Company, Samson's real concern was how to turn public recognition into the financial support
needed to grow the company. Expansion plans for 1992 alone
would require $14 million in capital spending. Intermedia needed
access to public equity markets.

Intermedia Becomes The First U.S. CAP To Go Public

At Bear, Stearns & Co., Inc., Tom Lord, co-head of the Technology Group, organized a conference on the CAP industry.
Hundreds of people from the financial community attended, even
though there were no publicly traded U.S. companies in which to
invest. Lord realized that there was a latent market for CAP equities
and began working to groom Intermedia for an Initial Public
Offering (IPO). While Denver-based IntelCom had gone public earlier, it had been formed on the shell of an existing Canadian company. Intermedia would be the first CAP start-up company to IPO
on the U.S. market.

Lord was brash, out-spoken and aggressive, but he could also bring
people together. Kolsby liked him immediately. "Without Tom," he
said, "it (Intermedia's IPO) would not have happened." Under
Lord's pushing and prodding, an offering document was hammered
out. Bear, Stearns & Co. prepared to underwrite an offering on the
NASDAQ that would represent about a 33% ownership of
Intermedia's equity.

Creating the offering was challenging. By year end 1991,
Intermedia's revenues had climbed to $5.2 million; but it still lost
nearly a million dollars. Working capital was a negative one million
dollars, long-term debt was $9.5 million and shareholder's equity
was a negative $7.5 million.[48]

In the cable and cellular industries, where, as with CAP companies, large sums of money were being invested in the creation of networks of durable value, it had been possible to get investors to focus more on cash flow than on bottom-line profitability. The argument was that as long as heavy investment in network infrastructure continued, the enterprise would not show a net profit but was, rather, creating value for the future.

Tom Lord used this argument persuasively. What should be of interest, he proposed, was whether the operations were moving toward generating more cash than they consumed. Although not an accountant's technical definition of "cash flow," a commonly used and related metric is Earnings Before Interest, Taxes, Depreciation and Amortization (EBITDA).[49] Progress toward a positive EBITDA indicated a movement toward a viable, self-sustaining business. EBIDTA had been increasingly negative for Intermedia since its inception and reached a negative $2 million in 1990. But, by making temporary cuts in staffing, network construction and other expenditures, Intermedia was able to show a marginally positive (plus $15,000) EBIDTA at year-end 1991.

Based on these results a preliminary prospectus for Intermedia's IPO was prepared that offered 2.5 million shares at $10 per share[50,51]. The offering included the sale of two million shares by Intermedia and half a million shares by the selling shareholders, including some of the holdings of the more nervous venture capital firms and Kolsby.[52]

Reworking The Prospectus

However this proposed offering would not fly. Intermedia's first quarter 1992 results came out and EBITDA had again swung negative, although only slightly (-$5,000). Furthermore the IPO market, which had been red hot in January, had cooled; and some IPOs were being canceled or postponed in early 1992.[53]

The prospectus was re-worked by Tom Lord at Bear, Stearns & Co. The proposed selling by existing shareholders, anathema to Wall Street in an IPO, was eliminated. Restrictive convenants relative to the New York Life's $10 million holdings were removed. The number of shares in the offering was reduced to 2.3 million, and the price was lowered to $8 per share.[54]

Even with these improvements, the IPO required a great deal of confidence in Intermedia's future by investors. Intermedia's tangible book value per share before the offering was 92 cents. If the new offering succeeded, the tangible book value would rise to $3.06, so that investors paying the IPO $8 price would experience an immediate dilution of $4.94 per share.[55]

Launched

The success of this trail blazing offering was watched nervously by other CAPs. Knowing that the ability to tap the equity and debt markets was the only way they were likely to raise enough capital to build networks that could challenge local telephone markets, they were anxious for the Intermedia IPO to succeed.

The Intermedia stock opened weakly on April 30, 1992.[56] The offering was under-subscribed; and the after-market price fell below the offering price, something that investment bankers strive hard to avoid. For the remainder of the year the stock traded below $8 and reached a low of $5.75.[57,58]

However, entering 1993 Intermedia's stock price firmed and began a steady climb as investor enthusiasm for telecommunications and start-up companies re-emerged.[59] By the third quarter of 1993, the stock reached $18.50, more than double the offering price. The offering had staggered into the air but now had clearly taken wing, and the equity markets were open to CAPs.

With their equity interests diluted to only a few percent of the stock by the time Intermedia Communications went public, the founders, Samson and Kolsby were only modestly rewarded for their pioneering, entrepreneurial efforts. However, Intermedia, their collective brain-child was now on its way and would ultimately rise to become a major force among competitive telecommunications providers.

****

III. The Founder Of Indiana Digital Access & Ohio Linx

Cliff Arellano, Natural Salesman

Cliff Arellano was born in California in 1934 of Hispanic parents. Short and swarthy with a wild mop of jet black hair, he did not have the appearance of the prototypical, 44-long, IBM salesman. But friendly, sincere and enthusiastic, Arellano excelled in sales from the beginning of his career.

His college training was limited to two years at Ball State, but he had a natural affinity for high technology and was drawn to dealing in its products. He sold data communications products for the Data 100 Corporation until 1978 when the company was acquired by Northern Telecom. Although Northern Telecom was promoting the idea of advanced products for an emerging voice and data digital world, the Data 100 sales staff was not given new products and was limited to selling only their aging data product line. Disappointed, Arellano left to seek more opportunity.

With his love of selling, he formed a partnership with an older engineer who didn't. Their enterprise, Business Telephone Systems, was an interconnect company and a distributor of Northern Telecom PBXs. Although Arellano knew nothing about voice products such as PBXs, he was studious; and his technically-savvy partner taught him. They made a highly effective team and soon sold $15 million worth of equipment and reaped the reward of a 7% commission.

Northern Telecom was so impressed by the success of Business Telephone Systems that they bought the company. However, Northern Telecom quickly decided that the salesmen were making too much money and cut back the commission schedule. Arellano left to start his own company.

Communications Products, Inc.

Arellano mortgaged his house and put together approximately $50,000 to form Communications Products, Inc. It was a family company consisting of Arellano, his wife, son and daughter. Communications Products, Inc. benefited from the confusion surrounding the break-up of the Bell System and the divestiture by AT&T of the operating companies. The RBOCs were permitted to sell equipment such as PBXs, but only through the awkward process of establishing separate subsidiaries to their core telephone business. In addition, most RBOCs had few personnel trained in engineering and installing systems of this type.

While the RBOCs could buy products such as PBXs at lower prices through volume discounts, they often worked through smaller companies such as Communications Products to avoid regulatory hassles. This made a great deal for Arellano when the RBOC would market to the customer, take the order and then acquire the equipment through Communications Products.

Communications Products would configure and engineer the system to meet the customer's needs, order the switch from Northern Telecom and deliver the integrated system. Technicians from the Bell company would carry out the physical installation and premise wiring. With a 50-60% mark-up on equipment, no inventory and almost no marketing or labor expense, Communications Products, Inc. achieved very high margins. This deal appeared too good to last, and Arellano assumed that the Bell companies would ultimately buy directly from Northern Telecom and not require his services. He began to look for his next business opportunity.

Exploring The CAP Business

Arellano tracked down the leading figures in the CAP business. He found friendly and helpful receptions. In 1986, he flew to New York to see Bob Atkinson and find out more about how TCG was conducting its operations. Atkinson showed him the satellite farm on Staten Island, the shared tenant service PBX serving the Teleport industrial park and the TCG POP in the World Trade Center. Arellano was dazzled. "Boy," he said, "maybe I can do some of this."

He drove to Chicago to meet Tony Pompliano and tour the Chicago Fiber Optic network then under construction. He visited Scott Brodey in Washington, D.C. to see the operational ICC network. Also while in Washington he sought out Andy Lipman at the law firm of Pepper, Hamilton and Scheetz. Arellano had read an article by Lipman in *Telephony* magazine about the opportunities presented by telecommunications deregulation and about dealing with such practical issues as obtaining access to telecommunications rights-of-way.

Arellano was greatly encouraged by Lipman's enthusiasm and by his suggestion that the entrepreneurs who were seeking to start competitive telecommunications companies should form an ad hoc advocacy group. This eventually became the Association for Local Telecommunications Services (ALTS), and Arellano served as its Treasurer for many years.

Arellano was eager to start but needed to raise money before he could go further to create a company. He had, however, formed some definite opinions about the kind of company he wanted. First, he did not want to invest a great deal of up-front capital in a network, as Brodey had done in Washington, D.C. He wanted to build in response to customer orders. Second, he did not agree with the prevailing opinion that only the largest cities had enough dedicated access and private line demand to support a facilities-based competitive company. He wanted to create the company in his home city of Indianapolis, Indiana, even though it was only the 31st largest metropolitan area in the United States.

Pursuing Time Warner

After meeting with several potential investors, including an independent telephone company and long distance reseller, Arellano held discussions with Time Warner and their local cable operator, American Cablevision of Indianapolis. Their initial responses were not enthusiastic. Time Warner said that they had tried offering fiber-based, dedicated transport in New York on their Manhattan Cable system; and it hadn't been very successful. Their cable system in Kansas City was preparing to do something similar, with an operation called Kansas City FiberNet, but they were not very excited about its potential.

Arellano, however, was persistent and kept pushing the issue with the Time Warner personnel. He insisted that a carefully-managed competitive telecommunications business would do well. Time Warner invited him to their corporate headquarters in Denver for further discussions. Working with Time Warner's analysts in Denver, a mutually acceptable business plan was devised which included benchmarks for performance over the next three years. It was agreed that if Arellano could meet the benchmarks, he would receive an 18.5% equity share of the new company.

Indiana Digital Access

The company was named Indiana Digital Access and incorporated in Indiana on September 30, 1987. It was owned through a complex series of partnerships by Time Warner's American Television and Communications cable company, headquartered in Denver, Colorado. Time Warner's local cable operation, American Cable-vision of Indianapolis, would be responsible for operations. Arellano would be responsible for sales and marketing; and his company, Communications Products, Inc., was the minority owner.

Arellano received a visit from Ron Vidal of Kiewit Telecom and his AT&T partners. They proposed to build the Indianapolis fiber network for Indiana Digital Access for an estimated $10 million. However, American Cablevision presented a lower cost option. Indiana Digital Access contracted with the cable company to construct the network by overlashing the fiber on its existing aerial coaxial cables and by placing fiber in its existing conduits. The estimated construction cost was a tenth of the Kiewit proposal.

Communications Products, Inc. did the engineering and provided the terminal equipment. The cable company installed the core network fiber and provided network maintenance. Actual construction of fiber from the core network to the customer's building was deferred until after the customer had signed a contract.

Indiana Digital Access intended to target long distance traffic, both POP-to-POP and POP-to-end user, which was under FCC jurisdiction. Nevertheless, it applied for and was granted a Certificate of Territorial Authority by the Indiana Utility Regulatory Commission in January 1988, probably to aid in future possible right-of-way issues.

The first customer circuit was placed in operation in July 1988. The customers signed up for three to five years on non-cancelable contracts with 20% annual returns built into the lease terms. Unlike most other competitive telecommunications companies, Indiana Digital Access, with very little overhead and pre-sell expense, was quickly showing an operating profit. Within a year, Indiana Digital Access had achieved all the benchmarks projected for the first three years of operation. Time Warner was very pleased with the results which encouraged them to create similar operations in Kansas City and their other cable systems.

Ohio Linx

By 1991, Arellano was growing restless and wanted to control and operate his own competitive telecommunications company. One of his carrier customers in Indianapolis mentioned that they had a need for ten to twelve DS-3 circuits in Cleveland, but that there was no CAP company there offering an alternative to the local phone company. Arellano loaded a measuring wheel into his car and, with his son, drove directly to Cleveland, arriving late at night. In the middle of the night, they walked down the deserted major streets of the city, rolling the wheel along and calculating the amount of fiber to be ordered.

Still retaining his interest in Indiana Digital Access, Arellano formed his own company, Ohio Local Interconnection Network Exchange Company - doing business as Ohio Linx (Ohio Local Interconnect Network eXchange). The company was incorporated on April 3, 1991, to pursue the opportunities in Ohio[60]. Arellano turned to the equipment vendors seeking funding for his new company.

Telco Systems, an early CAP equipment supplier, was experiencing financial problems, and turned him down. He turned to Northern Telecom the major rival to AT&T for dominance of the North American telecommunications market. Northern Telecom, which was eager to identify new markets beyond the traditional carriers, agreed to lend Arellano $1.5 million. Before the contract was signed, however, Arellano received a call from a representative of AT&T Credit Corporation. AT&T Credit Corporation, whose original mission was to help customers fund purchases of AT&T equipment, was eager to invest in start-up competitive telecommunications companies.

The AT&T agent said, "We'd like to do business with you. What's it going to take to get your business. You need 3-4-5-6 million, don't you?" Arellano replied, "Boy, those numbers sound good to me. If I could get six million, that would be great." Arellano indicated that there was a problem, however. He had designed his network around Northern Telecom equipment and he said, "Next week I am signing a deal with Northern Telecom for $1.5 million." "Wait," was the reply. "Don't do anything. I'll be there Monday morning. We'll work something out."

Within two days an agreement had been completed for AT&T Credit Corporation to lend Ohio Linx $6 million. It also permitted the use of up to half the money to acquire equipment from non-AT&T vendors, including AT&T's bitter rival Northern Telecom. The agreement was not without strings as it contained numerous benchmarks that had to be attained for the funding to be released in each stage of the company's development.

Ohio Network Construction

Arellano served as his own project manager for the construction of the Cleveland network. It was a new and uncomfortable role. There were numerous obstacles and delays, some of which he attributed to stonewalling and resistance by Ohio Bell, the local telephone company. Without the aid of a cable partner, as in the Indiana Digital Access network, construction was expensive and went slowly. The first customer was finally installed on the five-mile Cleveland network in mid-July 1991.[61]

Ohio Linx began the development of fiber networks in other Ohio cities—Dayton, Akron, Toledo and Cincinnati, Ohio. With Arellano dividing his time between construction management and marketing, sales ramped up very slowly. For the fiscal year ended March 1992, the company had sales of $146,803 and losses of $146,133. By the end of the second fiscal year in March of 1993, sales had only reached $318,000 with losses of $924,000; and the company was in violation of the covenants of its AT&T loan agreement.[62] The stress of simultaneously managing network development and trying to meet the benchmarks required by the AT&T credit facility were wearing on Arellano.

Time Warner Communications

In order to concentrate on Ohio Linx, Arellano sold his interest in Indiana Digital Access to Time Warner in July 1993. Time Warner used these assets in forming a national CAP, Time Warner Communications. Initially, Time Warner Communications consisted of three networks, Indiana Digital Access of Indianapolis, Indiana, Kansas City FiberNet of Kansas City, Missouri and MetroComm AxS of Columbus, Ohio. All of these networks were built in conjunction with the cable plant of the local cable television operators.

Let's Make A Deal

With AT&T Credit Corporation reluctant to release any more money, Arellano found himself searching for help. Finally he concluded, "I'm not a financially inclined person. I'm grounded in technical specifics and marketing. This business is so capital intensive that I'm spending all my time constantly trying to raise money."[63] With accumulated losses of just over $1 million, current liabilities of $3.5 million and AT&T Credit Corporation unwilling to advance any more funds from the credit facility, prospects for Ohio Linx looked grim.[64],[65] Arellano began contacting other telecommunications companies, including Teleport and MFS Communications, searching for a deal. Unexpectedly, he received a call from Intertel Communications. Denver-based Intertel, using a combination of network builds and acquisitions, was focusing on the second and third tier (250,000 to 2,000,000 population) U.S. cities and making a major bid to become the third largest national player behind Teleport and MFS.

The caller was Bill Maxwell, the CEO of Intertel Communications. "Hey Cliff," he said, "we want to do a deal with you." "Well," replied Arellano, "I'm about to sign something with Teleport." "Wait," said Maxwell, "I'll come there and I'll make a deal with you, right away." Arellano's terms included a $1 million cash payment, $1 million in stock, relief from the debt owned AT&T Credit Corporation and retention of a 20% equity position in Ohio Linx.[66] Intertel agreed to this on August 17, 1993, plus a three-year employment contract and a five-year buy/sell agreement .

Lessons Learned

Indiana Digital Access demonstrated that CAPs were not confined to the largest cities. CAPs could operate profitably in small markets provided low-cost rights-of-way were available and provided operations were kept lean. Arellano's Ohio Linx experience served to show the limits of what individual entrepreneurial drive could achieve. Building fiber-based CAPs to challenge incumbent telephone companies was going to take very deep pockets and significant resources. Most small entrepreneurs were not going to be able to bootstrap such resources. For them, merger or buy-out were probably the only viable options.

****

IV. The Founders Of FOCUS and Diginet Communications

Following their departure from Chicago Fiber Optics (CFO) in 1988, the original CFO operating group, John Lucas, Tricia Breckenridge, Carol Barrett, Dan Goggin and Jack Rabin began the development of a network in Philadelphia. Although a Philadelphia network had been under way while they were part of Chicago Fiber Optics, they were now in competition with the new CFO/MFS partnership; and a new start was required.

The Lucas group retained the FOCUS name and began the Philadelphia Fiber Optic network, which was conceived as the first in a series of urban networks under the FOCUS holding company structure.   In Philadelphia, they found a local financial backer, who was involved in the geothermal power business and understood the nature of an entrepreneurial venture from his exposure to Independent Power projects.

Rights-of-way were obtained, a deal was executed with Northern Telecom, including equipment financing, and a contractor was hired. Construction on the core network for Philadelphia Fiber Optics was begun to connect the major long distance carrier POPs in the metropolitan region.

Planning was also initiated for networks in other cities, but the Philadelphia network was running into trouble before it was finished. In addition to financial problems, the team was coming apart. The group became disenchanted with Lucas' leadership, and at a Board meeting they voted to remove him. The major backer supported the Board's decision, but soon decided that he could no longer provide money to complete the network. The cost of extending the network to customer locations was exceeding expectations, and his other investments in geothermal power were demanding his resources.

Philadelphia Fiber Optics did not declare bankruptcy but simply ceased operating due to a lack of cash. A new investor was found who wanted to continue with the FOCUS plan to build multiple cities. Part of the collateral for the investment was the Philadelphia Fiber Optic assets.   A right-of-way deal was negotiated with

Western Union for FOCUS to build a network in San Francisco. But before the deal was signed, MCI suddenly purchased all of Western Union's rights-of-way in every city; and the dream of building a national chain of urban CAPs ended for FOCUS.

Breckenridge, Goggin and Rabin formed a new company, FiberConnect, to build a CAP network in the western suburbs of Chicago and to salvage what they could of FOCUS. They obtained a franchise from the city of Oak Brook, Illinois to build a fiber network. Construction had not begun when they were approached by Diginet Communications to join forces.[67]

Diginet Communications Becomes A CAP

As noted earlier, Milwaukee-based Diginet Communications had been operating a long-haul fiber link along the Chicago and Northwestern railroad right-of-way between Milwaukee and Chicago since June 1985. Harold Sampson, the Milwaukee businessman who owned Diginet Communications, thought that he could develop more traffic on this long-haul fiber if it linked fiber CAP networks in downtown Milwaukee and downtown Chicago.

Sampson knew Breckenridge, who, at one time, had done work for one of his companies. Sampson offered to buy what was left of FOCUS and to absorb FiberConnect into Diginet Communications. He wanted their help to build the CAP networks and to market the services. Breckenridge was named Vice President of Sales and Marketing for Diginet.

By year-end 1989 the first phase of a five-mile CAP network in Chicago was completed, and the following year a four-mile network in Milwaukee.[68] The networks primarily linked the long distance carrier POPs in the two cities.

In Chicago the competition for the carrier business was particularly fierce. This competition focused on very high speed (DS-3) dedicated circuits. Although these high speed circuits were considered "special construction" and, as such, were not subject to tariffed pricing by Illinois Bell, a one mile circuit cost approximately $14,000 per month when CAP competition began. With Diginet Communications, MFS and, later, Teleport competing with Illinois Bell for the market in Chicago, prices steadily eroded. Short-haul DS-3 prices went from $14,000 to $7,000 to $3,000 and, briefly, to less than $1,000 per month. Diginet Communications' sales for 1990 climbed to $3.5 million but then seemed to stall, increasing only slightly in 1991 and 1992.[69],[70],[71] Hope for profitability faded, and Diginet Communications was in financial distress.

Without more equity the company would be in default on its loans from Northern Telecom. Negotiations were held between Sampson and Northern Telecom. Northern Telecom began to shop for a buyer for Diginet. Sampson reduced operating expenses to a minimum while looking for a buyer. Breckenridge and the entire sales team were laid off. On February 22, 1993, TCG announced that it had agreed to acquire Diginet Communications for an undisclosed amount.

Breckenridge remained active in the CAP industry, later serving as Vice President of Corporate Development for Rochester-based FiberNet USA and then as Executive Vice President of Business Development for New Jersey-based KMC Telecom.

****

V. The Founder Of Eastern TeleLogic

Gary Lasher

Gary Lasher had a very advantageous point from which to observe the emergence of CAPs. In a twenty-year career with Continental Telecom, moving from engineer to executive, he had held a variety of positions ranging from Vice President of Operations of the regulated telephone company to President of the engineering and construction company. Then, in 1987, he became Executive Vice President and Chief Operating Officer of Private Satellite Network, a venture company in New York that engineered, constructed and operated satellite-based private broadcast television networks for major corporations.[72]   When Private Satellite Network did work in New York City, Lasher came into contact with TCG. Lasher saw TCG evolve from a satellite-oriented business model to a fiber-optic-network-oriented model.

Lasher was intrigued by the growing opportunities for fiber-based CAP networks. He became involved with Scott Brodey's Institutional Communications Company CAP in Washington, D.C. and served on its Board of Directors. Lasher became so impressed with the emerging potential of the CAP business that he decided to strike out on a CAP venture of his own.[73]

Eastern TeleLogic

One of ICC's investors, Regional Financial Enterprises, Inc. (RFE) of New Caanan, CT, was willing to provide seed money for the new venture. "RFE and I decided on Philadelphia," Lasher said.[74] On July 3, 1986, Eastern TeleLogic Corporation was incorporated with Gary Lasher as President.[75]

As they had for ICC, Hackman and Baring searched for investors for the new CAP. A group of venture capitalist investors agreed to fund Eastern TeleLogic. This group included the Edison Venture Fund, Le Groupe Videotron Ltee., Morgan, Holland Ventures, New York Life Insurance and Regional Financial Investment Partners .[76]

Big Network Or Small Network?

As an experienced construction project manager, Lasher drew up and issued a formal Request for Proposal, seeking a builder for the

Eastern TeleLogic fiber network. The plan called for a large network, over 100 miles in length.   The network would encircle
Philadelphia and pass through the major suburban business centers
and industrial parks. The estimated cost of the network was in the
range of $25 to $30 million.

Kiewit Telecom received the RFP and wanted to build the Eastern
TeleLogic network. However, Vidaland Crowe of Kiewit were
convinced that Lasher was proposing to build the wrong network.
They tried to persuade him to change his business plan. Rather than
build a sprawling regional ICC or TCG-type network, they suggested that he begin with a small ($4-$5 million) central-business-
district fiber network as Kiewit had built for Chicago Fiber Optic.

The Eastern TeleLogic network plan proposed the inclusion of a
tandem switch similar to the one in the ICC network. Kiewit
Telecom also counseled against the inclusion of such a switch because of the potential conflict it introduced with long distance customers of the CAP network.

Lasher considered this advice and dismissed it. He elected to pursue
his own "big network" strategy, including the tandem switch.
Kiewit Telecom was not selected to build the network.

Big Network!

Eastern TeleLogic's 108-mile network was built by Alta Telecom, a
U.S. subsidiary of Alberta Telephone of Canada. Alta Telecom also
became an investor in Eastern TeleLogic. Northern Telecom made
equipment funding available to Eastern TeleLogic. The network
included a Northern Telecom DMS-250 tandem switch and other
Northern Telecom equipment including cable and multiplexers.

Construction began in October 1988, and the network became operational in July 1989. It linked 120 buildings in Philadelphia's
Center City and 180 business locations in the northern and western
suburbs. The network also linked twenty-two long distance carrier
POPs.[77] "Some companies wire a city; we wire a region," Lasher
told the press.[78]

Learning from ICC's experience, Eastern TeleLogic marketed its
long distance switched access services carefully in a way that did not
alienate their long distance carrier customers. This task was made

easier by the fact that Eastern TeleLogic, unlike ICC, was geared more toward serving large corporate customers than long distance carriers.

Eastern TeleLogic Growth

In 1990, its first full year of operation, Eastern TeleLogic achieved estimated revenue of $4 million.[79] By 1992, revenue had reached an estimated $10 million dollar level; but its growth had slowed dramatically.[80],[81]

With $42 million dollars invested, the venture capitalists wanted to see strong quarter-by-quarter revenue growth. As a founder of ALTS and a highly respected industry spokesman, Lasher was considered one of the strongest operating executives in the CAP industry. But, without the regulatory freedom to address a wider range of telecommunications services, the Philadelphia market had its limits, even for a "big" network; and Lasher felt pressed to meet his backers' expectations. Even when Eastern TeleLogic had achieved a very impressive penetration of nearly 25% of the addressable dedicated access market, its revenues were still only $11 million.[82]

Rival CAP MFS entered the Philadelphia market. Rumors that MFS was rebuffed in attempts to acquire Eastern TeleLogic were unconfirmed. MFS built a small network in Philadelphia, but Lasher was dismissive of their competitive efforts. "We eat their lunch," he said. "In the Philadelphia area, MFS has 24 buildings, we have 240 buildings (on net). We're a local company. We have more investment in the community."[83]

Comcast CAP

Even a strategy of locally extending a fiber network is capital intensive. Eastern TeleLogic needed to be associated with an entity with synergistic interests in telecommunications if it were to gain enough financial backing to continue to grow its network. That backing came from a cable television multiple system owner, Comcast Corporation of Philadelphia, PA.

With broad interests in communications, including cellular as well as cable, and in the future possibilities of delivering telecommunications services over fiber-cable systems, Comcast announced in July 1992 that it had signed an agreement to buy controlling interest in

Eastern TeleLogic.[84] In November 1992, Comcast closed the deal to acquire 51% of Eastern TeleLogic and placed its interest in the hands of its own CAP company called Comcast CAP.[85]

Part of TCG ... What Role Now?

With increased financial backing, Lasher was able to expand the Eastern TeleLogic network mileage; and revenue began to exhibit healthy growth.   However, the operation of Eastern TeleLogic as an independent entity was coming to an end. Comcast was taking an equity interest in TCG. As part of that process, TCG acquired 49% of Comcast CAP, and thus 25% ownership in Eastern TeleLogic for $6.5 million dollars in 1993.[86]

Lasher maintained that he was comfortable in a partnership with TCG, particularly if the alternative were MFS. "We have a relationship with TCG. We've always had one. ETC (Eastern Tele-Logic) and TCG do not compete head to head. MFS and ETC do."[87]

In November 1993, TCG acquired the remaining 75% of Eastern TeleLogic from Comcast for $233 million, and Eastern TeleLogic became a subsidiary of TCG.[88] The price reflected the value that Lasher had created. The "big" network concept had worked. The network now reached 525 miles, encompassing Camden, New Jersey and Wilmington, Delaware, as well as Philadelphia. There were nearly 400 buildings on-net and revenue was in excess of $25 million.

A TCG spokesman said, "We certainly would look to have Gary continue his leadership of ETC."[89] A passive role in someone else's CAP was not a role for Lasher, however. Within a year, he was off to pursue other entrepreneurial ventures.

****

VI. The Founder Of Electric Lightwave And GST Telecom

John Warta

John Warta had an early introduction to competitive telecommunications when, in December 1986, he became Senior Vice President for Marketing, Sales and Corporate Development at NorLight, the fiber optic network subsidiary of five Midwest utilities.

When Warta left NorLight after two years, he continued to work with utilities. He formed Vancouver, Washington-based Pacwest Network to help utilities pursue telecommunications opportunities, including marketing their rights-of-way for fiber optic network development. Pacwest participated in projects involving 3,000 miles of fiber.

Electric Lightwave

In 1988 while engaged in a project with Portland General Electric, Warta co-founded Electric Lightwave, Inc. (ELI) to enter the CAP business directly. Electric Lightwave became a subsidiary of Pacwest Networks and initiated development of fiber networks in Seattle and Portland. As other entrepreneurs had found, bootstrapping the financing of a CAP network proved difficult. After two years of trying, Electric Lightwave was a four-employee company struggling to build its networks. To obtain the capital required for expansion, Warta sold controlling interest to Citizens Utilities in July 1990 for a commitment of $10 million. Warta remained as CEO of Electric Lightwave.

Connecticut-based Citizens Utilities is a utility holding company with diversified interests in telecommunications, electric, gas and waste water services in sixteen western States.

Electric Lightwave opened its Seattle and Portland fiber networks in 1991 and had its first significant revenues ($1.2 million) in 1992, after four years of effort.[90] Looking forward to future entry into full local telephone service, Electric Lightwave initiated lobbying efforts with the Washington and with the Oregon Public Service Commissions. While waiting for authority to enter local switching, Electric Lightwave installed a tandem switch for long distance access in its Portland network in 1993.[91] Network expansion also continued in 1993 with local fiber networks under construction in Salt Lake City, Sacramento and Phoenix, as well as a long haul fiber network from Phoenix to Las Vegas.[92]

RBOC, U S WEST took the Washington Utilities and Transportation Commission to court over its intent to grant Electric Lightwave full authority to offer local, switched service. The case went all the way to the Washington State Supreme Court, which ruled that the Commission is not required to protect local telephone service as a monopoly franchise.[93] Following the court ruling, on March 24, 1994, Electric Lightwave was certified to provide local service. It installed a switch in Seattle and became the first CAP west of the Mississippi to offer switched local telephone service, and Electric Lightwave was on its way to become a major player in the competitive industry.

John Warta was not around to enjoy the accomplishment. Chaffing under the lack of ownership control, Warta had pulled up stakes in June 1993. Resigning as President, CEO and Director of Electric Lightwave, he was on his own again and reactivated his consulting company, Pacwest Network.

GST Telecom

Warta was not out of the CAP industry for long. Within a year he had formed a new company, GST Telecom, as a joint venture between Pacwest Network and Greenstar Telecommunications, Inc., a Canadian company listed on the American Stock Exchange. Greenstar had ties to IntelCom. One of Greenstar's founders and director, W. Gordan Blankstein, had also been associated as a founder, officer or director with IntelCom's predecessor companies: Canuck Resources, Teleport Denver and InterTel Communications.

Greenstar Communications had investments in long haul fiber network projects, telephone equipment manufacturing and a joint venture with IntelCom to develop a local fiber network in Phoenix.[94] John Warta was named President and CEO of GST Telecom, Inc. in June 1994. Like Electric Lightwave, GST Telecom would grow into a major regional CLEC. By the time GST Telecom would go public in November 1997, it would have networks in seven western states and Hawaii and revenue in excess of $100 million.

Footnotes Chapter 6: Entrepreneurs

[1] "Teleport Eyes New Satellite Feeds," *The Denver Business Journal,* Feb. 23, 1987, v38, n22, s1, 1.

[2] Ibid.

[3] "Developer to Launch Satellite 'Teleport'," *Rocky Mountain Business Journal,* August 18, 1986, v37, n46, s1, 1.

[4] "Uplink Services Provide Uplift to State, Wide Variety of Firms" *The Denver Business Journal,* Aug. 18, 1987, v38, n47, s1, 20.

[5] "Developer to Launch Satellite 'Teleport'"...

[6] "Calling All Consumers: Now It's True About Your Phone Service, Too: Let the Buyer Beware," *Denver Business,* Sept. 1988, v11, n1, s1, 24.

[7] "Uplink Services Provide Uplift to State.

[8] Investment Summary Prepared For Intertel Communications, Inc. by TPL/The Investor Relations Co., Jan. 1991, 6.

[9] "Developer to Launch Satellite 'Teleport'"..

[10] Developer to Launch Satellite 'Teleport'"..

[11] "Calling All Consumers.."

[12] "Intertel Communications, Inc.," *Wall Street Transcript,* Sept., 2, 1991, 102.388.

[13] Ibid.

[14] "Intertel Communications, Inc., Formerly Canuck Resources Corp.," *Standard & Poor's Corporate Descriptions,* 1992.

[15] Ibid.

[16] Investment Summary Prepared For Intertel Communications, Inc. by TPL/The Investor Relations Co., Jan. 1991, 6.

[17] "Intertel Communications, Inc.," *Wall Street Transcript,* Sept., 2, 1991, 102.388.

[18] "Teleport Denver Acquisition Update," Company Press Release, Sept. 18, 1990.

[19] "Canuck Resources Changes Name to Intertel Communications," *Business Wire,* Dec. 17, 1990, s1, 1.

[20] "Northern Telecom Completes $18 Million Loan to Subsidiary of Intertel Communications," *Business Wire,* Dec. 18, 1990, s1, 1.

[21] "Teleport Denver Calls For Bids on Fiber Network and Signs a Major Network User Contract," *Business Wire,* Sept. 20, 1990, s1, 1.

[22] Intertel Communications Inc., Second Quarter Report, March 31, 1992.

[23] Evans would ultimately leave Intertel to found and run his own company, Convergent Communications.

[24] The EMC category was experimental and soon discontinued by the AMEX.

[25] "Intertel Begins U.S. Trading On American Stock Exchange Emerging Company Marketplace March 18," *Intertel Communications Press Release,* March 18, 1992.

[26] "Intertel Gains Listing On American Stock Exchange," *Network World,* Industry Update, April 13, 1992.

[27] 1992 Annual Report of Intertel Communications, Inc., 19.

[28] Ibid. , 9.

[29] Corporate flyer: ICI Facts, August, 1990.

[30] Florida Digital Network declared bankruptcy in 1987. Kolsby would create another company of the same name in 1998.

[31] Entrepreneur Advises Losing The Ego," *Business & Finance Section, Tampa Tribune,* Feb. 15, 1993, 1.

[32] Ibid.

[33] "The Rise Of The MAN Handlers," *Data Communications,* Oct. 1989, 68.

[34] Ibid.

[35] "Enterprising Women," *Readers Digest,* November, 1996, 110.

[36] Ibid.

[37] Ibid.

[38] Corporate flyer: ICI Facts, August, 1990.

[39] "MANS Are Martin Marietta's Near-Term Market Window," *Telephone News,* May 2, 1988.

[40] "Intermedia Initiates Orlando MAN This Month," *Fiber Optic News,* May 9, 1988, 8.

[41] Prospectus, Intermedia Communications of Florida, Bear, Stearns & Co. Inc., April 30, 1992, 14.

[42] Ibid., 28.

[43] Ibid.

[44] "Florida Regulates LAACs As An IXC With Interstate Privileges," *The Long-Distance Letter,* Jan. 1989.

[45] Ibid., 15

[46] Tampa was GTE territory, and GTE had higher access tariffs than Southern Bell. GTE was less aggressive in its pricing response but in 1991 dropped its DS-1 rate by 17%. As a result the Tampa network moved toward being cash flow positive more rapidly than the Orlando network.

[47] Preliminary Prospectus, Intermedia Communications of Florida, Bear, Stearns & Co. Inc., April ( ) 1992, 41.

[48] Prospectus, 5.

[49] "Cash flow" includes other items, the primary one being an allowance for working capital.

[50] Preliminary Prospectus, 4.

[51] Ibid. , 11.

[52] Ibid. , 41.

[53] "The Trials of Going Public," *Communications Week,* May 25, 1992, PNN1.

[54] Prospectus, front cover.

[55] Ibid. , 12.

[56] Intermedia trades under the symbol, ICIX, on the NASDAQ.

[57] "Second Offering to Fuel ICI's Competitive Punch," *Tampa Bay Business Journal,* vol. 13, No. 40, Oct. 1-7, 1993.

[58] "Southern Bell Competitor Plans Big Push With Stock Sales," *Daily Business Review,* (formerly Miami Review) Aug. 1993.

[59] Ibid.

[60] "1992 Alternate Local Transport.. a Total Industry Report," (Glastonbury, CT, Connecticut Research, 1992), 153.

[61] Ibid.

[62] IntelCom Group Inc. Preliminary Prospectus, Paine Webber Inc., C.J. Lawrence/Deutsche Bank. Hannifin, Imhoff Inc., May 6, 1994, F-39.

[63] "Sale of Ohio Linx Could Portend Things Yet to Come," *Local Telecom Competition Report,* Sept. 29, 1993.

[64] IntelCom Group Inc. Preliminary Prospectus, F-38.

[65] Ibid. F-43.

[66] Ibid. F-12.

[67] "FiberConnect And Diginet Join Forces: Constructing Bypass In Chicago Area," *Fiber Optic News,* Oct. 17, 1988.

[68] "Diginet Expands Alternative Access Networks With Service In Milwaukee," *Fiber Optic News,* Jan. 15, 1990.

[69] "1991 Alternate Local Transport ... a Total Industry Report," (Glastonbury, CT, Connecticut Research Report, Feb. 1991), 68.

[70] D&B - Dun's Market Identifiers, DN = 12-159-1242, November, 1990.

[71] "1992 Alternate Local Transport.. a Total Industry Report," (Glastonbury, CT, Connecticut Research, 1992), 56.

[72] D& B - Dun's Financial Records, DN = 17-419-1676, Dec., 1990.

[73] "Eastern TeleLogic Burrows In Delaware Valley For The Long Term," *Local Competition Report,* November 1, 1993, 7.

[74] Ibid.

[75] "The ALTS, An Emerging Industry," (Glastonbury, CT, Connecticut Research Report, 1989), 57.

[76] "1991 Alternate Local Transport ... a Total Industry Report," (Glastonbury, CT, Connecticut Research Report, Feb. 1991), 74.

[77] Ibid.

[78] "Building Bridges Over Bypass," *Telephony,* Jan. 15, 1990, 32.

[79] "1991 Alternate Local Transport ... a Total Industry Report."

[80] "1993 Annual Local Telecommunications Competition ... the ALT Report" (Glastonbury, CT, Connecticut Research, 1993), VII-14.

[81] Ibid.

[82] Beyond Transport," Paper presented by Gary Lasher, Jan. 14, 1993 at a TeleStrategies Conference.

[83] Eastern TeleLogic Burrows In Delaware Valley For The Long Term," 10,

[84] "Comcast Plans Acquisition," *Wall Street Journal,* July 17, 1992.

[85] "Comcast Closes 51 Percent Purchase of Local Loop Carrier in Philadelphia Area," Press Release, Nov. 13, 1992.

[86] Preliminary Prospectus for Teleport Communications Group, Inc., Merrill Lynch & Co., Morgan Stanley & Co., Donaldson, Lufkin & Jenrette, Lehman Brothers, Deutsche Morgan Grenfell, June 3, 1993, F-15.

[87] Eastern TeleLogic Burrows In Delaware Valley For The Long Term," 10.

[88] "Comcast, Teleport Acquiring Eastern TeleLogic," *Cable World,* Nov. 4, 1996, 28.

[89] Ibid.

[90] Electric Lightwave, Inc. Prospectus, November 24, 1997, 25.

[91] Ibid., 40.

[92] Ibid., 41.

[93] "Electric Lightwave, Inc. Chronology," Undated Press Release by Electric Lightwave, Inc.

[94] "Teleport Denver To Expand To Metropolitan Phoenix, Suburbs," *Telco Competition Report,* February 8, 1993, 10.

7. WINNING THE HEARTS & MINDS

Charting The Course For A New Century

By the late 1980s, the importance of telecommunications to the U.S. economy was becoming increasingly clear. Politicians began to be interested in being identified with its policy-shaping decisions.

There had been no comprehensive U.S. national policy assessment in two decades, and President Reagan wanted one carried out. The administration's Assistant U.S. Secretary of Commerce, Alfred Sikes, was given the task. Sikes had a long background in telecommunications and telecommunications regulation. He had served as the Administrator of the National Telecommunications and Information Administration (NTIA) from 1986 to 1989. Sikes initiated a comprehensive review and forecast of telecommunications in the US, which would be published under the title, "*NTIA TELECOM 2000: Charting The Course For A New Century.*"

John Shapleigh & Scott Bonney And The TELECOM 2000 Report

Sikes did not want a purely academic nor too bureaucratic a viewpoint to be reflected in the study. He wanted a realistic and useful evaluation of the future. He wanted the authors to have some practical experience in telecommunications. He recruited John Shapleigh, the former Chairman of the Missouri Public Service Commission, to lead the effort. Shapleigh was an attorney with experience in politics and telecommunications.

In addition to his background as a state regulator, Shapleigh had worked as an executive in the competitive long distance industry. He had been Vice President and General Counsel of LDX NET, a high-technology, long distance company that had built and operated a state-of-the-art, 1,800-mile, fiber optic network. From his own office, Sikes assigned a young policy advisor, Scott Bonney, to work for Shapleigh on the study. Bonney had been brought into the Department by Sikes because of his background in regulated utilities and his first-hand knowledge of the utility industries. Bonney had worked for an electric utility, American Electric Power, and a telecommunications company, GTE.

149

He had done the nitty-gritty work of rate design and technical cost-
ing with American Electric Power; and he knew the network, regulatory and business issues through work at GTE's SpaceNet satellite
company and GTE corporate.

During the course of the work on the report, Shapleigh and Bonney
were visited by the two Bobs—Atkinson and Annunziata—from
TCG. They wanted to explain their business and to be certain that
competitive local telecommunications companies such as TCG and
their potential significance in the emerging telecommunications
world were not overlooked in the TELECOM 2000 report.
Annunziata also issued an invitation to Shapleigh to speak before the
World Teleport Association in Cologne, Germany the following fall
and to present the preliminary findings of the study.

The massive Telecom 2000 report was released on October 23,
1991. It noted that:

> Some 36 different firms are now offering or planning
> to provide alternative local telecommunications ser-
> vices in more than 38 cities in 26 states ... the clear
> benefits that have stemmed from the introduction of
> competition into the ... (long distance) ... and ...
> (telephone equipment) ... markets provide promise
> that similar benefits will follow from local ...
> (telephone) ... competition.[1]

The report suggested that the State Public Utility Commissions,
which regulate local telephone service, should take the lead in developing regulations to encourage and facilitate local telecommunications competition. In particular, the authors urged that local telephone companies be required to interconnect with their new
competitors and to link their networks at the telephone companies'
central offices.

The report laid down the rationale for new policy directions and, in
its conclusion, issued a call to action.

> ... the soundest way for government to encourage
> efficient infrastructure development is through re-
> moval of unnecessary regulation and promotion of a
> competitive telecommunications marketplace.[2]

Dispersal

Upon completion of the study, the principals involved all dispersed. Before the Reagan administration came to an end in 1988, Sikes was nominated to the position of Chairman of the Federal Communications Commission. Shapleigh, excited by the findings of the TELECOM 2000 report, was eager to return to his home town of St. Louis and try his hand at starting-up his own competitive company.

Bonney had always considered his sojourn in Washington, D.C. as temporary. He intended to return to his old company, GTE. However, Bonney found that GTE was relocating its headquarters from Stamford, CT and moving to Texas. With strong ties to the East Coast, he had no desire to live in Texas. When Atkinson invited him to join TCG as Director of Regulatory Affairs, Bonney accepted.

Missionary Work

For the next two and a half years, Atkinson and Bonney were the entire regulatory department for TCG as it battled for regulatory and legislative change to open local telecommunications markets to competition. The major goal was to win the hearts and minds of the regulators.

This was no easy task. Atkinson and Bonney considered themselves to be in a "missionary mode" to both educate and persuade the regulatory community. Education was necessary because many regulators had only a slight grasp of the details of the workings of the telecommunications industry.

Public utility commissioners in some states were responsible for the regulation not just of telephone service but also for water service, electric service, taxi service, *etc.* Most commissioners served only part time. Furthermore, they were often appointed for their political connections, not their industry knowledge. The TCG approach was to patiently play the role of educator and to win trust and to persuade by not pushing a hard-sell approach.

A further problem for Atkinson and Bonney was that recent history did not support their position. The two most recent "experiments" with introducing competition into the local telephone market were generally conceded to have been disasters for consumers. These "experiments" were alternate operator service and competitive payphones. Both businesses had attracted unscrupulous elements who had engaged in deceptive practices and price gouging. Regulators had been besieged with complaints and with horror stories about people getting unexpected bills for hundreds of dollars for using a non-telco payphone in a bus or airport terminal. Suggestions for any further experimentation in opening of local telephone service to competition were greeted with skepticism.

Right And Goodness Are On Our Side

Bonney was impressed with Atkinson's almost religious zeal about opening markets to competition. It was clear that Atkinson firmly believed in his mission with passion, and he infused that passion into everyone around him. For Bonney, it helped bolster his spirits in the face of what sometimes seemed an impossible task. The resources of the telephone companies were so vast, including deep pockets and legions of lawyers and lobbyists. The possibility that tiny TCG and its allies could prevail against them in winning regulators to their point of view had a quixotic flavor.

Bonney was spending nearly seventy-five percent of his time on the road, meeting and talking with state utility commissioners. Whenever he was about to leave on one of these trips, Atkinson would grab him by the shoulders, look him in the eye and say, "Now Scott, don't forget. The facts are on our side on this thing. Right and goodness are on our side. I mean, everything America stands for in terms of giving people choice and having the competitive market be the determinant of technologies, services and like that. All of that is on our side. So when you go into these battles of ideas, just remember that you've got right on your side."

On the issue of being outnumbered by the army of Bell lawyers and lobbyists, he counseled. "Scott, don't worry about it because we have the strength of a hundred because our hearts are pure. We are on the right side of this issue."

It was clear he believed it.

Picking A Venue: The Light Will Shine Down

Responsibility for telecommunications regulation in the United States is divided between the federal government and the individual state governments. Regulatory issues involving long distance traffic were the responsibility of the Federal Communications Commission. However, traffic could be physically local and still be jurisdictionally "long distance" and hence under FCC:jurisdiction over long distance control. For example, delivering traffic to long distance carrier POPs, which is what most competitive companies did, involved local transport of traffic that was under federal jurisdiction. Issues related to this traffic required filings and, mostly paper, pleadings to the FCC in Washington, D.C.

Other local telephone service issues were within the jurisdiction of the state Public Utility Commissions. State utility issues involved mostly open hearings with extensive cross examinations and evidentiary processes. Such proceedings were time consuming, both in their execution and in the time required to travel across the U.S. to each state being contended. Atkinson preferred the venue of battles in arenas of the individual states to pleadings before the FCC
It was his strong belief that the full exposure of ideas revealed in the open hearing process would ultimately show the rightness of the position TCG espoused. As he put it, "The light will shine down and illuminate the truth."

The New York Regulatory Battle-Ground

A handful of PUCs across the country are typically on the leading edge of change. These set the tone and establish the precedences that later become adopted by the utility commissions of the other states. The New York Public Service Commission (NYPSC) has historically been one of the most advanced and technically knowledgeable PUCs in the country. In the late 1980s, the NYPSC was conducting a "Competition Proceeding" to examine the implications of allowing competition in local telecommunications.[3]

Having failed to get voluntary interconnection with New York Telephone through negotiations, Atkinson brought the issue to the NYPSC. In December 1986 he asked that the TCG interconnection issues be made a part of the "Competition Proceedings," and in January 1987 they were.

Dr. Gail Garfield Schwartz, who had been appointed to the Commission in 1985 by Governor Mario Cuomo, was named Deputy Chairman in 1987 and served in that position until 1992. Dr. Schwartz, bright, articulate and proactive, was a strong supporter of competition and of incentive regulation. She said, "We regulators in New York made an early policy decision. It was to encourage competition wherever it might be viable, while protecting captive customers from the abuses of the remaining monopoly bottleneck."[4]

In addition to a Ph.D. from Columbia University in urban and regional development and a Master's degree from New York University, Dr. Schwartz had been a post-doctoral fellow at Harvard University. The author of three books and numerous articles, she understood issues in depth and had served as an advisor to the Congressional Office of Technology Assessment.

Her theory was that, "A lot of monopoly with a little competition around the edges will not bring many competitive benefits to consumers, but lots of competition with a little monopoly at the core, will ... In New York, therefore, we have been defining the core natural monopoly which we will continue to regulate fully."[5]

Through the National Association of Regulatory Utility Commissioners (NARUC), her influence was felt by other state PUCs. She was particularly considered a leader for her work on NARUC's Communications Committee, and her views carried weight with its members.

"Comparably Efficient" Interconnection

In May 1989 the NYPSC issued a landmark ruling ordering New York Telephone to interconnect with local competitors like TCG.[6] For the first time, a local telephone company had been ordered by its state regulators to interconnect with a competitive local telecommunications company.

In his report to the NYPSC, Administrative Law Judge, J. Michael Harrison, who presided over the hearings, actually ruled against TCG's proposal for collocation in New York Telephone's central offices. He claimed that he found no basis for requiring New York Telephone to interconnect with Teleport. However, the Commission itself disagreed and overruled the Judge's finding.[7] Commissioner Schwartz noted the significance of the ruling. "It breaks new ground because it advances competition in the local exchange area, by 'invading' the central office."[8]

The order provided an option for "physical collocation" of competitor equipment in the telephone company's Central Office or for "virtual collocation"— provided that such an interconnection could be made "comparably efficient" to physical collocation.[9] "Comparably efficient" was defined to mean technically and economically comparable to actual physical collocation.

The interconnection order was limited, as it applied only to dedicated circuits; and permission for TCG to interconnect for switched traffic, a potentially much greater market, was not granted at this time.[10]

The meaning of "comparably efficient" left room for disagreement. New York Telephone and TCG signed a Memorandum of Understanding in June 1989 in an attempt to resolve specifically the "economic comparability" aspect.

However, in July 1989, New York Telephone filed the first version of its "Optical Transport Interconnection Service" which provided for virtual collocation but essentially ignored the agreements in the Memorandum of Understanding. New York Telephone began making revisions to the tariff in iterative negotiations with TCG and the NYPSC.

If You Command the Vocabulary, You Command The Concept

TCG realized that in addition to pressure on the regulatory and legislative fronts, the effort to turn opinion toward a "pro-competition" direction required a public relations effort. Bonney and Atkinson had been handling "external affairs" in addition to their regular duties, but a full-time public relations person was needed.

In 1989, TCG was contacted by Roger Cawley, a NYNEX employee then on strike duty, offering to do public relations work for TCG. Cawley was hired and began issuing press releases and increasing trade press coverage.

Cawley strongly believed that words mattered. He believed in what he called the "Orwellian principle that if you command the vocabulary, you command the concept." TCG's stance would be that it should be the one to frame the debate and, if necessary, even invent new language to describe emerging ideas.

The MFS Interconnection Initiative

On November 14, 1989, MFS launched its own initiative aimed at nationwide interconnection and collocation based on the work of its attorney, Andy Lipman. Unlike the TCG effort, this initiative was aimed at the FCC, not the state PUCs.

At a press conference at the National Press Club in Washington, D.C., MFS CEO Tony Pompliano announced that a petition had been filed at the FCC and at the Department of Justice (DOJ). The petitions asked that the RBOCs be forced to offer interconnection at cost-based rates, terms and conditions.

MFS requested that either physical or virtual collocation be offered on a tariffed basis. While the FCC had been reluctant to act on TCG's earlier petition, with the NYPSC action, they now decided to ask for public comment on the MFS petition.

This put the industry on notice that the FCC would probably require interconnection between RBOCs and CAPs.

Not Whether, But How

Bonney noticed that an important shift had occurred. In the telephone industry conferences and meetings in which he had participated, the idea of competition in the local telephone market had routinely been openly attacked by incumbent company supporters. Somehow, this was no longer happening.

A crucial change was now apparent. Without overtly recognizing it, the majority had adopted the CAP presumption that competition was the natural state and that monopoly was an unnatural and passing state. The debate had moved from discussions of *whether* competition should be allowed to *how* competition should be implemented. The first phase of the missionary effort had succeeded in shifting the ground of the debate.

Virtual Collocation Is Like Virtual Sex

The New York Public Service Commission was faced with continuing disagreements between TCG and New York Telephone over the Optical Transport Interconnection Service (OTIS) tariff. Although the Commission clearly preferred the parties work out a solution themselves, they had, under Richard Stannard, the Director of the Communications Division, the in-house resources for technically knowledgeable intervention.

Prodded by Stannard's staff, the two parties conducted iterative negotiations that produced a revised tariff. In January 1990 the NYPSC found New York Telephone's revised OTIS tariff in compliance with its order of the previous May.

Some technical issues were still outstanding; and a Task Force, established to address them, continued until June 1990.

TCG had indicated its willingness to accept virtual collocation, as long as it provided "comparably efficient interconnection" (CEI). After four months of frustration in trying, Teleport had no operational circuits installed under the OTIS interconnection tariff. MFS had insisted that only physical collocation was workable. Atkinson and Lipman submitted joint comments to the Task Force which moved to a more common position.

> ...the Joint Commenters *(TCG & MFS)* would strongly prefer to have actual collocation in NY Tel's central offices. This is because CEI allows a hostile competitor—NY Tel—to exercise far too much control over the cost, capabilities and characteristics of its competitors' services. Therefore, even if NY Tel provides CEI in the fairest and most neutral manner possible, NY Tel will always have a disturbing conflict between its own interests and those of its rivals.[11]

One major disagreement was over the right of TCG to control network monitoring and supervision over the fiber linking their network to the CO, including the terminating electronics in the CO. The Task Force seemed to find in favor of TCG but also conceded New York Telephone's ultimate responsibility for network integrity. The resolution was murky. The Task Force suggested that virtual collocation might never be equivalent to physical collocation.[12] New York Telephone dissented from the Task Force findings.[13]

In September 1990, sixteen months after the NYPSC's favorable interconnection ruling, TCG made its first CO collocations. OTIS "virtual collocations" were established in six New York Telephone COs.[14] Numerous implementation issues intruded. New York Telephone opposed the application of the OTIS interconnection tariff to PBX trunk circuits. They maintained that such trunk circuits were never intended to be covered by this tariff. This issue was in contention for eight months.

Some critics said that comparable efficient interconnection via virtual collocation was a sham that could never work because there were too many opportunities for gamesmanship by the telephone companies. These proponents of physical collocation said that virtual collocation was about as satisfying as virtual sex.

Pressured by strong appeals to the NYPSC from interested corporate end users, New York Telephone finally agreed, in November 1990, that TCG could provision digital PBX trunk service under the tariff. New York Telephone and TCG sent a joint letter to Stannard indicating that they had reached agreement in principle and asking that the Commission hold in abeyance TCG's outstanding complaints against New York Telephone until a final agreement could be reached.[15]

In December 1990, NYNEX threw in the towel on the whole "virtual collocation" issue and agreed to offer actual, physical collocation in New York and Massachusetts.[16] However, New York Telephone suggested that actual implementation might be limited. In their view, opening the central office for collocation would result in perhaps one hundred or more companies seeking entry.

They asserted that physical collocation in these circumstances would be totally impossible due to space limitations. This assertion was vigorously countered by Stannard, who called it a "red herring."[17] Stannard said that, "If *(CAPs)* demanded space for 100 collocation stalls and there was a supply of only 50 such stalls, there would be a way to build the other 50."[18]

On To Chicago

TCG carried the interconnection fight to other states and sought to broaden the application of interconnection beyond dedicated circuits to circuits carrying switched traffic. Filings were made in California and Illinois; but the focus of the battle settled on Chicago, the headquarters location of midwest RBOC, Ameritech.

Atkinson and Bonney began working on issues in Illinois in July of 1989, long before TCG had initiated construction of its Chicago network. They established contacts with regulators, Illinois Bell personnel and at Ameritech, the RBOC parent of Illinois Bell Telephone.

Meeting with Joe Wojcik, Senior Director of Carrier Services for Ameritech, they suggested that Ameritech adopt the "New Jersey" collocation arrangement. This initiated a series of carefully worded, "Dear Bob" and "Dear Joe" letters between Atkinson and Wojcik. Knowing the high probability that issues would end up in litigation, each side tried to establish a documented record that seemed to reflect an open-minded willingness to work together while still not yielding any ground.

> Mr. Robert C. Atkinson
> Senior Vice President, Regulatory
> and External Affairs
> Teleport
>
> Aug. 4, 1989
> Dear Bob:
>
> Thank you for visiting us last week and providing us with the information on your agreement with New Jersey Bell. We will review this information and get back to you in the very near future ...I am sure you will agree that pricing is the key issue in our developing relationship and also recognize our need to provide parity treatment to our customers. I hope by last week's opening of dialogue, we

can work to meet the needs of both
companies ...

Joseph T. Wojcik
Senior Director - Carrier Services
Illinois Bell

After reviewing the TCG agreement with New Jersey, Wojcik wrote
to Atkinson that this was not the basis for an interconnection arrangement for Ameritech. Furthermore the idea that inter-connection
of the TCG and Illinois Bell networks was needed in order to provide diversity and to guard against another "Hinsdale-like" outage,
was firmly stiff-armed.

Aug. 23, 1989
Dear Bob:

Thank you for sending the information regarding your agreement with
New Jersey Bell. However, it does
not appear to relate to the types of
services we discussed in our meeting.

As I understand it, your agreement
with New Jersey Bell deals with the
swapping of facilities...we are well
along in the downtown area on the
installation of the Ameritech Network
Protection Plan which precludes the
need for an agreement of this type.

Oct. 4, 1989
Dear Bob:

... I appreciate your sending the copy
of the New Jersey Bell Tariff page. It
provided the missing link... I have
reread...the agreement and ... Tariff,
and I cannot agree to using these as a
basis for an agreement between our
companies...I again make the offer to
work with your designated contact on
the development of specific pricing...

Shuttle Diplomacy

Atkinson and Bonney continued their missionary work. They visited Terry Barnich, the Chairman of the Illinois Commerce Commission, to explain the details of the interconnection issue. They also laid out the TCG experience in New York and the actions of the New York Public Service Commission. Barnich was impressed by the logic of pro-interconnection arguments. After the visit, Barnich picked up the phone and called Dick Brown, the President of Illinois Bell. "Dick," he said. "Let me buy you a cup of coffee."

Barnich indicated that he found the arguments for interconnection put forward by TCG to be persuasive. "I have seven votes on the Commission that will support this idea," he told Brown. "Now the Commission could write an Interconnection Arrangement or Illinois Bell and TCG could write one voluntarily." "Who," he asked, "do you think would do a better job?" Barnich was bluffing. He did not know, in fact, whether the other members of the Commission would support his view.

Brown, who was known in Ameritech for his intelligence and sharp analytic skills (He later became CEO of information technology giant, Electronic Data Systems) but was also openly criticized by traditionalists within Ameritech for promoting ideas which were "too radical," may have suspected that Barnich was bluffing. However, it didn't matter. He was already moving to the view that going "proactive" on the TCG interconnection issue and demonstrating a willingness to accept competition was the best strategy for Ameritech. He believed that this would permit the negotiation of greater regulatory freedom for the telephone company. He began lobbying inside the company to change the corporate direction. Ameritech, he felt, should seek some kind of *quid pro quo* deal.

Atkinson tried again with a new letter and phone calls to Wojcik.

Jan. 17, 1990
Dear Joe:

Despite your Oct. 4 letter, I wonder
whether some changed circumstances

> might cause Illinois Bell to reconsider
> ...The first changed circumstance is
> the Illinois Commerce Commission's
> Sept. 22 Order granting (TCG) ... a
> Certificate of Service Authority... The
> second changed circumstance is New
> York Tel's optical inter-connection
> arrangement ... Please let me know
> whether IBT will consider the "New
> York" type of arrangement...

The result was a cautious reply that exuded cooperation but yielded
no progress.

> Feb. 9, 1990
> Dear Bob:
>
> Following our conversation of
> February 2, regarding your most re-
> cent letter, I felt a written response
> reaffirming our willingness to work
> with you yet explaining the many
> sides to this issue would be appro-
> priate... in our interpretation, the ICC
> order granting (TCG) a certificate of
> authority to provide "direct,
> unswitched services in the Chicago
> Exchange area," does not determine
> (TCG)...to be an independent tele-
> phone company...Finally, I hope you
> did not mean to imply... that Illinois
> Bell is unwilling to work with (TCG)
> toward a fair resolution of these
> issues ...

This exchange of correspondence was augmented by attempts by
Annunziata to contact Ameritech's top man, Chairman and CEO,
William Weiss, to pursue directly the possibility of an acceptable
quid pro quo.

Mr. William L. Weiss
Chairman and Chief Executive Officer
Ameritech

March 6, 1990
Dear Mr. Weiss:

I read your recent speech to the
Federal Communications Bar Association with great interest...I was
particularly impressed by your
statement that "Ameritech favors open
competition in the local exchange"
and I hope that these words will soon
be matched by action...Teleport
Communications—Chicago...has
been attempting to negotiate a fair,
competitive interconnection with
Illinois Bell for over a year ... I
would very much appreciate your
personal involvement in establishing a
(TCG)-IBT interconnection arrangement that is a necessary pre-requisite
to the local competition you welcome.
...I would like to meet with you personally to reach agreement in principle on an interconnection arrangement, including the *quid pro quos*
that IBT would seek and which
(TCG) could support. ...

Robert Annunziata
President and Chief Executive Officer
Teleport Communications Group

Weiss did not respond to Annunziata's request to meet personally,
but other meetings between Ameritech and TCG were held in
Chicago. TCG seized eagerly on the fact that the idea of a *quid pro
quo* was discussed and not rejected outright. However, the definition of a suitable *quid pro quo* still seemed illusive. At TCG, there
was a feeling that if a *quid pro quo* could be established, the successful negotiation of an interconnection agreement would follow
naturally.

April 10, 1990
Dear Joe

Thank you for arranging the April 2 meeting. Howard Bruhnke and I found it to be most useful. ...I would like to summarize the meeting in the following way ... (Item) 3. The fundamental reason blocking development of a competitive IBT-(TCG) interconnection is that IBT wants some sort of a "quid pro quo" from regulators in return for a competitive inter-connection ... Our view is that Item 3—the *quid pro quo*—is the <u>real</u> issue ... While Mr. Weiss has yet to reply to Mr. Annunziata's proposal *(to discuss the quid pro quo issue)*, we will renew the suggestion based on our April 2 session ...

Annunziata again extended an invitation to Chairman Weiss to meet personally to arrive at an agreement on the substance of the elusive *quid pro quo.*

April 10, 1990
Dear Mr. Weiss:

Since I wrote to you on March 6, representatives of our companies *(have met)* ...the major result of the April 2 meeting was to identify that agreeing on a suitable *quid pro quo* for IBT and/or Ameritech in return for a competitive interconnection was <u>the</u> key issue. This, of course, is precisely the issue you raised in your recent FCBA speech.

Determining a *quid pro quo* that both our companies could support will be

challenging, to say the least. It is also
a task that must ultimately be undertaken by senior executives with deci-
sion-making authority. I would
therefore like to renew the suggestion
...that I should meet with you to
reach agreement ...

The *quid pro quo* was not, in fact, the major issue. Within
Ameritech, there was not general agreement that any such deal with
TCG should be pursued. There was some irritation at executive
levels that the discussion had been allowed to progress to this point.
The interaction with TCG now had high-level attention at Ameritech.
Responsibility shifted to a new team.

Wojcik wrote one last letter to Atkinson trying to recap the situation
and announcing the changes on the Ameritech side.

May 21, 1990
Dear Bob

Thank you for your letter of April 10

... regarding the New Jersey "arrangement," we agreed to re-examine
it; which we have done. Our position
remains unchanged...With regard to
Item three (the *quid pro quo)* I
disagree with your depiction of what
occurred during our meeting. (TCG)
originally had suggested an
exploration of the "*quid pro quo*" ...
we did not make a commitment to
provide you with a list of our regulatory requirements. To do so would
be unproductive because the regulatory issues ... *(cannot)*... be negotiated between (TCG) and IBT ... I
understand that Mont Williams has
responded to Mr. Annunziata's letter
to Mr. Weiss and ...*(will)* ... meet

> with Mr. Annunziata ...As a closing
> note ... I have moved on to new
> responsibilities. My position has
> been filled by Mr. Thomas
> Bainbridge ...

Atkinson dutifully wrote a letter to the new team leader, but frankly
acknowledged that he did not now expect the issues with Ameritech
to be settled by amicable negotiation.

> Sept. 14, 1990
> Dear Mr. Bainbridge
>
> Joe Wojcik advised me in his May 21
> letter that you would be assuming his
> responsibilities ... he indicated that
> Illinois Bell was waiting for some
> technical and operational information
> ...developed from our actual and
> planned interconnection with other
> local exchange carriers. Enclosed
> please find the following.
>
> 1. Interconnection Schematic ...
> 2. Interconnection Electronics ...
> 3. Operation Procedures ...
>
> Frankly, based on our prior discus-
> sions with IBT and Ameritech, I do
> not expect IBT to voluntarily offer
> (TCG) an interconnection agreement
> which will permit (TCG) to compete
> fairly with IBT for "central office ac-
> cess services"... My expectation ... is
> that IBT would prefer that the
> interconnection issue be *(resolved by)*
> the Illinois Commerce Commission
> ... If this is the case, please just tell
> me ...

Further correspondence from Atkinson related to changes that TCG was making in the Chicago network to incorporate SONET technology.

Oct. 11, 1990
Dear Mr. Bainbridge:

As we discussed briefly during our telephone conversation, I would like to provide you with an update ...(of our) ... interconnection requirement. I hope this change will make it possible for IBT to provide (TCG) with an efficient interconnection arrangement ...

Correspondence between Atkinson and IBT shifted to the regulatory arena.

Oct. 19, 1990
Mr. John Ake
Vice President, Regulatory
Illinois Bell Telephone

Dear John:

During our meeting last Friday you expressed interest in receiving more information about the interconnection arrangement between Teleport Communications (TCG) and New Jersey Bell (NJB). The purpose of this letter is to provide you with that information ...We have been seeking a similar arrangement with Illinois Bell since late 1988. The enclosed copies of my two latest letters to Tom Bainbridge (September 14 and October 11) summarize our outstanding requests...Please let me know if you require any additional information.

Formal Complaint Against Illinois Bell

On December 12, 1990, Teleport Communications Chicago filed a formal complaint against Illinois Bell with the Illinois Commerce Commission. The complaint, among other things, included the charge that:

> Local network interconnection is critical to emerging competition, and IBT's failure to provide competitive interconnection has resulted in a significant reduction of customer choice and a competitive imbalance in the marketplace. Repeated attempts by (TCG) to achieve the requested Interconnection Arrangement with IBT on a voluntary negotiated basis have proved futile. (TCG) thus believes that formal regulatory relief is necessary ...[19]

TCG wanted action now. They documented their long history of fruitless attempts to negotiate an agreement with Ameritech.

> (TCG) has been attempting to obtain a competitive and efficient interconnection with IBT for nearly two years through meetings and correspondence with IBT and Ameritech representatives. To date, these meetings and correspondence have not resulted in any meaningful proposal from IBT...

Illinois Bell Negotiates

At the corporate level, Ameritech began to warm to embracing, at least rhetorically, the possibility of competition. Chairman and CEO of Ameritech, William L. Weiss began to speak of a pro-competitive strategy. Illinois Bell President Dick Brown pushed the pro-competition message vigorously, "I share the view that competition is just as inevitable in the local exchange as it was in the interexchange (long distance) market—that we should all focus our energies to transition the local exchange carriers so we can participate successfully in a competitive environment."[20]

Seeing the hand writing on the wall, and knowing the inclination of the Illinois Commerce Commission, Ameritech decided it was time to let Dick Brown's Illinois Bell company negotiate a workable interconnection agreement with TCG. Illinois Bell asked the ICC to stay proceedings on the TCG complaint so that the parties could negotiate a settlement. Those discussions led to an agreement between Illinois Bell and TCG to "interconnect" the TCG fiber network with IBT central offices in Chicago although a few unresolved problems remained.[21] The agreement was limited to only non-switched private lines and special access services, but the atmosphere was upbeat.[22] Atkinson noted that IBT had negotiated in a straightforward manner and shown a sincere interest in resolving problems. "Unlike," he observed, "some other telephone companies who have been gaming the regulatory process to avoid honestly confronting this competitive issue."[23]

Ameritech CEO Weiss documented Ameritech's new official stance "... (it is) my position ... that I welcome full, free and fair competition in all information industry markets ... we intend to be relentless in our pursuit of policy changes that will promote the development of a fully and rationally competitive information industry."[24]

The Free Trade Zone Proposal

Without question New York and Illinois were the two states leading the way toward the introduction of competition for local telecommunications. A friendly rivalry had grown up between the Illinois Commerce Commission (ICC) and the New York Public Service Commission in adopting measures to promote competition.

Illinois Commerce Commission Chairman Terrence Barnich decided that it was time for his state to make a more dramatic move relative to competition in Chicago than the New York Public Service Commission had attempted for New York City. He reasoned that

> ...the transition from a regulated monopoly model to a competitive model has been slow to evolve. And while many states have adopted regulatory policies that encourage local telephone competition, they have done so at the margins, and no state has developed a competitive model or opened up a single local exchange to full competition. Regulators, in general, have unfortunately applied a "Mr. Coffee" approach of trying to drip-feed competition into the industry.[25]

Regulatory groundwork in Illinois, dating back to the early 1980s
had created the opportunity for dramatic action; and Barnich proposed to seize the moment.   Under Illinois law, the Illinois
Commerce Commission in 1991 could classify as competitive on
either a statewide or more geographically-restricted basis those
services for which there was more than one provider.   Barnich
proposed that the entire downtown Chicago Loop area (Metro
Statistical Area 1) should be declared a "Free Trade Zone" where all
telecommunications services could be offered competitively.[26]

Barnich unveiled his proposal at a conference in Washington, D.C.
on November 1, 1991.[27]   Barnich was only scheduled for a brief,
fifteen minute presentation; but he wanted to present his case and
spoke for nearly an hour.   The concepts in the "Free Trade Zone"
proposal were warmly and enthusiastically embraced by members of
the competitive industry in the audience.

The CAPs quickly jumped on Barnich's message.   Roger Cawley,
in charge of public relations for Teleport, played a particularly active
role in spreading the word.   He said, "It may be the first time a
chairman of a regulatory body, which sometimes tend to protect local companies, has said he welcomes competition in the market."[28]
MFS President Royce Holland called Barnich's statements "a very
visionary proposal that probably will make Chicago ...the telecommunications capital of the world."[29]   Teleport President Robert
Annunziata said that "while New York has been a path-breaker,
Illinois is upping the ante."[30]   Annunziata also observed, "The message out of Illinois and New York is simple.   We're being told to get
ready to go after the final frontier."[31]

Introducing Switched Service

As part of TCG's expansion plans into Chicago and Boston, TCG
proposed to include AT&T 5ESS switches in each network.   In
Chicago, Scott Bonney, who had emerged as the TCG spokesman
for obtaining new network certifications, began work to obtain approval for the switch.   TCG intended to test the waters with the first
application for actual switched services.

Bonney probed to find what type of switched service competition
Ameritech might be willing to live with.   It appeared that Ameritech
would not oppose a TCG application for authority to offer switched
service as long as it did not include basic dial tone service such as

POTS (Plain Old Telephone Service). TCG carefully choreo-
graphed its moves with Ameritech. The idea was to move the
camel's nose a little further into the tent without incurring a huge legal battle with Ameritech.

The application was made under Section 13-405 of Illinois' new
statute permitting limited switched service competition with protection for "universal service." TCG discussed every possible enhanced, switched service offering including switched data, specialized services for businesses and switched access, but stopped short
of basic local telephone service. Ameritech apparently would not
object if TCG wanted to offer "Centrex" service which was a central
office switch service which emulated that offered by a shared PBX.

Ameritech thought that they had an understanding with TCG that
they would never attempt to offer basic dial tone service. The TCG
filing, however, would be hedged. It would say that the range of
switched services discussed was what was intended to be offered,
"at this time." As to whether future offerings would have an impact
on Ameritech's financial viability in their local dial tone business,
TCG was offering no assurances.

"Teleport Plans Tough Assault on Illinois Bell"

On Thursday, November 21, 1991, Bonney was working in the
TCG New York office when he was summoned into the office of
Roger Cawley. Cawley had John Keller, a staff reporter for the
Wall Street Journal, on the phone. Although TCG's planned filing
was still a couple of weeks away, he had gotten wind of it and was
preparing a story. Together, Cawley and Bonney fielded the reporter's questions. Keller was looking for an eye-catching lead. He
apparently wanted it to be something about, "TCG offers competitive telephone service against Illinois Bell."

Bonney and Cawley answered carefully and somewhat warily.
They discussed the data services, the specialized services, the
Centrex and the shared-tenant service type offerings. The reporter
pressed for more. He said, "If that's all you want to do, I don't
know why you're putting in this 5ESS ($1.5 million) switch. It
seems like overkill."

Finally Bonney responded, "Look, you can read into this what you
want, but we're not making that kind of investment to switch around

a bunch of data services. We're making this investment to become the second telephone company in Chicago."

The Wall Street Journal story ran on Friday under the headline, *"Teleport Plans Tough Assault on Illinois Bell."*[32] The story included Bonney's explanation that the first step in Teleport's Chicago expansion would be to install a multi-million dollar switching center that would provide Centrex-type and shared-tenant services to businesses in Chicago. It also included the comment from Illinois Commerce Commission Chairman, Terrence Barnich that, "Teleport is going to ask for permission to provide a public switched service ... (that) would ultimately mean the break up of the local monopoly. This will be the most significant event since divestiture. And I would give them permission to do it."[33]

Most importantly, the story contained the direct quote from Bonney that, "Our ultimate goal is to become the second phone company in the Chicago area ... and in all the other areas in which we now operate." Ameritech was furious and felt they had been deceived.

Whatever You're Doing, Stop It!

Bonney arrived at work on Monday to find an uproar. His office was located between that of Atkinson and John Scarpati, the TCG CFO. The two were shouting at each other. Heat had come down from the Merrill Lynch corporate office, particularly from the financial departments. Answers were demanded as to why TCG was upsetting a major Merrill Lynch customer, Ameritech.

Ameritech CEO, Bill Weiss, had made a direct call to fellow Penn State alumnus, Bill Schreyer, Chairman and CEO of Merrill Lynch. Weiss indicated his surprise and displeasure to open his morning paper and read that a company owned by Merrill Lynch was attacking his company. After all, Merrill Lynch served as a financial advisor to Ameritech and was paid millions of dollars in fees by Ameritech for its services.

The "second telephone company" comments by Scott Bonney were singled out. Another call from Ameritech's financial organization to Merrill Lynch's delivered the message that they should expect no more business from Ameritech.

So?

Bob Annunziata was not immediately available since he had gone to Italy to confer with the Vatican on a proposed satellite communications network. Atkinson and, particularly Scarpati on the financial side, were taking the heat from the Merrill Lynch organization. Scott Bonney's young career at TCG looked to be in jeopardy.

Calls to Bob Annunziata in Italy finally got through. Annunziata was apprised of the frantic status at TCG and that the people at Merrill Lynch were demanding answers. "We've got people all over us because of this Wall Street Journal article which says we are taking business away from Ameritech." Annunziata's response was calm. He said, "So?" It was suspected that he was not displeased to finally have this issue sharply drawn with Merrill Lynch management.

Annunziata pointed out that this was not an ambush. Ameritech had frequently made statements to the effect that it expected to face competition in the telephone business and welcomed it. His advice to Atkinson and Cawley was to gather all the pro-competition statements they could find from previous Ameritech speeches and publications and fax them all over to Merrill Lynch headquarters.

"We've Got To Go The Other Way"

At Ameritech, Dick Brown, the President of Illinois Bell did not react to the news about TCG with anger. He was the man with the vision of the *quid pro quo*. He saw opportunity in the situation. He told others in Ameritech, "We've got to go the other way on this thing because I have a list of ten things that would really be beneficial to us and would really impress our shareholders in terms of regulatory flexibility. I can sail right through with this."

Brown argued to Chairman Weiss that TCG, with good management and solid financial backing, was here to stay and was the competition that Ameritech had always known was coming. He favored interconnecting with them, so that they would not build around the Illinois Bell network, and, also, so that their presence as viable competitors could be used to win regulatory concessions from the Illinois Commerce Commission.

Brown asserted, "Let's have the party at our house. Let's have all that traffic from Teleport coming into our central offices. What more could you want? Forget the idea that they are the enemy. These are big time future customers of ours."

"All that," he offered, "and we can come to the Commission and claim the need for regulatory relief because we now have competition." Internally, Brown had copies of the Wall Street Journal article circulated within the company. "See," he said, "We do have competition. Here it is. Let's get moving."

The heat on TCG corporately, and Scott Bonney individually, lasted less than two days. A call from Ameritech's financial department to their counterparts at Merrill Lynch retracted the earlier threat to withhold business.

Ironically, Dick Brown would hire Scott Bonney in 1992 and make him Vice President of Regulatory and External affairs in Illinois to oversee the company's program of opening its markets to competition. Dick Brown was promoted to be one of three Vice Chairmen contending to inherit Chairman Weiss's top position at Ameritech

A Revitalized Association For Local Telecommunications Services (ALTS)

The efforts of competitive companies to prevail in the regulatory arena were hampered by industry fragmentation. TCG had carried the regulatory fight in New York and Illinois essentially on its own. MFS was pursuing its initiative with the FCC. Other competitive companies were appearing individually before state and local regulatory bodies, on an ad hoc basis.

Atkinson realized that a more unified industry-wide effort would be both more effective and more efficient. The natural vehicle for this was the Association for Local Telecommunications Services (ALTS). The organization was still being run part-time by Atkinson. It needed a dedicated, full-time leader with strong regulatory and political skills.

John Shapleigh's first attempts to start-up competitive companies in St. Louis were not successful. He promoted "The Business Network" which had nearly completed raising its debt and equity funding when investors were frightened off by news of a pending rival fiber network project backed by greater resources. Shapleigh called the "two Bobs" at TCG looking for his next move.

Atkinson had a ready suggestion. Would Shapleigh be interested in running ALTS, the trade association? "What does the job pay?" Shapleigh wanted to know. "Nothing," said Atkinson, "but you will learn a lot."

Two Small Tasks

Shapleigh took over as the first full-time head of ALTS in November 1990. He was immediately faced with two tasks. Number one on the agenda was the submission of a document to the FCC. In response to MFS' November 14, 1989, petition for inter-connection, the FCC had put out a Notice of Proposed Rule Making (NPRM), asking for industry comment. This was the initial step toward an FCC regulatory action on interconnection. ALTS needed to draw-up and submit a well-reasoned, formal industry response to the NPRM document. Shapleigh organized the ALTS submission.

The second task was to unify the industry. Although MFS and TCG worked co-operatively in the regulatory area, this was primarily due to mutual respect between Andy Lipman and Bob Atkinson, who held the similar responsibilities within MFS and TCG, respectively.

These two major companies, which between them comprised the bulk of the competitive local telecommunications industry, had many common interests, but also numerous points of conflict, as they both sought to be the dominant national player. MFS had dropped out of the ALTS organization, and Shapleigh's goal was to bring them back. For ALTS to be effective, he knew that these two companies needed to be unified behind the trade association.

The primary policy advocate for MFS was Lipman. Shapleigh lobbied Lipman to have MFS rejoin ALTS; but it became clear that this was not considered a regulatory policy issue at MFS, but rather a business strategy issue.

The decision would have to come from the business side of MFS. Shapleigh called on Rick Weidinger, Vice President of Business Development for Kiewit Communications. He took Weidinger to lunch in New York City and tried to impress upon him the importance of everybody being inside the tent on major policy issues. Personal diplomacy did not yield any immediate results.

Generating Momentum

Shapleigh organized a first major ALTS conference and exposition for May 21, 1991, in Washington, D.C. It was the largest gathering to date of competitive local telecommunications companies, their customers, investors, suppliers, competitors and regulators with approximately 350 attendees.

Shapleigh brought in his old friends from Missouri — Senator John Danforth and FCC Chairman Al Sikes — as well as Congressman Jim Cooper. Cooper was introducing new telecommunications reform legislation which could greatly benefit competitive companies. The meeting was a great success.

It was apparent from the number of attendees, the eagerness of equipment vendors to sell to the industry and the status of the invited speakers, that the industry and ALTS were gaining significant visibility and influence. Big things were in motion, and MFS was not at the party. On June 21, 1991, Doug Bradbury, MFS Senior Vice President of Corporate Affairs announced that MFS was rejoining ALTS.[34]

Please Call Me A CAP

The FCC rule-making process moved toward implementation, aided by a united ALTS front. One day in 1992, Lipman, Atkinson and Shapleigh gathered in a hearing room on the 8th floor of the FCC building. There was no established terminology in general use for designating competitive local companies. Shapleigh and crew were listening to the FCC Chairman and Commissioners talking about "alternative access providers" and "alternative access carriers" being allowed to collocate in RBOC Central Offices.

They mutually realized that an FCC order would soon be issued and the industry would be stuck with whatever label was applied to them in the wording of the order. They also realized that they did not want that label to be "alternative." Competitive companies hoped to ultimately evolve to become their customers' primary carrier, not a secondary carrier.

Shapleigh met with Chairman Sikes and Chief of the Common Carrier Bureau Firestone, both of whom he had known at NTIA. Shapleigh expressed his appreciation that the FCC was going to issue the collocation order. However, he requested that in the order would they please not refer to the competitive carriers as any type of "alternate" carrier.

Sikes asked for a recommended name. Shapleigh conferred with Lipman and Atkinson, and they settled on "Competitive Local Carriers" (CLC). It seemed to have a nice ring to it. Shapleigh liked it. He thought that with the word "competition" in it, it seemed as American as apple pie.

But when the proposed CLC name was presented to Sikes and Firestone, they looked horrified. The word "local" was totally unacceptable to them. The States, not the FCC, had jurisdiction over local telecommunications. Any FCC order regulating something with "local" in its name was unthinkable. It would create massive protests from State PUCs and ignite their perennial suspicion that the FCC wanted to preempt their areas of responsibility.

Lipman, Atkinson and Shapleigh conferred again and finally settled on the term, Competitive Access Provider(CAP). The term CAP had been in use in some parts of the industry since 1991, but now it was written into the FCC order; and it became the official designation applied to the industry.

(Several years later, as CAPs evolved into providers of switched local service, they would become known by the then more appropriate title, "Competitive Local Exchange Carriers" - CLECs.)

Victory: An FCC National Collocation Interconnection Order

On September 17, 1992, the FCC enacted its interconnection order, requiring all telephone companies with revenue greater than $100 million per year to offer interconnection to "all interested parties" by June 1993.[35] Somewhat surprisingly, the order called for physical collocation, except where lack of space in the central office might necessitate virtual collocation.

FCC Chairman Alfred Sikes had opposed physical collocation as unnecessary and too intrusive. In his opinion this ruling was legally vulnerable to a challenge that it constituted illegal confiscation of local telephone company property. Despite his reservations, however, he supported the ruling.[36]

A jubilant Royce Holland at MFS said, "This decision is a beachhead for further dismantling of the entire $90 billion local exchange monopoly over the next few years."[37] He proclaimed that this decision would be marked in the history books as the "beginning of the end of the 80-year-old local exchange monopoly."[38]

Although the FCC collocation order only applied to what was called "special access," dedicated transport from the Central Office as part of a POP-to-end user path carrying long distance (interstate) traffic, it was a watershed event. Concurrent with the release of the order, the FCC indicated that it was beginning a new NPRM on the financially larger issue of interconnection for switched access service.

These actions by the FCC relative to interstate service, combined with actions by states like New York and Illinois for intrastate service, established the principle that interconnection of competing networks was in the public interest and would, one way or another, be policy in US markets.

The week following the FCC action, the ALTS Board of Directors met in the Bank of America building in San Francisco. The meeting room was on an upper floor with a commanding view. Looking out the window, Shapleigh could see clouds below.   "We thought we'd arrived in heaven," he said. "Little did we know the long hard journey we still had ahead."

TCG's Atkinson was more circumspect. "We must not misunderstand it and read too much into it," he said. "Interconnection will not increase competition. It allows us to use the local loop, not compete with it. We're still bound by the line-of-business restrictions. We can't do switched access. The FCC's decisions create the steps to competition, but do not make competition."[39]

Footnotes Chapter 7: Winning the Hearts & Minds

[1] As quoted in "Local Telecommunications Competition, The Challenge of Change," *The 7th General Assembly of The World Teleport Association*, Yokohama, Japan, Nov. 20, 1991, 6.

[2] Ibid. 6.

[3] New York Public Service Commission Case 29469.

[4] "Infrastructure, Competition and Policy," Telecommunications Free Trade Zones: A Model for Local Exchange Competition Conference, Sponsored by the Annenberg Washington Program of Northwestern University in Conjunction With the Illinois Commerce Commission, Evanston, IL, March 30, 1992, 1.

[5] Ibid. , 2.

[6] State of New York Public Service Commission, Opinion 89-12, Case 29469, Proceeding On Motion of the Commission to Review Regulatory Policies for Segments of the Telecommunications Industry Subject to Competition, May 16, 1989.

[7] Ibid., 25.

[8] Ibid., Appendix C, 1.

[9] Ibid., 25-26.

[10] Ibid. , 30.

[11] "Joint Comments of Metropolitan Fiber Systems and Teleport Communications in Support of Task Force Findings,"
NYPSC Comparably Efficient Interconnection Task Force Findings, April 19, 1990, 5.

[12] "CEI Task Force Findings," Transmittal from Dennis Taratus, Chair - CEI Task Force to John J. Kelliher, Sec. NYPSC, March 15, 1990, Finding VII.

[13] Ibid. , "Dissenting Position of the New York Telephone Co., Appended.

[14] "The New York Experience: Central Office Collocation and Interconnection," Atkinson, Telecommunications Reports' Central Office Interconnection II Conference, Washington, DC, Feb. 14, 1991.

[15] Letter to Richard Stannard, Director, Telecommunications Division, NYPSC, Nov. 7, 1990.

[16] "NYNEX Agrees To Collocate Alternative Carriers' Gear," *Network World,* Dec. 10, 1990, 2.

[17] "Unbundling the Basic Access Line: The New York Experience," *KMB Video Journal,* recorded Boston, Feb. 1991, v7, No. 2.

[18] Keynote Address by Andrew C. Barrett, FCC Commissioner, Telecommunications Reports' Central Office Interconnection II Conference, Washington, DC, Feb. 14, 1991.

[19] Complaint of Teleport Communications Chicago, Inc., Teleport *Communications of Chicago v. Illinois Bell Telephone Co.,* Illinois State Commerce Commission Docket No. 90--0444, Dec. 12, 1990, 6.

[20] Presentation before the National Association of Regulatory Utility Commissioners by Richard H. Brown, Washington, E.C., February 25, 1991.

[21] Advice No. 4771, Illinois Bell Tariff Ill. C.C. No. 15, Revised pages 242,248, 283, 286:1; Original pages 283.1, 286.2-286.6, 357.3-357.10; Filed February 20, 1991; Effective April 7, 1991.

[22] "Illinois Bell Offers Ties For Alternate Carriers," *Computerworld,* March 4, 1991.

[23] "Teleport Communications-Chicago And Illinois Bell Telephone Reach Interconnection Agreement For Chicago Central Offices," TCG Press Release, Feb. 20, 1991.

[24] "It's Time To Make Things Happen: Monopoly, Competition And Regulation In The Local Exchange," Presentation to the Probe Research Conference by William L. Weiss, New York, NY, April 10, 1991, 2.

[25] Terrence L. Barnich, Craig M. Clausen, Calvin S. Monson, *Telecommunications Free Trade Zones: Crafting A Model For Local Exchange Competition,"* (Springfield, IL: Illinois Commerce Commission Monograph, January 1992), 3

[26] Ibid.

[27] Presentation at a TeleStrategies Conference by Terrence L. Barnich, Washington, D.C., November 1, 1992

[28] "Phone Face-off Pushed For Chicago." *Chicago Sun Times,* November 23, 1991, 30.

[29] Ibid.

[30] "Cracking The Bells." *Information Week,* November 18, 1991, 13

[31] Ibid.

[32] "Teleport Plan Tough Assault On Illinois Bell," *The Wall Street Journal,* November 22, 1991, B1

[33] Ibid.

[34] "Metropolitan Fiber Systems Joins ALTS," MFS Press Release, June 21, 1991.

[35] Expanded Interconnection With Local Telephone Company Facilities, Report & Order, CC Docket No. 91-141, FCC Rcd. 7369 (Sept. 17, 1992).

[36] "FCC Mandates Physical Co-Location," *Telephony,* Sept. 21, 1992, 3.

[37] "Federal Communications Commission Takes First Step to Dismantle Local Exchange Monopoly," MFS Press Release, Sept. 17, 1992.

[38] "FCC Mandates Physical Co-Location,"

[39] "Challenges Continue To Confront Competitive Access Industry," *Local Competition Report,* November 16, 1992, v.1, no. 2, 3.

8. RIVALS

MFS & TCG: Natural Rivals

After Crowe and Holland were rebuffed in their 1987 visit seeking an alliance with Annunziata and Atkinson, the lines were drawn. It would be a contest. With both MFS Communications and Teleport Communications Group pursuing a national expansion strategy, the two companies were to be natural rivals. They would build competing fiber networks in the major cities of the United States. Their first head-to-head meeting would be in Boston, considered to be the toughest city in the United States to build a network.

Teleport Tries To Maintain Its Lead

Annunziata knew that others would follow the trail that TCG was blazing, and he was impatient to replicate the successful New York network in other major US cities before competitors could get there. However, it was just difficult to justify to Merrill Lynch that they should make large, aggressive investments in something so far removed from their core business.

While an investment in the telecommunications infrastructure in their headquarters city of New York might be rationalized, the commitment of funds to expand beyond New York was controversial within Merrill Lynch. Attempts to get the Company to commit to a $100 million, multi-city capital expansion program met resistance.

The alternative to complete internal funding was to find joint venture partners in each city. Many of TCG's New York customers had branches in Boston, making it an obvious choice as the first expansion city. A suitable and willing partner, mutual fund giant Fidelity Investments was available.

However, the very month that Merrill Lynch and Fidelity Investments agreed to form a new venture to develop a network in Boston, the financial picture suddenly darkened.[1] The "October 1987 Crash" was the largest New York stock exchange point drop ever. Merrill Lynch's earnings per share fell by more than 70% in 1987 and did not really resume their previous growth until four

181

years later. Even with joint ventures, TCG would have to scrap for funding.

Merrill Lynch committed to provide funding of $3 million for the joint venture, and Fidelity committed to provide $2 million.[2] Merrill Lynch Teleport Technologies, Inc. (MLTTI) was made the general partner with 60% ownership of Teleport Communications - Boston, and Fidelity Communications Limited Partnership owned the remaining 40%.

Entering 1988, TCG was still optimistic that MLTTI would be able to form other joint ventures and build networks in as many as fifteen major cities over the next two years.[3] Specific cities mentioned as possible sites included San Francisco, Los Angeles, Houston, Chicago, Washington, Philadelphia and Boston.[4]

It was rumored that MLTTI might form joint ventures with competitive carriers already in operation. The FOCUS' Philadelphia Fiber Optic network in Philadelphia and the Institutional Communications Corporation's network in Washington, D.C. were mentioned as possible alliances.[5]

Snow, Shoppers, Traffic and Construction

Entering the 1980s, there were very few urban cable systems. Cable was considered to be about "better reception" and was relegated primarily to suburban areas. Urban construction, where cable had to be placed in conduit under the street rather than hung on utility poles, could easily cost ten times as much as suburban construction. It seemed unlikely that urban neighborhoods would pay more than $3 to $5 per month for a cable service just to improve the quality of reception of programs that were "free" over the air.

A few cable pioneers thought that cable was about more than "better reception." They envisioned programs not available by broadcast as well as movie channels, public interest, education and pay-per-view. One of these pioneers was Chuck Dolan, whose CableVision of Boston held the local franchise in that city.

Banks would not lend money for a speculative venture such as an urban cable system. The technique Dolan used to raise money was to use limited partnerships. These partnerships could take advantage of special tax write-offs. In order for the investors to receive their write-off, the system had to be up and running and serving real customers. Dolan had raised the money on the promise to have the system operational before year end. In October of 1982 he found that he was stopped by a city-imposed moratorium.

The streets of downtown Boston are crooked and narrow. Traffic is generally congested and difficult, but it is doubly so during the holiday shopping season. In addition to the shopping crowds, movement in winter streets was hampered by the usual New England snows. Given the combination of snow, traffic and shoppers, the city did not want the added burden of street construction. Therefore, there was a moratorium on all street construction, except for emergencies, from Thanksgiving through New Year's Day.

It looked as if CableVision were not going to be able to meet its obligations to its investors and was in a desperate situation.

David McCourt

David McCourt grew up in an Irish family of seven children in the Boston suburb of Watertown. His grandfather and father had been in construction; and the John McCourt Company, which was organized in 1915, was a very successful international contractor.

After high school McCourt had wanted to become a Boston cop. His father advised him, "OK, but you've got to be a smart cop. You have to graduate from college first." McCourt went off to Georgetown and studied sociology.

The McCourts also knew the political structure of Boston and were friends of the influential O'Neill family. McCourt took a summer job in Washington, D.C. in the office of the powerful House Speaker, Tip O'Neill.

Returning to Boston after college, McCourt worked in the family construction business, but didn't feel it was his calling. One day he read an article in the paper that derided the CableVision plan for an urban cable system and its current dilemma.[6] He turned to his friend, Tom O'Neill, Tip O'Neill's son, for advice on the political problem.[7] They concocted a plan. They would leverage the fact that the mayor had the power to allow construction, even during the moratorium, for reasons he deemed an "emergency."

A Christmas Present For East Boston

David McCourt formed his own cable construction company, McCourt Cable Systems, on October 7, 1982.[8] He then went to Chuck Dolan of Cablevision and told him that he could get the permits to begin the construction of the cable system and could probably meet the year-end deadline to have the first phase operational. Dolan said that if McCourt could deliver, the construction contract was his.

Boston's Mayor, Kevin White, had a political problem. He had been a prominent promoter of the expansion of the City's major airport, Logan International. His constituency in East Boston was enraged. Every time a plane took off over their neighborhood from the extended airstrip, their television reception was disrupted.

McCourt went to the Mayor with the news that CableVision was going to build an urban cable system that would eliminate television interference and that they might be persuaded to build the first segment of the system in East Boston. Furthermore, the system could be in place before Christmas, if construction started right away. The Mayor was delighted to present such a holiday gift to soothe his irritated constituents. He announced that the system would be built.

When McCourt applied to the city for a permit to begin building, it was granted without challenge. The first phase construction was completed in time for Christmas. The whole system ultimately took three years to complete.

A Bite On The Nose

McCourt's triumph in building the urban cable system in "the toughest street construction" city in America dimmed when a dispute arose with Dolan and CableVision over payment. The dispute dragged on to the point that McCourt was forced to lay off his workforce and sell his equipment, even his pickup truck.

One night McCourt was drinking with his friends at Sevens, a pub on Beacon Hill in Boston. Tom O'Neill and developer, Donald Chiofaro, who built International Place, the tallest building in Boston, were in the crowd. Chiofaro grew tired of McCourt complaining about Dolan. He reached across the table, grabbed

McCourt by the tie and said, "If somebody bothers you David, this is what you do" and bit him on the nose.[9]

McCourt got the message. He went out and began digging up the cable he had laid for CableVision. CableVision quickly made a financial settlement with McCourt.

Looking For The Next Opportunity

Contractors normally live from job to job. Workers are kept on the payroll, and cash flows out until the next contract is landed. Since McCourt had been forced by necessity to essentially dismantle his company, he did not have these costs. Therefore, the cash settlement left him with an unaccustomed amount of cash in his pocket, but almost no company. McCourt looked for new business opportunities that could leverage his cable experience.

Unlike New York, which is a "vertical city," Boston is a "horizontal city." Large companies in Boston typically have operations housed in multiple buildings. McCourt found business opportunities in constructing private networks to connect the buildings of companies like Bank of Boston and Digital Equipment.

Each job involving city streets required a permit. Mike Adams, McCourt's Chief Engineer, spent considerable time at the Department of Public Works obtaining the necessary permits. One day in 1987, Mike met someone from Kiewit at the Commissioner's Office. He had been sent by Crowe to explore the possibility of building a fiber network in Boston, and he tried to hire Adams on the spot. McCourt and Kiewit were each now aware of the other's existence.

A MAN For Boston

McCourt had already begun developing the idea of creating a Metropolitan Area Network (MAN) in downtown Boston. Instead of building these private networks for corporate clients, McCourt thought, why not build a shared network, which he would own, and sell capacity to many corporate users?

He had discussed the idea with his friend, powerful Boston attorney, Edward McCormack. McCormack, a former State Attorney General and close associate of Mayor Kevin White, was well connected in Boston politics and very active in commercial real estate. McCormack thought the MAN idea was great, and the two agreed to form a company to develop it.

The city objected to granting permits for this activity. They saw no regulatory standing for such a company to gain access to the city streets for rights-of-way. They said, "You are not a utility or a phone company or a cable company. You are not proposing to act as a private contractor. We don't know what you are. We don't know whether you have the right to dig up the streets, so we're shutting you down."

McCourt went to city hall and made a presentation about the MAN concept and how it could boost the general welfare and enhance downtown Boston as a place for companies to locate their operations. The city was impressed and proposed that the network should be built by and owned by the city. It took several months for McCourt to convince them that he should be allowed to build and own it.

Teleport Communications—Boston

With the backing of Fidelity Investments, one of the largest corporations in Boston, MLTTI was hopeful that the joint venture, Teleport Communications - Boston (TCB), could launch its network quickly. Paul Chisholm, a well-known telecommunications manager in Boston, and then serving as Vice President of Telecommunications for Shawmut Bank, was chosen as Vice President and General Manager for TCB.[10] In March 1988, TCB submitted its application to the Massachusetts Department of Public Utilities for a "Certificate of Public Convenience and Necessity" to operate as a telecommunications carrier.[11]

Both New England Telephone and Cablevision intervened. New England Telephone did not oppose certification of TCB but required written answers to a long list of questions. Cablevision sought to have the PUC require that the TCB fiber network interconnect with their network so that they could fulfill their obligation to the city to provide a Commercial Institutional Network for the urban center. The PUC declined to require TCB to do this.

Dealing With The Street Issue

Responding to these questions took time, but even more time was required to deal with the tight control which Boston maintained over opening streets to lay cable. With narrow and congested streets, Boston was concerned with the number of different companies seeking to dig them up.

The Public Works Commissioner, Joseph Casazza, tightly enforced city policy on street management. On August 4, 1988, the city established the Public Improvement Commission (PIC) and under the PIC policy street openings were controlled and companies interested in laying conduit and cable were encouraged to combine their actions in a shared project under a designated "lead contractor." This would require a process of advertising proposed street openings and negotiating with any companies interested in participating.

Teleport Communications - Boston indicated that it would seek authority from the city to place conduit and fiber cable under the streets using the PIC process. Teleport, however, also had another strategy, which was to lease conduit and cable from its Western Union ally.[12]

Western Union, a minority owner of the Teleport New York network, claimed ownership of buried network assets in nearly every major U.S. city. These were in eclectic condition, ranging from rotting, wooden pipes to fiber cables in metal conduit. In some cases, the location and/or condition of these assets was uncertain.

Western Union also claimed authority from rights granted in the 19th century to use these assets without local government interference. These claims had worked in the building of the New York network, but were contested in other cities. Western Union sought a blanket permit from Boston to upgrade and improve its ancient network facilities under the city streets. McCourt was outraged.

McCourt argued that it had taken his company over a year to win its first permit for the construction of MAN facilities from the city, and the process limited him to obtaining street-by-street approvals. Now Western Union, on behalf of Teleport, was seeking a blanket permit which would cover the entire city.

This, McCourt asserted, was unfair. The new competitors should be required to go through the same process which McCourt had done. Otherwise, he said, he would still be filling out permit applications and Teleport would have completed its network.

McCourt said to Casazza, "Do you think that Western Union suddenly thinks that its over one-hundred-year-old business is going to rejuvenate itself, or do you think something else is going on here?" The processing of Teleport Communications - Boston's requests suddenly slowed down. TCB would finally deliver service to its first network customer in Boston, Fidelity Investments, on May 5, 1989.[13]

MFS—McCourt, Inc.

On July 28, 1988, McCourt adopted a formal organization of his MAN company, Corporate Communications Network, Inc. with himself as President and Edward McCormack as Treasurer.[14]

In August 1988 the city announced a new requirement for installing fiber under Boston streets.. Although Commissioner Casazza said that he knew of no other city which did so, Boston would require that companies laying conduit for fiber must install extra capacity and give it to the city.[15] The city would be free to either use this capacity for its own purposes or to rent it to companies that might come to town later and wish to have network facilities.

Over breakfast at the Harbor Hotel on Rose Wharf, McCourt worked out an agreement with Jim Crowe and Royce Holland to join forces. In September 1988 a letter of intent was signed for MFS and Corporate Communications Network to form a 50/50 joint venture, MFS-McCourt, Inc. to develop a CAP in Boston.

TCB finally received certification in October 1988 and was designated a "lead contractor," but the chance to initiate installation of a network in Boston in 1988 had passed. More ominously, MFS had caught up. TCB now faced competition from the formidable MFS-McCourt team, which filed its own application for certification with the Public Utility Commission on November 15, 1988.[16] Furthermore, even before filing for certification, MFS-McCourt showed its aggressiveness by initiating construction by holding a "ground-breaking" ceremony and running a fiber cable between buildings at 75 State Street and 200 State Street.[17]

An emerging real estate recession in Boston was pressuring McCormack, and he decided to withdraw from Corporate Communications Network. McCourt incorporated a new entity, McCourt Fiber Network, Inc. on December 23, 1988, to take the place of Corporate Communications Network, Inc.[18] The MFS-McCourt joint venture reorganized in January 1989 and refiled its application for certification on February 2, 1989, with a new ownership structure.[19] In the new organization, McCourt Fiber Network, Inc. owned 17.5% of the common stock and MFS owned 82.5%.[20]

On April 13, 1989, MFS-McCourt was designated a lead contractor for the newest portion of the downtown Boston fiber development in the heart of the financial district.[21]

Furious Opposition

Teleport originally filed a tariff for its dedicated transport services that actually proposed to charge more than the incumbent New England Telephone Company because it intended to offer higher quality, higher reliability service. When MFS-McCourt filed its proposed tariff, it was well below both the New England Telephone and the TCB rates.

TCB mounted a furious opposition to MFS-McCourt. TCB sought and obtained status as an intervenor in the certification hearings. TCB told the Department of Public Utilities:

> TCB is concerned that the financial analysis and projections contained in the Applicants' filing do not appear to make economic sense ... As a competitor of the Applicant, TCB may be damaged if the Applicant is permitted to commence operations in the commonwealth while charging such uneconomic rates.[22]

TCB bombarded MFS-McCourt with questions and demands for greater disclosure.

In April 1989, TCB formally asked the PUC to deny MFS-McCourts' request for certification.[23]

1. Certification should be denied because MFS-McCourt's documents on their face are insufficient ...

2. MFS-McCourt lacks the financial and other resources and competence necessary to conduct a viable operation in Massachusetts ... TCB will seek to prove that the proposed operation will run at a loss, will not be viable, and is likely to fail, leaving numbers of unhappy large business users in its wake.

3. MFS-McCourt's failure will not be in the public interest, and will not be in the interest of TCG because, rather than resulting in more business for TCB and other alternative private line carriers, MFS-McCourt's weakness and instability will cause potential business users to avoid <u>all</u> alternative carriers entirely and, to be safe, to place <u>all</u> their traffic with the dominant carrier, New England Telephone (NET) ...

4. Therefore, TCB will ask the Department to employ a standard of certification that will tend to weed-out weak and unstable carriers such as MFS-McCourt before they are permitted to hold themselves out as carriers certificated by the Department ...

5. ... Failure, or poor performance, by any alternative carrier, therefore will injure all other alternative carriers, and will, in the long run, benefit only NET, by confirming its monopoly position. ...

TCG eventually retreated from its claim that MFS-McCourt had insufficient financial resources but still maintained that future problems could arise and that any certification should contain restrictions.

On June 14, 1989, the Massachusetts Department of Public Utilities granted a certificate of public convenience and necessity to MFS-McCourt. While requiring that MFS-McCourt refile its tariffs, the certification was granted without special restrictions.

Clashing At ALTS

This MFS - TCG rivalry became apparent at ALTS. MFS criticized almost every initiative that the industry association had been pursuing under TCG's leadership. MFS CEO Pompliano laid out his complaints in a statement issued early in 1989.[24]

He disagreed with the priority that TCG had given to collocation interconnection in the RBOC central offices.[25] Many of the ALTS members actually agreed with MFS on this. They were not at the same stage of development as TCG and did not really share TCG's concern about the severity which the lack of interconnection at the central office placed on their addressable market and growth potential. Most CAPs were struggling to get their first networks up and were more preoccupied with becoming operational than they were with growing the business.

Pompliano was also critical of the focus of the resources of ALTS on opposition to RBOC filings for the use of Individual Case Basis (ICB) pricing[26]. RBOCs were permitted by regulators to use ICB pricing for non-standard communications offerings (*e.g.*, very high speed transport and "dark" (unlit) fiber offerings) if they were so infrequently used that there was insufficient data on which to establish standardized, tariff rates.

As long as these services were not offered on a tariffed basis, CAPs had no "price umbrella" from which to discount their competing offerings. RBOCs could then set the price for a given job on an individual case basis; and potential competition could be driven out of specific markets without the need to lower prices throughout an RBOC's total service area, including locations where there was no competition.

While acknowledging that central office collocation interconnection and ICB pricing were important issues for CAPs, Pompliano argued that it was more important for the industry association to address a broader range of issues centered on anti-competitive actions by the RBOCs.

Pompliano pledged MFS to the following course:

> During 1989, MFS will attempt to take a much more active leadership role in ALTS and will try to influ-

ence the members to address the broader issues in a cohesive manner that will highlight RBOC's anti-competitive posture to the public and to regulators.[27]

Even while suggesting a bigger role for MFS in ALTS, Pompliano also raised the question of whether there was really a commonalty of interest for MFS with the other members of the organization. MFS, he pointed out, was moving aggressively to expand into multiple cities while he saw "no parallel activity from the balance of the ALTS members."[28]

This was generally viewed as a thinly veiled dig at TCG's failure to launch operations beyond its New York - New Jersey network.

MFS Withdraws From ALTS

MFS didn't wait long before deciding that its efforts to exert influence on the ALTS were destined to be ineffective. MFS concluded that this was essentially a TCG controlled operation. In April 1989, MFS resigned its membership and withdrew from the ALTS organization.

MFS CEO Pompliano said:

> Although the Association for Local Telecom Services provides a good service by acting as an industry watchdog, we believe that the strong influences directing the organization have run contrary to our goals, interests and philosophy of service. In many cases, ALTS centered its activity on issues pertaining to the Northeast.
>
> We believe that other issues, such as averaged pricing and switched access, are more far-reaching. Also, because ALTS was led by our competition, it made our presence in the association awkward, at best.[29]

MFS On A Fast Track

TCG had established the competitive industry, but MFS was determined to beat it out in a national expansion race.[30] While aided by the Kiewit experience in construction and project management, it was primarily the availability of reliable internal funding from the parent company that allowed MFS to move quickly to build new networks.

MFS was driving a stake in the ground by rolling out small, central-business-district fiber networks. By March of 1989, construction of the Philadelphia and Baltimore networks was nearing completion and Minneapolis was underway.[31] With the completion of these networks, the confidence grew at Kiewit. It seemed reasonable that by keeping costs under control, networks could be built and sold for at least the invested capital. The downside risk to speculative network builds did not seem great, and there was good up-side potential.

The Kiewit company decided to increase its investment in new networks to at least the level of the old $80-million-plan and perhaps higher. This was too rich for the blood of the CFO investor group, who didn't want their contribution to exceed $20 million.

In June 1989, Kiewit bought them out. Their 20% interest in the venture was converted to preferred stock, and they retained ownership and control of the Chicago network. MFS ran the Chicago network under a management agreement.

Internal Strains

While MFS was succeeding in implementing a very rapid expansion program, there were strains and problems within the organization. No Kiewit people were incorporated into the Pompliano team, and there was a culture clash between the two groups. Pompliano did not like the rigid, milestone-oriented, project-style mode of operation preferred by Kiewit.

Kiewit didn't like Pompliano's bombastic style and disorganized reporting. Monthly progress reports underwent frequent changes in form. It was difficult for Holland and other Kiewit personnel to determine just what progress was being made.

Pompliano's attitude seemed to be, "I have the telecommunications expertise, and you do not. Send the money, and don't meddle; and we will deliver in due time." For Kiewit, speed was imperative. In order to avoid delay, the friction with Pompliano was ignored, and he was allowed to operate in non-Kiewit style. However, although rapid expansion was underway, Crowe was not satisfied that developments were going smoothly and was concerned about meeting projected schedules.

You're Mine And I'm Yours

After it became clear that MFS was going to pursue the competitive telecommunications business in earnest, and build its own networks nationally, it became impossible for Kiewit Telecom to win network construction jobs for other competitive companies. As a result, Ron Vidal had abandoned the effort and had gone to work in other parts of the Kiewit organization.

One day as Vidal was walking down the hall of the Omaha headquarters building he was stopped by Jim Crowe, who called him into his office. "Ron," he said, "There is something wrong in our new network build-outs. I want you to pick a city, go find out what isn't working and fix it. Then we'll apply it to all the cities."

Vidal picked Boston because both he and his wife had grown up on the East Coast. "However," he said, "I don't just want to fix it. I want to stay and run the business as the City Manager." Crowe said that he preferred to have Vidal in Omaha; but that, if he could sell himself to Pompliano, he could go ahead and try.

Vidal met with Pompliano and asked to be put in charge of the Boston network, which was under development. Pompliano was skeptical. "Have you ever sold telecom services before?" he asked. "No," Vidal replied. "Well what makes you think you can sell?" Pompliano began asking numerous questions about Vidal's Kiewit Telecom experience. "Look," Vidal said, "Just hire me for the job. If I'm no good, fire my ass and I'll go back to Kiewit." Vidal became the first Kiewit employee to go to work as an MFS employee.

Arriving in Boston, Vidal found the MFS operation in confusion. The local MFS point man got lost trying to show him around the streets of the city. He also found a disgruntled partner, David McCourt, who was used to running his own business and was unhappy with all the directives coming out of Chicago.

At 11:00 one night, McCourt received a telephone call at home from Crowe in Omaha. McCourt, at once, began to vent his frustration on Crowe. "Pompliano says we've got do to this and that and the other thing. Pompliano says ... " Crowe interrupted. "Let me make one thing clear. You are *my* partner in this deal. You're mine and I'm yours. If you have any issues with this deal, talk to *me*." McCourt felt it was a turning point and the beginning of a close working partnership between himself and Crowe. He also felt it was a turning point in Crowe's relationship to Pompliano.

With the completion of its first two-mile loop in the Boston financial district in July 1989, MFS found itself, for the first time, in actual head-to-head competition with TCG. Their rivalry was no longer abstract because now their networks both accessed the same buildings, and they were marketing to the same customers.

In the Fall of 1989, TCG announced its intention to open new networks in Los Angeles, San Francisco, and Houston. These were all cities that were also targeted by MFS.

Network Communications, Inc.—Houston

As home of the Johnson Space Center, Houston, Texas emerged as a high-tech center. The future of broadband data transmission and the need for fiber optic local telecommunications networks were apparent early to some of its citizens.

The group incorporated Network Communications, Inc. in June 1986 and applied to the city for a franchise to build a fiber, metropolitan area network to provide digital communications links to businesses within Houston. A non-exclusive, ten-year franchise was granted in February 1987.[32] The franchise required that Network Communications, Inc. pay fees to the city; but, two years later, none had been paid since the construction of the network was still not underway.

In October 1987, Royce Holland came to see Network Communications President, F. Scott Yeager and tried to persuade him to merge his company with MFS. Yeager wanted to continue on his own. MFS incorporated a shell, MFS of Houston, in September 1988 but did not proceed to build a network immediately. TCG actually began development first. In January of 1989, Teleport Communications Houston, Inc. submitted its application to the city for a franchise.[33]

Network Communications, Inc. President, Yeager wrote to the City Council opposing the TCG application.[34] Yeager pointed out that, in oral presentation to the Council, TCG admitted that it had conducted no detailed study to assess the size of the potential market in Houston.[35] He further noted that the incumbent telephone company, Southwestern Bell, Network Communications and another local company, Phonoscope, all now had the right to build networks in Houston. If the TCG application were granted, it would become the fourth company. Yeager suggested that before granting TCG a franchise, the Council should consider whether the Houston market was large enough to support all these competitors.

The city responded that it was not its responsibility to ensure any company's profitability; and that, in any event, it did not have the power to grant exclusive franchises.[36] Yeager threw in the towel and agreed to merge Network Communications into Metropolitan Fiber Systems of Houston.[37] In August 1988, construction got underway; and by year-end 1989 the network was in operation.[38]

Meanwhile TCG would not have an operational network in Houston until 1991.

TCG's Expansion Program

TCG felt itself being outflanked. In September 1989 TCG said that, in addition to its operating networks in New York and Boston, it would expand nationally and expected to be in several more cities by year end.

At MFS Pompliano was scornful. He responded with some hyperbole, "Merrill Lynch said it was building a network in Boston three years ago. We started there in December, and it will be done next month. It's hard for me to take (Merrill Lynch's) comments seriously."[39]

By year end 1989, MFS had new networks operational or partially operational in seven cities: Philadelphia, Baltimore, Boston, Minneapolis, San Francisco, Los Angeles and Houston. TCG had networks operational in New York and Boston and under development in San Francisco, Los Angeles and Houston and certification in Chicago.[40,41]

Clashing Before The Washington, D.C. Public Service Commission

In Washington D.C. Institutional Communications Company was belatedly filing for certification with the District of Columbia PUC, even though it had been operating in the District for some time.[42] The ICC application hearing was consolidated with that of TCG and MFS, which were also applying for Certificates of Public Convenience and Necessity to offer limited local service.

The TCG/MFS rivalry showed up during the hearings. On Dec. 13, 1989, MFS filed a motion to interject an additional issue in the District hearing.[43] MFS pointed out that ICC had recently joined a marketing consortium called NatMet. In addition to ICC, NatMet was composed of CAPs: TCG, Eastern TeleLogic and Intermedia Communications of Florida.

MFS claimed that it introduced the issue of NatMet into the hearings to raise the issue of "whether the members of NatMet will be able to offer services over ICC's facilities without being granted a certificate of public convenience and necessity." The members of NatMet were highly annoyed by the MFS move and were more inclined to see MFS' action as simply meddlesome.

NatMet had been organized as an umbrella organization to facilitate national marketing for its members. In the industry, it was widely assumed that NatMet was an attempt to counter the marketing advantages which MFS was gaining from its rapidly expanding, multi-city national presence.

Annunziata, who had been elected President of NatMet, said that NatMet hoped to include all CAPs as members. When reporters noted that MFS was conspicuously absent from NatMet, Annunziata replied that MFS had not been invited to join because the four who did join had like-minded philosophies and similar high standards. Asked whether this meant that he thought that MFS didn't have high standards, he replied that he could not say because he was not familiar with MFS' networks.[44]

In practice, NatMet had difficulty in being effective. Organized in December 1989, it didn't close its first piece of business until May 1990 when Eastern TeleLogic arranged for access facilities for the Colonial Penn Group in Pennsylvania and in Florida, where it used the facilities of Intermedia Communications.[45] With disparate network equipment, which interfered with a uniform service offering, and with little financial incentive to organize coordinated sales and marketing, NatMet never achieved significant results.

The D.C. Commission ruled that the issue of NatMet could be introduced, but its consideration would be narrowly limited "to the impact that ICC's participation in NatMet would have on the intra-District services ICC offers or proposes to offer."[46]

MFS President, Tony Pompliano issued a peevish statement saying that MFS was building its own national network and had no interest in joining NatMet. He wondered aloud why any company with national ambitions would join such a consortium. "I guess," he said, "its their (TCG's) way of saying that they no longer have national ambitions."[47]

Crowe And Holland Take Command Of MFS

Despite the launch of their respective national expansion programs both MFS and TCG faced internal problems. For MFS, tension grew between the Kiewit organization and Pompliano. For TCG questions had arisen within Merrill Lynch as to why they should be in the telecommunications business at all.

At MFS, as Royce Holland and other Kiewit personnel became better acquainted with MFS operations, they grew more optimistic about the prospects for competitive telecommunications. Holland and Crowe, particularly, began to see the possibility of creating a "second MCI success story" rather than simply carrying out a speculative construction venture.

At the same time, they grew more critical of Pompliano's management style and ability to perform as company spokesman. Not only did Pompliano's telecommunications expertise seem less indispensable, but the role of CEO in the evolving company was also changing. MFS was increasing its pressure on the regulatory and public relations fronts. The senior spokesman for MFS needed to carry the ball in public presentations and hearings. This put a premium on the CEO's skills as an articulate and polished public speaker. The Kiewit group began to doubt that this was Pompliano's strong suit.

At TCG, the pressure was building within the corporate parent, Merrill Lynch, to sell this non-core business. Fidelity Investments, whose subsidiary was TCG's partner in the Boston network, knew of Merrill Lynch's desire to sell and was, at the same time, increasingly interested in expanding its involvement in the telecommunications business.

Ned Johnson and Jim Kirby of Fidelity flew their corporate jet to Omaha for discussions with Walter Scott, Jim Crowe and Royce Holland at Kiewit about combining forces to jointly acquire TCG. MFS did not yet have a New York network, and the possibility of gaining control of the extensive TCG network was very attractive as an accelerated way to enter the premier U.S. local market.

Johnson and Scott represented a powerful combination of wealth. Johnson, considered a master marketer, had helped his father build Fidelity into a mutual fund giant. He had been a member of the Forbes 400 since 1985. Scott, who's quiet accumulation of wealth had gone largely unnoticed, would become a member of the Forbes 400 in 1996.

A follow-up meeting, addressing the details of joint venture, was held at the Cleveland airport in February of 1990. Senior management was an issue. Johnson asked Scott, "Do you have anybody to run this thing, if we can put it together?" Scott replied, "Well, no we sure don't. I don't believe our guy can even handle what he's got now." Johnson indicated that he was not certain that Annunziata was quite ready for such large responsibility, either. Kiewit and Fidelity were not able to formulate a joint venture proposal and finally decided not to make an offer for TCG.

Scott's comments were not lost on Crowe. Crowe quickly reorganized MFS with himself as Chairman and Pompliano in the largely honorary role of Vice Chairman of the Board. Royce Holland was installed as the new CEO and President. Holland soon became the visible public figure and spokesman for MFS. An effective leader and articulate speaker, he would become one of the most recognized personalities in the CAP industry.

"Do You Want Me To Say Goddamn Twice?"

The change in leadership at MFS did not lessen the rivalry with TCG. While those on the front lines of the regulatory battles had no trouble cooperating, it was a different story at the management level. Lipman, Atkinson and Bonney worked in a cooperative mode. Lipman pursued the MFS Interconnection Initiative from an interstate perspective with the FCC, while Atkinson and Bonney worked on the same issues in the intrastate arena with the state PUCs. Differences in regulatory strategy and on many other issues sometimes produced outbursts of anger from senior executives at MFS and TCG.

One day Ron Vidal was summoned to Holland's office in the Oak Brook, Illinois tower and told, "Go down to that goddamn Staten Island and tell that goddamn TCG that if they don't get in line we're going to make their life miserable." "Yes, sir," Vidal replied. "Let me be sure I understand. You want me to say goddamn twice?"

Arriving at TCG headquarters on Staten Island, Vidal met with Atkinson. "Bob," he said. "My company is upset that you guys at TCG keep filing regulatory stuff that undercuts what we file." "Well," Atkinson responded. "The trouble is that you guys have your heads up your asses." "Well," said Vidal, "they think you have your head up your ass, and if it doesn't stop, we are going to make your life miserable."

When Vidal returned to MFS headquarters he was greeted by Holland, "I bet you had a good time up there in Staten Island." "I really didn't." Vidal responded.

MFS, France Telecom, British Telecom: Shopping For TCG

Merrill Lynch began to actively seek buyers or outside investors for TCG. Northern Telecom, France Telecom and British Telecom considered investing in TCG. France Telecom and British Telecom, powerful European telephone monopolies, were very eager to gain entry into the huge American market, but only if they could play on a national scale.

By the end of 1990, TCG had opened networks in San Francisco, Chicago and Los Angeles, which, together with its New York and Boston networks, gave it a total of five major cities operational. MFS had added Pittsburgh to its list of operational cities and had taken a controlling interest (80%) in the Chicago network for a total of nine cities. A combination of the two companies would create a powerful national presence.

France Telecom and British Telecom individually approached MFS about partnering to make a joint offer for TCG. France Telecom and MFS could not agree on a proposal for the relative percentages of ownership. However, British Telecom and MFS, after eight or nine months of negotiation, came together to bid for TCG.

"He's Not As Good Looking As Kim Basinger"

MFS opened discussions with TCG. Crowe and Annunziata made the rounds visiting the TCG and MFS networks on the Kiewit corporate jet. Annunziata was less than enthusiastic about being acquired by MFS. It seemed likely that he would have a subordinate role in the new company.

MFS was uncertain whether Annunziata would meld with their management team. Scott, Crowe and McCourt met at a construction industry dinner at the Hilton Hotel in New York and discussed the issue. McCourt was dispatched to have dinner with Annunziata and make an evaluation.

McCourt had lunch with Annunziata but was distracted by the presence of popular movie star, Kim Basinger, at the next table. Returning from the meeting, McCourt was asked his assessment of Annunziata. "He's not as good looking as Kim Basinger," McCourt responded. The consensus was that Annunziata had been running his own show for a long time and probably would not take a subordinate role. In any event, it seemed unlikely that the chemistry of the Crowe-Holland management team could be superseded.

Negotiations with Merrill Lynch on the purchase price were stalled at a small differential. Merrill Lynch wanted $155 million. The MFS/British Telecom partnership only offered $145 million. The $10 million gap, which would seem insignificant in introspect, was never closed. To Annunziata's relief, the negotiations ended without a deal.

British Telecom: Shopping For MFS

British Telecom still badly wanted to enter the U.S. market, and now discussed buying MFS. They wanted to buy both WilTel, a fiber-based long distance carrier, and MFS. British Telecom indicated that they were willing to buy 50% of MFS for an amount equal to Kiewit's entire capital investment to date ... approximately $100 million. The proposal was that both Kiewit and British Telecom would then invest more equity and build out 50 to 60 U.S. cities; and, that in three to four years, British Telecom would buy the remainder of MFS, based on the then appraised value. It was a no-lose proposition for Kiewit with significant up-side potential. It was, in fact, a variation of the original speculative, construction project idea which Kiewit had entertained.

Walter Scott considered the offer in June of 1991. Holland offered his opinion that MFS should pursue a higher risk course and keep building on its own. He was now firmly convinced that there was literally the opportunity to duplicate in the local market the success that MCI had found in the long distance market.

He was also convinced that, while MCI struggled for 20 years to penetrate the long distance market, the local market could be cracked within the next two years. This was reinforced by the fact that in May 1991 the FCC had issued its Notice of Proposed Rule Making to allow central office interconnection.

Scott had been conditioned by the construction business. The ability to assess risk and to take disciplined risks was endemic to bidding large construction projects. Twice in its history, once during the building of the St. Lawrence Seaway and once during the building of a tunnel connecting Copenhagen to the mainland of Denmark, unexpected construction problems had nearly destroyed the Kiewit company. Only hard scrambling by the company saved it from these near disasters; but, as a result, it gained a great deal of confidence.

Scott decided to decline the British Telecom offer and to take the riskier course of continuing to build MFS networks. It turned out to be a sage choice and confirmation for the judgment of Omaha investment guru, Warren Buffet, who regarded Scott's business acumen as "sensational."

TCG And MFS: Rolling Up CAPs

By June 1991, after Shapleigh had brought some harmony to the CAP industry and MFS and TCG were working within the industry association, ALTS, the competition between the two companies continued, but on a less strident note. As they planned their entry into each city, both MFS and TCG made "make or buy" decisions. By year end 1991, MFS had constructed new networks in New York and Dallas and purchased an 85% interest in ICC and its Washington, D.C. network for a total of 12 major city networks operational.

In Dallas, TCG purchased the assets of DFW/MetroLink, a CAP start-up that had declared Chapter 7 bankruptcy. Together with a new network constructed in Houston, TCG had seven major cities operational.

In 1992, MFS acquired an 80% interest in the Atlanta network developed by Kolsby's Metrex Corp. MFS also built its fourteenth network covering northern New Jersey. TCG added no new networks in 1992 but significantly expanded existing ones, more than doubling its route-miles.

Both TCG and MFS continuously asserted that *they* were the "largest" CAP. TCG claimed the most route-miles of fiber, and MFS claimed the most cities served. These, and other statistical measures, were typically subject to disagreement and conflicting claims. For example, there was disagreement over the way in which "cities" were being counted. Since some of TCG's larger networks included many communities, by TCG's count, their networks served 10 Metropolitan Services Areas (MSAs) and over 50 communities.

MFS Communications Goes Public

In 1993, MFS ultimately turned to the public equity markets to fuel its expansion. On May 20, 1993, an Initial Public Offering of 11,000,000 MFS shares at $20 per share, representing 20% ownership of the company, was managed by Salomon Brothers, Inc. and Bear, Stearns & Co. Inc. Kiewit retained majority ownership and, in addition, bought an additional 2,000,000 shares at the IPO price.[48]

The offering was very successful and was over-subscribed, with orders for more than 70 million shares, which greatly encouraged other CAPs to consider going public. Demand for the stock continued strong; and the price, which never fell below the IPO level, had nearly tripled by the third quarter.

Given the success of the offering, MFS brought out a secondary offering of four million shares at $50 per share, on September 14, 1993, using the same investment bankers. As a result of these two offerings, MFS raised over $400 million in 1993. MFS now not only had a large amount of capital but also a highly desirable stock to use as fuel for its national expansion by either constructing or acquiring networks.

Cable Company Interest In Telecommunications

Other than the telephone companies, only cable operators had "a wire to the home" in most of America. Cable companies had long been regarded as natural candidates for future competition with local telephone companies to provide residential, local telephone service. However, there were near-term regulatory, geographic and technology barriers to such competition. On the regulatory front, switched, local service was still the exclusive monopoly franchise of the local telephone companies. The dedicated transport service, which was open to competition and being pursued by CAPs, served business and carrier customers.

Geographically, the placement of cable networks, primarily serving suburban, residential areas, did not position them to readily serve these CAP customers.

On the technology front, cable networks were primarily "one-way" systems. Cable systems were originally built to broadcast television signals "downstream" to the customer. The systems were constructed of coaxial cable in a "branching tree" topology. Multiple amplifiers in series were used to boost the signal. There might be 30 or 40 of these amplifiers in cascade between an end user and the "head end" of the cable system. In order to use the cable itself to deliver telephone service a number of changes in the technology of the system would be needed.

These included installing two-way amplifiers and reducing the total number of amplifiers in cascade. This reduction was necessary to increase system reliability and to decrease the funneling and concentration of noise in the upstream channel. Such changes, including the use of fiber optic trunking, were being incrementally incorporated to upgrade cable service but would take years of effort and billions of dollars to produce a platform able to support telephone service.

However, without waiting for these changes in their networks, cable operators could enter the CAP business at once, leveraging their rights-of-way. They could simply deploy extra fiber cable exclusively for dedicated transport CAP services. In theory, with a foothold in the CAP services, cable operators would be better positioned to expand out of basic video service and into local telecommunications, as regulatory changes permitted.

Cable Companies Invest In TCG And Buy Out Merrill Lynch

John Dillon, Senior Vice President and Chief Financial Officer of Cox Enterprises, a major cable systems owner, read about TCG in the Atlanta Journal and contacted Wayne Fox at Merrill Lynch to inquire about the opportunity for Cox to invest in TCG. As a result of subsequent negotiations, Merrill Lynch sold Cox a 12.5% ownership in TCG in June 1991 and an option to obtain control of TCG.[49]

In February 1992, cable operator TCI bought 49.9 % of TCG[50] from Merrill Lynch; and Dillon said his company was, "actively considering whether or not to exercise our option." He sought to play down the idea of competition with the telephone companies, saying, "Teleport isn't a direct competitor to the phone companies. It has built its business on not being the local phone company."[51]

In March, Cox exercised its option to expand its ownership to 51.1%, buying out Merrill Lynch's remaining interest.[52] Dillon was still guarded about the cable groups' ultimate goals in telecommunications. He said, "We envision a bigger horizon for Teleport, but right now, we plan to let it keep on keeping on."[53]

In 1993, Cox and TCI, sold 20% of TCG to cable operators, Comcast and Continental Cable. As a result of these transactions, ownership of TCG was in the hands of four of the largest cable companies in the United States with a total of 16.5 million subscribers. Over the next three years, the cable stockholders of TCG would invest $770 million in growing the company.[54]

TCG entered into multiple network expansion projects using cable rights-of-way and fiber deployment, not only with its owners and their subsidiaries but also with other cable operators.

TCG formed a new division, Affiliate Services, and located it in Denver, the headquarters city of many major cable companies. Affiliate Services was established as the umbrella organization for specific joint ventures between TCG and the local cable operator in various cities. In June 1993, TCG announced that it had signed letters of intent with eleven cable companies to build networks in Detroit, Miami, Providence, Phoenix and St. Louis as joint ventures with Affiliate Services.[55]

The TCG/MFS Race At Year End 1993

Boosted by the funding and partnership relations with the cable in-dustry, TCG's network deployment accelerated in 1993. MFS had nearly caught up with TCG in 1992 in terms of route-miles of fiber deployed; but, in 1993, TCG pulled clearly ahead. In terms of ma-jor cities with operational networks, however, MFS retained its lead.

TCG & MFS Major City And Fiber Route-Miles Operational

Year	TCG Major Cities	TCG Route-Miles[56]	MFS Major Cities[57]	MFS Route-Miles
1987	1	45	0	0
1988	1	58	1	3
1989	2	227	7	49
1990	5	273	9	127
1991	7	400	12	373
1992	7	891	13	858
1993	13	1,952	13	1,298

Source: FCC, Company Reports and Connecticut Research Inc.

MFS and TCG Dominate The CAP Industry

With the issues of ownership and financing settled for the moment, TCG and MFS continued their competition to build-out networks in the major U.S. cities with renewed energy.

In terms of revenue, MFS and TCG were, by far, the dominant members of the CAP industry. MFS had total revenue of $141 million in 1993; but half of this revenue came from its Network Systems Integration group, which built fiber networks and related construction. In terms of telecommunications service revenues, TCG and MFS were nearly even. TCG had service revenue of $82 million and MFS had $70 million.

CAP industry revenue reached $309 million in 1993. There were nearly thirty CAPs with revenue producing networks by 1993; but MFS and TCG, combined, still accounted for nearly half of the total industry revenue.[58]

<u>Competitive Local Service Revenue</u> ($millions)

Year	TCG Rev.	Per Cent Industry	MFS Rev.[1]	Per Cent Industry	Industry Rev.
1985	1	100%	0	0%	1
1986	3	100%	0	0%	3
1987	6	75%	0	0%	8
1988	11	55%	0	0%	20
1989	20	61%	0.4	1%	32
1990	28	42%	9	14%	66
1991	47	38%	23	18%	124
1992	57	27%	48	23%	210
1993	82	26%	70	23%	309

(1) Excludes MFS Network Technologies

Source: Company reports, Connecticut Research, Inc. estimates for TCG 1985-1989 and industry total revenue

We're Number One

Both MFS and TCG laid claim to being the CAP industry leader. Either claim was valid based on carefully selected parameters from the universe of: major cities served, metropolitan areas served, route-miles of fiber, fiber-miles (route miles times fibers per cable) buildings on-net, revenue, voice grade circuits, *etc.*

In any event, the two stood head and shoulders above the other participants in the industry. In effect, between them, they defined the CAP industry. Neither company would eclipse the other. Both continued to open networks in major cities across the country, and neither was forced to close or defer a network due to the other's competitive presence.

The bulk of the $80 billion local telecommunications market was still controlled by the incumbent local telephone companies. The RBOCs were the CAPs' real competition: not other CAPs.

Footnotes Chapter 8: Rivals

[1] Application Of Teleport Communications - Boston For A Certificate Of Public Convenience And Necessity, (DPU Case 88-60), March 3, 1988, Exhibit 8.

[2] Ibid.

[3] "Firm Forms Bypass Net Subsidiary," *Network World,* v4, No. 51, Dec. 28, 1987, 1.

[4] Ibid. , 8.

[5] Ibid.

[6] Steve Rosenbush, *Telecom Business Opportunities,* (Newport, RI: Aegis Publishing Group, Ltd., 1998), 165.

[7] Ibid., 166.

[8] Response of MFS-McCourt To Information Requests of Teleport Communications-Boston, (DPU Case 88-229/88-252), TCB-8, March 21, 1989.

[9] Rosenbush, 166.

[10] Application and Initial Tariff of Teleport Communications - Boston, Mass. DPU Dockets 88-60 & 88-71, Response to Information Request, CableVision 1-10, July 1988.

[11] Application Of Teleport Communications - Boston For A Certificate Of Public Convenience And Necessity, (DPU Case 88-60), March 3, 1988.

[12] Application and Initial Tariff of Teleport Communications - Boston, Mass. DPU Dockets 88-60 & 88-71, Response to Information Request, CableVision 1-19, July 1988.

[13] Teleport Communications Group 1989 Annual Report, 12.

[14] Response of MFS-McCourt To Information Requests of Teleport Communications-Boston, (DPU Case 88-229/88-252), TCB-8, March 21, 1989.

[15] "Private $ Building City Net: Offbeat Policy Will Give Hub Conduit," *Boston Business Journal,* v6, n46, s1, January 9, 1989, 1.

[16] Application Of MFS-McCourt, Inc. For A Certificate Of Public Convenience And Necessity, (DPU Case 88-229), November 15, 1988.

[17] "First Private Communications System to Link Downtown Buildings," Press Release, MFS-McCourt, November 3, 1988.

[18] Response of MFS-McCourt To Information Requests of Teleport Communications-Boston, (DPU Case 88-229/88-252), TCB-3, March 21, 1989.

[19] Request For Leave To Amend Application For Certification, (DPU Case 88-229/88-252), February 27, 1989.

[20] Ibid. 3.

[21] "Metropolitan Fiber Systems - McCourt Selected By City Of Boston To Construct New Section Of Downtown Boston Underground Fiber Optic Network," MFS Press Release, April 13, 1989.

[22] Petition of Teleport Communications - Boston To Intervene, (DPU Case 88-229/88-252), February 15, 1989.

[23] Statement of Relief Sought By Teleport Communications - Boston, (DPU Case 88-229), April 14, 1989.

[24] "A Message From The President," *MFS Network,* v1, No. 1, First Quarter 1989, 3.

[25] Ibid.

[26] Ibid.

[27] Ibid.

[28] Ibid.

[29] "MFS Withdraws From ALTS," *Fiber Optic News,* May 22, 1989.

[30] "Metropolitan Fiber Systems, Inc. (MFS) Comes Out Of The Closet," *Fiber Optics Weekly Update,* Sept. 1988, v8, No. 44, 1.

[31] Application Of MFS-McCourt, Inc. For A Certificate Of Public Convenience And Necessity, (DPU Case 88-229/88-252), Pre-filed Testimony of Royce J. Holland, March 9, 1989.

[32] City of Houston Ordinance 87-66, February 18, 1987.

[33] Teleport Communications New York Response To The City's Application And Qualifying Questionnaire, January 10, 1989.

[34] Letter to the City of Houston from Network Communications, Inc., February 27, 1989.

[35] Questions submitted to the Houston City Council by F. Scott Yeager of Network Communications, Inc., March 13, 1989.

[36] City of Houston, "Response to Network Communications Letter To Council Members," February, 28, 1989.

[37] Articles of Merger And Joint Agreement, July 6, 1989 (Filed with the Office of the Secretary of State of Texas August 15, 1989).

[38] "Fiber Optic Network Vies For Local Access Market," *Houston Business Journal,* Dec. 4, 1989, 25.

[39] "Weaving An Alternative," *Telephony,* September 11, 1989.

[40] "Teleport Communications Group Announces Three Additional Fiber Optic Networks," TCG Press Release, September 22, 1989.

[41] "Teleport Communications-Chicago Becomes First All-Fiber Local Carrier To Receive Ill. State Certification," TCG Press Release, September 25, 1989.

[42] "Application Of The Institutional Communications Company For A Certificate Of Public Convenience And Necessity," (Public Service Commission Of The District Of Columbia Formal Case No. 867), October 10, 1989.

[43] "Formal Case No. 892, In The Matter Of The Application For A Certificate Of Public Convenience And Necessity Of Teleport Communications Washington, D.C., Inc., Metropolitan Fiber Systems of Washington, D.C., Inc., And The Institutional Communications Company," Order No. 9418, January 23, 1990, 20.

[44] "Bypass Companies Group To Offer One Contact, Uniform Quality," *FCC Week,* December 11, 1989.

[45] "National Metropolitan Networks," *Fiber Optic News,* May 7, 1990. 7.

[46] Formal Case No, 892, 22.

[47] "Bypass Companies Group..."

[48] Prospectus MFS Communications Company, Inc.. Salomon Brothers, Inc., Bear, Stearns & Co., Inc., May 19, 1993.

[49] "Cox To Invest In Fiber-Optics Network Firm," *Wall Street Journal,* June 20, 1991, B4.

[50] "Cable Giant TCI Agrees To Buy Teleport Stake," *Wall Street Journal,* February, 19, 1992, B1.

[51] Ibid. , B5.

[52] "Cox Enterprises To Acquire Merrill Lynch's Remaining Interest In Teleport Communications Group," TCG Press Release, March 4, 1992.

[53] "Cable TV Concerns To Own Local Telephone Company," *New York Times,* March 3, 1992, D21.

[54] Preliminary Prospectus, Teleport Communications Group, Inc., Merrill Lynch & Co., Morgan Stanley & Co., Donaldson, Lufkin & Jenrette, Lehman Brothers, Deutsche Morgan Grenfell, June 3, 1996, 45.

[55] "Teleport Communications Group And Eleven Major Cable Companies To Build Local Fiber Optic Telecommunications Networks," TCG Press Release, June 7, 1993.

[56] (1) 1987 and 1988 are FCC numbers. TCG claimed 150 miles complete in 1985, difference may be "sheath-miles" vs. route-miles due to multiple cables.

[57] 1988 is CFO network

[58] "*1993 Local Telecommunications Competition.... the 'ALT Report',*" (Glastonbury, CT, Connecticut Research, 1993), II-5.

9. TRIAL BY FIRE AND WATER

Network Reliability: A Continued Concern

Concern for network security and survivability did not fade following the Hinsdale fire of May 1988, but rather it continued to grow in importance. Subsequent mishaps in long distance networks kept concerns alive. In November 1988, an AT&T fiber cable was cut in New Jersey blocking 3.5 million calls; and in January 1990, a software problem in the AT&T network disrupted half the country's long distance service. Topping it off in September 1991 the loss of power to a key AT&T switching center in Manhattan affected phone traffic up and down the East Coast and effectively knocked-out the Ronkonkoma Air Traffic Control Center that handles all flights within 200 miles of New York City.

Regulators and politicians were alarmed and outraged. Congressman Edward Markey (MA) demanded that the General Accounting Office prepare a report for his Subcommittee on Telecommunications and Finance on the frequency and causes of all network outages for the years 1990 and 1991.

In a letter to the House Government Operations Committee, Federal Communications Chairman, Al Sikes, wrote, "So far the impact of (past) outages has been measured in hours wasted and dollars lost; I want to take every step necessary to make sure the future outages are not measured in terms of property destroyed and lives lost."

A Crack In The Ceiling

Back in Illinois, a new incident was brewing which would threaten the local networks of both Illinois Bell and its CAP competitors.

The murky waters of the Chicago River which run around the edge of Chicago's downtown Loop District go largely unnoticed except on March 17, St. Patrick's Day, when the water traditionally is turned a bright green for the day by the City.

In September 1991, the Great Lakes Dredge and Dock Company of Oak Brook, Illinois, set to work driving wooden pilings in the river

213

under the Kinzie Street bridge.[1] The pilings were intended to shield the bridge abutment from accidental damage due to collisions with river traffic.

Forty feet below the surface, masonry fell from the ceiling of the tunnel that housed the fiber optic networks of MFS Communications, Teleport and Digital Direct, a subsidiary of cable operator, TCI. A crack twenty-feet long appeared in the tunnel ceiling.

In mid-January 1991, an employee of the cable company found the crack while inspecting the tunnel and made a video tape of it.[2] On the tape, a worker slogs through knee deep mud and water in the tunnel and, breathing heavily, gasps out, "This is a cave-in!"[3]

According to Chicago Mayor, Richard M. Daley, city workers first heard about the crack in February 1991, but did not find it when they went to look. On March 13, 1991, employees of MFS Communications guided city inspectors to the location.[4] Measurements quickly established that they were directly under the river and that the silt oozing into the tunnel must be coming directly from the river bottom.

On April 2, 1991, Louis Koncza, the city's bridge engineer wrote a memo to John LaPlante, the acting transportation commissioner, saying "This wall failure should be repaired immediately due to the potential danger of flooding out the entire freight tunnel system, which is quite extensive."[5]

A Hole In The River

Engineer Koncza estimated that repairs, using masonry bulkheads, would cost about $10,000. When no contractors were found willing to meet this price, LaPlante put the job out for bids. He was still waiting for bid responses when, on April 13, 1991, the tunnel ceiling collapsed, sending the river surging through the tunnels. The Mayor fired LaPlante. LaPlante later said, "I think he is a good mayor. I think he did what he had to do."[6]

A giant whirlpool formed in the river. Like water draining from a bathtub in the northern hemisphere, the whirlpool circulated counterclockwise under the influence of the Coriolis force. An estimated 250 million gallons of water poured into Chicago's tunnel system.[7]

The Loop Goes Dark

No one was trapped in the tunnels, and there were no fatalities or injuries; but the water rapidly flooded the sub-basements and basements of 120 buildings. Thirty electrical transformers shorted out when they became submerged.[8] To prevent further damage to equipment, the local electric utility, Commonwealth Edison, cut power to the buildings.[9]

Office workers began evacuating the buildings, groping down darkened stairwells, carrying boxes and files in stifling air. Approximately 200,000 people were displaced, including 7,000 from the Sears Tower, bringing business to a halt and sending workers home.[10] For some the trip home was complicated by the fact that the subway had also been flooded and was unserviceable.

The Chicago Board of Trade was hard hit. Despite redundancy safeguards that included five independent electrical feeds into its two buildings, all power was lost.[11,12] By Wednesday, traders operated an abbreviated, two-hour session in the dark with flashlights in trading pits made hot and clammy without ventilation[13].

At least thirty companies activated their remote, back-up computer sites; but the problem was not really damage to computer centers, it was the loss of occupiable office space for workers.[14,15] Furthermore, it became increasingly apparent that modern businesses, with a greater reliance on LANs and distributed file servers, require more than simply main frame computer back-up.

At street level, all appeared calm and normal. There was no trace of water, and business seemed to have been halted by an invisible force ... a flood with bone-dry streets. Estimates of possible business losses ranged widely from $150 million to $1.5 billion.

Plugging The Hole

Efforts focused on plugging the hole in the river. Initial attempts, including dumping truck loads of cement and gravel and even sand bags and old mattresses, into the yawning whirlpool, produced no obvious results.

These efforts gave way to a plan to drill 54-inch diameter vertical shafts into the tunnel on each side of the river and lower concrete plugs to seal off the damaged area.[16] Completing one shaft slowed, but did not stop the flow of water.

Divers in cages were lowered into the swirling water to inspect the situation, but were hampered by the cold water and the limited visibility. Only able to see six inches ahead in the murky water, they operated mostly by feeling their way along. Entering the tunnel, they vacuumed the floor in an attempt to provide a way for fresh concrete to stick to the surface.

Water leakage into the tunnel was not completely stopped until nearly a week after the break, but the flow was sufficiently reduced for recovery operations to begin much earlier. By week's end, power had been restored to all but eleven buildings.[17]

Telecommunications Impacts

At Arthur Andersen's office, where 450 tax specialists were laboring to meet the April 15 filing deadline, the water smashed the walls of an electrical vault in the basement and also wiped out the packet-switched data network equipment used to deliver its North American payroll.[18,19] Generally, however, little direct damage to telecommunications equipment was done by the flood waters.

Most problems stemmed from the loss of electrical power. Some companies shut down their PBXs and communications systems, fearing that erratic power surges might damage the equipment.[20]

The on-going problem for the next several days would be providing telephone service for workers displaced from their offices. Camping out in hallways, cubicles and hotels, the refugees borrowed, shared and scrounged telephones wherever they could.

The MFS Network Survives

Linking over 100 buildings in the Loop area through the tunnel system, MFS Communications was potentially in the most exposed position of any carrier. MFS' fiber cable itself was in a relatively secure situation since the cables ran through four-inch diameter metal pipes attached to the ceiling of the tunnel. Even exposure to water was not of great concern since the cable was of a gel-filled, water-proof design.[21]

The original layout of the MFS network included dual control centers—a primary center in the basement of the Insurance Exchange Building and a secondary center on the first floor of the Prudential Center. The cost of this added redundancy had been debated within MFS as a possible unnecessary expense, but was retained anyway.

A year prior to the flood, the Prudential node was converted to the main node due to the higher rent at the Insurance Exchange Building. This was a fortuitous move, since the Insurance Exchange node basement location was completely inundated in the flood.

The MFS system switched smoothly to its own back-up power and operated in this mode for twelve hours until commercial power was restored.[22] MFS' only equipment failure occurred in a LaSalle Street building that had its multiplexer electronics in the basement. By the time these were destroyed by the rising water, the building had already been evacuated.

MFS found itself suddenly thrust into the public eye. Journalists were looking for something sensational, especially on the Daley administration that was holding multiple daily press conferences to deal with its first major embarrassment. CEO Royce Holland was contacted by a reporter who offered to give MFS its first ever publicity in the Wall Street Journal if he would detail mistakes and dish the dirt on the city. To his credit, Holland declined, saying he had nothing to add to the information already revealed by the city. He was simply relieved that the MFS network had come through the crisis intact, although there remained concern that it could yet be damaged during on-going recovery operations.[23]

The Teleport Network Survives

Teleport had not yet created an extensive Chicago network and had only twenty-six Loop buildings on-net via the tunnels.[24] Like MFS, the Teleport cable was in metal conduits and was capable of operating even if submerged.

Teleport's most tense moment during the flood came when officials wanted to cut Teleport's fiber cable at its point of entrance into the basement of the Chicago Board of Trade. Water was spraying into the basement through the conduit, and city officials wanted to cut off and cap it. Although they were finally dissuaded, Teleport quickly rerouted its service to customers in the area as a precaution.[25]

The Illinois Bell Response

Illinois Bell had learned some valuable lessons from past crises and had created a dedicated Emergency Operations Center on the 16th floor of the company's headquarters in downtown Chicago to respond to network emergencies.[26]

Notification of the flood was received at 8:30 Monday morning, and by 8:45 the Emergency Operations Center was in service. It operated around the clock, monitoring trouble spots and sending out aid to customers. Even Illinois Bell President, Dick Brown, determined that this would not be another "Hinsdale," served in the emergency command post.

No central offices were in danger, and the Illinois Bell network did not use the tunnels to deploy its copper or fiber cables. The points of vulnerability were where equipment in basements could be flooded. Nine buildings lost phone service because terminating cables were submerged. Technicians were dispatched to the Chicago Board of Trade Building to build a sandbag barricade around the threatened Illinois Bell Centrex switch in the basement that served the building.

The major task, however, was in providing emergency phones for the office workers operating out of temporary locations. In days Illinois Bell provided call forwarding for 2,000 business lines, and installed 4,000 Centrex lines and 4,000 other temporary lines.

Whose Advantage?

Unlike the Hinsdale fire, the Chicago Flood did not seem to yield any particular advantage to CAPs or to Illinois Bell. CAPs did charge that, immediately after the flood, Illinois Bell marketing personnel were suggesting to their customers that they should be glad their telephone and data traffic were not passing through the CAP fiber submerged in the tunnels.

Any possible marketing edge quickly disappeared. On May 6, 1991, U.S. Army Corps of Engineer workers, drilling into the tunnels to pump out the remaining water, accidentally sliced through two fiber cables and one copper cable of Illinois Bell.[27] Investigation revealed that the Engineers had been misled by Illinois Bell maps showing the location of the cables which were off by five feet.

Illinois Bell pointed out that this fiber, which had been installed after the Hinsdale fire as a part of the Ameritech Network Protection plan, was self-healing so that no customers lost service.[28] Service on the copper cable, however, was interrupted.

For telecommunications managers, the bottom line was to again emphasize the importance of network redundancy and the need for back-up power. For carriers, some remaining network vulnerabilities were illuminated. For industry observers, the beneficial impact of competition on network and service reliability was now clearly observable.

New York: Home Of The Trillion Dollar Gamble

For increasingly communications-dependent businesses, the potential economic impact of wide-spread network outages was becoming a chilling prospect. Nowhere was the concern greater than in New York City, the nation's commercial hub. To raise an awareness of just how great the economic stakes could be, a consortium of government and business representatives formed an advocacy group, the "New York City Partnership, Inc."

The Partnership and the consulting firm, Booz, Allen & Hamilton, Inc., published a report, "*The $1 Trillion Gamble: Telecommunications and New York's Economic Future*," in June 1990. Their study concluded:

> A loss of telecommunications service for just one day in the Manhattan central business district could disrupt $1 trillion in financial transactions—an economic impact that would ripple through the U.S.[29]

The report recommended that diversity and redundancy be used to protect networks. Diversity seeks to build enough routing options and flexibility into the network so that if any part fails, traffic can be routed around the problem. Redundancy focuses on backup facilities such as auxiliary power supplies. However, the Partnership report also noted, "A telecommunications network cannot be made 100% disaster-proof." It recommended that planning also be undertaken for "disaster recovery."

The City established a Mayor's Task Force on Network Reliability under William Squadron, the Commissioner of the city's Department of Telecommunications and Energy. The Task Force negotiated a Mutual Aid and Restoration Agreement, signed in February 1992 by fourteen telecommunications carriers. One facet of the agreement was "the Bridge," a conference call link to facilitate coordination and cooperation among them in event of an emergency.[30] In less than a year these arrangements would be put to the test.

Teleport And The "Five Nines"

This emphasis on high reliability communications provided a bonanza for Teleport Communications Group and its fiber optic networks. As TCG found increased customer focus on high reliability, it improved its network and promoted the low outage statistics of its self-healing, diversely- routed fiber.

Before fiber, communications networks with an availability of 99.9% were considered "leading edge." However, 99.9% availability meant that the circuit could be out of service for nearly 9 hours over the period of a year. For critical data traffic this was not acceptable.

During 1988, its first year of service, TCG achieved a network availability of 99.9942%. This meant that the average circuit outage was 30.2 minutes for the year. By 1991, TCG had improved this to 99.9995% or less than three minutes of outage for the year. TCG made this achievement of "five nines" (99.999%), a benchmark goal for all its networks.[31]

NYNEX Loses Its Sense Of Humor

With the "high reliability network" and the "you need a backup network" messages, TCG was taking a significant share of the market for high speed fiber transport in Manhattan. According to New York Telephone, TCG had over 25% of the DS-1 market in the commercial center of New York City by 1992. These market share losses, although not financially damaging, were beginning to sting New York Telephone's pride.

TCG convinced many corporations with critical telecommunications needs to put at least some of their traffic on TCG's self-healing fiber. Since 1988, TCG had been using the cartoon of an upside-down bell filled with eggs, one of which had tumbled out and cracked. The accompanying slogan read, "Don't put all your tele-com eggs in one basket."

The real Bell logo was a revered symbol and registered trademark of the Bell System for more than 100 years. It was considered such a potent marketing tool that the seven RBOCS had fought a pitched battle to wrest the rights to it from AT&T during the breakup of the Bell System in 1984.

Finally, in March 1990 Terrence McAllister, lawyer and spokesman for an annoyed NYNEX, declared "It's our bell and no other com-pany has the right to use it in any way shape or form."[32] McAllister said that he had told TCG to stop using the logo and that, even though TCG had depicted the logo in an uncharacteristic color (orange) and position (upside down), it still was a violation of the trademark and was "objectionable."

Roger Cawley, TCG's manager of public affairs told Wall Street Journal reporter Jill Bullock that the Bell symbol was being used so that consumers could compare the two companies. "The broken egg," he said, "represents the risk to customers if they were to to-tally depend on just one telecommunications system for their busi-ness needs. No system is 100% effective."[33] On the issue of mis-appropriating the Bell logo Cawley said, "Our symbol must not look too similar to NYNEX's or they would have contacted us long be-fore now."[34] As to the threat of legal action by NYNEX, he re-sponded, "If they can't take a joke, too bad!"[35]

There was no legal action.

Teleport's New York Network Node Stronghold

In addition to self-healing architectures, redundant electronics and diversely routed fiber, network security also means physically se-cure network nerve centers. The most secure spot for the critical

TCG network node in New York City was fairly obvious. The fiber network converged on the World Trade Center complex in the heart of the financial services industry in lower Manhattan. The massive, 110-story, twin towers soar 1,350 feet and are anchored in bedrock 70 feet down.

By placing the network central node in the lowest level basement, the sixth-level (B-6), TCG placed the facility in a seemingly impregnable fortress-like location. Nothing short of a major cataclysmic event was likely to breach this stronghold.

Targeting The World Trade Center

The Friday morning of February 26, 1993, was cold and gray in New York. The weather forecast called for an increasing threat of snow with one to three inches possible. Onshore wind gusts whipped around the World Trade Center creating wind-chill much below the nominal temperature in the mid 20s.

A rented yellow Ford Econoline panel van from Ryder moved down the street and turned into the parking garage of the World Trade Center at 12:02. The van was followed closely by a burgundy Corsica.[36] There were two men of Middle Eastern origin in the van. The driver, a former New York taxicab driver, had flown in from Dallas two weeks earlier. He had come in response to an urgent call from a boyhood friend who needed his driving experience. In the van's cargo bed were 1,200 pounds of an explosive chemical mixture brewed from urea, nitric acid and sulfuric acid. The van made its way down two levels to B-2 and pulled into a Port Authority parking slot near the center of the garage, next to a concrete block wall. The Corsica pulled up behind them.

On the other side of the wall were Port Authority facilities that controlled many of the building's functions. There was also a conference room that was used by several Port Authority employees as a lunchroom. To be certain of a detonation, the men lit four, parallel, long-delay fuses. Jumping into the Corsica, they exited the garage with just minutes to spare.

"A Bomb Went Off!"

At noon, five Port Authority workers gathered in the conference room and opened their lunches. Shortly after noon, William Lavin left his colleagues and walked upstairs to the street level to see if the snow had begun. It saved his life.[37]

Four levels below the truck in the B-6 basement, Mike Aldridge, the New York City Operations Manager for TCG walked out of his office with a memo in his hand. He was about to drop it off on a subordinate's desk. The time was 12:18. Aldridge saw the lights flicker. Papers flew into the air, and he was knocked to the floor. A concussion and muffled roar shook the room.

Above on B-2, Lavin's four colleagues in the lunchroom were killed instantly. The cinder block wall separating the room from the parking garage was converted into high speed shrapnel. Damage to the eyes of one of the victims showed that he did not even have time to blink.[38]

In the B-6 TCG node the building's lights went out, and the emergency lights came on. Aldridge jumped up, grabbed a phone and called the Network Operations Center (NOC) on Staten Island. Jim McRobbie answered the phone. Aldridge shouted, "A bomb went off!" He did not know why he instinctively said "bomb." In fact, he really didn't know what had happened.

It even crossed his mind that the battery plant in the next room, used as a back-up power supply, might have exploded. "If it did," he thought, "I'm going to get fired." McRobbie thought it was a joke and started to laugh. Aldridge swore and re-dialed to reach Rod Resky in charge of the NOC. On the control panels in front of McRobbie, reality hit as alarm lights began to flash. Soon circuit monitors throughout the NOC were flashing like lights on a Christmas tree. "A bomb went off down here. There is smoke, we are evacuating," Aldridge shouted. "Get out! Get everyone out of there! Tell them to drop everything and get out of there," Resky responded. Aldridge dropped the phone.

Evacuation

The first impulse was to run. Restrained only momentarily by practiced fire drill procedures... check to see that no one is in the restroom, take a head count ... 20 men rushed the elevator. B-6 suddenly seemed more like a claustrophobic trap than a fortress.

Outside plant engineer, Tom Fenner said, "Immediately we did what everybody in grade school is taught not to do in such circumstances. We ran."[39] Pushing the elevator buttons produced no response. Not only was the elevator destroyed, everyone then remembered that the elevator was the wrong move in an emergency.

There were two stairwells out of B-6 leading up toward the street. The north stair was obviously damaged. Bricks were falling down, and it appeared impassable. The south stair to Liberty Street was usable, but pitch dark and smoke filled.

The men felt their way up the stairway in the blackness. When they reached the B-2 level, they heard a man crying. He had been pulling into a parking space in the garage when the blast blew him out of his car. Tom Fenner, tying a fire hose around his waist as a safety line, tried to crawl through the rubble to reach the victim but could not. They called to him to hold on and that they would bring rescue workers.

Reaching the top of the stair, they stepped out onto Liberty Street. It was cold and snowing. Aldridge did a quick nose count. Port Authority workers were alerted to the injured man in B-2. Everyone ran for the pay phones in the lobby to call home. It was 20 minutes since the explosion. Aldridge called Resky in the Staten Island Network Operations Center to report that the Teleport personnel were out safely. He also reported that speculation among Port Authority workers was that a huge building rectifier or electrical transformer had exploded. However, no one was yet sure just what had happened. It was cold on the street, and Aldridge and four technicians made a quick trip back down to the TCG node to scoop up coats and cell phones. It was 30 minutes since the explosion.

The explosion in B-2 had occurred directly beneath the Vista Hotel, a 22-story structure between the two towers. The Port Authority established an emergency command center in the lobby of the hotel in order to direct the fire and rescue operations. The lobby windows of the World Trade Center had blown out, and the marble facade of the hotel had been pulverized. Walking through the lobby to the command post involved walking on a crunchy mixture of marble and glass.

Counting noses again, Aldridge realized that his lead technician was missing.   He had gone back down to retrieve his paycheck from the pocket of his shirt that had been left hanging on a coat hook. Aldridge climbed once more back down the stairs and found the technician absorbed in his work. He was lying on his back and holding a penlight in his mouth. He had patched into a live circuit and was giving a technical status update to personnel in the Staten Island network control center.

Aldridge commended his dedication and ordered him out.

Dreams Of Carnage

Across the Hudson River, the bombers watched the World Trade Center towers from a vantage point on the New Jersey waterfront. They could just detect traces of smoke rising from the World Trade Complex but, to their disgust, the towers remained standing. It had been their hope, they later told the FBI, to topple one of the towers into the other.

Although only 55,000 people actually had offices in the towers, the conspirators had thought that, with the complex filled with mid-day visitors and patrons, they might be able to kill as many as 250,000 people.[40] Most of their plans were on a grandiose scale. When the ring leader was finally captured two years later in Islamabad, Pakistan his laptop computer contained outlines of the action steps for: a kamikaze attack on CIA headquarters in Langley, Virginia, the assassination of President Clinton with phosgene gas, the murder of Pope John Paul II and the coordinated and simultaneous destruction of 12 American jetliners in flight.[41]

Where The Hell Is The Backup Power?

While the equipment in the node had automatically and successfully switched over to battery backup when the power went out, some circuits were out of service. From monitoring information in the Staten Island NOC, it was apparent that some circuits had lost both their primary and secondary fiber paths, while others had not.

Two of the eighteen cables running from the TCG node had been damaged by shrapnel, and the cable linking the node with Tower I of the World Trade Center was completely destroyed. Passing within thirty feet of the center of the blast, this fused-silica fiber, despite having a melting point above 2,000 degrees Fahrenheit, had simply been vaporized.

Customers were beginning to call in to report loss of service. Unless electrical power could be restored soon, it was possible that all service would be lost. The batteries were only designed to provide emergency power for a few hours, and it was vital to switch to auxiliary diesel power generation as soon as possible.

Following the retrieval of the lead technician, Aldridge and others made one more trip down to the node to recover their personal computers and test equipment. The presence of the Teleport node in B-6 was unknown to most people, and building security had not yet prevented them from coming and going at will up and down the Liberty Street stairwell.

Five of the eight main power cables feeding the complex had been severed and, at the request of the fire department, all remaining power to the building was being shut down at 1:30. Teleport had a $50,000 per month contract with the Port Authority for emergency backup power. Aldridge was concerned because the Port Authority's diesel-powered generators had not yet come on. He pressed the Port Authority to find out when the power would be available. He did not know that the Port Authority control center had been destroyed in the blast. When he was finally given an estimate that power would be available at 4:00, his concern deepened. Aldridge feared that TCG's batteries would not be able to last until then.

Building security began to tighten, but at 2:00 Aldridge talked the firemen into letting his team return to the TCG node. A fireman came along. The technicians began pulling redundant cards and shutting down all but the most critical equipment to save battery power. The fireman was nervous. There was concern over the possibility of more explosions. He said, "Do you really think it's a good idea to be down here?" The TCG technicians felt that they had a responsibility to keep their network operating.

A Little Water

Water began seeping into the basement, slowly at first. The water had not worried Aldridge at first. The electronics in the node were on a raised wooden platform, eighteen inches above the floor. The heavy bank of rectifiers, however, was sitting directly on the concrete floor. The backup generators would provide alternating current power, and the rectifiers would be needed to convert the power to the direct current required to run the telecommunications equipment.

If the water rose and covered the rectifiers, the backup power would be useless, even if the diesel generators came on. Flooding to that degree seemed to be a remote threat. There were sumps in the basement to collect spilled water; and the basement itself was huge, covering acres. The real problem seemed to be that the backup generators weren't being fired up. Why wasn't the Port Authority turning them on? Everything was in confusion. Some people seemed dazed. Aldridge couldn't get an answer.

"The Shit Is Hitting The Fan"

Disrupting telecommunications did not appear to be an objective of the bombers. Indeed, it later appeared that they, along with most inhabitants of the World Trade Center, were unaware of the existence of the Teleport network node in B-6. However, the placement of the bomb had, by chance, effectively raised communications havoc.

Bob Atkinson was sitting in his office on the 3rd floor of the Teleport One building at the Staten Island Teleport facility. Someone ran in and said, "We've been bombed." They rushed down to the Network Operations Center on the second floor and saw the alarm signals lighting up the room.

Bob grabbed a telephone and called Bill Squadron at the New York City Department of Telecommunications and Energy in Manhattan. It was 12:24. "Bill," he said, "remember that Mutual Aid Pact. This is the call. The shit is hitting the fan. There has been a huge explosion at the World Trade Center." "Is that what it was," Squadron replied, "I heard the noise from my office, but I didn't know what it was. I'm activating The Bridge." By 12:44 the conference bridge was activated and the representatives of the fourteen carriers began exchanging information and passing aid requests.[42]

Trapped

High in the towers, the shock of the explosion was muted.[43] The lights flickered and went out. The smoke came quickly.[44] Elevators stopped between floors.[45]   Rumors were rampant. Office workers grabbed their phones.[46] It was not clear whether evacuation by walking down the stairs would lead to safety or straight into a raging inferno.[47] Some people headed for the roof and others threw chairs through the windows to get air. Because of damage to the Port Authority control center, there were no public address system announcements or instructions.[48]

A consensus somehow formed to walk down the stairs, and people herded in that direction. The stair wells were unlighted, smoke-filled, stifling and packed with people feeling their way down step by step. At each floor landing, progress stopped as more people crowded into the stairwell. The walk from the top floors to the street took hours. Some were sobbing. Some were choking and vomiting. New Yorkers rose to the occasion. People were generally orderly and grousing about the lack of any direction or guidance from some "authority." Occasionally there would be a cry of "pregnant woman on the right," and room would be made to let her pass through.[49]

Struggling To Maintain Phone Service

TCG was not alone in struggling to keep its network up. New York Telephone had its own battle to fight. While the node in B-6 was the heart of TCG's New York network, it primarily contained the electronics for dedicated circuit traffic. TCG's two AT&T 5ESS digital switches were not in the World Trade Center but in the nearby World Financial Center. These Central Office grade switches had originally been installed there by Merrill Lynch to serve as giant, private PBXs before being acquired by TCG. Although the switches were not directly touched by the explosion and smoke, they were impacted by the loss of some trunk circuits that passed through the B-6 node.

The situation was different for New York Telephone. Their POP was on the 10th floor of Tower II where they had three switches; a Northern Telecom digital DMS-100 and two older analog switches, AT&T 1AESSs. They served 40,000 switched lines and 30,000 dedicated lines.[50] The volume of traffic on these switches surged after the explosion as people on the upper floors of the two towers clung to the phone as their lifeline—calling to find out what had happened, calling for help or calling to reassure loved ones. Over the next few hours of the crisis, New York Telephone's switches would carry 700,000 calls.[51] While the switches were well away from the explosion, the loss of power caused them to invoke backup power. New York Telephone had three backup generators that, like the TCG node, were remotely located in the B-6 basement. One had a wall fall on it, but the other two started and came on-line. After half an hour of operation on diesel generator power, cooling water in B-6 was cut. Without water, New York Telephone was forced to switch to battery backup power.

It was uncertain whether these batteries would last more than three hours. No one knew how long evacuation of the towers would take or when new auxiliary power might be available. It was important to stretch the batteries to their maximum life. The switches had been configured in "dual mode" with hot standbys for many of the electronic components for redundancy.[52] The decision was made to go to "simplex mode" to reduce battery drain. Technicians began pulling cards and shutting down non-critical circuits. Operation in this mode would continue for six hours. Dedicated fiber circuits had to be shut down to preserve switched service.

These moves succeeded. Phone service in the complex was maintained during the crisis. Emergency auxiliary power, supplied by Consolidated Edison, arrived just as the batteries were beginning to fail.

The Teleport Node Goes Dark

TCG's need for backup power was becoming urgent. Over "The Bridge" both AT&T and MCI offered to provide portable generators. On Staten Island, Annunziata could not stand idly by any longer and decided to take matters into his own hands. A generator was loaded into a truck, and Annunziata headed into Manhattan with a police escort. Traffic into Manhattan was blocked. It was slow going. Emergency traffic was able to move only by driving the wrong way through the Battery Tunnel.

At 4:50 pm , MFS and other carriers reported through "The Bridge" that they were beginning to lose circuits that passed through the TCG node.[53] The batteries were giving out.

At 5:00 TCG reported that it was now in an extreme emergency situation. Also at 5:00 the Port Authority reported that damage to their chillers and exhaust system meant that they would not be able to turn on backup power. It was clear that the TCG node would have to shut down. Calls began going out to customers. Abrupt loss of power could damage telecommunications electronics, and a controlled shutdown process was initiated.

By 6:30 the shutdown was complete. The TCG node went dark.

Commercial power began to be restored to parts of the building at 7:30 when the undamaged feeders were switched back on. It was too little, too late for TCG. The TCG node remained dark.

Annunziata finally arrived at the World Trade Center at 8:00 pm. He was greeted by the sight of rescue workers who were bringing out body bags. The news was grim. The TCG network was down. Even if the network had still been live, the generator in the truck was useless. Water in the TCG node had covered the rectifiers on the basement floor. Without the rectifiers, the alternating current provided by the generator could not be converted to the direct current required by the network equipment.

The Problem Is Water

The problem for TCG was the water. It continued to rise. It was almost up to the eighteen-inch, raised wooden floor which supported the equipment racks. If it continued to rise, it would destroy TCG's valuable electronics.

It had been expected that the Port Authority's large sump pumps in B-6 could be used to limit any significant flooding, but the pumps were now under water; and it was learned that they could not be started when submerged. There was a frantic search for a way to get rid of the water. Annunziata even discussed with the Port Authority the possibility of knocking a hole in the wall and draining the water into the subway system.

Back at the Staten Island facility, Al Hansen, Senior Vice President of Operations for TCG, took command of NOC operations from Rod Resky and sent him into the city to see what could be done there. Resky made the trip in a police car which made its way through the Holland Tunnel. He arrived at the World Trade Center about 9:30, just as rescue workers were announcing that the evacuation of the towers was complete.

Coming down West Street, the scene seemed surreal. Trucks, emergency vehicles and flashing lights surrounded the darkened towers. Through the broken windows, the Port Authority command center in the hotel lobby could be seen. Under the glare of the emergency lights, the large equipment being maneuvered inside the building looked to Resky like giant bugs or alien space machines. Resky felt he was on a battle field. He saw Annunziata, waved and went over to his boss. Annunziata looked distraught.

Resky went down the stairwell with a flashlight. He was shocked by the violence reflected by the bomb crater. Back at the NOC there had been unconfirmed rumors of chunks of concrete ripped from the building, but these stories had been discounted as gross exaggerations. Now he saw that it was all true and more. The bomb crater gaped 60 feet wide and over 100 feet long. It penetrated four levels from B-1 to B-4. The wall to PATH subway station was smashed through. Blocks of concrete were thrown out of the crater.

Resky found Aldridge in the node wearing a pair of boots and standing in water. Aldridge said, "They say there may be another bomb down here, but we've been too busy to worry about it." Resky made a quick trip to a nearby sporting goods store and bought a pair of green fisherman's hip waders that he would wear for the next three days.

Could This Be The End Of The TCG Story?

They talked about how distressed Annunziata looked and what might become of TCG. Both wondered if this could be their "Hinsdale" or worse. In the Hinsdale fire, Illinois Bell, after all, only lost one out of hundreds of Central Offices. The World Trade Center node was the heart of the entire TCG New York network, and the New York network accounted for the bulk of TCG's business.

TCG had built its reputation on super reliable networks. Never-fail network reliability was the keystone of TCG marketing. All the work of the last nine years, their credibility and the company were at risk. Could this be the end of the TCG story?

They located an eighteen-inch, ruptured water pipe that was causing the flooding. Resky went to the Port Authority command post, found two maintenance workers who knew him and led them to the broken pipe. By the time the flow was cut, the water in the control room had risen to within inches of the bottoms of the equipment racks. The situation was stabilized. Now the arduous recovery could begin.

Recovery

The TCG contingent did not feel relieved at this point. Previously, they had been reacting to events which were largely out of their control. Now the ball was in their court, and they felt that the company's survival depended on how quickly they could restore customer service. Certainly a sustained outage, even if a fraction of the Hinsdale Central Office outage, was unthinkable.

The good news was that it was Friday, and most business activity was curtailed for the weekend. The real pressure from customers would come on Monday morning. If the network were still down, the serious damage to the company would begin.

"The Bridge" stood down from emergency status at 8:49 pm, but messages continued to be exchanged until 2:27 am.[54] Before the "Bridge" shut down, AT&T made an important commitment. They would bring a set of rectifiers to the Liberty Street entrance leading to the TCG node. A diesel generator could be run out in the street and the conversion to direct current done there and transmitted to the B-6 control room. This would only work if a very large cross section copper wire could be run down the stairwell to the node. Otherwise the voltage drop for the direct current power would be too great to operate the node electronics. (With alternating current, a voltage drop could be compensated for with a step-up transformer, an option not available for direct current.)

O'Kane Electric a family-run electrical contractor, responded to TCG's phone call. By 11:00 pm they had rigged some light-duty alternating current power down from the generators in the street, lashing the cables to the stair railing. By 2:00 am they had the node wired for lights and critical power as well as lighting in the halls and stairwell.

Work began to reduce the water level in the control room. Husky salvage workers from Crescent Salvage manhandled a 300-pound pump down the stairwell. The pump's effectiveness was limited, however, due to its four-inch diameter hose, the distance to street level and tendency of the water to freeze as it reached the street.

In spite of the dangerously cramped and damp conditions, electric workers also began to overlash the bulky copper cable on the stair rail to carry the dc power down from the street. By 7:00 am Saturday morning a heavy cable was in place and hooked up to the four rectifiers from AT&T on the top landing. Electronics could now be powered up and tested in the B-6 node. By 11:00 am the temporary cable had been replaced by a more substantial bus bar system, and by noon the work of turning up and restoring customer circuits was begun.

Standing water was still a problem, and the TCG technicians were working wading in it. Progress at elimination of the water was enhanced by pumping into the building's drainage system rather than all the way up to the street level, but the process would still require another three weeks before all the water was removed and the control room was dry.

The remaining problem was to deal with the damaged fiber cables. Although two diversely routed conduits led to the external network from the node—one north to Vessy Street and one south to Liberty Street—it had not seemed necessary to continue that diversity all the way to the B-6 node. The two conduits met at a common splice box on B-2 and ran down a common conduit to B-6.

The five-foot by three-foot box, containing the splices and coils of extra fiber, was, by chance, near ground zero for the explosion. The box had been blown apart, and the cables dangled out. Worse than direct destruction, some fiber cables, which looked perfectly okay, were impregnated with tiny pieces of shrapnel from the blast; and these produced intermittent transmission problems that were difficult to diagnose. A temporary wooden structure was built around the splice box to protect it during the clean-up operations. Tom Fenner directed a five-man re-cabling team that included TCG technicians flown in from Denver. New fiber was spliced and cables were rerouted. By Monday morning most customer circuits were back in service, but in a patched together, fragile configuration that might fail at any moment.

TCG personnel felt that they were literally in a desperate fight to save their company. There was real fear that TCG's business, based on high reliability, never-fail networks might have come to an untimely demise.

The work continued at a heavy pace to convert the "lash ups" and temporary fixes into a more stable mode of operation. Electronics had to be restored, tested and put back into service. Circuits were re-wired and cables rerun. TCG technicians worked in the node around the clock. The work was exhausting and uncomfortable. Living and sleeping in the flooded node was difficult. Food was pizza or take-out grabbed at spare moments. The restroom in the node was inoperative, and going to the bathroom meant a weary climb of seven flights of stairs to the lobby level.

Sleep was at a premium. Aldridge got two hours sleep in the first 49 hours. After three exhausting days, Fenner feel asleep in his chair in the middle of giving a status report.[55] Resky lived in B-6 for a week, and Aldridge did not get home until March 18th.

The prodigious TCG effort was a success. Customer restoration was so rapid that there were few complaints. The precarious nature of the recovery was largely invisible to customers and to the public.

Teleport publicity down-played the critical role of the B-6 node and emphasized that TCG had five other nodes throughout the city. From most trade press stories, it was not even evident that TCG had experienced any circuit outages.

New York Telephone Takes The High Road

New York Telephone, for its part, brought in 150 technicians to work in the World Trade Center complex. Over the weekend, they rerouted lines and installed thousands of new lines. Their network was essentially restored by Sunday. However, forwarding numbers to the new locations of World Trade Center-based companies setting up temporary offices turned up some problems. New York Telephone's old analog 1AESS switches, which had been in place in the towers since they were built, were technologically obsolete and could not forward all their numbers.

By Monday, March 1, 1993, the switch node was determined to be unstable and was bypassed completely. By Wednesday, New York Telephone had installed call forwarding on 4,083 lines, activated 1,700 new business lines and 176 high speed data lines.

The camaraderie which existed among the carriers during the emergency began to dissipate as the emergency passed. The taunting of the upside down bell logo still rankled at New York Telephone. Some telephone personnel began to grouse privately that the TCG node was under-engineered, and that TCG didn't deserve to come out of the crisis with such good press. However, at the executive level, the company refrained from any such public remarks.

Beginning on March 1, New York Telephone addressed the public relations issues through a series of eight, full-page "World Trade Center Crisis Updates" in the New York press. In the final Update on March 24, 1993, they took the high road and stressed the importance of their own network:

NOW THAT IT'S WINDING DOWN, HERE'S WHERE WE'RE WINDING UP

... we thought we'd pass on some of the learning we've gained as a result of this extraordinary emergency.

The network is a lifeline.

In the hours after the explosion, the New York Telephone public switched network was, for many of those trapped in the towers, the only link to the outside world. While we've always understood that our network is a vital component of New York's infrastructure, this life-and-death experience was, for us, both a source of pride and a source of deep humility. While the network survived and thrived this time, we are keenly aware of our responsibility to remain vigilant ... crisis preparedness cannot be overstated. In the case of our own network, years of advanced planning and investment went into the redundant systems and diverse routing, without which the outcome might have been much different ...[56]

Captured and Convicted

The renter of the van used to transport the bomb was quickly apprehended when he returned to the Ryder Truck Rental to reclaim his $400 deposit. He had reported the van stolen at 10:00 pm on February 25, 1993, the night before the blast. Therefore, he expected to be able to get his deposit refunded. Since he held only a child's airline ticket and did not have enough money to upgrade to an adult ticket, he needed the refund money before he could flee the country.[57] The conspirators had not imagined that the identity of the van in the explosion would be discovered so quickly. However, the FBI, working quickly, found a vehicle identification number on the shattered axle of the van and traced it to the rental company.

Four of the conspirators were convicted in 1994 and each was sentenced to 240 years in prison.[58]   The two primary bombers were captured in 1995 in Pakistan and Jordan, respectively. They were convicted by a federal jury in Manhattan in November 1997 and received life sentences.[59]

Lessons Learned

Direct physical damage to the World Trade Center buildings was estimated at around $550 million, but business dislocation lasted for a month. As with the Chicago Flood, business losses were much larger but nearly impossible to assess.

There were a number of lessons about network reliability coming from the World Trade Center and Chicago Flood experiences. One was that, because of water, the deepest location in the ground might not be the safest place for locating a telecommunications network center. Another was the realization that even greater diversity in network routing and redundancy in network elements was required than had previously been imagined.

TCG initiated a prolonged re-engineering of its networks, with the deployment of fiber shadow circuits and advanced SONET fiber technology. With these enhancements, TCG could electronically re-route any of its circuits so that no single node loss could, in the future, bring the network down.

TCG, along with the entire competitive telecommunications industry, had weathered its most severe crisis. The World Trade Center bombing did not become a public relations "Hinsdale" for CAPs. In fact, the impact was just the opposite. Regulators and legislators, in addition to telecommunications-dependent companies, now grasped the reality behind, "Don't put all your eggs in one basket."

The travails of both New York Telephone and TCG in New York and of Illinois Bell Telephone, MFS and TCG in Chicago also underlined the fact that no system is 100% effective. It was clear that rational public policy required interconnection between the rival networks of telephone companies and their new competitors. The battle for "hearts and minds" of regulators and policy-makers to require network interconnection was all but won.

The battle for adoption of an interconnection policy would now begin in earnest.

Footnotes Chapter 9: Trial By Fire & Water

[1] "Chicago Mayor Fires An Aide Because Of Flood," *The Wall Street Journal,* Wednesday, April 15, 1992, A8.

[2] Ibid.

[3] Ibid.

[4] Ibid.

[5] Ibid.

[6] "Rain Thwarts Effort To Plug Chicago Tunnel Leak," *New York Times,* April 16, 1992, A12.

[7] *New York Times,* April 14, 1992, A1.

[8] "Work On Chicago's Flood Progresses At A Slow Rate," *The Wall Street Journal,* Friday, April 17, 1992, C12.

[9] "Down And Out In Chicago," *Information Week,* April 20, 1992.

[10] Ibid.

[11] Ibid.

[12] "The Great Chicago Flood," *Information Week,* April 20, 1992.

[13] "Chicago Refugees Look For Place to Call 'Office'," New *York Times,* April 17, 1992, A12.

[14] The Great Chicago Flood,"

[15] "Disaster Recovery -- Chicago Users Bail Out," *Communications Week,* April 20, 1992.

[16] Chicago Mayor Fires An Aide Because Of Flood,"

[17] Down And Out In Chicago,"

[18] "Telecom Managers Scramble During Flood," *411 Newsletter,* April 20, 1992, 1.

[19] "Down And Out In Chicago,"

[20] "Disaster Recovery -- Chicago Users Bail Out,"

[21] "Chicago Flood Forces Evacuation From Buildings With Fiber," *Fiber Optic News,* April 20, 1992.

[22] "Carriers Regroup In Flood Aftermath," *Telephony,* April 27, 1992, 12.

[23] "Metropolitan Fiber Chicago Network Remains Fully Operational," *CCMI New Bureau,* April 17, 1992.

[24] "Worst Of Chicago Loop Flood May Be Yet To Come," *Telephony,* April 20, 1992, 8.

[25] "Carriers Regroup In Flood Aftermath,"

[26] "Past Crises Had Illinois Bell Prepared For The Worst," *Telephony,* April 20, 1992, 9.

[27] "Army Engineers Slice Two Illinois Bell Fiber Cables; Service Restored," *Fiber Optic News,* May 18. 1992.

[28] "Illinois Bell Net Saves The Day," *Network World,* May 11, 1992, 6.

[29] "*The $1 Trillion Gamble: Telecommunications and New York's Economic Future,*" The New York City Partnership and Booz, Allen & Hamilton, Inc., June 1990.

[30] "N.Y.C. Telecommunications Disaster Pact Pays Off In First Crisis," *Common Carrier Week,"* March 8, 1993.

31 Richard G. Tomlinson, "The Impact Of Local Competition On Network Quality," in William H. Lehr, *"Quality And Reliability Of Telecommunications Infrastructure"* (Hillsdale, New Jersey: Lawrence Erlbaum Associates, Inc., 1994), 213-224.

32 "Actually, It's Pretty Hard to Put Eggs in the Right-Side-Up One," *Wall Street Journal*, March 13, 1990, B3.

33 Ibid.

34 Ibid.

35 Ibid.

36 "The FBI Files," Discovery Channel, October 27, 1999.

37 "For Victims And Investigators Of Trade Center Bombing, Relief But Scant Sense Of An End," *The New York Times,* November 13, 1997.

38 "2 Convicted In Plot To Blow Up N.Y. World Trade Center,"

39 "We Felt The Building Move," TCG 1994 Annual Report.

40 "Trade Center Conspiracy's Who And Why Are Solved, But Not Mystery,"

41 Ibid.

42 "Mutual Aid Plan Appears To Work After N.Y. Bomb Blast," *Telecommunications Week,* March 8, 1993.

43 "Ordinary Lives Hurtled Into The Extraordinary," *The New York Times,* Saturday, Feb. 27, 1993.

44 "First, Darkness, Then Came The Smoke," *The New York Times,* Saturday, Feb. 27, 1993, 1.

45 "Blast Hits Trade Center, Bomb Suspected; 5 Killed, Thousands Flee Smoke In Towers," *The New York Times,* Saturday, Feb. 27, 1993, 1.

46 First, Darkness, Then Came The Smoke," *The New York Times,* Saturday, Feb. 27, 1993, 22.

47 Ibid.

48 "Size Of Blast 'Destroyed' Rescue Plan," *The New York Times,* Saturday, Feb. 27, 1993.

49 "First, Darkness, Then Came The Smoke,"

50 "Carriers Unite To Restore Service After World Trade Center Bombing," *Communications Week,* March 29, 1993.

51 "N.Y.C. Telecommunications Disaster Pact Pays Off In First Crisis,"

52 In "hot standby mode" duplicate sets of electronics are powered up and active. If the primary set develops a fault, service is automatically switched to the standby set with essentially no discernible disruption.

53 "Mutual Aid Plan Appears To Work After N.Y. Bomb Blast,"

54 Ibid.

55 "We Felt The Building Move,"

56 For example, *New York Times,* March 24, 1993.

57 "The FBI Files,"

58 "Trade Center Conspiracy's Who And Why Are Solved, But Not Mystery,"

59 "2 Convicted In Plot to Blow Up N.Y. World Trade Center,"

10. FROM CAP TO CLEC

CAP Status In 1993

Although MFS and TCG dominated the emerging CAP industry, many smaller companies were attempting to establish themselves. However, in absolute terms their numbers declined slightly in 1993, as more were absorbed into the larger CAPs than were created as new start-ups. By year-end 1993, approximately thirty-one companies were providing competitive local access services via either microwave or fiber networks. Most were generating tiny revenues. Only nine CAPs had annual telecommunications service revenues in excess of $2 million.

Largest CAPs In 1993 By Telecom Revenue ($million)[1]

	Competitive Company	Telecom Revenue	Total Revenue
1.	Teleport Communications Group	$82.4	$82.4
2.	MFS Communications	70.0	141.1
3.	Eastern TeleLogic	11.0	11.0
4.	Bay Area Teleport	9.9	9.9
5.	Intermedia Communications of Florida	8.3	8.3
6.	IntelCom Group	6.0	33.9
7.	LOCATE (microwave)	5.0	5.0
8.	Electric Lightwave	3.7	3.7
9.	Mtel Digital Services (microwave)	2.5	2.5
	Others (21)	10.8	10.8
	Industry Total	$209.6	$308.6

CAP Market Niche

In 1993, the CAP industry had total revenues of $309 million and total telecom services revenues of $210 million. Nearly all of the telecom services revenues were for dedicated transport either for long distance access or private line service.[2]

Since dedicated transport is only a small part of the total local telecommunications market, CAPs were serving only a small fringe of a large market. In fact, the total U.S. market for local telecommunications services in 1993 was $93 billion.[3] Dedicated transport for access and private line accounted for less than $6 billion or only 6.5% of this total market.[4] Furthermore, CAPs could not even address all of the dedicated transport market since the extent of their networks was limited and telephone company circuits were not generally available to CAPs for economic resale. CAPs were truly niche service providers.

Concentrations of dedicated transport demand were not homogeneously distributed but were concentrated primarily in major urban centers where large corporate facilities were clustered and where long distance carriers required high-speed trunking among multiple local points of presence. Therefore, it is not surprising to find that the CAPs with large revenue in 1993 had most of their networks located in the major cities.[5]

Operational CAP Networks In 1993

Competitive Access Provider Co.	Cities Operational
Teleport Communications Group.........	Boston, Chicago, Dallas, Houston, Los Angeles, Milwaukee, New York, Oakland, Omaha, San Diego, San Francisco, San Jose, Seattle
MFS Communications....................	Atlanta, Baltimore, Boston, Chicago, Dallas, D.C., Houston, Los Angeles, Minneapolis, New York, Philadelphia, Pittsburgh, San Francisco
Eastern TeleLogic.........................	Philadelphia
Bay Area Teleport........................	San Francisco Area, Sunnyvale, Oakland
Intermedia Communications..............	Jacksonville, Miami, Orlando, Tampa, St. Pete.
IntelCom Group...........................	Cleveland, Charlotte, Denver, Phoenix
LOCATE (Microwave)....................	New York
Electric Lightwave........................	Seattle, Portland
Mtel Digital (Microwave)................	Los Angeles Area

CAP Optimism In 1993

In 1993 CAPs were optimistic and were not discouraged by the fact that they had penetrated only a small portion of the limited address-able market open to them. This optimism was shared by investors, as the stock prices of the three publicly traded CAPs rose sharply. By August of 1993, the shares of MFS Communications, IntelCom Communications Group and Intermedia Communications of Florida had risen from their lows of the year by 158%, 170% and 475%, respectively.

In large part, this optimism stemmed from the expectation that an in-creasingly de-regulatory environment would soon result in larger segments of the telecommunications markets being opened to com-petition. In June 1993, the FCC interconnection order of September 1992, requiring collocation, became effective and was expected to increase the CAP addressable dedicated transport market five-fold, from $500 million to $2.5 billion.[6] In August 1993, the FCC ex-panded its interconnection order to include the transport element for carrying local switched access to long distance carrier POPs. But, what is more important, there were unmistakable signs that the switched services market, where the bulk of the revenue in local telecommunications lay, would open to competition.

Entry into most of these new markets would require that CAPs ac-tually install and operate their own telephone switches. With the ownership of switches and the regulatory right to provide switched services, CAPs hoped to be able to address the bulk of the nearly $100 billion local telephone market.

PBX Switches

There had always been limited ways in which CAPs could provide switched services. A CAP a large corporation or anyone else, could own and operate a PBX (private branch exchange) switch. From the mid 1980s, in most states, one could apply for "shared tenant service" status and share a PBX among several users. The PBX was not an integral part of the public switched telephone network, but rather sat on the edge of the network. It interfaced to the tele-phone company's public switched network via PBX "trunk" cir-cuits.

End users on the PBX could access its features, such as dedicated trunks to long distance carrier, least cost routing and voice mail. Related groups (*e.g.* members of the same company) on the switch could use the PBX as an intercom and call each other with abbreviated dialing. In most jurisdictions, however, a call between unrelated users could not legally be completed within the PBX switch. Such a call would have to be sent out to the local phone company's central office, switched and then sent back to the PBX. In this regard the shared PBX which TCG operated in the early 1980s in the Staten Island Teleport satellite park enjoyed unique status because it was permitted by the New York Public Service Commission to complete calls between unrelated parties within the park.

However, business opportunities for CAPs involving shared PBXs never developed into a large revenue opportunity.

Tandem Switches

The other sense in which CAPs had been involved in switched service was by owning and operating "tandem" switches. A tandem switch does not connect directly to end user telephones but operates to route traffic in the network between switches.

For example, by providing trunk circuits to a PBX and having dedicated links to several long distance carrier POP switches, a tandem switch could give the PBX end user the opportunity for low-cost switched access to multiple long distance carriers. This would give the end user the flexibility to use whichever carrier was most cost-effective for the time of day, type of call being made, etc. Both ICC in its Washington, D.C. fiber network and Eastern TeleLogic in its Philadelphia fiber network installed their own tandem switches for this purpose.

Real Telephone Service

In no sense did operation of a shared PBX or a tandem switch make a CAP a "telephone company." The defining service of a telephone company is local switched service or "dial tone." The right to provide this service was the core monopoly franchise of the local telephone company.

State Public Utility Commissions traditionally guarded this franchise from encroachment in order to protect "universal service" and maintain low-cost, basic "dial tone" service – also known as "Plain Old Telephone Service"– for residential customers. It was generally conceded that "universal service," defined as affordable, ubiquitous, residential telephone service, was a desirable societal goal. The tariffed rate system was loaded with hidden subsidies which had the effect of raising business and long distance access rates in order to maintain lower residential "Plain Old Telephone Service" rates.

While regulators might allow limited local service competition in market niches like dedicated transport, they were not ready to throw open the bulk of switched services to competition. Telephone companies constantly warned that each competitive inroad threatened their revenue stream and, hence, threatened "universal service."

Real Central Office Switches

Even if CAPs had been permitted by regulators to install central-office-grade switches and act like miniature telephone companies, delivery of switched services was not easy. Providing local switched telephone service is much more complex and costly than providing dedicated transport.

Everything about switched service operation is more expensive. The technology of a central office switch requires technicians with a higher degree of training than that required to service dedicated transport electronics. The per-minute usage billing required for switched services is much more complex than the flat-rated, monthly billing of dedicated transport circuits. Customer service, marketing and maintenance to support and deliver switched services all require a much greater investment in staffing, training and support systems than does a CAP operation.

Despite all these barriers to entry, many CAP leaders soon realized that it would be necessary to find a way to enter competitive switched services if they were to avoid being permanently confined in a limited revenue niche of the telecommunications market.

These aspirations by competitive providers to deliver a broader range of services were implicitly contained in the initial proposal to the FCC that the industry should be called "Competitive Local Carriers" (CLCs) rather than "Competitive Access Providers" (CAPs).

TCG Acquires Central-Office-Grade Switches

As it had in creating the CAP business, TCG led the way in moving the competitive industry into the ownership and operation of central-office-grade switches. TCG had never incorporated a tandem switch in its operations because it thought that would put them in conflict with their best customers, the long distance carriers, as such a move had done for ICC. They did, however, have experience with shared PBX switches since the early days of providing shared tenant service at the Staten Island teleport facility.

TCG formed a switched services subsidiary, TC Systems, Inc., in November 1989.[7]   Its first task was to build and operate a private, digital, switched network for the Port Authority of New York and New Jersey using a large PBX switch. In February of 1990, TC Systems purchased two central-office-grade AT&T 5ESS switches from TCG parent, Merrill Lynch, and transferred the responsibility for their operation to TC Systems.[8]

These switches had been acquired by Merrill Lynch and installed in the World Financial Center near the World Trade Center during boom times in the brokerage business. Although built to be central office switches, they had been operated by Merrill Lynch as "high-end" PBXs. With the brokerage business contracting, the switches were greatly under-utilized. The two switches were fully equipped for 24,000 and 35,000 lines, respectively; but only 9,600 lines were activated to serve Merrill Lynch employees. It now seemed prudent for Merrill Lynch to "outsource" both the switches and the telephone operations.

TC Systems applied for and received authority to operate these switches as "shared PBXs" and by year end 1991 was serving 27,000 lines to 30 customers. Annunziata made it clear that TCG had its eye on the total local telephone market. He said, "We expect to get as big a share of that $100 billion market as we can."[9]

As state regulations permitted, TCG deployed more central-office-grade switches and expanded its range of switched service offerings. By year end 1993, TCG had switches operating in Chicago and Boston.[10]

"The Other Local Telephone Company"

In New York City, Teleport announced on July 13, 1994, that, using the regulatory freedom recently granted by the New York PUC, it was offering the first full-scale, peer-level competition for the local switched telephone service of business users.[11]

Agreements with New York Telephone not only covered interconnection with the TCG network but also provided for mutual compensation between the two carriers for calls originating on one network and terminating on the other.[12] Although impediments still remained to broad, full scale competition for local switched service, the initial step had now been taken.

By year end 1994, in addition to the four large AT&T 5ESS switches in New York City, Boston and Chicago, TCG had pre-emptively installed two more 5ESS switches in San Francisco and Los Angeles, awaiting regulatory approval to begin operation.[13] TCG's revenue from switched services reached $40.2 million for the year and accounted for one third of its total revenue.[14]

The CAPs Are Dead: Long Live The CLECs

With his company well launched into switched services, Annunziata pronounced in April of 1994 that the end had come for CAPs. He observed,

> CAPs have been at risk since day one. The simple truth is that a company can't survive only on 'access services' such as private lines, special access lines and the local transport of switched access, provided over a few miles of fiber optic cable in a city's downtown business center. To be viable, a company must develop a product line as broad as the traditional local telephone company, which means, offering switched services, data services, pay phones and other services ... Let me hasten to add that TCG and a few other companies thought of as CAPs are not endangered because they are no longer CAPs. They are or have already evolved well beyond providing only competitive access services.[15]

Annunziata not only announced the end of the CAP industry, but he also proposed a new name for its successor. Since local telephone companies were known as Local Exchange Carriers or LECs, he suggested that competitive local carriers ought to be called CompLECs.[16] However, the "CompLEC" label didn't stick. Ultimately the name that stuck was CLEC—standing for Competitive Local Exchange Carrier. Now every CAP that installed its own switch, and even some that didn't, wanted to be called a *CLEC*.

CLEC Deployment of Central Office Switches

MFS Communications and LOCATE joined TCG as CLECs in the New York City market in 1993; and by year end 1995, fourteen CLECs had 70 switches in operation in many cities. Unlike TCG, LOCATE and MFS did not deploy AT&T switches. LOCATE installed a Siemens Stromberg-Carlson EWSD™ in its Manhattan microwave network, and MFS Communications installed an Ericsson AXE™ switching platform as far away as New Jersey to serve New York City remotely over its fiber network.

Central Office Grade Switches Deployed By CLECs 1991-1995

Company	1991	1992	1993	1994	1995
Teleport Commun. Group	2	2	4	6	21
MFS Communications	0	0	1	12	16
IntelCom Group	0	0	0	2	13
MCImetro	0	0	0	0	10
City Signal/US Signal	0	0	0	1	1
Brooks Fiber Properties	0	0	0	0	1
LOCATE	0	0	1	1	1
CableVision Lightpath	0	0	0	1	1
ACC National Telecom	0	0	0	0	1
Electric Lightwave	0	0	0	0	1
NEXTLINK	0	0	0	0	1
Jones Lightwave	0	0	0	0	1
McLeod	0	0	0	0	1
Time Warner Commun.	0	0	0	0	1
	2	2	6	22	70

Sources: Company Reports and Connecticut Research, Inc.

MFS Intelenet Switched Services

MFS Communications moved rapidly to embrace CLEC operations. In October 1993 MFS formed a switched services subsidiary, MFS Intelenet, which they called "the nation's only full service telecommunications company designed exclusively to meet the needs of small to medium-sized businesses."[17]

Apparently unconcerned over possible negative reactions from long distance carriers, MFS Intelenet differentiated its switched service offering from TCG's by announcing that it intended to offer "both local and long distance service through one carrier, over state-of-the-art facilities."

In fact, it was this strategy that led MFS to select the Ericsson AXE™ digital switch. This modular platform could be configured to incorporate both local and tandem switching functions and could even be expanded to operate as a gateway switch for international calls. MFS initiated a rapid deployment of these switches and by the end of 1994 had a dozen in operation.

Not content to slowly acquire switched service customers, MFS targeted for acquisition companies which had a base of existing telephone customers. MFS identified shared tenant service operators as one such class of prospective targets. In May 1994, MFS acquired Centex TeleManagement, a shared tenant service operator with over 11,0000 telephone customers in nine states.[18] MFS also acquired RealCom Office Communications, a shared tenant service operator with 3,800 customers in eighteen major cities.[19]

For 1994, Intelenet's switched services accounted for $116 million or 51% of MFS Communications' revenue. By 1995, it was $266 million or 53%.[20]

IntelCom Group: A Small Company With Big Ambitions

The small CAP company that seized the opportunity to move into switched services most aggressively was the Denver-based IntelCom Group. In 1993, IntelCom Group was a distant third in industry rank, behind MFS and Teleport in overall revenue, and only in sixth place in CAP revenue

IntelCom Group announced that it intended to lead the competitive industry in the roll-out of central-office-grade switches. It began operation of its first two AT&T 5ESS switches in Denver and Cleveland in 1994 and by the following year had thirteen in service. Only Teleport and MFS had more switches.

Along with this move into CLEC operations, IntelCom continued its previously initiated program of aggressive national expansion of fiber networks through acquisition and construction. IntelCom Telecom Services President Bill Maxwell said, "We intend to continue our expansion into new markets while we roll out our switched services strategy. This accelerated growth will sacrifice profitability in the near term but build long-term enterprise value."[21]

The roll-up of CAP networks, which began in 1993 with Cleveland-based Ohio Linx and Charlotte-based Privacom, accelerated in 1994.[22] IntelCom Group acquired Bay Area Teleport in the San Francisco Bay area and Mtel Digital Services

in the Los Angeles area, as well as the fiber networks of FiberCap in Melbourne, Florida, Conticom in Denver and Mid-American Cable in Louisville, Kentucky. In addition, IntelCom began construction of fiber net-works in Akron, Boulder, Colorado Springs, Columbus and Nashville.

A "Carrier's Carrier"

IntelCom positioned its switched service offering as switched access termination for long distance carriers. This was a strategic fit with IntelCom's carriers' carrier market positioning.

This offering avoided the necessity of long and painful struggles with state PUCs for certification as a local switched services provider, since long distance service was under FCC jurisdiction and open for competition. IntelCom could offer termination of long distance switched access in any state without seeking PUC approval.

IntelCom said, "It is important to stress that the decision to aggressively pursue switching is based on what we can do today in the market, not what we expect from regulators tomorrow. That will be a nice bonus when—not if—it arrives."[23]

Switched service revenue did ramp-up quickly for IntelCom. By the end of 1994, the President of IntelCom's Telecommunications Services, Bill Maxwell, reported, "We are at the beginning of what we expect to be an explosive growth curve in switched minutes, with a (fiscal) first quarter annualized run rate of approximately $2 million with very minimal market penetration."[24] This annualized run rate expanded to $4 million and then to $10 million in the following two quarters. By the final quarter of 1995, IntelCom was switching 235 million minutes of use.

IntelCom's Top-Line Revenue Growth

IntelCom drove its revenue growth with three lines of business: Telecommunications Services (CAP & CLEC), Satellite Services and Network Services.

While Telecom Services' revenue did achieve robust growth as networks and switches were added, the other business lines grew also. Telecom Services' revenue tripled to $18.7 million in 1994 and increased from contributing 18% of IntelCom's total revenue to a 25% share.

IntelCom Chairman, Bill Becker, commenting on the revenue growth at year-end 1994 said, "We continue to deliver strong top-line growth—the 15th consecutive quarterly revenue for the company. In particular, our CAP operations are now the fastest-growing segment of our business."[25] By 1995 IntelCom's total revenue reached $122 million. Telecom Services' revenue more than doubled to $40 million but, with strong growth in all sectors, still accounted for only a third of IntelCom's total revenue.

The Bottom Line Pain

The downside of a carrier's carrier strategy, which offers wholesale switched termination service, is that it is a low margin business. As the company noted, "We have repeatedly stated that initial margins in switched services will be modest, especially when we connect through Bell central offices for our long distance customers."[26]

IntelCom also observed that its expectations were that this situation would improve, " ...we expect to significantly improve our margins over time as we achieve more favorable interconnection arrangements with the Bell companies we do business with and, ultimately,

when we see full, effective competition in the local telephone exchange."[27] However, the strain of maintaining its expansion
program and investing in a switched services business without
current profits put a tremendous drain on the company's cash flow.
New capital financing was urgently needed.

IntelCom Group: Under New Management

IntelCom Group changed management. In April 1995, Becker announced that a three-member executive committee had been formed
to run the company. "These changes will help IntelCom meet its
operating and financial performance objectives," he said. "It also
will allow me to focus on strategic opportunities for the company."[28]

Three days later, Becker announced that he would resign and
that the company was seeking a new President and CEO and that the
Directors were considering a plan to reorganize as a U.S. rather than
Canadian company.[29]

On May 30, 1995, IntelCom announced the appointment of J.
Shelby Bryan, a lawyer with experience in cellular telecommunications and investment banking, as its new CEO and President.[30]
Bryan would say later, "(IntelCom) was a troubled company, and I
was asked by investors to come to Denver and help the situation ...
What (IntelCom) lacked when I came along was the capital to go after that (CLEC) market, because this is a capital-intensive business."[31]

In his first report to shareholders in June 1995, Bryan noted that the
year-to-date revenue growth was up 113% over the same period the
previous year. However, he cautioned, "While these numbers reflect a continuation of IntelCom's top-line growth of recent years,
this momentum alone is no longer sufficient to accomplish our business objectives ... We are going to focus on Telecom Services...
Our ambition is to grow this business into a significant telephone
company. We will look to sell assets that no longer fit our core focus..."[32]

Bryan also informed the shareholders that he had already begun to
deliver new financing including a $20 million dollar commitment
from Morgan Stanley & Co, followed by a $300 million private
placement of senior notes and a $30 million preferred stock private

offering.[33] Over the next three years, Bryan would help IntelCom Group raise more than $1.5 billion to fuel its growth. IntelCom refocused and emphasized the expansion of its networks as regional clusters in California, Colorado, the Ohio Valley, the Southeast and Texas. It abandoned the pursuit of a national footprint and sold off networks in markets such as Melbourne, Florida, where it had only a nominal presence.

IntelCom began selling its teleport facilities, and Satellite and Network Services were de-emphasized. Aggressive switch deployment continued, and switched services expanded to include local dial tone and long distance service for business customers.

MCI Tries To Be A CLEC

Long distance carrier, MCI Communications had been a major customer of the competitive access providers from the beginning of the CAP industry, contributing a significant percentage of CAPs' revenues for dedicated access. However, MCI paid the bulk of its access dollars to local telephone companies. By 1993, MCI was paying $5.4 billion a year for local access, with 99.6% of the revenue going to the LECs.[34]

In March 1990, MCI had acquired a significant set of local access facilities when it bought Access Transmission Systems from Western Union.[35] This sale marked the final exit of the once formidable Western Union company from any form of participation in telecommunications transmission.

The Access Transmission Systems' assets included rights-of-way and underground conduit, some over one hundred years old, that had been accumulated by Western Union in more than 100 cities during the hey-day of its telegraph business. Some of the conduit was difficult to locate or had decayed, but some had been modernized and contained up-dated fiber cable or active optical systems. In all, the purchase included fourteen million feet of conduit and three million feet of fiber cable.

MCI had been the largest customer of Access Transmission Systems, leasing its facilities to create fiber connections to large customers' locations. At $30 million, the purchase made sense since MCI had been paying more to lease a small fraction of the facilities than Western Union was asking as a sale price for the whole collection. In 1993, MCI formed a strategy to use these and other assets to enter the CLEC business directly.[36] The plan was formally announced in January 1994 as part of a massive, six-year, $20-billion-plan to upgrade the company's networks and attack the LEC monopoly over local phone service.[37]

The New CLEC: MCImetro

The formation of MCI's CLEC, MCImetro, was part of the larger announcement by MCI Chairman, Bert Roberts, on January 5, 1994. Roberts indicated that MCI would spend $2 billion of the $20 billion upgrade program through MCImetro to wire up local-phone access networks in twenty cities. These were all major cities where service was dominated by the RBOCs. Roberts made his objective clear, "We want to be a local phone company and expect to be."[38]

MCI indicated that it intended to deploy advanced digital switches such as the Northern Telecom DMS 100 and the Siemens Stromberg-Carlson EWSD and ultimately deliver a full range of switched services, including voice, data and video.[39]

Although only four states—New York, Massachusetts, Illinois and Washington—then allowed a full range of switched local service, MCI intended to change that. Gary Parsons, the MCI executive tapped to run MCImetro, said, "One of our primary responsibilities will be to have those regulations changed. Somebody has to take the initiative to force competition to occur."[40]

The RBOC response was that regulators should now allow them to enter the long distance business. Ameritech President Dick Notebart said, "Here is a major long distance company verbally opposed to our entrance into long-distance services while at the same time it voices interest in entering the local-services market."[41] MCImetro declared that it intended to function as an even handed and fully competitive CLEC, selling local access services to all customers, including its long distance arch rivals, AT&T and Sprint, at the same rates as it sold to its parent company, MCI Communications.[42]

Although MCImetro would be a new competitor to the existing CLECs, they did not view its creation as a negative for the industry. MFS Communications Chairman, Jim Crowe, thought that MCI's entry "ratifies our business plan and the strategic value of our net-work."[43] TCG's Bob Atkinson saw the formation of MCImetro as the beginning of a massive migration of long distance access traffic off RBOC networks and onto CLEC networks. "That," he said, "can only be good for Teleport."[44]

Most important to the CLECs, however, was the prospect of MCI's legal and lobbying muscle joining the CLEC industry's efforts.[45] As the giant slayer which had taken on AT&T and won, MCI was revered by CLECs as the epitome of the successful challenger to entrenched telecommunications monopoly.

The prospect of having MCI's formidable legal legions and legislative lobbying muscle actively promoting CLEC issues was viewed with glee.[46] MFS Vice President of regulatory and legal affairs, Andy Lipman, expressed his pleasure at MCI's involvement and said, "We invite them to join us at the barricades. There is still 99% of the (local exchange market) which is closed to us."[47]

Within a few months of the MCImetro announcement, Heather Gold, the President of ALTS, the competitive industry association, noted that MCI had already dedicated considerable resources to the fight for opening local markets to competition and had supported the association's positions on telecommunications bills proposed in Congress.[48]

MCImetro Roll-Out

MCI's early announcements indicated that the first phase of the $2 billion MCImetro roll-out would begin with construction of a network in Atlanta, Georgia, and would include twenty major cities within two years.

Some industry observers were skeptical of this aggressive roll-out plan and suggested that MCI might be bluffing. They opined that MCI might just be posturing for the shock and public relations effect.[49] Rumors began to circulate within the industry that there was no evidence of the type of serious advanced planning and ordering required to support a major network construction project. Sources at MCI's equipment supplier, Northern Telecom, said that no requests for proposals had been received except for equipment for the Atlanta network.[50]

By the second quarter of 1994, the downtown Atlanta network was operational. The network was providing only unswitched service but MCImetro was optimistic.   MCImetro CEO, Gary Parsons, stated that his company would not only spend $2 billion to build networks in the twenty largest cities but also would commit "multiple billions of dollars" more to the local market.[51]

MCImetro COO, Nate Davis, asserted that his company was moving aggressively behind the scenes. He noted, for example that MCImetro was not solely reliant on the Western Union facilities, but was actively developing 1,300 miles of right-of-way from unannounced acquisitions in addition to 1,200 miles of the Western Union assets.[52] He told a telecommunications conference audience that by the third quarter of 1994, MCImetro would be deployed in six cities.[53]

However, the enormity of the task that MCImetro had set for itself began to become apparent. Due to logistical constraints, MCImetro spent only $100 million on network construction in 1994 and by year-end had networks operational in only four cities: Atlanta, Boston, Dallas and Los Angeles.[54]

While the Western Union assets were useful for quickly deploying fiber backbone, they were of little use in the more difficult and time-consuming task of gaining the rights-of-way and building access required to link buildings to the network. Furthermore, entry into local switched service posed major impediments. As a long distance carrier, MCI had no experience in installing and operating local, central office switches; and winning certifications for switched service was an arduous state-by-state process.

MCImetro Revenue Ramp-Up

Despite start-up difficulties, MCImetro persevered. By the end of the third quarter, MCImetro had networks in seventeen cities with seven switches and 2,234 miles of fiber. Revenue quickly ramped-up to $22 million by the second quarter of 1995. The bulk of this revenue was for dedicated access but, with the installation of MCImetro's first local switch in Baltimore in the second quarter of 1995, revenue from switched services began to contribute.

In Baltimore, MCImetro installed a DMS 500, a new digital switching platform developed by Northern Telecom for the CLEC market. The DMS 500 combines the functionality of a Class 5 central office switch with that of a tandem switch. Many of the parts are interchangeable with the existing DMS 100 central office switch and the DMS 250 tandem switch. This combination is not only more efficient, it was a better match for the CLEC business model than the traditional large LEC model.

MCImetro had seven switches and networks operational in seventeen cities by the end of the third quarter of 1995. Revenue for the quarter reached $29 million. Things, however, were not going well. The revenue was illusionary, and the costs were burdensome. Other long distance carriers were generally not willing to buy access from MCImetro, and the so-called "revenue" was simply a shift of money from one pocket to another. Money simply transferred from MCI Communications' core business to MCImetro.

MCImetro was originally structured to be fully staffed with its own engineering, operations and sales force. MCI changed course and decided to fold all sales functions into the core company's established sales force which would pitch bundled local and long distance services primarily to MCI's business customers.[55]

MCImetro was a drag on MCI's stock price.[56] By August 1995, MCI Chairman Bert Roberts was publicly discussing ways to ease the financial pain.[57] This included joint ventures, partial sale of MCImetro or spinning it off from the core business with its own tracking stock.[58]

By November, MCI decided to reorganize MCImetro as a unit within MCI Communications, rather than a separate subsidiary.[59] MCImetro CEO Parsons was assigned to other projects. MCImetro COO, Nate Davis, continued to run operations but now reported to the head of MCI's network business unit.

MCI emphasized that it was not altering its strategy for entering the local exchange markets and would continue to invest capital in building fiber networks but would seek to rely more heavily on resale of LEC facilities.[60] It was, after all, by reselling AT&T service that MCI had originally entered the long distance business. MCI bitterly challenged regulators that if they truly wanted a competitive local exchange market to develop, they must allow CLECs to purchase for resale wholesale LEC local service at discounts of 30%.[61]

MCImetro completed the year 1995 with revenue of $108 million, ten local switches and networks operating in 25 cities. Either these networks had been scaled back or MCI had never really meant that it intended to spend the entire $2 billion in phase one. MCImetro capital expenditures over the 24 months totaled $365 million.[62]

MCImetro Disappoints

For most CLECs, MCI's performance had been a disappointment. While they had contributed resources in support of industry issues, the leadership had been unexpectedly weak. Eager to clear regulatory hurdles before the Maryland PUC and begin operation of its Baltimore switch, MCI negotiated a reciprocal compensation (charge for terminating traffic that originated on the competitor's network) agreement with Bell Atlantic which CLECs considered onerous.[63] When a modified form of the Maryland deal was invoked to set the terms for reciprocal compensation in Pennsylvania, it was clear that an unwanted precedent had been established; and CLEC criticism of MCImetro became vocal.[64]

CLECs were also upset by MCI's call for deep-discounted wholesale rates for re-sold LEC local service. While CLECs favored discounts, they feared that if excessively generous terms were granted, the value of CLEC alternative networks would decrease. If companies like AT&T and MCI could enter the local exchange market by merely reselling LEC service, they would have no need for CLEC facilities.

If, as was more likely, the state PUCs rejected MCI's call for deep discounts, MCI (and with it the whole competitive industry) simply came off as appearing weak. It suggested that CLECs were fundamentally unviable without unreasonably biased rules in their favor. This was not the bold leadership that CLECs had expected of MCI. MCI was no longer the reckless, risk-it-all entity of Bill McGowan's heyday.

MCImetro was not MCI's only problem. The company's position gyrated wildly as it stopped and started two different wireless strategies and an on-line service. In response to the charge that its behavior was erratic, MCI CEO Bert Roberts told *Business Week* magazine that these changes demonstrated a strength—flexibility. "We're quick to move forward and quick to pull back when we have to," he said.[65]

Business Week's response: "Now, Roberts just needs to hope that it takes the local phone companies longer to figure out the long-distance market than it takes MCI to figure out its new businesses."[66]

City Signal

City Signal of Grand Rapids, Michigan played an important role in the transition of CAPs to switched service CLECs. City Signal had its origins in a GTE Corporation design project for a fiber network to carry traffic between long distance carriers' Points of Presence in the Grand Rapids area. In June 1989, after a two-year design effort, GTE decided not to carry out the project.

One of the proposed customers, long distance reseller TeleDial America, formed City Signal to carry out construction of the network. Both TeleDial America and City Signal were controlled by Ron VanderPol. One of the original network designers, Brad Evans, became President of City Signal.

The Grand Rapids network became operational on October 1, 1990. By 1994, City Signal had eight networks in four states. The networks included four tandem switches. From the beginning City Signal included tandem switching in its network to provide switched access for TeleDial America and other long distance carriers.

On April 5, 1994, City Signal announced that it intended to compete for local switched service and was applying to the Michigan State Public Service Commission to provide basic local and toll service in the Grand Rapids area under Michigan's newly passed Telecommunications Act.[67] City Signal President Brad Evans said, "Local telephone service is the next logical step in our ongoing commitment to Grand Rapids telecommunications users ... City Signal's entry into the local phone service market will complement our current product line and provide a full range of service options for our customers."[68]

Surprisingly, City Signal claimed that it would even provide broad phone service, not just for business and multi-line users, but even for single residential telephones. It proposed to do this by leasing local loops from Ameritech's Michigan Bell Telephone Company. Evans said that City Signal would file tariffs for basic residential rates that were five percent lower than those of Ameritech and business rates that were twenty percent lower.[69] An Ameritech spokesman said, "We'll open up the local loop, and in turn we want the freedom to compete in the long-distance arena ..."[70] He also suggested that City Signal should be required to contribute to subsidize universal service as well as provide for emergency services and services for the handicapped, such as the hearing impaired.

City Signal/US Signal

To carry out its new strategy City Signal and TeleDial America were combined into a single entity, US Signal. Jim Voelker the Vice Chairman of City Signal became the President of US Signal. Voelker, had co-founded a national fiber optic carrier's carrier, Digital Signal. He had served as its CEO from 1985 to 1990 and hence knew the requirements of both the local and the long distance markets.

He knew what he wanted from his switch vendor. In order to deliver local services, City Signal planned to replace its Grand Rapids tandem with a grouping of local and tandem switches—DMS 100/200/250—from Northern Telecom. However, Northern Telecom, realizing that this need for combined local and tandem capability was an emerging requirement for CLECs in general, created a new product, the DMS 500 multi-functional switch platform, incorporating elements of the entire DMS family of switches.

City Signal's out-of-state networks were offered for sale. Networks in Detroit and Indianapolis were sold to TCG; and networks in Memphis and Nashville were sold to NEXTLINK,a new CLEC owned by billionaire cellular pioneer, Craig McCaw, in January 1995. In April 1995, Jim Voelker left US Signal and moved to Seattle to become the President of NEXTLINK.

Entry into residential phone service proved elusive and unfeasible under existing conditions. However, entry into business phone service, particularly for colleges and hospitals was successful; and by August 1995, US Signal was serving 1,000 business lines on its Grand Rapids switch and had orders pending for 2,800 more business lines.

U S Signal entered into discussions with the aggressively expanding Brooks Fiber Properties which wanted to acquire only the CLEC operations. An agreement was reached to sell the City Signal assets to Brooks, and the transaction was completed in January 1996.

Brooks Fiber Properties

The most unexpected company to emerge as the competitive industry made the transition from CAP to CLEC was St. Louis-based Brooks Fiber Properties. In 1993, following his two-year stint as President of the industry association, ALTS, John Shapleigh was still searching for a way to become a player in the competitive telecommunications industry. Shapleigh felt he knew how to create a successful competitive company but did not know where to find the money to fund it.

Among others, he talked with two wealthy St. Louis area businessmen, Robert A. Brooks and James C. Allen. In 1992 they had sold their cable company, Cencom Cable Associates, which they founded in 1982, to Crown Media (an affiliate of Hallmark Cards, Inc.) for nearly $1 billion. At the time Cencom Cable was the 21st-largest cable company in the country, and Brooks was serving as its Chairman and CEO while Allen was President and COO.

Brooks was looking for his next opportunity through Brooks Telecommunications Company which he had founded in 1991. Brooks Telecommunications, however, was not addressing CLEC opportunities; it was considering a range of possibilities from cable system construction to rural telephone company acquisition to international fiber network construction. Shapleigh kept feeding Brooks and Allen data about the growing CLEC industry, hoping to gain their attention. That happened in September 1993 when MFS Communications went public. The tremendous response to the MFS IPO had venture capital investors and investment bankers excited about finding more CLEC investment vehicles. Now actively courted by venture capitalists, Brooks, Allen, Shapleigh and their associates created a formal business plan and formed Brooks Fiber Properties, Inc.

Brooks Fiber Properties, Inc. was formed on November 10, 1993, and initially capitalized with $41 million from seven venture capital firms—Centennial Funds, Burr, Egan, Deleage & Co., Fleet Equity Partners, Media/Communications Partners, One Liberty Group, Norwest Equity Partners and Providence Media Partners.[71]

Brooks Fiber's Small Market Strategy

Since Brooks Fiber Properties was late to the CLEC game, they decided that they would avoid the major cities where the large, established competitors were established. Instead, Brooks Fiber Properties would acquire or build networks in Tier II and Tier III cities (population 2,000,000 to 250,000).

Brooks set a goal of attaining networks in ten cities per year and moved quickly with a series of acquisitions in its target markets. On January 31, 1994, it acquired from Massachusetts-based FiveCom Associates, Inc. an operating network in Springfield and networks under development in Hartford and Providence. On October 14, 1994, it acquired Phoenix FiberLink with networks in California, a long-distance resell business and a telemanagement business.[72]

New network construction was also begun in Oklahoma City, Oklahoma, Little Rock, Arkansas and Knoxville, Tennessee. From a standing start at the beginning of the year Brooks Fiber Properties ended 1994 with networks operational in five cities, three cities under construction and revenue of $2.8 million. On March 15, 1995, Brooks Fiber Properties acquired PSO/ MetroLink, Public Service of Oklahoma's network in Tulsa. Brooks Fiber developed a close relationship with MCImetro, and in September 1995 the two companies entered into an agreement to jointly develop and expand the existing Brooks network in the San Jose area.[73]

Brooks entered switch services in 1995, installing a switch in its Sacramento, California, network and through acquisition of City Signal and its switch in Grand Rapids, Michigan. By year-end, Brooks had networks operational in 11 cities, under development in ten more and revenue of $14 million. The pro forma 1995 results for Brooks, including the Brooks Telecommunications Company and City Signal acquisitions, yielded networks operational in 13 cities, under development in twelve more and total revenues of $23.3 million.

On The Road To Riches

Although members of the competitive communications fraternity routinely made disparaging remarks about the marketing abilities of the LEC monopolies, there were, within the vast telephone industry, energetic individuals with relevant marketing skills and latent entrepreneurial instincts. Brooks Fiber decided to tap this source for a new President and Chief Operating Officer.

In April 1995, Brooks Fiber recruited D. Craig Young from Ameritech where he was the Vice President of Sales Operations for Custom Business Services. Prior to joining Ameritech, Young had held several similar positions with another RBOC, U S WEST, for seven years. In his RBOC positions, Young was not involved just in marketing but had management responsibility for voice and data sales, engineering and pricing activities for large commercial and government customers and full profit and loss responsibility for more than $650 million in revenue and direction of a work force of more than 400 employees.[74]

That a small start-up CLEC like Brooks Fiber could attract such high-level talent from a secure position in a major RBOC was significant. As the competitive industry grew, the lure of exciting roles and the potential reward of stock and options in CLECs destined to go public proved powerful incentives to drain talent from the traditional carriers into the new industry.

Competitive Industry Revenue Growth In 1994 & 1995

During 1994, the leadership of the competitive industry was making the transition from CAP to CLEC; and by 1995 the CLEC industry was in full swing. With the transition, MFS and TCG still dominated, as they had the CAP industry.

Leading Competitive Companies Ranked By 1994 Total Revenue[75]

	Company	Revenue ($million)
1.	MFS Communications	$286.7
2.	Teleport Communications Group	100.0
3.	IntelCom Group	73.9
4.	Intermedia Communications of Florida	14.3
5.	Eastern TeleLogic	12.0
6.	Electric Lightwave	8.2
7.	LOCATE (Microwave)	6.0
8.	Brooks Fiber Properties	2.8
9.	City Signal	2.6
10.	PSO/MetroLink	2.5
	Others (31)	26.4
	Industry Total	$535.4

<u>Lending Competitive Companies Ranked By 1995 Total Revenue</u>

	Company	Revenue ($million)
1.	MFS Communications	$583.2
2.	Teleport Communications Group	134.7
3.	IntelCom Group	122.4
4.	MCImetro	108.0
5.	Intermedia Communications of Florida	38.6
6.	GST Telecom	22.6
7.	Brooks Fiber Properties	19.9
8.	Eastern TeleLogic	17.0
9.	Electric Lightwave	15.7
10.	NEXTLINK Communications	7.6
	Others (26)	<u>76.7</u>
	Industry Total	$1,146.4

Industry revenue exceeded $1 billion for the first time in 1995. Although this was only 1% of the $100 billion local telephone market, it represented an important milestone and a sign that the incumbent telephone companies would eventually face significant competition in their core markets. With just seventy central-office-grade switches in service and local switched service competition allowed in only a few states, CLEC revenue from switched services was nevertheless growing rapidly.

In addition to adding switched services revenue, CLECs had become much more complex and diversified than CAPs had been. Not only did some CLECs derive revenue from lines-of-business, such as systems integration, which were not necessarily telecommunications services, the services themselves had become more varied. CLEC Telecom Services now included revenue from sources such as long distance, resold carrier services, shared tenant services and data services in addition to the services traditionally associated with telephone companies.

CLEC Service Mix In 1995

MFS epitomized the increasing complexity of CLECs. MFS' total revenue of $583.2 million included contributions from MFS Network Technologies whose construction projects ranged from network development to automated highway systems.

Of the $498.2 million in Telecom Services revenue, only 35% came from its American CAP network operations. The acquired shared tenant service companies—Centex TeleManagement and RealCom —accounted for 49%. Data services accounted for 10%. Switched services and international operations each contributed 3%.

Overall the CLEC industry Telecom Services Revenue for 1995 was $1.1 billion. The breakdown by category shows that the original CAP revenue sources—dedicated access and private line—were still predominate, but with revenue from long distance and switched services (including reselling) becoming increasingly significant.

<u>1995 CLEC Industry Telecom Services By Category</u>[76]

Telecom Services Category	Revenue (%)
Dedicated Access & Private Line	47%
Long Distance	23%
Local Switched Service	15%
Switched Access	7%
Data Services	6%
Miscellaneous Telecom Service	2%
	100%

Footnotes Chapter 10: From CAP To CLEC

[1] Sources: Company financial reports and Connecticut Research, Inc. estimates.

[2] "ALT/CAP Access & Switched Services Market," *Connecticut Research Report On Competitive Telecommunications,* January, 1, 1994 v.2, No. 1, 1.

[3] Tier I LEC revenue from *The Armis Analyst 1994 Yearbook* by Coyle Research, Lake Bluff, II, 4, plus non-Tier I LEC and CAP revenue estimates by Connecticut Research.

[4] "The Access Market - Part II & The Private Line Market," *Connecticut Research Report On Competitive Telecommunications,* March, 1, 1994 v.2, No. 3, 1.

[5] *FCC Deployment Update, End Of Year 1993,* Industry Analysis Division, Common Carrier Bureau, FCC, 39-41 with edits by Connecticut Research Inc.

[6] "FCC Opens Local Exchange To Alternate Carriers," *Lightwave,* November, 1992, 1.

[7] TCG Press Release, November 28, 1989.

[8] "Unit Of Teleport Communications Purchases Telephone Switches And Agrees To Manage Internal Communications Of Merrill Lynch," TCG Press Release, March 13, 1990.

[9] "The Local Call Goes Up For Grabs," *The New York Times,* December 29, 1991, Section 3.

[10] "Teleport Communications Group's New Digital Switch Delivers Enhanced Local Switched Service To Chicago; Businesses To Benefit From Superior Disaster Avoidance Capabilities," TCG Press Release, May 26, 1993.

[11] "Teleport Communications Group Launches 'The Other Local Phone Company™' For New York," TCG Press Release, July 13, 1994.

[12] "TCG Is Nation's First Competitive Local Carrier To Obtain Peer Telephone Interconnection; Agreement Reached On Mutual Compensation," TCG Press Release, July 1, 1994.

[13] "1994 Local Telecommunications Competition" (Glastonbury, CT, Connecticut Research, Inc.) 1994, VII-97.

[14] TCG Preliminary Prospectus, Merrill Lynch & Co., Morgan Stanley & Co., Donaldson, Lufkin & Jenrette, Lehman Brothers, Deutsche Morgan Grenfell, June 1996, 4.

[15] "Competitive Access Providers (CAPs) Termed 'Endangered Species' Unless CAPs Pursue New Vision, Says Robert Annunziata, President Of TCG And Founder Of The $Billion Dollar CAP Industry," TCG Press Release, April 7, 1994.

[16] "Redefining Local Exchange Competition," The Fifth Annual Conference On Local Exchange Competition, sponsored by Telecommunications Reports and Telco Competition Reports, Washington, D.C., April 8, 1994.

[17] "MFS Intelenet Launches Full Service Phone Company Providing Both Local And Long Distance," MFS Press Release, October 5, 1993.

[18] "MFS And Centex Sign Merger Agreement," MFS Press Release, May 2, 1994.

[19] "MFS Communications Company Announces Merger Agreement With RealCom Office Communications; Will Become Part Of Intelenet," MFS Press Release, May 17, 1994.

[20] Preliminary Prospectus For MFS Communications Company, Inc., Salomon Brothers, Inc., Goldman, Sachs & Co., Smith Barney Inc., UBS Securities, June 5, 1996, 39.

[21] "IntelCom Group Announces Record 3rd Quarter Revenues Of $16 Million, Up 95 Percent From A Year Earlier," IntelCom Group Press Release, Aug. 10, 1994.

[22] 1994 IntelCom Group Annual Report, 14.

[23] Ibid., 5.

[24] "IntelCom Group Announces Record Second Quarter Revenues Of $25.9 Million, Up 124 Percent From 1994 Quarter," IntelCom Press Release, May 17, 1995.

[25] "IntelCom Group Announces Record First Quarter Revenues Of $24.6 Million, Up 151 Percent From 1994 Quarter," IntelCom Group Press Release, Feb. 15, 1995.

[26] 1994 IntelCom Group Annual Report, 5.

[27] Ibid.

[28] IntelCom Group Press Release, April 24, 1995.

[29] "IntelCom Group Announces Search For President And Chief Executive Officer; Reorganization As U.S. Company," IntelCom Group Press Release, April 27, 1995.

[30] "IntelCom Group Appoints Cellular/PCS Pioneer As New President And Chief Executive Officer," IntelCom Group Press Release, May 30, 1995.

[31] "Turnaround Bound," *tele.com,* March 22, 1999, 48-49.

[32] IntelCom Group 1995 3Q Report.

[33] Ibid.

[34] "MCI's Entry Into Local Exchange Market Could Speed Telecom Industry Changes," *Telco Competition Report,* January 6, 1994, v.3, no.1, 4.

[35] "MCI Buys WU Unit," *Telephony,* March 12, 1990, 3.

[36] "MCI Is Planning Local Networks In Major Cities," *The Wall Street Journal,"* December 12, 1993.

[37] "MCI Proposes A $20 Billion Capital Project," *The Wall Street Journal,"* January 5, 1994, A3.

[38] Ibid.

[39] "MCI Metro Deploys Switches For Local Fight," *Telephony,* March 13, 1995.

[40] Ibid.

[41] "MCI Is Planning Local Networks In Major Cities,"

[42] "MCI Proposes A $20 Billion Capital Project," *The Wall Street Journal,"* January 5, 1994, A4.

[43] "MCI Planning Local Networks In Major Cities,"

[44] "MCI's Entry Into Local Exchange Market Could Speed Telecom Industry Changes," *Telco Competition Report,* January 6, 1994, v.3, no.1, 2.

[45] "MCI Makes $2B Local Call," *Network World,* January 10, 1994, v.11, no.2, 95.

[46] Ibid.

[47] "MCI Metro Asks For Authority To Offer Switched Local Services In Five States," *Telco Competition Report,* October 13, 1994, v.3, no.21, 3.

[48] Ibid.

[49] "MCI's Local Plans Get National Attention From Anxious Telcos," *Telco Business Report,* March 14, 1994, 7

[50] *Telco Business Report,* March 14, 1994, 9.

[51] "MCI Details Local Plans," *InformationWeek,* May 2, 1994, 16.

[52] "MCI Metro Updates Peach Of A Plan For Local Loop Service," *Local Competition Report*, May 2, 1994, 4.

[53] "MCI Metro Updates Peach Of A Plan For Local Loop Service," *Local Competition Report*, May 2, 1994, 3.

[54] "MCI Seeks New Financing Plan For Venture," *Network World,* August 14, 1995, 16.

[55] "*1998 Annual Report On Local Telecommunications Competition,"* (Chicago, IL: New Paradigm Resources Group, Inc. and Connecticut Research, Inc., 1998, MCI - Pg. 2 of 18.

[56] F. J.. Governali, MCI Communications Report, CS First Boston, October, 24, 1995.

[57] "MCI Restructures, Plunges Into Wireless," *Telephony,* August 7, 1995.

[58] "MCI Seeks New Financing Plan For Venture," *Network World*, August 14, 1995, 15.

[59] "MCImetro Tariffs Approved By Maryland PSC," *Telecommunications Reports*, November 13, 1995.

[60] Ibid.

[61] "MCI Reveals Local Market-Entry Plan, Future Arguments For State Commissions," *Telecommunications Reports,* September 2, 1996.

[62] MCI Communications Corporation Form 10-K, December 31, 1996, 13.

[63] "MCImetro Tariffs Approved By Maryland PSC," *Telecommunications Reports,* November 13, 1995.

[64] "PA. PUC OKs Controversial Reciprocal Compensation Approach," *State Telephone Regulation Report,* December 14, 1995.

[65] "MCI Is Swarming Over The Horizon," *Business Week,* February 19, 1996, 69.

[66] Ibid.

[67] "City Signal Seeks Competition In Basic Telephone Service," City Signal Press Release, April 5, 1994.

[68] Ibid.

[69] "Alternate Provider Ready To Challenge Ameritech In Michigan," *Local Competition Report,* April 18, 1994, 4.

[70] Ibid. , 5.

[71] Prospectus for Brooks Fiber Properties, Inc. Senior Discount Notes, Goldman Sachs & Co., Bear, Stearns & Co. Inc., Salomon Brothers, Inc., February 16, 1996, 5.

[72] Ibid., F-13.

[73] Ibid., 22.

[74] Ibid. 49.

[75] Sources: Company financial reports and Connecticut Research, Inc. estimates.

[76] "1995/6 Local Telecommunications Competition," (Glastonbury, CT, Connecticut Research, Inc.) 1995, I-5.

11. THE INTERNET SURPRISE

Its All Just Ones and Zeros ... Isn't It?

For many years, the, "data business," however one might choose to define that term, was a source of envy and frustration for all telecommunications carriers, including long distance carriers, LECs and CLECs. It was not that traditional carriers were not in the data transport business. AT&Tleased its first modem (a device for sending digital data over an analog network) in 1958, thereby inaugurating data transmission over the public switched network[1].

Over the intervening years, data traffic became an increasing component of both switched and unswitched networks. Much of the volume on the public switched network was really composed of fax or modem data traffic. In the dedicated transport world, the market was driven, to a degree, by the growing needs of high-speed data applications such as computer networking and LAN interconnection.

Communications strategists generally supported the assumption that all communications would ultimately be carried in digital form; and it became an industry cliché that, "Once it's digital, it doesn't matter if its voice, data or video ... It's all just ones and zeros." The invocation of that phrase was the precursor of many business failures. Nevertheless, pundits predicted that one day AT&T and IBM would fight it out for dominance of a unified voice/data/video universe. Something else happened.

Evolution Toward An All-Digital Public Network

As anticipated, the public switched telephone network evolved from a totally analog system to a system that was increasingly digital at the core—switches and trunk circuits—and only analog on the edges, at the local loop and individual telephone level. The Bell System's last big push as a monopoly under AT&T was an attempt to bring the local loop and the telephone into the digital world. AT&T began the promotion of a national roll-out of this service, called Integrated System Digital Network (ISDN).

Ubiquitous deployment of ISDN would have created a totally digital system in which every telephone was a digital device and both voice and data would flow as co-mingled bits through the network from beginning to end. The Bell System initiative was disrupted by divestiture, and ISDN became a niche service rather than a universal replacement for basic telephone service.

AT&T's agreement to breakup the Bell System and divest itself of the RBOCs was, at least in part, intended to free it from the presumed more pedestrian business of local telephone operations so that it could enter more quickly into the glamorous world of computers and data communications.

It did not go well. AT&T's failed attempt in the mid-1980s to commercialize the computers developed in its famous research laboratories was a major disappointment. A subsequent attempt to become a force in the computer industry, through acquisition of the NCR corporation, proved disastrous. .

LEC Irritation And RBOC Frustration

The problem for most telecommunications carriers was that they were not participating in the high-margin, high-growth aspects of the "data business."

It was particularly irritating to the LECs that all around them companies with some kind of relationship to data communications were experiencing sustained annual revenue growth that often exceeded 20-30%. Meanwhile, their telephone businesses seemed limited to a 5-6% annual revenue growth, basically constrained by an underlying annual population growth rate of 2-3%. Even with expanded telephone usage and a few enhanced services, LECs had a very difficult time envisioning greater than single-digit growth of their annual revenues.

RBOCs, in particular, barred by the terms of the Bell System breakup from manufacturing, could only watch in frustration as a company like Cisco Systems could start from nothing and build a multi-billion dollar business in a few years by producing a router - a device allowing communication between LANs with different protocols. Cisco Systems, formed by a group of computer scientists from Stanford University to commercialize the technology they developed to integrate a campus-wide network of LANs, shipped its first router in March 1986. In less than eight years, Cisco had revenue in excess of $1 billion with operating margins above 40%. In a dozen years, the market capitalization of Cisco's common stock would exceed $200 billion ... equal to 50% of the combined stock market value of all the RBOCs.

The obvious solution to achieving better growth rates seemed to be for the telecommunications carriers to capture more of the revenue related to data communications and enhanced data services. Most carriers formed and reformed organizations and departments devoted to the "data business," but without obtaining significant additions to their core telecommunications revenues. Success in the "data business" proved illusive.

What We Need Are A Few Good Technologies

The technologists had some suggestions. What was needed were new network technologies that would be more efficient, support higher transport speeds than traditional switched voice circuits, be more flexible than point-to-point, dedicated lines and offer more opportunities for added features and services. What was needed were technologies to overlay or replace the existing circuit-switched telephone network.

There were a number of candidate technologies generally lumped under the titles packet-switching or cell-based switching. In a circuit-switched network, the whole capacity of a circuit is available for the duration of the call, whether or not anyone is speaking (or sending data). Most of the time the line is idle, waiting for something to transmit.

Like voice traffic, most data traffic is intermittent, not continuous. In fact, data traffic tends to come in "bursts," requiring a great deal of capacity on the line but only for a brief time. Unlike voice traffic, which requires real-time transmission, data bits can wait for a pause in transmission because the computer at the other end can store and process and doesn't care if the bits do not arrive in real-time or even in the right order.

Packet-switching is a technology which exploits these characteristics of data traffic and forms the data into groups of packets, each containing its own routing information. By interweaving (multiplexing) the packets, multiple data "conversations" can share the same physical circuit, making full use of its capacity. Because each packet carries its own addressing, packets can travel multiple physical circuits to arrive at the same destination (virtual circuit), making full use of all network transmission paths and bypassing circuit outages.

Multiple packet-switched technologies, with different characteristics, began to be developed to meet a variety of data transmission needs. These included frame relay and Asynchronous Transfer Mode (ATM)—each of which was born in the development of the standards for ISDN—and Internet Protocol (IP) and Switched Multimegabit Data Service (SMDS).

Switched Multimegabit Data Service (SMDS) was the technology selected by the RBOCs and funded for development in their jointly-owned Bellcore Research laboratory. This highly functional, high-speed switched data service, though expensive, was viewed as the ultimate technology that would put the RBOCs in the driver's seat as the future providers of enhanced data communications services.

Dreaming Of A Shared IP Network

Dr. Michael Viren came to the world of data communications by an indirect route. Educated as a mechanical engineer and a Ph.D. economist, he spent ten years in academia, teaching at the University of Kansas and the University of Missouri-Columbia. He worked for a while as the Director of the Utility Division of the Missouri Public Service Commission where he wrote their state order to de-tariff telephone equipment after the *Carter Phone* Decision.

A project linking the University of Missouri's computer local area networks (LANs) over router-based wide area networks (WANs) proved to be more fun. Viren migrated to the world of data communications and started his own consulting company, designing and building LANs and WANs all over Missouri, Iowa, Nebraska and Wisconsin.

Most of his customers had at least one remote business office which needed a link between its LAN and a computer center at headquarters. Viren conceived of a shared WAN based on the Internet Protocol (IP) as a low-cost means to provide data transport for these customers. IP was the protocol that had been invented by ARPANET's Bob Kahn and Vint Cerf in 1974 at the Advanced Research Project office of the Department of Defense to link disparate computers over a collection of networks. ARPANET, a national network linking university and other major computer centers, began operating in 1969[2] and ultimately became *The Internet.*

Unable to raise enough capital to build his dream network, Viren went to work in August 1986 for the GTE telephone company as a specialist in WANs and LANs. He tried to persuade GTE to bring out IP networks as a data service offering. GTE was not interested and decided to retreat from the few data transport services they had started. Viren's area was shut down, and he was offered openings in the GTE operations in Indianapolis or Tampa. It had been a cold winter; Viren's family chose Florida.

Viren found GTE's telephone operations in Florida to be slow and bureaucratic. In bids for high-speed, dedicated circuits, they kept getting beaten by an up-start, small competitive communications company called Intermedia Communications of Florida. He went to see them and found he had some contacts. The General Counsel, Jim Burt, was his former student; and Richard Anthony, the Senior VP of Marketing and Strategic Planning, was the former assistant city manager of Columbia, Missouri.

Although Intermedia Communications was one of the oldest competitive companies, it was still struggling to establish itself. It had not made the transition to CLEC and was almost totally dependent on dedicated transport service offerings which were under price pressure. Intermedia established its prices as discounts below the tariffed prices set by its major competitors in Florida, BellSouth and GTE. The price umbrella was collapsing. A DS-1 circuit, which had been a $1,000 a month when Intermedia entered the market, was now down to $350 a month. Furthermore, Intermedia, a one-state operation, was vulnerable to larger multi-state CLECs like MFS and TCG that were beginning to move into Florida.

Intermedia liked Viren's idea of a shared IP WAN, as a new product offering; and he was hired in February 1991 as Director of Product Development. Along with other duties, such as writing software to support the company's back office operations, Viren set to work on development of a shared data network.

The telecommunications industry was buzzing with discussion about advanced data offerings, primarily for interconnection of the now ubiquitous corporate LAN. It was apparent that most corporate personal computers would be attached to LANs and that these LANs would have communications links, including high-speed data links to other LANs. It seemed clear that some packet technology would be the big winner in this application. A telecommunications company providing the offerings might become an important player in data service. However, it wasn't clear which technology to choose.

Looking For The Right Box

It was hard going. Available equipment was too expensive. The best Viren could find was made by StrataCom of Campbell, California. It supported frame relay, but not IP or SMDS; and it cost the equivalent of $1,200 per digital voice circuit. Viren had calculated that his network would need to produce five cents per month for every dollar of invested capital. At this price, the service would need to produce $60 per month per digital voice circuit just to cover the cost of the box. Something four times cheaper was needed.

Williams Telecommunications Group (WilTel), using the StrataCom equipment on its national fiber and digital microwave network and serving customers with enough nodes to make the economics work, became the first long distance company with a frame relay offering.[3] Frame relay is related to a much older packet-switched technology called X.25. Developed in an era of low quality networks, X.25 has a protocol containing extensive error checking and re-transmission of damaged packets.

Frame relay, taking advantage of networks upgraded with fiber optics and other lower-noise transmission, foregoes extensive checking and relies on intelligence in the computer to determine that re-transmission is needed. In the event of a problem, packets are simply discarded and all unacknowledged packets transmitted again. These simplifications greatly speed up the transmission process.

More carriers began to bring out offerings. By Fall of 1991, frame relay was being offered by five long distance carriers: WilTel, BT Tymnet, CompuServe, Graphnet and Sprint; and MCI had announced service for early 1992. Even two RBOCs, NYNEX and

Pacific Bell, had announced that they would tariff frame relay offerings in 1992.[4]

A year had passed and Intermedia still had no data networking offering. Viren decided to give up looking for the right box and, for now, simply try to be a reseller of a carrier's service. The obvious carrier was frame-relay pioneer, WilTel. WilTel had used frame relay to transform its image from simple fiber transport supplier to high-tech data communications company. Dr. Viren went to visit WilTel in an attempt to negotiate a deal for Intermedia to purchase frame relay transport at wholesale rates and resell the service at retail. WilTel turned him down flat.

Cascade Communications

As he was leaving the WilTel building, Viren was stopped by two engineers who said that they thought that they could supply the equipment for Intermedia to create its own cost-effective, frame relay network.

One of the engineers was Gururaj "Desh" Deshpande, who was starting his own company which, in August 1991, he named Cascade Communications. Deshpande's basic conviction was that all the PCs in the world would one day be linked to each other over a large public network. "It didn't really matter if it was IP, frame relay or ATM. I simply knew in 1990 that every computer would have to get connected to every other computer in the world."[5]

"Desh" set out to develop a multi-functional switching platform that could address all the different packet technologies. By January 1992, "Desh" was ready to demonstrate his switch. At the ComNet '92 show in Washington, D.C., he invited Viren to come to his hotel room at the Hyatt for the demo. He had rigged up three prototype boxes—two in the bedroom and one in the bathroom. The estimated price, the equivalent of $200-300 per voice channel, met Viren's requirement precisely.

Viren placed the first order for what would be called the Cascade STDX-6000 in June 1992. (Cascade Communications was the world leader in frame relay equipment when it was acquired by Ascend Communications in 1997.)

Wait 'Til The Sun Shines

Viren ordered equipment for installation in Orlando, Tampa and Miami; and Intermedia initiated its frame relay offering in August 1992. Viren trained the sales force himself and sent them out. There were no sales. The customers did not understand the offering.

Viren called on the prospective customers himself to see what the trouble was. The idea of replacing dedicated, point-to-point circuits with frame relay seemed odd to the customers. Viren went to a blackboard and sketched a cloud with several customer locations linking into the cloud via short local dedicated links ... only one for each location. The cloud designation was a standard device to indicate that, within the frame relay network, the transmission path was not constrained to a fixed physical link but that the data could move through the network over multiple paths, forming a virtual circuit ... each port could support multiple virtual circuits.

Viren thought he had gotten through. However, the prospect pointed to the cloud and asked a pointed question in all seriousness.

 "What happens to the cloud if the sun comes out?"

Frame Relay Gains Recognition

Customers began to learn more about frame relay. Frame relay was a hot topic at conferences and seminars. Feeling pressured by the long haul carrier offerings, the seven RBOCs made a joint commitment to frame relay in a May announcement and, during 1992, all tariffed frame relay service offerings. They made it clear that this unexpected move was an interim measure in response to competition and that they were still committed to the "more elegant" solution, SMDS.

Telephony magazine commented editorially that, "To their credit, the (RBOCs have) regrouped and agreed to provide frame relay, in addition to SMDS, in order to meet customers' needs."[6]

Frame relay was no longer completely unknown. After trying all year, Viren finally closed Intermedia's first frame relay sale in December 1992. The customer was a computer store with branches in Tampa, Orlando and Miami. Rushing the installation to completion before Christmas, Viren went home for the holiday feeling smugly pleased with himself.

After several days, he received a call at home from an engineer in the Intermedia Network Control Center. "You know that stuff you sold to the computer store?" he said. "Well I haven't had time to look at the manual yet but there is this red light blinking in the control room and I don't know what it means."

What it meant was that the system had been out since the day after it was installed. Fortunately, the customer had not yet tried to use the system. Viren talked the engineer through the reset process over the phone. Frame relay education, he concluded, was needed in-house as well as with the customer.

Can Frame Relay Save The Company?

Intermedia began to gain some frame relay business, with ten orders in January and ten more in February. In March 1993, Intermedia landed its first out-of-state customer, linking its frame relay network to the gateway of Internet Service Provider, PSI, in Atlanta.[7]

The new cash from frame relay was a Godsend. Revenue from the core dedicated access business continued under pressure. GTE dropped the price umbrella on a DS-1 dedicated circuit down to $150 per month.

Intermedia CEO, Bob Benton, was 63 and ready to retire. David Ruberg was recruited as the new President and CEO. When he arrived in May 1993, Ruberg was almost immediately visited by Jim Crowe of MFS. He wanted to buy Intermedia and threatened that if Ruberg refused, MFS would crush his company. Ruberg found that one of the few bright spots in Intermedia's picture was the new frame relay offering. He worked with Viren to reposition the marketing from a technology approach to an application approach.

Changing Frame Relay Sales Strategy

The two major markets for frame relay were expected to be LAN interconnection and the replacement of the dedicated links for customers with IBM SNA private computer networks. The SNA opportunity had been expected to be large. It was estimated that nearly half of all the data traffic on private networks was IBM SNA.

IBM had conditioned corporate computer managers to demand only dedicated lines in their SNA computer networks. Use of any other transmission would invalidate the IBM service agreement for the network. SNA was an aging computer networking architecture with most transmission at a very slow 9.6 kilobits per second. Replacement of the dedicated lines with frame relay offered an immediate improvement in speed to 56 kilobits per second with a more redundant and less expensive network.

However, even after IBM endorsed the use of packet switching, computer managers were wary of abandoning their familiar dedicated line networks. Sales were difficult. Intermedia decided to de-emphasize the large corporate SNA computer network application. Instead, lower-tech, commercial businesses with multiple locations within the state of Florida (for example law firms) were targeted for LAN interconnection. Intermedia also began working with the state of Florida, on an experimental basis, to show them how their network applications would run better on frame relay.

Although the focus was on in-state applications, potential frame relay candidates frequently had remote locations to which they wanted interconnection. To broaden the reach of Intermedia's frame relay offering, Viren looked to interconnect Intermedia's frame relay network with those of other carriers. The Frame Relay Forum, an industry consortium, had defined standards for a Network-to-Network Interface (NNI) allowing direct interconnection between frame relay networks of different carriers.

Viren tried, without success, to interest BellSouth in establishing a mutual NNI interconnection. Finally GTE, which had joined the frame relay parade in mid 1993, agreed to interconnect with Intermedia's frame relay network. This interconnection in Tampa was the first NNI between a LEC and a competitive company. (In just a few years, the trend would reverse. As its density of nodes in Intermedia's network increased, RBOCs Bell Atlantic and BellSouth, and many other carriers would actively seek to establish NNIs with Intermedia Frame Relay backbone network.)

By year-end 1993, Intermedia had 100 frame relay nodes in 37 cities. By leasing circuits to connect its nodes, Intermedia was able to derive revenue from cities where it had no fiber network, even locations outside the state of Florida. The revenue from "enhanced data services," primarily frame relay, grew to account for a small but measurable 4% of Intermedia's revenue in 1993.[8]

Expanding Intermedia's Reach

Across the country a few small, regional data communications and specialized carrier companies were offering frame relay. Viren organized a meeting of some of these companies—EMI, PacNet and Norlite—at a trade show. Five companies—Intermedia, EMI Communications of Syracuse, NY, PacNet of Seattle, Insinc of Vancover, British Columbia and Southwest Network Services of Austin, Texas— finally agreed to form the UniSPAN Consortium[9] in May 1994. Later the membership would change.

With 30 frame relay switches among them serving 800 customer nodes, the consortium members felt that they were positioned to deploy a higher density of switches in their regions than the large long distance companies would have.

Since a major cost component of frame relay service was the dedicated link from the customer's location to the frame relay "cloud," the consortium expected to be able to offer lower prices due to their higher density of nodes.[10] The consortium would offer national coverage by linking to their two nearest neighbors through NNI gateways. The consortium provided customers one point of contact for ordering and billing, even though their traffic might traverse multiple networks.

The first consortium customer, turned up on May 9, 1994, was an East Coast cable television provider with three nodes in EMI's territory and two in Intermedia's. The consortium network was not without problems. NNI was designed for close switch connections. The link between EMI's frame relay network and Intermedia's stretched all the way from Orlando, Florida to Washington, D.C. and experienced frequent outages. To improve service, the consortium members decided to link their networks in Chicago, where each of the members would locate one of its own switches.

A CLEC First: Intermedia's Frame Relay Success

The degree of Intermedia's success with its frame relay offering was unprecedented, not just to relative CLECs, but for telecommunications carriers in general. By year-end 1994, it was providing frame relay service through 12 frame relay switches to 900 nodes in 336 cities. Intermedia upgraded its switches and expanded its capability to provide cell-based Asynchronous Transfer Mode (ATM) as well as frame relay packet switching.[11]

This didn't mean that Intermedia abandoned all other growth paths. Intermedia acquired a long distance reseller late in 1994; and in early 1995 acquired another CLEC, FiberNet, Inc., with networks in Cincinnati, Ohio and Raleigh-Durham, North Carolina and networks under development in Huntsville, Alabama and St. Louis, Missouri.[12,13] While these additions added significant revenue, the exciting part of Intermedia's revenue growth was its ability to tap the data market.

Revenue from these data services was suddenly producing 16% of Intermedia's 1994 revenue and growing rapidly. Intermedia had demonstrated that data services could produce more than just an incremental addition to the core telecommunications business and could extend Intermedia's business reach far outside the state of Florida.

No Pain, No Gain

Intermedia's success in data services did not come pain free. In the midst of its rapid growth in 1995 problems arose which CEO David Ruberg feared would bring his company to its knees.

A major frame relay customer of Intermedia was a company that did call verification through equipment placed in prisons. This fast-growing company was pulling Intermedia along with it, and soon the company had sixty to seventy prison nodes along the East Coast. When the volume got high, the frame relay network began to experience sudden crashes. When a frame relay network gets congested, either because a switch buffer or interconnecting trunk circuit capacity is exceeded, it simply discards packets. Automatic re-transmission of packets results in "packet storms," if traffic isn't rerouted quickly through the network.

This exposed a weakness of the UniSPAN consortium. The systems were composed of a mix of equipment and linked by trunks operating a variety of speeds. There was no unified network management capability that could "see" through the network to facilitate problem detection and network reconfiguration.

The problem of network crashes was finally overcome by installing upgraded Cascade Communications switches and by developing an end-to-end management capability called ViewSpan. The ViewSpan development was started by EMI, but finished by Intermedia. This experience prompted Intermedia to acquire EMI and to create a more homogeneous network and to reduce its dependence on the UniSPAN consortium.

While frame relay delivered low cost, high speed data transport with great efficiency due to its simplicity, that same simplicity made it vulnerable. Catastrophic crashes of frame relay networks would continue to plague carriers in the future (AT&T in April 1998, UUnet in November 1998 and MCI WorldCom in July 1999).[14]

Developing "Native Speed" LAN Interconnection Offerings

Computer users linked by a LAN to other computers or resources such as printers enjoy a high speed connection which carries their data traffic at very high speed. Computer users at remote locations can be linked to the LAN through a communications gateway, but over relative low speed circuits which impair their ability to exchange data with users or facilities on the LAN. As LANs became ubiquitous in the business world, it was assumed that there would be an increasing interest in linking remote users to the LAN at its full or "native" speed.

 introduced one of the first data offerings in New York City. It was called LAN EXTENDER, and was an integrated product to interconnect early (4 megabits per second) IBM Token Ring LANs at native speed.[15] Whether due to the sales force's lack of familiarity with data or the customers' unwillingness to buy data products from a communications company, the product launch was not successful. There were no sales.

MFS attempted to develop a complete set of native speed LAN inter-connection offerings. MFS designed its offering using the fastest available LAN technology, FDDI, which operates at 100 megabits per second. By using FDDI, MFS could offer interconnection at speeds up to and including native speeds for the three most popular LANs in use, IBM Token Rings at 4 megabits per second and 16 megabits per second, respectively, and Ethernet at 10 megabits per second.

MFS announced its new LAN service on August 20, 1991. The service was only operational on MFS' Houston fiber network, but was planned for roll-out in other cities based on customer demand. The major customer in Houston was the Baylor University Medical Center which needed to connect Ethernet LANs in separated facili-ties and had high-speed requirements including transmission of medical imaging data.

In the announcement, MFS CEO Royce Holland said, "The rapid growth of LANs, the increase in distributed processing and the need for more data delivered to the workstation all have combined to cause the metropolitan area to become a communications bottleneck … While other technologies for transmitting high-speed data have been proposed, including SMDS and SONET, these services still remain in the testing stage …"[16]

FDDI had been developed for LAN operation, and extending it into a wide area WAN application presented some problems. These in-cluded security, integrity, distance and delay characteristics.

Technology Transfer Associates of Houston, which designed the MFS product, dealt with these issues by sending the data over the FDDI LAN in the form of IP packets. Using higher level protocols, TCP/IP, developed for ARPANET, the packets could be routed so that a given site only received those packets meant for it. Routing also allowed packets to pass through gateways to other LANs via wide area technologies.[17]

WilTel representatives at the MFS press conference indicated that they would support access to their frame relay network from MFS' FDDI gateway. This, they said, would allow MFS to bring its ser-vice to cities that were otherwise inaccessible to them. They noted that although their current frame relay network was limited to DS-1, it would soon be upgraded to DS-3 (45 megabits per second).

MFS packaged its LAN service as a user-friendly "turn-key" offering. MFS retained ownership of all equipment, including responsibility for any associated routers, bridges, protocol converters and multiplexers.

They found that this was not enough. Customers, conditioned by full-service computer companies like IBM, expected more of a data communications vendor than just a LAN connector. They expected the vendor to be involved in re-architecting and segmenting LANs, installing bridges and routers prior to linking them and to deal with a myriad of issues, including software problems at higher protocol levels.

It was soon apparent that real success in data services such as LAN interconnection would require staffing technical experts and would draw the telecommunications carriers deeply into computer technology. The resource commitment required was daunting.

MFS Takes The Plunge Into Data Services

MFS was contacted by Al Fenn, Vice President of Business Development and Planning for British Telecom North America, Inc. British Telecom:Tymnet was one of the pioneers attempting to establish itself as a major provider of frame relay service in the United States.

Fenn had also served as President of Tymnet which was the nation's leading X.25 packet switched public data network. His message was simply that by combining packet switching over long haul fiber with its local fiber networks, MFS had a unique opportunity to build a national data communications business. Fenn nominated himself as the man to lead a dedicated business unit to exploit this opportunity.

On January 10, 1992, MFS announced a newly formed company, MFS Datanet, Inc. with Al Fenn as its President. MFS Datanet's stated mission was to, "...develop and market advanced data services..(and)..be responsible for the further development of the MFS high-speed LAN connectivity services introduced last year."[18]

Is There A Market For Native Speed LAN Interconnection?

There was no overwhelming reception for MFS' high speed LAN metropolitan-area interconnection service. Few customers had two locations in a given city that were on an MFS local network and which needed to be linked at native LAN speeds.

Datanet revenues did not ramp up quickly. MFS never directly reported Datanet revenues but did acknowledge that by the fourth quarter of 1992 they were still "immaterial.[19]"

Undeterred, MFS decided that the answer was more investment to expand the offering and to extend its reach by leasing high-speed long distance lines to reach between cities. They reasoned that while customers might not have multiple local, on-net locations whose LANs needed interconnection, it seemed likely that there were potential customers who would like to link the LANs in offices in two different major cities, for example, New York City and Chicago.

In December 1992 MFS announced that it would begin offering, "the first commercially available nationwide network designed specifically to allow companies to interconnect geographically dispersed LANs at native LAN speed." MFS declared that initial service would link Washington, D.C., New York City and Chicago; and that fourteen other cities, served by MFS local networks, would follow over the next five months.[20]

Fenn noted that his company would be flexible and migrate to whatever was the best emerging technology. He said, "MFS Datanet's (LAN interconnect) services function independently of, but in concert with, the still evolving services and standards of SONET, SMDS, Frame Relay and ATM. This protects the customer against network obsolescence caused either by changing requirements or advancing technology."[21]

MFS Finds An ATM Switch

MFS decided that the emerging Asynchronous Transfer Mode (ATM), cell-based switching technology was the right vehicle to carry the high speed LAN interconnection between cities. ATM transport is flexible and scaleable and can carry real-time voice, data and video traffic. While frame relay was still limited to DS-1 speeds, ATM could scale-up to speeds well above the currently fastest FDDI LAN speed of 100 megabits per second.

The problem with rolling out an ATM service was that equipment was not available. Although fourteen companies had announced their intentions to build ATM switches, none were yet commercially available.

Fenn narrowed his search for an ATM switch to two companies. One was under development by BBN Communications of Cambridge, Massachusetts, which had been the leading manufacturer of X.25 packet switches. The other was from a more obscure source, MPR Teltech, the Burnby, British Columbia - based research and development arm of Canadian carrier, BC Tel Group.

Although the MPR Teltech switch was barely emerging from its development stage, it did have twenty site installations; and MFS decided to go with it. Whether BC Tel had the resources for commercial manufacturing was questionable. However, Newbridge Networks of Kanata, Ontario, stepped in to acquire the rights to the MPR Teltech switch in October 1992 and manufacture the switch.[22]

Newbridge was a struggling T-1 multiplexer manufacturer that had nearly gone bankrupt in 1991.[23] Its gamble on the MPR Teltech switch was fortuitous and became one of the linchpins of a remarkable ascendancy to the ranks of a premier provider of equipment to the telecommunications carrier marketplace. The Newbridge version of the switch became the highly successful 36150 Mainstreet ATM switch.

Yes, But Is There An ATM Market?

By December 1992, MFS had ATM switches installed and linked over DS-3 speed (45 megabits per second) lines between Washington, D.C., New York and Chicago.[24] However, only readers of the data communications press knew that the links were ATM-based. MFS maintained a curious silence over the fact that it was using this technology, possibly because it was so far out on the leading edge that it feared failure of the equipment.

By March 1993, MFS was not only operating a core ATM network of switches in the three cities, it had also completed an agreement to link the rest of its fourteen cities through interconnection with WilTel's network.[25] In the May 19, 1993, prospectus for its initial public stock offering, MFS stated tersely that it expected to offer high speed data communications between the networks of all of its cities by the third quarter of the year. There was not a single mention of ATM.

MFS broke its silence on August 4, 1993, and revealed that it had installed and was operating a fully functional, fourteen-city, Asynchronous Transfer Mode (ATM) network.[26] MFS offered testimonials from satisfied customers including a bank that used the service to backup its New York data center in Chicago. The bank said that data transfer operations which previously required nine hours were completed in thirty minutes.[27]

Less noted, but more important, was the testimony of an obscure Internet service provider, UUNET Technologies of Falls Church, Virginia. UUNET, operating a service called Alternet for business users, was providing Internet access for 350 corporate LANs.[28] By moving to MFS' ATM service, they could provide a very fast backbone network whose capacity was scaleable to its customers' needs.

ATM-Based LAN Interconnection For The World

Entering 1994, MFS announced a new five-year, sixty-city expansion plan, including twelve cities outside the United States, with data services being a major driver.[29] MFS President & COO Royce Holland said that MFS' rapid expansion was driven by the need for high-speed data communications and international connectivity.

MFS still saw high-speed LAN interconnection as its primary data service. In fact, it labeled its ATM offerings as a family of "High-Speed LAN Interconnection Services." Fenn told reporters that "High-speed LAN use has put emphasis on ATM."[30] He predicted an explosion of demand for high-speed interconnection and a migration to nearly universal ATM transport that could threaten the market for dedicated leased lines.

Despite MFS' enthusiasm for high-speed LAN interconnection, customer response was not overwhelming. By the time the international link was opened, the service had been offered for seven months; and little more than fifty customers had signed-up.[31]

On February 9, 1994, MFS Datanet initiated international ATM service linking MFS' New York and London offices.[32] MFS indicated that service would soon be expanded to Western Europe and to the Pacific Rim, and that High-Speed LAN interconnection would be offered on an international basis. No long distance carrier yet offered international ATM service, and only WilTel and Sprint had domestic offerings. Industry consultant, Daniel Briere, President of TeleChoice, Inc., noted, "MFS is in a kick-butt mode."[33]

MFS deployed APEX ATM switches from General DataCom, Inc. of Middlebury, Connecticut for its international service, partially because they could interface at European digital protocols. This led to speculation that the 36150 Mainstreet switches from Newbridge Networks might be deficient. Although MFS Datanet denied that they had experienced problems, the rumors continued to circulate and resurfaced later in the year when Newbridge projected lower-than-expected earnings. Newbridge's market capitalization dropped more than $1 billion in one day of frenzied trading.[34]

By May, 1994, MFS' Holland still insisted that MFS Datanet's offering remained focused on LAN-to-LAN connectivity. He called LAN interconnection the "fastest-growing segment of the market," but declined a request to break out revenue figures for the MFS Datanet subsidiary. He did concede that the company was examining other options and noted that the ATM platform was extremely flexible and could support a broad range of services ... including frame relay.[35]

Frame Relay Rules

Frame relay did not turn out to be a transient phenomenon among data communications technologies to be swept aside by ATM or SMDS, as many had predicted. Despite its inability to deliver full native LAN speed connectivity, it remained the favorite technology to replace traditional dedicated lines.

AT&T, the largest U.S. frame relay provider, was swamped with a wave of orders in 1994. By mid-year the unexpected rush was producing long installation delays. To meet the demand, AT&T began an aggressive roll-out program in 1995, installing new frame relay switches at the rate of two a day.[36]

The demand for frame relay transport, whether for LAN interconnection or other data transport applications, greatly exceeded the demand for full native-speed LAN interconnection. MFS moved to meet the market. MFS added Cascade's B-STDX 9000 Multi-service-WAN platform to feed frame relay traffic to its Newbridge Mainstreet and General Datacom APEX ATM switches. On June 21, 1994, MFS Datanet announced that it was offering the first frame-relay-over-ATM service.

Fenn said, "Our Frame Transport Service is ideal for customers who made a commitment to frame relay services yet want a smooth, easy and investment-free migration path to ATM technology as user applications and traffic requirements expand."[37] He also acknowledged, "We had been getting a lot of frame relay requests, and we looked at that and decided to come out with frame relay transport because it rounds out our high-speed interconnection services."[38]

While MFS Datanet's frame-relay-over-ATM service did offer advanced features over standard frame relay transport, MFS rivals privately derided it. MFS, they said, had misjudged the market and had gone a "bridge too far" due to Crowe's infatuation with high technology. Some suggested that MFS' international ATM network would soon become an embarrassingly expensive white elephant.

Suddenly The Internet Drives Data Communications

Carriers everywhere were hit with a surge of data communications business. It was not high-speed LAN interconnection, nor the replacement of dedicated lines by frame relay, nor the migration of IBM SNA-based private data networks that drove this unexpected surge. It was the Internet.

As with nearly everyone, MFS did not see it coming. It wasn't part of a strategic plan. It just happened. MFS' Royce Holland admitted to friends that MFS had been blind-sided. They simply woke up one morning and realized that a good portion of their business was the result of Internet-related events. Some of this was simply demand for traditional leased line and dial-up services, and some was from new opportunities associated with Internet Service Providers who were suddenly flocking to collocate their equipment in the POPs of MFS or any other welcoming CLEC with available space.

On February 15, 1996, MFS Chairman and CEO Jim Crowe gave Wall Street the news during his quarterly Analyst Teleconference. He said:

> ... something *over 25%* of all of MFS' incremental new sales are derived from Internet related services. That's up from *essentially zero* at the beginning of 1995. That's a startling statistic from our point of view. And we think it's one that has significant implications for our future.[39]

Crowe saw a direct analogy between the emerging Internet Service Provider's business and that of a long distance carrier.

> What we call an Internet Service Provider ... is really an Internet long distance company. They lease long haul facilities, add switches—albeit packet switches —rather than circuit switches—and provide service over a long haul backbone using those switches. All of the access to their networks still occurs in the same fashion that access occurs to the voice long distance network. That is substantially through the RBOC network, either using dial-up connections or leased lines ...I would submit to you that, just as in the voice world, when the players are able to bundle local and long distance Internet service provision, there will be a realignment. There will be tremendous opportunity for those that have facilities in the bottleneck portion of that equation which continues to be the local loop...Our facilities in the local loop are no less valuable for the provision of Internet services than they are for the provision of voice services...MFS has the opportunity to see margins that are very different from (those of existing Internet Service Providers).[40]

The Telecommunications Industry Finds A Mass Market For Data

The whole telecommunications industry could now take a different approach to data communications marketing. Rather than the arduous sale of specialized LAN links to fussy, demanding and skeptical computer managers of large corporations, new customer groups had emerged. The last traces of the priesthood of the glass room were being swept away.

Across the board, the CLEC industry increased its efforts in data communications services. TCG, which had begun to experience some success with its re-launched LANLINK offering,[41] now joined the ATM parade. On March 29, 1995, TCG announced that it would offer ATM-based LAN switched data services on a national basis.[42] The service rollout began in New York in July using Cisco Systems' Lightstream ATM switch.[43]

In the new, bandwidth-hungry, frenetic, Internet-driven world the demand was for high-speed circuits as quickly as you could provision them and any old way you could provide them. This was more like the mass market that telecommunications carriers had traditionally enjoyed in the voice world.

In this new world, the value of a separate organization, dedicated to meticulous data communications and systems integration expertise, was no longer obvious. In the third quarter of 1995, MFS Datanet ceased to operate as a separate entity and was folded into MFS Telecom under Ron Beaumont.[44]

The Scramble To Provide The Internet Infrastructure

On the national scene the need to beef-up the elements of the emerging Internet had become apparent, and a dawning awareness of the future dimensions of the prize had carriers fighting for a piece of the action. Efforts to upgrade the National Science Foundation's NSFnet and the Department of Energy's ESNet produced a cat fight among the major long distance carriers.[45]

Every contract was challenged by the losers. AT&T successfully protested the award of a contract to Sprint for upgrading ESFNet because Sprint's proposal was based on an ATM switch that had not yet been built.

Sprint, in turn, attacked the award of a contract to MCI for upgrading NSFnet on the grounds that MCI was simply using federal funds to develop its commercial ATM network.[46]

In addition to scrapping over the Internet backbone, the long distance carriers also fought to win the contracts to provide the Network Access Points ("NAPs") which were, as Sprint noted, "The large-scale switching and management centers for all commercial traffic on the Internet, which is growing at an estimated rate of 20% per month."[47]

The MFS ATM Network Wins

But MFS, with its advanced deployment of ATM switches, was better positioned to win the NAP business than either the LECs or the long distance carriers. By year-end 1995, Crowe was able to report to shareholders the key role that MFS had quietly assumed in Internet gateways.

He said, "The company plays a major role in making the Internet available to users across the nation through sales of data transmission services to Internet service providers. MFS Datanet is also one of several companies that manage the operation of Network Access Points ("NAPs"), through which traffic on the Internet must pass in order to move from one Internet service provider's system to another. MFS developed and manages NAPs that are known as MAE East in Washington, D.C., MAE West in San Jose, California and MAE Chicago in Chicago, Illinois."[48]

A Warning From Bill Gates

During the summer of 1995, Walter Scott, CEO of Peter Kiewit Sons', attended his friend Warren Buffett's biannual executive multi-day retreat. In a mansion outside Dublin, Ireland, Scott and the thirty other rich and powerful participants heard a startling present-ation from Bill Gates and his wife, Melinda French.

Their message was that the Internet was going to be huge beyond anyone's dreams. Gates was moving to reposition Microsoft to meet this new reality. He asserted that traditional telephone powers were going to be hurt by the Internet sucking away data and voice traffic. "Afterwards I sat down with Bill and talked with him about it," Scott said, "my gut feeling was, if you weren't part of it, you were going to be left behind."

Scott was concerned about the potential impact on MFS' core business. Back in Omaha he huddled with Crowe to discuss how MFS should react to the explosive growth of the Internet. Crowe initiated Project Silver to study the situation and to propose an MFS strategy. The Project Silver team visited 20 to 30 Internet Service Providers; Crowe personally went to six.

The conclusion from Project Silver was that MFS needed to do much more than provide telecommunications services to Internet Service Providers. MFS decided that it needed to *"be"* an Internet Service Provider and that it needed to get there fast.

MFS would have to buy its way in and acquire a leading Internet Service Provider without delay. The Internet, they concluded, was the future.

Footnotes Chapter 11: The Internet Surprise

[1] Hyman, Toole and Avellis, "The New Telecommunications Industry: Evolution And Organization," (Public Utilities Reports, 1987), 126.

[2] "It's A Packet World," *Business Communications Review,* September 1996, 14.

[3] "WilTel First To Deliver Frame Relay," *Network World,* April 1, 1991, 1.

[4] "Frame Relay: Who Has Announced What?," *Business Communications Review Frame Relay Supplement,* October , 1991, FR 18.

[5] "The Accidental Seer," *The Red Herring,* March, 1977.

[6] "Subverting The Network," *Telephony's Data Communications Series: The Data Challenge,* June 15, 1992.

[7] "Intermedia Announces Interconnection Services To The Internet; Predicts Product Will Help Business, Science And R&D In Florida," Intermedia Press Release, March 1, 1993.

[8] Prospectus for Intermedia Communications Of Florida, Bear, Stearns & Co., Merrill Lynch & Co., Morgan Stanley & Co., May 8, 1996, 25.

[9] "Regional Carriers Set To Challenge Current Frame-Relay Services, Costs," *Info World,* May 16, 1994.

[10] "Consortium Aims To Take On Big Three In Frame-Relay," *Communications Week,* May 23, 1994.

[11] "Intermedia Communications Doubles Frame Relay Capacity In Southeast Network To Meet Intensified Customer Demand," Intermedia Communications Press Release, April 4, 1994.

[12] "Intermedia Communications To Acquire Long Distance Carrier, Phone One," Intermedia Communications Press Release, November 10, 1994.

[13] "Intermedia Communications Acquires FiberNet," Intermedia Communications Press Release, February 16, 1995.

[14] "Frame Relay Disaster Recovery," *Research Report On: CLEC Issues,* New Paradigm Resources, v.7, No. 9, September 1999, 2.

[15] 1992 Alternate Local Transport ... A Total Industry Report, (Glastonbury, 1992, Connecticut Research), 174.

[16] "Metropolitan Fiber Systems Launches First Commercially Available High-Speed Communications Network," MFS Press Release, August 20, 1991.

[17] "MFS Makes A MAN Out Of FDDI," *Data Communications,* October ,1991, 57-62.

[18] "Al Fenn Joins Metropolitan Fiber Systems As President Of Newly Formed MFS Datanet Inc.," MFS Press Release, January 10, 1992.

[19] MFS Communications, Inc. Form 10-K, December 31, 1993, 27.

[20] "MFS Datanet Announces First National Service For High-Speed Interconnection Of LANs and Custom Networks," MFS Press Release, October 5, 1992.

[21] Ibid.

[22] "Newbridge Acquires ATM Switch," *Communications Week,* October 26, 1992, 123.

[23] "Newbridge Pushes Ahead," *Communications Week,* November 15, 1993, 28.

[24] "MFS Datanet, Inc.," MFS Corporate Fact Sheet, April 1993, 2.

[25] "LAN-Speed Links Available Now," *LAN Times,* March 8, 1993, v10, no. 5.

[26] "MFS Datanet Unveils The First National ATM Network: A New Era In Communications Begins," MFS Press Release, August 4, 1993.

[27] "Customers Give A Thumbs-Up To First National ATM Data Network," *Investor's Business Daily,* August 25, 1993, 1.

[28] Ibid.

[29] "MFS Expanding To 60 Markets; Data Drives Growth, Executives Say," *Telecom Data Report,* January 17, 1994.

[30] Ibid.

[31] "MFS Goes Global With ATM Service," *Network World,* February 14, 1994, 65.

[32] "MFS Datanet Announces World's First International ATM Service. New Global ATM Service Links U.S. and U.K. Initially," MFS Press Release, February 9, 1994.

[33] "MFS Unveils Worldwide ATM Service," *InfoWorld,* June 6, 1994.

[34] "Newbridge Predicts First-Quarter Losses," *Communications Week,* August 8, 1994.

[35] "MFS Reports Increased 1st Quarter Revenues; Service Expanding To European Locations," *Telecom Data Report,*
May 23, 1994.

[36] "Behind The Big Bang," *Data Communications,* February, 1995, 62.

[37] MFS Datanet First To Support Frame Relay Over ATM, New Frame Transport Service Provides Frame Relay Connectivity Over MFS' Fiber Optic ATM Network," MFS Press Release, June 21, 1994.

[38] "MFS Datanet Unveils Frame Relay-Over-ATM; Service Enables Access Speeds Up To MBPS," *Telecom Data Report,* July 4, 1994.

[39] MFS Communications Company, Inc., Fourth Quarter 1995 Analyst Conference Call Transcript, February 14, 1996, 4.

[40] Ibid. , 11.

[41] "Bank of New York Adopts Teleport Communications Group's LANLINK Data Service," TCG Press Release, May 18, 1993.

[42] "TCG Launches Enhanced, ATM-Based Switched Data Services; Offers Highest Speed Connectivity, Superior TCG Quality," TCG Press Release, March 29, 1995.

[43] "Teleport Steps Into Switched ATM Services," *Communications Week,* April 3, 1995.

[44] MFS Communications Company, Inc., Third Quarter 1995, Analyst Conference Call Transcript, October 31, 1995, 4.

[45] "Error Requires Resolicitation Of ESNet; Sprint Protests MCI's NSFnet Backbone Award," *Telecommunications Reports,* March 14, 1994.

[46] Ibid.

[47] Sprint Press Release, March 10, 1994.

[48] MFS Communications, Inc. Form 10-K, December 31, 1995, 4.

12. WAR OF THE WORDS

Multi-Front Assault

The growth of CLEC revenue did not occur in a vacuum. CLECs could only market their services in arenas that had been pried open by gains made on the regulatory and legislative fronts. While advancing technology enabled services, burgeoning marketing skills promoted them and expanding organizational structures delivered them with increasing cost effectiveness, the CLEC industry continued to operate within the confines of a niche in the vast world of telecommunications. As the industry developed, it increasingly embraced the Teleport philosophy that success in the continuous war to stretch the boundaries of its niche required a multi-front assault. This was a battle that needed coordinated efforts in public relations and intellectual initiatives, as well as the direct actions on the regulatory, legal and legislative fronts. CLECs began to assign more resources to this war of words.

Planting The Seeds Of Change

During the 1980s, the early struggle for entry into local service competition had focused on gaining interconnection with the LEC networks. As the 1990s dawned, Teleport realized that physical linkage at the central office was not sufficient. True interoperability, which would allow calls to flow back and forth seamlessly between CLEC and LEC networks, required physical, logical, financial and administrative "interconnections." Led by TCG the CLEC industry promoted a four-phase vision of how competition had evolved and how it should be allowed to continue to evolve to embrace the entire spectrum of local telecommunications services.[1]

In the first phase, these providers had primarily been in the "access" business and were appropriately called Competitive Access Providers (CAPs). The CAPs had installed their own fiber networks and served large business and long distance carrier customers with dedicated private lines. These "anchor tenants" helped pay for the cost of installing these backbone networks. Little interaction with the incumbent telephone companies was required except to collocate some equipment in central offices or to lease high-speed dedicated lines from the telcos to reach customer locations that were not on the CAPs' fiber networks.

In the second phase, CAPs became CLECs by installing their own central-office-grade switches and offering switched services in addition to dedicated transport and private line service. Now the interaction with the telephone companies had increased dramatically since local telephone calls, including 911 calls, had to be exchanged seamlessly between the LEC and the CLEC networks. As CLECs offering a wider range of services, competitive companies could now afford to serve medium-sized as well as large business customers. However, instead of needing only to lease a few high-speed, dedicated lines from the LEC, CLECs might require hundreds of analog local loops from the LEC to reach the dispersed locations of their smaller, lower-volume customers. The hundreds of millions of local loops represented the ultimate bottleneck facility; and without the right to buy selected "unbundled" elements (including loop, port and switching functions) of the LEC local loop at wholesale rates, CLECs contended, it would be a very long time before most customer locations could be served cost effectively by LEC competitors.

In phase three, CLECs foresaw the possibility of moving, for the first time, beyond an exclusive focus on the large and medium-sized business market. Provided that CLECs could develop sufficient economies of scale on their own networks, it appeared that it would then be feasible to offer services to smaller customers who were located conveniently near these networks. It was conjectured that the incremental costs associated with serving this class of small customers might make such business profitable. In this manner, small business customers or even residential customers grouped in apartment buildings and similar high-density locations might become part of the "addressable market" for CLECs. In the fourth and final phase, CLECs would be in a position to take on the biggest and most costly challenge—bringing choice and competitive alternatives to the mass market, including "Plain Old Telephone Service" to widely dispersed residential consumers.

Teleport's Nine Points

Teleport addressed in more detail the "soft issue" requisites for dial-tone competition, such as number portability and network unbundling, which Illinois Commerce Commission Chairman

Barnich's "Free Trade Zone"proposal of November 1, 1991, had put on the table.[2] In a November 14, 1991, speech[3] in New York, Teleport CEO Annunziata laid out a nine-point list of conditions that his company considered necessary as a prerequisite for the development of viable local exchange competition.

Annunziata noted that although Teleport had negotiated and implemented central office interconnections with LECs in five states, "no local exchange service competition exists today and it cannot develop in the future without these (nine) interconnections."[4] He called central office interconnection the first of the nine required steps and said, "But without the other eight conditions, central office interconnection will provide benefits to only a few, sophisticated users of private line services in a few cities. The broader interconnection we seek will stimulate the development of a technologically advanced, low cost and highly reliable local public telecommunications infrastructure that is composed of a number of competing networks seamlessly interconnected with each other."[5] Annunziata enunciated the nine points as:

<u>Physical Interconnections</u>

1. *Cost-based, unbundled local loops* between a subscriber's premises and the telephone companies' Local Serving Offices (Central Office).

2. *Cost-based central office interconnection arrangements* and cost-based connections between unbundled, cost-based loops and the Central Office interconnection arrangement.

3. *Local telephone number portability* so that subscribers can exercise free consumer choice by changing from one local exchange carrier to another without sacrificing their existing telephone numbers.

<u>Logical Interconnections</u>

4. *Equal access to and equal status in LEC's Signaling System 7 systems,* including databases and network routing processes (i.e., the LEC's traffic routing systems treat TCG's Class 5 switches no differently from a LEC Class 5 end office).

5. Equal access to and equal status in LEC's tandem switching and interoffice networks (i.e. the telephone companies' switching systems treat TCG's Class 5 switches no differently from a LEC Class 5 end office).

6. Integration of TCG's competing Class 5 and Class 4 (tandem) switches into LEC's local traffic routing plans with the integration accomplished through unbundled switching and facility elements at cost-based rates.

Financial And Administrative Interconnections

7. Unbundled, cost-based LEC rates to terminate local calls originated on TCG's systems that are delivered on TCG's networks to the LEC's Class 5 Local Serving Office or Tandem switch (i.e. a local service "access charge").

8. Payment by LECs for TCG's termination of LEC originated local calls on TCG's systems.

9. Cooperative engineering, operational, maintenance and administrative practices and procedures.

Teleport initiated and sustained a public relations campaign to promote these nine "points" and to fix them in the minds of regulators and legislators. The nine points were refined, polished and reiterated. TCG widely distributed wallet-sized calendars with the nine points printed on the back.

These demands shocked some LEC executives who had persisted in the belief that CLECs were merely about competition for access services (*i.e.* bypass) and, thus, basically a marginal threat relative to the bulk of telephone company revenues. As the TCG manifesto made clear, CLECs were insisting they be granted a peer or co-carrier status with their Class 5 central office switches fully integrated with the LEC network.

With such full hardware and software integration, including network signaling, routing tables and operational support systems, a CLEC switch would look and act just like a LEC switch in the network. One enraged RBOC executive said, "CLECs have been an irritant until now, but this — this is total war!"

They viewed it as outrageous that CLECs should expect to be allowed to lease the telephone companies' own network facilities in order to compete against them. But the CLECs responded that this was exactly how competition was successfully introduced into the long distance market. MCI, Sprint and other long distance companies purchased transport on AT&T's network at wholesale rates until they were strong enough financially to build their own network facilities.

CLECs maintained that the transition to a fully competitive market should occur by gradual deregulation of the LECs as their market power from the control of bottleneck facilities declined. TCG noted, "Fair competitive terms are not a new idea in the evolution of telecommunications in the United States...Federal and state regulators gave AT&T more pricing flexibility as its market share declined. The experience in the (long distance) market since divestiture has proven the validity of this approach. Gradual regulatory relief as competition grows is the correct model for the local exchange market."[6]

Growing Strength Of The CLEC Braintrust

Industry leaders TCG and MFS expanded their efforts to influence change in the telecommunications regulatory structure. CLECs would never be able to match the numbers of lawyers, economists and lobbyists serving the telephone companies. But CLECs could enlist a small number of elite individuals with strong industry backgrounds.

At MFS, Andy Lipman,now at the Washington, D.C., law firm of Swidler & Berlin, was made Senior Vice President for Legal and Regulatory Affairs while still retaining his partnership at the law firm.[7] In his new position at MFS, Lipman was given responsibility for directing and implementing legal and regulatory affairs, MFS lobbying efforts and the expanding in-house legal and regulatory staff. Lipman was made chair of a new MFS steering committee charged with further developing the company's regulatory policy and strategy. Meanwhile, at Swidler & Berlin his telecommunications practices staff grew to fifteen persons.

MFS also expanded its in-house staff and recruited a key legal counsel from the Federal Communications Commission. Cindy Schonhaut was named Director of Regulatory and Legislative Affairs at MFS on September 9, 1991.[8] In the previous eleven pivotal years at the FCC, Schonhaut had served as a member of the task force that implemented the original access and divestiture tariffs, the primary liaison between the FCC's Common Carrier Bureau and the state regulatory agencies and legal advisor to FCC Commissioner Andrew Barrett. At MFS, Schonhaut would be responsible for representing MFS' views before State and Federal legislatures and regulatory agencies.

Just as the TCG team of Atkinson and Bonney had done, MFS fielded its own missionary team to visit state regulators to deliver a package of diplomacy, education and persuasion on both the need for and the mechanics of transitioning to a competitive local telecommunications market. The MFS team of Royce Holland, Andy Lipman and Cindy Schonhaut became known in some circles as The Gang of Three. Regulators were impressed by the intellectual firepower displayed by The Gang of Three. Although Holland and Lipman were two of the most visible personalities in the CLEC industry, it was Schonhaut, with a deep understanding of PUC operations, that often left the greatest impression on the minds of regulators.

At TCG, Bob Atkinson commanded an increased staff. TCG was particularly pleased when they were able to hire Dr. Gail Garfield Schwartz, deputy chairman of the New York State Public Service Commission, after she stepped down from her post in June 1992. On September 1, 1992, she became TCG's Vice President of Government Affairs.[9]

Annunziata called the appointment a "coup for TCG that symbolizes the seriousness and growing maturity of the competitive local carrier industry. We are fortunate to have someone of Ms. Schwartz's national stature and expertise join us. There is no question that Ms. Schwartz's background, intellect and national prominence will play an incalculable role in educating the public, policy makers and regulators about the vital need for competition in the local telecommunications marketplace."[10]

Dr. Schwartz said, "This is an opportunity to paint on a much larger canvas. The issue of paramount importance to this country's economy is an efficient, modern telecommunications infrastructure. The best way to get the best, to the most, the quickest is by relying on the market."[11]

During his two-year tenure as the "*pro bono*" President of the Association of Local Telecommunications Services, John Shapleigh had used his political connections to increase the contacts between the industry association and influential politicians and regulators. He had been successful in recruiting people such as Senator John Danforth, Congressman Jim Cooper and FCC Chairman Al Sikes to speak at ALTS meetings. Shapleigh's departure in December 1992, to become Vice President and General Counsel for Brooks Telecommunications Corporation, removed the Association's most direct link to Congressional allies.

In an attempt to continue to exert influence on the national political scene, the members of ALTS issued a white paper, "Telecommunications Policy '93," with Dr. Schwartz as the principal author, and sent it to the White House and selected members of Congress. In a preemptive strike against expected LEC lobbying in Washington, D.C., the paper was also sent to President-elect Bill Clinton and Vice President-elect Al Gore.[12]

Calling For Action

"Telecommunications Policy '93" presented the case for opening local telecommunications markets to full competition. In a direct appeal to Vice President Gore's known interest in an "information super highway," the paper argued that its provisions, if enacted, would accelerate private investment and "contribute to the national telecommunications 'super highway'—which is in fact a 'network of networks'."[13] The White Paper noted that:

> The history of telecommunications during the last three decades demonstrates conclusively that competition does achieve national objectives, better than regulated monopoly can do. Both political parties have supported the emergence of competition, first in customer equipment, next in long distance service. Now is the time to move swiftly and unequivocally to a fully competitive local exchange market.[14]

To implement the recommendations of the White Paper, it included a three-part action agenda consisting of:

1. removing all barriers to entry
2. providing for the shared use of facilities
3. establishing a national fund to subsidize low-income consumers (to be called the Universal Service Assurance Fund)

The removal of entry barriers focused on establishing network interconnection. "The history of telecommunications is the history of interconnection, and ample legal precedent exists for extending full interconnection requirements to the local exchange."[15]

The report asserted that at the current, painful, rate of progress, interconnection would not be generally achieved for decades.

> The ALTs (CAPs) have been seeking voluntary interconnection since 1985, without success. They have sought before regulatory agencies mandatory interconnection since 1986 and have been granted such opportunities, under different—and limited circumstances in five states (New York, New Jersey, Illinois, Massachusetts and California) and by the FCC. However, local exchange carriers take every opportunity to delay implementation of regulators' orders, and ALTs (CAPs) have not yet achieved cost-based interconnection anywhere.[16]

The Antitrust Division of the Justice Department was asked to take note that, "Numerous examples of LEC anti-competitive behavior have been documented. For example, ALTS can point to LECs' failure to provide interconnection once agreed to."[17]

But the major call for action was to the Congress. "It is time for Congress to focus on the terms and conditions of marketplace entrance and exit."[18] Rather than allow matters to proceed on a state-by-state basis, Congress was urged to establish a national policy for interconnection and to remove all barriers to local competition. "Removing these barriers can be accomplished solely by (state) regulators, but it is unlikely they will do so in a timely fashion without a Congressional mandate and Executive Branch direction."[19]

Personal Diplomacy

But clearly ALTS needed more than policy papers. It needed to make its physical presence felt in Washington. On March 8, 1993, ALTS installed a full-time, salaried President, Heather Burnett Gold.[20] As the former Vice President of the long distance trade group, the Competitive Telecommunications Association, Ms. Gold was well versed in communications and in lobbying Congress.

In addition to representing ALTS positions and testifying before legislative groups, Heather Gold introduced the members to the power of personal lobbying. Few CLEC executives had previously met their Representatives and Senators. Now, when ALTS meetings convened in Washington, D.C., members, prompted by Ms. Gold, took the time to visit their respective legislators.

Awareness of the CLECs and their issues began to rise inside the Beltway.

Railing Against The "POT Bay"

The addition of direct lobbying did not replace attempts to frame the debate on telecommunications issues through "White Papers." TCG initiated a series of such papers beginning on June 4, 1993, with a report, "The 'POT Bay:' Several BOCs Attempt To Obstruct Interconnection … Again" by Dr. Gail Garfield Schwartz.[21]

TCG railed against the requirement imposed by some LECs that a new device, POT Bay, (not to be confused with POTS - "Plain Old Telephone Service" - the acronym POT Bay stood for Point-Of-Termination Bay) to be used between the collocator's equipment and the main distribution frame where telco cables terminate in the central office. TCG argued that this device served no real function other than to raise additional barriers of expense, inconvenience and signal degradation for the CLEC.

Southwestern Bell Telephone, which had the highest proposed tariff for a "POT Bay" with an non-recurring charge of $21,863 and a monthly fee of $329, modified its tariff on the day the paper was published to a non-recurring charge of $2,743 and a monthly fee of $41.34. Although Ameritech, BellSouth, NYNEX, Pacific Bell and Southwestern Bell insisted that the "POT Bay" was a necessary device, their position was weakened by the fact that Bell Atlantic and GTE required no such device.

Exorcising The Ghost Of The "Protective Coupling Device"

The TCG paper characterized the imposition of the "POT Bay" as another in a long line of Bell tactics of erecting unnecessary barriers to prevent access to the telephone network.[22] In a criticism that stung, TCG drew an analogy between the "POT Bay" and the infamous and now discredited "protective coupling device" which AT&T had invoked to impede the connection of non-Bell manufactured equipment to the public telephone network.

When the *Carterfone Decision* of 1968 first gave customers the right to attach "foreign equipment" (as AT&T labeled it), to the telephone network, the Bell Systemhad responded by requiring that a "protective coupling device" be inserted between the user equipment and the network to prevent "harm to the network." This device, which could only be leased from the Bell System, was ultimately found to be a useless and unnecessary sham.

The "protective coupling device" requirement was replaced for a time by a program of certifying equipment to be attached to the network. Ultimately however, during the U.S. antitrust suit against AT&T, the presiding Judge, Harold Greene, found that the "protective coupling device" was merely an attempt to foreclose competition by erecting an unreasonable barrier to network interconnection.[23]

Ameritech responded to TCG's complaints in November 1993 and eased, but did not eliminate, its "POT Bay" requirement. It did, however, allow the collocated CLECs to own the device and to maintain it within their own collocation space.[24]

Under continuing pressure and criticism from their state PUCs, the telephone companies successively modified, or discarded, the "POT Bay" until it was no longer an odious burden for the CLECs. The heat went out of the issue although later legislation would allow for an "inter-connection element."

The real importance of the "POT Bay" dust-up was the nature, intensity and effectiveness of the CLEC protest. The telephone companies were now on notice that they were living in a new environment. Tactics employed by the industry in the past to defend its network turf would now be challenged by a knowledgeable CLEC industry which could aggressively project its viewpoints. On the intellectual battlefield, the CLECs could bring a spotlight to even relatively minor issues and be reasonably certain that their arguments would be heard and responded to by regulators and legislators.

The White Paper Campaign: The Pen Is Mightier

From 1993 to 1995, the TCG authors issued a dozen "White Papers" addressing key issues in local competition. These were intended either to draw attention to RBOC actions or inactions that the CLECs considered anti-competitive or to suggest the framework for resolution of outstanding issues created by migration to a competitive telecommunications environment (e.g. Universal Service). These included topics such as:

> •*The "POT Bay:" Several BOCs Attempt To Obstruct Interconnection ... Again*, June 1993

> •*Telco Fiber Fiascoes: Will Accelerated Infrastructure Programs Be The Next Nuclear Power Plant Debacles ?*, July 1993

> •*Universal Service Assurance: A Concept For Fair Contribution And Equal Access To The Subsidies*, December 1993

> •*The Unlevel Playing Field: Asymmetric Market Power Demands Asymmetric Regulation*, March 1994

> •*Wither The CAPs ?*, June 1994

> •*Interconnection Compensation - The Critical Issue For Local Exchange Competition*, October 1995

While some of the material in this avalanche of paper had relevance to near-term actions in progress before state PUCs, the real target was to set the stage for future developments on a national scale. On the national level, the first target was to influence policy decisions at the Federal Communications Commission. The ultimate goal was to shape the results of the widely anticipated Congressional action to rewrite the basic laws for national telecommunications.

Coming To Terms With Divestiture

Throughout the decade of the 1980s and into the 1990s, there were numerous attempts to address modernization of the fundamental legislation underpinning telecommunications in the United States— The Communications Act of 1934.

Congress had tried, unsuccessfully, in the 1980s to involve itself in national telecommunications policy making during the events leading to the breakup of the Bell System and the divestiture of the RBOCs by AT&T. A swarm of bills was introduced in both the House and the Senate, many related to the protection of "Universal Service" (*i.e.* preservation of low-cost, basic residential phone service), but none were passed before AT&T and the Department of Justice reached the divestiture agreement that seemed to end the matter.

After the divestiture settlement, Representative Tim Wirth of Colorado, Chairman of the House Telecommunications sub-committee, and a long-time AT&T foe, introduced House Bill, H.R. 5158, in March 1982 to limit the operations of the newly freed AT&T. The bill provided for separation and partial outside ownership of AT&T's long distance network. It proposed rules preventing AT&T from competing with the seven newly-formed RBOCs, and it proposed the transfer of some lucrative lines-of-business from AT&T to the RBOCs. H.R. 5158 produced an uproar in Congress. AT&T mounted a massive lobbying campaign against it, and AT&T's competitors enlisted Ralph Nader to support it. In the middle of the fight, MCI's Bill McGowan switched sides, going from backing the bill to opposing it. AT&T won the day. In July 1982, an embittered Wirth gave up saying, "In my eight years in this body, I have seen nothing like the campaign of fear and distortion that AT&T has waged to fight this bill."[25]

Telecommunications Life Under The Czar

With the demise of H.R. 5158, national telecommunications policy was essentially in the hands of Judge Harold Greene, the U.S. District Court Judge responsible for administering the divestiture agreement. Former FCC Chairman Richard Wiley said, "Judge

Greene has become the man of the hour. His decision...will chart the future of the telecommunications industry like nothing else—because there will be nothing else."[26]

There was speculation that Greene had readily embraced the divestiture proposal partially because he wanted to avoid congressional interference. One Department of Justice lawyer said,"...Greene was protecting his turf from Congress while simultaneously creating a kingdom for himself."[27] The Judge, however, did not totally accept the divestiture terms as proposed by AT&T and the Department of Justice. Seven months of hearings were held, with many parties suggesting changes, before the Judge settled on what became known as the "Modified Final Judgment" or "MFJ" (although Judge Greene never used this designation).

One important change came as a result of intense pressure from the American Newspaper Publishers Association whose members feared that AT&T might enter and monopolize electronic publishing. Over the objections of both AT&T and the Department of Justice, Judge Greene imposed a seven-year ban on AT&T with regard to electronic publishing over its own transmission facilities. One government lawyer said:

> That decision had the consequence of gaining for divestiture almost complete editorial support in the United States. Almost every newspaper in the country came out in favor of the deal, despite the fact that there was no real popular support for it (divestiture).[28]

Greene also made changes that sweetened the deal for the RBOCs. He allowed them to retain the Yellow Pages, a very profitable $2 billion business; and he allowed them to sell, but not manufacture, telephone equipment. He also awarded them the exclusive use of the well-established Bell logo.

With the formal breakup of the Bell System on January 1, 1984, life under the MFJ began. Access payments to LECs from AT&T and the other long distance carriers replaced settlement payments between AT&T Long Lines and the local operating companies. RBOCs were prohibited by the MFJ from offering long distance and information electronic services and from manufacturing.

The MFJ also required that RBOCs obtain waivers for entry into other lines of business. For next several years Judge Greene was continuously petitioned for rulings from RBOCs seeking interpretation of the MFJ or relief from line-of-business restrictions. Over time, some of the initial restrictions were removed or modified; but Congress and the RBOCs became increasingly unhappy over the role of Judge Greene in controlling the industry as "The Telecommunications Czar."

Congress still needed to modernize the outdated Communications Act of 1934.

Congress Spins Its Wheels

Attempts to "free" the RBOCs from the constraints of the divestiture agreement came quickly. In November 1985, barely a year into operation under the MFJ, two Representatives, Tom Tauke, a Republican from Iowa, and Al Swift, a Democrat from Washington, introduced a bipartisan bill for RBOC relief. The bill would have allowed the RBOCs to manufacture telephone equipment and to provide information services. The bill died without action. They tried again in 1989 with the same result.[29]

In 1986, Senate Minority Leader, Bob Dole, attempted to introduce a sweeping re-write of the telecommunications law. He introduced the "Federal Telecommunications Policy Act of 1986" in the Senate. It too died without action.

In 1988, John Dingell, the powerful Chairman of the House Energy and Commerce Committee introduced a House Resolution to allow the RBOCs into manufacturing and electronic information services. Again, no legislation resulted.

Senator Ernest Hollings, Democrat of South Carolina, tried to help the RBOCs by supporting a bill in 1989 that would allow their entry into manufacturing. Hollings introduced a new version of the bill with strict safeguards. This bill gained wide support and passed in the Senate by a vote of 71 to 24 in June 1991. A companion bill in the House gained more than 100 cosponsors, but the session ended with no legislation.

During 1992 and 1993, numerous bills were introduced into both the House and Senate which sought either to allow or to prevent RBOCs from certain actions. Despite protracted hearings and debates, all such bills died without enactment. Over time it became a well-founded joke among Capitol Hill legislators that delay in re-writing the 1934 Act or in amending the MFJ was animated by the desire to preserve the flow of immense campaign contributions from all the interested parties to the legislators.[30]

Wrestling With The Universal Service Issue

As discussions of relaxed regulation progressed to discussions of creating a totally open, competitive local telephone market, arguments focused on the issue of "universal service." The idea that the price of basic residential telephone service should be kept so low that telephone service would be universally available—even in low-income homes and high-cost areas—had existed since the passage of The Communications Act of 1934. In fact, it had been promoted by Vail to policymakers as a rationale for the Bell System to be allowed to operate as a monopoly.

An extra cushion was built into business telephone rates and long distance access rates which, in theory, allowed the telephone companies to subsidize low-cost or below-cost residential phone service. LECs argued that a transition to competitive local telecommunications would destroy this system of implicit subsidies. Without these revenue sources, they argued, local residential rates would soar, forcing many low-income consumers off the network. It was also possible, they asserted, that telephone companies might be forced to abandon or reduce the quality of service to whole communities of low-income or high-cost users.

Although critics claimed that these concerns were greatly exaggerated, threats to universal service weighed heavily with legislators as they considered re-writing the national telecommunications laws. FCC Chairman Reed Hundt, appointed by President Bill Clinton, pointed out the need to move beyond rhetoric and mythology and grapple with facts. "As we reform federal and state rules," he said, "we have to demythologize the debate. For example, there is a myth that low-income consumers don't use long distance services to the same extent as everyone else. That's just not true."[31] He also observed that implicit subsidies don't necessarily flow as intended. "(Long distance) access charges, set way above cost, don't just pay for phone service to those who can't afford it. They are also helping to pay the cost of providing a little-used telephone line to your neighbor's beachhouse."[32]

There were also Public Utility Commission studies that challenged whether the much touted subsidies existed any longer in the light of the declining cost of network technology. Studies by the PUCs of Illinois, New Hampshire and Maine found that in their states the prices of residential local service were covering or exceeding the cost of providing the service.[33],[34],[35]

TCG complained that in early moves toward deregulation telephone companies were permitted to assess surcharges such as "Universal Service Elements" on services provided to CLECs. TCG's Annunziata said, "But I have no idea whether any of these above-cost (charges) ... are actually used to support a needy consumer or a consumer in a high-cost area. It may very well be that we are supporting a telco's fleet of limousines or paying for corporate strategy meetings at posh resorts."[36]

TCG proposed that a new system of support for Universal Service be adopted in any new legislation. The key elements would be that all carriers would pay in proportionally and would be permitted to extract explicit subsidies from the fund for supporting eligible customers.[37]

As deliberations moved toward rough consensus on formation of such a fund, concern shifted to the definition of a proper definition of "universal service." Congressmen from rural areas became concerned that if only basic "Plain Old Telephone Service" were covered by universal service, rural areas might never see the high-tech services expected to emerge in a competitive era. With regard to advanced voice and data features, they did not want to see the country segmented into the "haves" and the "have nots."

Great Expectations For 1994

As 1994 approached there were great expectations of a new telecommunications law. Although there were still many legislative initiatives afoot, Democrats and Republicans had gotten together on most of these to present bipartisan, compromise proposals.

In the Senate Daniel Inouye, Democrat from Hawaii, and John Danforth, Republican from Missouri, were co-sponsoring a bill. In the House there was a similar bill sponsored by Edward Markey, Democrat of Massachusetts, and Jack Fields, Republican of Texas. Also in the House, John Dingell, who had been supporting legislation to free the RBOCs, was now proposing a compromise bill co-sponsored by fellow Democrat, Jack Brooks of Texas, who had supported greater restrictions on the RBOCs.

The compromises seemed to have quieted a great deal of the arguing among the competing carriers. Congressman Markey said, "The stars are now aligned for historic legislation in 1994, there's no question about it."[38]

An RBOC Victory On Physical Collocation

The CLEC string of victories on central office collocation which culminated in the FCC Interconnection Order of September 1992, received a setback in 1994. Originally the FCC had ordered the RBOCs and other telephone companies to allow CLECs to physically collocate their interconnection equipment in the telephone companies' central offices. The RBOCs, led by Bell Atlantic, had taken this ruling to court, charging that the FCC did not have the authority under the Communications Act of 1934 to make this mandate. It therefore constituted, they charged, an illegal "taking" of property from the telephone companies. On June 10, 1994, the three-judge panel of the United States Court of Appeals in Washington, DC ruled against the FCC essentially striking down the interconnection order.[39] The RBOC lawyers were ecstatic. Bell Atlantic General Counsel James Young said, "We're delighted with this court ruling. Instead of a flash cut to a completely competitive environment, there is now the opportunity to take a more deliberate approach. Today's decision prevents our competitors from setting up shop in our central offices."[40] CLEC stocks fell on the news, but the RBOC victory was not long lived. Giving the FCC the right to require physical collocation became an issue for the new Congressional legislation.

The "Information Highway" Administration Arrives

The in-coming Clinton administration, particularly Vice President Albert Gore Jr., wanted to make the modernization of telecommunications legislation a priority of its term. Gore had been promoting the concept of a "national information infrastructure" which gained cliché' status as "the information superhighway."[41]

The Vice President gave a much-heralded speech on telecommunications to the National Press Club on December 22, 1993; but surprisingly it contained no details for action by the Administration.[42] Gore said that the Administration would defer to the Congress which had done "a lot of heavy lifting and achieved significant breakthroughs."[43]

The Dingell-Brooks bill, "Antitrust Communications Reform Act" (H.R. 3626), would replace the MFJ, removing remaining line-of-business restrictions. It had the support of the RBOCs. The bill contained market entry tests that would allow RBOCs to enter the long distance market when there was "no substantial possibility that they could use their local facilities to impede competition."

The Markey-Fields bill, "Communications Competition and Information Infrastructure Reform Act" (H.R. 3636), would allow telephone and cable companies to enter each others' businesses. It also required that telephone companies open their networks to competition and provide network interconnection at technically and economically reasonable points.

Both bills were passed by the House on June 23, 1994.[44] The bills were consolidated into a single bill, the "Communications Act of 1994" (S. 1822) by the Senate Commerce Committee. The carefully crafted compromises which had eased the bills through the House came apart in the Senate. The combined bill contained stricter market entry provisions and increased network access requirements that generated RBOC opposition. Republican Minority Leader, Bob Dole, threatened a filibuster.

The bill's chief sponsor, Senator Hollings, raced to complete the legislation before the end of the session. In weeks of wrangling through the summer, he worked out a compromise with the RBOCs over terms of their entry into the long distance business. But they remained unhappy over other features including provisions that might delay their entry into cable television.[45] Ameritech and BellSouth, in particular, raised last minute objections. On Thursday, September 22, Senator Dole had a private meeting with Hollings and presented the changes desired by the RBOCs as "non-negotiable demands." On Saturday Hollings went to the floor of the

Senate and declared the bill dead.[46] He had reluctantly decided that the opposition made it impossible to push the bill through before the end of the 103rd Congressional session in October.

Discussions In Secret

The 1994 elections brought dramatic changes to the 104th Congress as Republicans took control of Congress with majorities in both the Senate and House. It was the first time Republicans had controlled the House in forty years.

Senator Larry Pressler, Republican from South Dakota, was installed as the new Chairman of the Senate Commerce Committee and immediately took up the telecommunications reform issue. Republican members of the committee held a two-day meeting with selected executives from all corners of the telecommunications industry on January 19-20, 1995, ending with a private dinner at which House Speaker Newt Gingrich delivered a speech.[47] These meetings drew fire from the Democrats who claimed that by locking them out and by not including consumer groups and state regulators, bipartisan support for future legislation was undercut.

Former Commerce Committee Chairman John Dingell submitted a written protest of these "discussions in secret" which seemed to be the "functional equivalent" of hearings. However, he observed sarcastically, that he had "no great quarrel with GOP members attempting to educate themselves on the issues."[48] Gingrich responded that the meetings were held privately so that the participants could talk freely about strategic plans and make candid remarks about regulatory agencies that they would not have made in open hearings.

House Telecom Subcommittee Chairman Jack Fields, Republican from Texas, felt that the meetings succeeded in producing a free-wheeling, give-and-take atmosphere in which a great deal of understanding was conveyed. Fields called this "the most unbelievable thing I've ever been a part of."[49]

This atmosphere provided a venue for directly influencing legislation. MFS President Royce Holland, who formed a strong bond with Congressman Fields, used the occasion to recommend that any bill be very specific on issues like interconnection. Vagueness, he argued, could result in protracted, complex rule making by the FCC.

The Republican Congress Gives It A Try

On January 31, 1995, Pressler's committee held hearings on a modified form of the Hollings bill as the "Telecommunications Competition Deregulation Act of 1995" (S. 652). The draft bill contained a "competitive checklist" of requirements that the RBOCs had to meet prior to entry into long distance. The "competitive checklist" looked suspiciously like TCG's "Nine Points."

In May, 1995, the Chairman of the Commerce Committee Tom Bliley, Republican from Virginia, introduced a companion bill, the "Communications Act of 1995" (H.R. 1555), in the House.

The Senate passed its bill on June 15, but the House continued to struggle over its bill throughout the summer year. In the House there was extended debate and numerous proposed amendments. Lobbying efforts by the RBOCs were successful in deleting provisions for quantitative market tests for determination of when their markets were open and for veto power by the Department of Justice over their entry into long distance. They were unsuccessful, however, at getting a "date certain" to replace the "competitive checklist" for market entry into long distance.

By August, the long distance carriers were contending that the bill had taken a form in which it would unfairly allow local phone companies into long distance service long before the local distance companies could challenge their monopolies in local service. President Clinton threatened to veto the bill because, he said, "Instead of promoting investment and competition, it promotes mergers and concentration of power."[50]

On August 4, 1995, the House passed its bill; and a House-Senate Conference worked the remainder of the year to resolve differences between the two bills. The Democrats and the Clinton administration were able to use the threat of a filibuster in the Senate to obtain major concessions from the Republicans. The long-distance entry provisions adopted some of the strictest elements of the two bills, and the RBOCs were unhappy. The House adopted the Conference Report on February 1, 1996, even though some of the Republicans grumbled that their leadership had given away too much. This almost led to a last minute revolt when Democrat John Dingell taunted them during the floor debate, declaring that the new bill was almost identical to the legislation which he had championed in 1994.

Passage Of The Historic Telecommunications Act Of 1996

On February 8, 1996, a bipartisan crowd of 400 legislators, staff personnel and industry executives jammed into the ornate, 100-year-old reading room of the Library of Congress in a festive mood to witness the signing of the historic "Telecommunications Act of 1996." President Clinton brought the same pen to the ceremony which President Eisenhower had used to sign the 1957 Interstate Highway Act.

The symbolism of the pen was to honor Vice President Albert Gore Jr.'s father, Senator Albert Gore Sr., who had written the Interstate Highway Act and to further the metaphor of the "information superhighway" that had become the Vice President's identifying issue. Gore engaged in a brief skit via video conference with comedian Lily Tomlin's character, Ernestine the telephone operator, who made reference to the "infomercial freeway."[51]

Senator Hollings thanked Judge Greene, whose hegemony over telecommunications would now end, for lighting the fires of competition and said that the Telecom Act would allow "the political side to catch up with technology." Expressing relief at having reached the end of the long, arduous road to enact the legislation he concluded by saying, "I'm going to Disney World."[52]

As he signed the bill the President said, "Today, with the stroke of a pen, our laws will catch up with the future."[53] The President expressed his hopes for the bill by saying, "We will help to create an open marketplace where competition and innovation can move as quickly as light."[54]

AT&T's CEO Robert Allen, attending the ceremony, said that his company would offer local, long distance and even television services to its customers in the near future. He indicated that AT&T would immediately start striking deals to lease telephone capacity from both RBOCs and CLECs and would also build local networks, possibly wireless, of its own. He said that AT&T would try to offer local phone service in every state and that it expected to capture one-third of the business now controlled by the RBOCs.[55]

In the same room, Bell Atlantic President James Cullen said his company would start offering long distance service outside its traditional region immediately and inside its region with a year.[56] In addition, he hinted that Bell Atlantic and NYNEX were seeking some kind of alliance that would soon give them control of the local phone market from Virginia through Maine.

The Competitive CheckList

The Telecom Act of 1996 contained both a carrot and a stick for the RBOCs. The carrot was the opportunity to enter the long distance market and to manufacture equipment. The stick was the requirement that they first open their local telephone monopoly markets to competition including making available physical collocation and unbundled network elements.

The Act gave RBOCs the right to immediately offer long distance service outside their local telephone operating area and established the requirements for their entry into long distance within their operating area. The right to entry into in-region long distance would be accompanied by the right to manufacture.

The key requirement was the demonstration that they had satisfied a fourteen-point "competitive checklist" of actions to open their networks to competition. Though couched in more abstruse language in the bill, the sense of the competitive checklist essentially incorporated the "nine points" which TCG had espoused.[57]

<u>The Competitive Checklist</u>

1. Reasonably priced interconnection of equal quality for all.

2. Access to network elements on an unbundled basis.

3. Access to poles, conduits and rights-of-way.

4. Right to lease unbundled local loops at wholesale rates.

5. Right to lease unbundled local transport at wholesale rates.

6. Right to lease unbundled local switching at wholesale.

7. Access to 911 and directory assistance.

8. White pages directory listing for all.

9. Nondiscriminatory access to telephone numbers.

10. Access to databases and network signaling needed for call routing.

11. Number portability.

12. Local dialing parity

13. Reciprocal compensation for local call termination.

14. Availability of all services at wholesale rates to resellers.

The RBOCs wanted to read these requirements as meaning that once they had opened their networks and met the checklist, as certified by a state Public Utility Commission, they would automatically be permitted to offer long distance in that state. There was, however, one more hurdle to cross. In the final step for an RBOC's entry into long distance, the FCC was required by the Telecom Act to certify that "the requested authorization is consistent with the public interest, convenience and necessity."[58]

This gave the FCC wide latitude to judge what was "consistent with the public interest." The FCC had a "track record" in this area. During the opening of the long distance market, AT&T continued to be subject to regulatory constraints that did not apply to the other long distance carriers. These constraints would not be lifted until the FCC ruled that AT&T was no longer "dominant." In judging when AT&T should no longer be regulated as the "dominant carrier," the FCC had relied in large part on a "market share" test. While the

RBOCs had lobbied successfully to prevent such an explicit test from being written into the Telecom Act of 1996 and made a part of the "checklist", there was nothing preventing the FCC from implicitly including such considerations in its determination of what was "consistent with the public interest."

CLEC Fears Of Pre-mature RBOC Freedom

The CLECs deeply distrusted the RBOCs. Although examples of overt network sabotage, such as MCIhad experienced while breaking the AT&TBell System's grip on the long distance market, were rare, CLECs that had won interconnection and other rights at the state Public Utility Commission level felt that the telephone companies covertly sabotaged them by slow-rolled service activation and excessive administrative delays. A process TCG dubbed "entanglement."

At an ALTS industry conference in May 1997, the President and CEO of ICG Communications, J. Shelby Bryan, articulated CLEC fears that only the carrot of long distance entry kept the situation from getting worse. Bryan said, "As soon as the (RBOCs) get into long distance, their incentive to cooperate with us is gone...We *have* to delay RBOCs getting into long distance, because—make no mistake—when they do, the whole competitive landscape changes."[59]

NYNEX Vice President of Regulatory Policy Jeff Ward responded to Bryan's remarks. He insisted that calls to ban RBOCs from long distance until local competition was established were unfounded because measuring market share or competition levels were not requirements under the Telecom Act of 1996. "Congress rejected the idea that market share or market entry tests should be conducted in order for RBOCs to enter long distance," he said. "All Congress said they (RBOCs) have to do is fulfill the 14-point checklist and make it possible for CLECs to operate—by making local loops available, for example."[60]

ICG Vice President of Regulatory Cindy Schonhaut, formerly with MFS, rebutted Ward's interpretation of the law. She acknowledged that, "The non-requirement of a market share test was allowed by a group of rural Senators from Montana, Alaska, South Dakota and Nebraska who thought certain rural areas might not get competition. They thought no one would show up, so they didn't require a competition test. However, that has not happened in one single state."[61] Schonhaut, a veteran of the FCC, implied that the agency would apply some form of market test even though one was not explicitly required by the Telecom Act.

The Action Moves To The FCC

Royce Holland's hope that the legislation would be so specific as to avoid protracted battles before the FCC was not met. The Telecom Act of 1996 left many implementation details and interpretations to the FCC. The action arena moved from Congress to the FCC. Ameritech CEO Dick Notebart observed that the lobbyists who worked to shape the bill "have hardly folded their tents and retreated. They have simply moved from Capitol Hill (to the FCC). I remain confident, though, that the FCC will stay true to the spirit of the law."[62]

It was not long before the RBOCs would learn how difficult it would be to obtain FCC approval for long distance market entry. Representative John Dingell became so frustrated with FCC Chairman Reed Hundt that he introduced a provision to restrict Hundt's travel to within fifty miles of Washington. Observers called it a "leash law." Dingell soon relented saying that his actions had served their purpose of gaining Hundt's attention.[63]

For the RBOCs, a "competitive telecommunications environment" meant allowing them to compete against the long distance carriers. For the FCC, as well as for the long distance carriers and the CLECs, a "competitive telecommunications environment" meant breaking the RBOC grip on bottleneck local network facilities.

As the FCC rejected petition after petition from the RBOCs over the next four years, their allies in the Congress fumed that the FCC was misinterpreting the will of the Congress. With each passing year a chorus of voices rose to complain that the Telecom Act was not working and that some drastic remedial action was needed.

Competition At The Speed Of Light ?

At the second anniversary of the passage of the Telecom Act, TCG CEO Bob Annunziata said, "Today, many observers are trying to assess whether the Act has been a 'success' or a 'failure.' … so far it is an 'incomplete success' and we are years away from being able to make a realistic judgment."[64] He blamed the slow progress toward a competitive market on a program of non-cooperation by the incumbent telephone companies. He asserted,

> ...the greatest barrier to local exchange competition is the anti-competitive attitude and behavior of the (telephone companies). Taking advantage of their monopoly position, the (telephone companies) have not hesitated to employ any tactic that would frustrate, delay, or otherwise impose substantial 'costs of entanglement' on would-be competitors seeking to interconnect with the (telephone company's) networks and to utilize (telephone company) facilities as part of CLEC service. This 'strategy of entanglement' has been perfected and shamelessly used by the (telephone companies) to discourage competition since the passage of the 1996 Telecommunications Act.[65]

Annunziata's suggested a remedy. "...It is up to state and Federal regulators to reduce the risk and cost of entanglement through swift, strong, and consistent application of the 'carrots and sticks' embodied in the Telecommunications Act."[66]

He pointed out that while CLECs could serve large business customers despite the cost of entanglement imposed through the lack of cooperation with the terms of the Telecom Act by the telephone companies, the ability to extend service to smaller businesses and to the mass market of residential telephone users could be effectively blocked by these tactics.

"The speed with which mass market competition develops," he said, "depends entirely on (telephone company behavior)...if the (telephone companies) continue to pursue the entanglement strategy, mass market competition will have to wait for the CLECs to build their own independent networks."[67] Such a process on a national scale would obviously take many years. While Congress, the RBOCs and the CLECs all fumed over the slow movement toward competition, not everyone shared their angst. For veteran industry observers who had witnessed MCI struggle for twenty years just to win the right to compete against AT&T's long distance fiefdom, the movement toward all-out competition in local telecommunications was moving at astonishing historical speed.

At the time of passage of Telecom Act of 1996, it had been widely speculated that NYNEX's New York Telephone might quickly become the first of the former Bell Operating Companies permitted to offer in-region long distance service. This speculation was based on the relatively advanced state of CLEC competition in New York City, led by MFS and TCG. But it would not be until December of 1999, after repeated rejections, that New York Telephone, now a Bell Atlantic Company, finally gained the FCC's ground-breaking approval to offer long distance service in New York state.[68]

The stage was now set for the creation of an all-out competitive telecommunications industry that would emerge quickly although, perhaps, not quite at the "speed of light."

Footnotes Chapter 12: War Of The Words

[1] Later summarized in the TCG White Paper, "Minimizing Entanglement, Maximizing Competition," February 1998, 6-8.

[2] Presentation at a TeleStrategies Conference by Terrence L. Barnich, Washington, D.C., November 1, 1992

[3] Probe Research, Inc. Conference, New York, November 14, 1991.

[4] "Framework For Consumer Choice In Basic Local Exchange Services Spelled Out By Teleport Communications Group President," TCG Press Release, November 14, 1991.

[5] Ibid.

[6] "The UnLevel Playing Field: Asymmetric Power Demands Asymmetric Regulation," TCG White Paper, March 1994, 11.

[7] "Metropolitan Fiber Systems Names Andrew D. Lipman Senior Vice President, Legal And Regulatory Affairs," MFS Press Release, August 12, 1991.

[8] "Metropolitan Fiber Systems Names Cindy Z. Schonhaut Director, Regulatory And Legislative Affairs," MFS Press Release, September 9, 1991.

[9] "Gail Garfield Schwartz Joins Teleport Communications Group; Former Deputy Chairman Of New York State Public Service Commission Takes Post As Vice President, Government Affairs," TCG Press Release, September 3, 1993.

[10] Ibid.

[11] Ibid.

[12] "ALTS Kicks Off White House, Congress Lobbying Effort," *Local Competition Report,* January 25, 1993, v.2, no. 2, 1.

[13] "Telecommunications Policy '93," A White Paper Prepared by the ALTS, 2.

[14] Ibid. , 5.

[15] Ibid.

[16] Ibid. , 14.

[17] Ibid. , 7.

[18] Ibid., 8.

[19] Ibid., 15.

[20] "Heather Gold Is New ALTS President," *Local Competition Report*, March 8, 1993, 11.

[21] TCG Opposes Bell Operating Companies' "POT Bay," Says Some BOCs Obstruct Interconnection Ordered By Regulators," TCG Press Release, June 4, 1993.

[22] Ibid., 4.

[23] United States v. AT&T, 524 Supp. 1336, 1352 (D.C. 1981).

[24] "Teleport Communications Group Releases Issue Paper On Central Office Interconnection Arrangements; Cites Ameritech Tariff As More Logical Approach," TCG Press Release, November 10, 1993.

[25] Steve Coll, "The *Deal Of The Century,...The Breakup Of AT&T,"* (New York: Atheneum, 1986), 354.

[26] Ibid., 356.

[27] Ibid., 357.

[28] Ibid., 361.

[29] "Congress' Role In Telecommunications Reform Has Been Negligible," *Washington Telecom News,* February 14, 1994, 4.

[30] Democratic Congressman from California, 1996.

[31] "Competition Is Key," Speech by Reed Hundt, Chairman FCC, Deloitte & Touche Consulting Group Telecompetition '95 Conference, Washington, DC, December 5, 1995.

[32] Ibid.

[33] "Local Competition and Interconnection," Staff Report to the Illinois Commerce Commission, July 2, 1992, 31.

[34] "Generic Investigation Into IntraLATA Toll Competition Access Rates," DE 90-002, Report of the New Hampshire Public Utilities Commission, June 10, 1993, 6-7.

[35] Testimony by David Gabel before the Maine Public Utility Commission on Behalf of the Commission Advocacy Staff, Docket No. 92-130, December 1992, 3.

[36] "CompLECs & Universal Service Assurance," Speech delivered by TCG President at the Third Annual Intelligent Network Summit, Sponsored by Telephony Magazine and Bellcore, June 1, 1994.

[37] Ibid.

[38] "U.S. Ready To Ease Its Legal Barriers In Communications," *New York Times,* December 20, 1993, A1.

[39] "F.C.C. Can't Force The Bells To Let In Rivals, Court Says," *New York Times,* June 11, 1996, 1D.

[40] "Court Overturns F.C.C. Rules On Baby Bells," *New York Times,* June 11, 1996, 47D.

[41] Ibid.

[42] "New Plan For Phone And Cable," *New York Times*, December 22, 1993, D1.

[43] Ibid., D2.

[44] "House Easily Approves Communications Bills," *New York Times*, June 29, 1994, D2.

[45] "Bill To Revamp Communications Dies In Congress," *New York Times,* September 24, 43.

[46] Bill To Revamp Communications Dies In Congress," *New York Times,* September 24, A1.

[47] "Closed Hearings Dent Bipartisan Alliances," *Interactive Week,* January 30, 1995, 35.

[48] Ibid.

[49] Ibid.

[50] "Clinton Vows To Veto Bill On Telecommunications Decontrol," *New York Times,* August 1, 1995, D1.

[51] *Warrens Telecom Regulation Monitor,* February 12, 1996, 4.

[52] Ibid., 3.

[53] "Communications Bill Signed, And The Battles Begin Anew," *New York Times,* February 8, 1996, A1.

[54] L.T. Knauer, R.K. Machtley, and T.M. Lynch, *Telecommunications Act Handbook* (Rockville, Maryland: Government Institutes, Inc., 1996), 8.

[55] "Communications Bill Signed, And The Battles Begin Anew,"

[56] "Communications Bill Signed, And The Battles Begin Anew," *New York Times,* February 8, 1996, B4.

[57] *Warrens Telecom Regulation Monitor,* February 12, 1996, 3.

[58] The Telecommunications Act of 1996, Title I, Part III, Section 271, (d), (3), (C).

[59] "ILEC Entry Into Long-Distance Should Be Delayed, CLECs Told," *Local Competition Report,* May 12, 1997, 4.

[60] Ibid.

[61] Ibid.

[62] *Warrens Telecom Regulation Monitor,* March 19 1996, 5.

[63] *Warrens Telecom Regulation Monitor,* September 16, 1996, 2.

[64] "Minimizing Entanglement, Maximizing Competition," February 1998, TCG White Paper, 1.

[65] Ibid., 3-4.

[66] Ibid. , 5.

[67] Ibid., 10-11.

[68] "Bell Atlantic Decision to Spark New Competition," *The Wall Street Journal,* December 23, 1999, A3

13. CONSOLIDATION

Competitive Industry Status In 1996 – Year One Of The Telecom Act

The passage of the Telecom Act in February of 1996 left the CLEC industry poised on the edge of a new era. National telecommunications law now had the intended result of a transition from a monopoly-dominated environment to one characterized by vigorous competition embracing local as well as long distance service.

Although 1996 was Year One of life under the new Telecom Act, few changes had actually been implemented until late in the year. The CLEC industry, still led by MFS and TCG, continued its established growth patterns. MFS alone rocketed past the $1 billion mark in 1996 and led the industry to total revenue in excess of $2 billion. Five CLECs now had revenues in excess of $100 million.

The seventy-eight identifiable players (those with actual revenue) were being joined by hundreds of freshly minted wannabes as a great variety of telecommunications-related companies and start-ups sought CLEC certification in the newly respectable industry that now had greater access to investment capital, raising more than $4 billion in 1996.[12]

Leading CLECs Ranked By 1996 Total Revenue[3] ($millions)

	CLEC	1996 Revenue
1.	MFS Communications	$1,238.5
2.	Teleport Communications Group	266.0
3.	ICG Communications (formerly IntelCom Group)	190.7
4.	MCImetro	178.0
5.	Intermedia Communications	103.4
6.	McLeodUSA	58.0
7.	GST Telecommunications	56.2
8.	Brooks Fiber Properties	45.5
9.	Electric Lightwave	31.3
10.	NEXTLINK Communications	25.7
	Others (68)	147.5
	Industry Total	$2,340.8

MFS Enters The Internet Business

MFS' Project Silver identified UUNET Technologies as the most desirable Internet Service Provider to acquire. UUNET was the largest and fastest-growing Internet Services Provider, in terms of both revenue and customer base, and was already collocated with MFS in many sites.[4]

UUNET was also owned 14.7% by Microsoft, and rapidly growing Microsoft Network was its largest customer. MFS CEO Crowe and Kiewit Chairman Walter Scott flew to Microsoft headquarters in Redmond, Washington to ask Bill Gates whether he would object to MFS buying UUNET. Gates gave his okay with his only condition being that UUNET CEO John Sidgmore should continue to run the operation.

On February 27, 1996, Jim Crowe and his vice president for Corporate Development, Rick Weidinger, went to the headquarters of UUNET Technologies in Fairfax, Virginia to meet with Sidgmore and Richard Adams, UUNET's founder, Chairman and Chief Technical Officer.[5] The discussions explored the mutual interests of the two companies. MFS needed UUNET's technical expertise in configuring and managing complex packet switched networks, and UUNET needed the broadband network, sales force and financial resources of MFS to maintain its place in the Internet race. Further discussions brought visions of even more synergism and of futuristic voice, data and video services which MFS could offer through UUNET's Internet expertise.[6]

Crowe wanted 100% ownership of UUNET. However, the size of the deal necessitated that MFS use its stock as the currency; and the UUNET board wanted cash. MFS refused. Urged on by the investment bankers, who envisioned an enthusiastic response by the stock market—to say nothing of a rich payday for themselves—the UUNET board relented and voted on April 26, 1996, to accept an all-stock swap that represented a 38% premium over the price of UUNET stock that day.[7] On August 12, 1996, the merger closed with MFS paying the equivalent of $2 billion in stock for UUNET.[8] The result of the merger was to create a powerful company with nearly $1 billion in pro-forma revenue and an annualized growth rate in excess of 100%.

The McCourt Initiative

Dave McCourt, MFS' partner in building and operating the Boston network, soon got restless after the construction phase was completed. In 1991, McCourt decided to go to the United Kingdom and to start over as a telecommunications contractor as he had been earlier in his career. There he found that deregulation had moved ahead of where it was in United States. The government in the United Kingdom had awarded franchises for the operation of hybrid cable—telephone networks. McCourt had three strategic ideas for wanting to be involved in building these systems:

(1) No one else knew how to build these systems, so the margins should be good.

(2) Building these systems would provide insight into the viability of competing in the residential (as opposed to the business) telecommunications market.

(3) Creating and staffing a telecommunications entity in the United Kingdom could provide the basis for market entry if MFS elected to go international.

McCourt told Kiewit Chairman Walter Scott about his overseas plans and asked whether Scott, through Kiewit or MFS, might be interested in being his partner in the venture. Scott's response was that if McCourt were just prospecting for work in the United Kingdom, he was not interested in spending Kiewit money for that. However, he said that if McCourt won a construction contract, then they could be partners.

McCourt formed McCourt Cable and Communications U.K. Ltd. and won a contract to design and build a hybrid cable-telephone system. Scott agreed to partner, and they formed McCourt/Kiewit International Partnership in 1992 as a 50/50 deal. The partnership built several systems and grew in size to 400 engineers. MFS began the installation of a network in London in 1993. With CLEC operations in London and other major European cities scheduled to begin in 1994, McCourt sold his share of the partnership to MFS.[9] Aided by this start, MFS' international telecom revenues grew very rapidly to $4.9 million in 1995 and reached $23.2 million in 1996.

McCourt was now convinced that he knew how to bring competitive telecommunications to the residential market using bundled telephone and cable services. On flight from the U.S. to the U.K. McCourt made a pitch to Walter Scott for the creation of a company that would be the residential telecommunications version of MFS and achieve the success that MFS had attained in the business telecommunications market. McCourt said, "Walter, I want to put a business plan together, but it needs to include a study of people's propensity to change phone and cable providers in their homes." Scott replied, "I'll give you $250,000 to do the business plan the right way."

RCN: Residential Communications Network

McCourt formed a partnership between himself and the Kiewit company called Residential Communications Network (RCN). The idea was to do for the residential market what MFS, with Kiewit's backing, had done for the business market. To move closer to the MFS analogy, McCourt developed a business plan for RCN and called it the MVS plan ... Metropolitan Video Systems. As the MVS plan was reviewed by the Kiewit Board, McCourt waited nervously outside.

One of the Directors emerged and asked, "What is it that you want to do with residential systems?" "Offer phone and cable television to the home," McCourt replied. "Phone and cable to the home!" he sputtered. "That doesn't sound like a real business. We've been contractors. To go from the construction business to telecommunications (via MFS) was hard enough. To go to residential cable television with HBO and Showtime and pay-for-view and all that— it seems too much. Jeez, maybe you should have called the business plan DGH ... Dave Goes Hollywood."

The Board approved the plan.

The Rise of WorldCom And Bernie Ebbers

In September 1983, Bernard J. (Bernie) Ebbers and friends, Bill Fields, David Singleton and Murray Waldron, had met in a Hattiesburg, Mississippi coffee shop to draw up a business plan for a company to resell AT&T long distance service. The waitress suggested the name for the company...Long Distance Discount Service, which quickly became better known as LDDS.[10] Ebbers was in the motel business and intended to be a passive investor in LDDS as a way to raise funds for buying more motels.[11] LDDS did not do well; and in April 1985 with the company teetering on the brink of bankruptcy, the Board asked Ebbers to take over as President. The mission was to sell the company, but no buyer was found. Ebbers decided that the only alternative was to turn the company around and make it grow.[12]

Ebbers, who liked to dress casually in cowboy boots and string ties, cultivated a laid-back image that hid a sharp and penetrating intellect. He often made reference to his eclectic, unpretentious early activities as a milkman, a basketball player, a gym teacher and a coach.[13] His success in building LDDS showed his true talent which was the rare ability to integrate acquired companies into existing operations. (Critics claimed that he didn't really integrate companies, but rather dictated how much profit each entity had to make each year and then left them alone to run themselves and figure out how to do it.)

LDDS began a roll-up of small and medium-sized long distance re-sellers. By 1994, after more than forty acquisitions, LDDS had revenues of $1.7 billion and was the largest reseller of long distance service in the United States.[14,15] Whatever his critics may have thought, he was certainly doing something right. The metric that pleased Ebbers the most was the fact that $100 invested in LDDS in 1989 was now worth $868.

Although LDDS, as the largest reseller of long distance service, got the most favorable volume-discounted rates from the long distance carriers, Ebbers decided that long-term success required the ownership of a physical network. Even though industry observers speculated that the country was awash in excess fiber capacity, Ebbers purchased WilTel Network Services and its national fiber network from the Williams Company in August 1994 for $2.5 billion.[16,17] By year-end 1995, LDDS had transformed itself into WorldCom and was carrying 19.4 billion minutes of long distance traffic on its own network and earned operating income of $249.5 million on revenues of $3.64 billion.

Jim Crowe Meets Bernie Ebbers

Although long distance carriers could use technology innovations and increasing traffic volumes to reduce the costs of the long-haul portion of their networks, they were still dependent upon the local telephone companies for the "last-mile" local link to the customer. Originating and terminating access charges paid to the local telephone companies could account for forty percent of the per-minute cost of the call.

Where CLEC local fiber networks could be used to bypass the telephone company's network, access charges could be dramatically reduced. As the fourth largest long distance carrier, WorldCom was a major customer of MFS Communication's local fiber networks. MFS, in turn, became a major customer of WorldCom. MFS had linked its ATM network between major cities over leased long-haul fiber circuits from WilTel. WorldCom acquired WilTel's national fiber network on January 5, 1995, and inherited MFS as a customer.

With their business ties between their two companies increasing, the senior executives of the MFS and WorldCom companies held a "get acquainted" meeting in Sandestin, Florida on August 14 and 15, 1995. WorldCom CEO Ebbers brought Scott Sullivan, his CFO, and Roy Wilkens the CEO of WorldCom's newly acquired WilTel division. Jim Crowe, Chairman and CEO of MFS, brought his President and COO, Royce Holland, and his CFO, R. Douglas Bradbury.[18] The meeting produced no immediate action, but each company went away impressed by the drive and aggressive vision of the other.

Bernie Calls

In May, 1996, Ebbers called Crowe to suggest that they explore joint commercial or strategic opportunities. They scheduled a meeting at MFS' headquarters in Omaha for May 21, 1996. Ebbers and Sullivan met with Crowe and two of his Vice Presidents, Frederick Weidinger, VP of Corporate Development, and Ron Vidal, VP of New Ventures. Views were exchanged on the CLEC business and the long distance business and the impact of the new Telecom Act.

They discussed the opportunities in international growth and in the pending entry of MFS into the Internet business through the acquisition of UUNET Technologies.[19] The May meeting was followed by a series of meetings over the next three months; and by August 1996 Ebbers revealed what he had in mind. He wanted local as well as long-haul fiber network facilities. He wanted to acquire MFS.

WorldCom Acquires MFS Communications

Crowe did not want to sell MFS. He had built the company from a start-up into the leading CLEC with annualized revenue of over a $1 billion and an international presence. He had just negotiated the UUNET acquisition and was excited about leveraging the new Internet opportunities using the MFS network. He was on a roll. Why quit now?

Kiewit Chairman Walter Scott had been convinced by Gates in 1995 that there was serious trouble ahead for the traditional telecommunications network. Crowe understood that concern. He believed that MFS' circuit-switched network would soon have to be rebuilt as an Internet Protocol packet-switched network or face decline. Even with UUNET's help, this could be a long, expensive and arduous process. He could see the attraction of a fresh start to design and build an all-new network without the burden of any legacy switches and equipment.

Ebbers was known to pay full price for assets he wanted, and he wanted MFS. Perhaps, Crowe concluded, MFS should sell now ... if the price were right. Crowe proposed a deal to Ebbers involving the exchange of one share of MFS stock for 2.1 shares of WorldCom stock.[20] On August 26, 1996, two weeks after the MFS/UUNET acquisition closed, WorldCom and MFS issued a joint press release prior to the opening of the NASDAQ stock market, announcing the formation of MFS WorldCom.[21]

At a stock swap of 2.1 to 1, the price tag for MFS was approximately $14.3 billion, which some observers suggested was too high. An analyst for Prudential Securities said, "Why does (WorldCom) have to pay such a premium? Either WorldCom was desperate or MFS thought it was worth a lot more."[22]

WorldCom's stock price dropped 26% in three days, but then recovered.[23] Ebbers, who was named President and CEO of MFS WorldCom, disagreed that he had overvalued MFS. "We are creating the first company since the breakup of AT&T to bundle together local and long distance services carried over an international end-to-end fiber network owned or controlled by a single company," he said.

First, since WorldCom, Inc.'s networks will connect to MFS' city networks, we expect to achieve significant cost savings from reduced line and access costs.

Second, the merger will eliminate duplication of capital spending programs, including those for undersea capacity, international facilities and MFS' planned U.S. intercity network.

Third, the combined company is uniquely positioned to take full advantage of the Congressional intent behind the Telecom Act...we expect these cost savings alone, including payment for originating and terminating both local and long distance calls, to substantially justify the merger.[24]

Crowe, the designated Chairman of the new MFS WorldCom, dutifully played his part. "Bernie Ebbers and WorldCom, Inc. are at the very top of all American companies in creating shareholder value. I look forward to joining Bernie's team and helping to continue that record," he said.

The merged assets of the two companies would create a powerhouse —billions in revenues, 500,000 business customers in North America, Europe and Asia and 30,000 miles of fiber networks. More importantly, however, Crowe noted, "Combined annualized third quarter revenues of $5.8 billion growing at 30 per cent per year, while impressive, does not fully capture the potential for future growth. The combined company has outstanding opportunities to increase growth rates in virtually all segments of the business. International and Internet-related business represents annualized revenue of approximately $1 billion currently growing at 100 percent per year."[25]

The merger was completed on December 31, 1996.

Teleport Communications Group Goes Public

It was clearly time for TCG to become a public company. TCG needed access to the equity markets, and the cable company owners wanted to monetize their $770 million investment and move on to other opportunities.

Ownership of TCG was creating barriers for the cable owners seeking mergers with telecommunications companies. As early as 1993, a proposed merger between RBOC Bell Atlantic and Tele-Communications, Inc., one of TCG's cable owners, raised questions about whether such a combination would be permitted.[26] Although the merger was never consummated, it was widely believed that TCI would be required to divest its ownership in TCG before the merger would be approved.

Now another cable owner, Continental Cablevision, wanted to sell out to an RBOC, U S WEST. Continental Cablevision's ownership in a CLEC created problems for RBOC ownership. TCG proposed to buy out Continental's interest in it with cash raised in an Initial Public Offering.[27] There were, however, significant structural issues to be resolved prior to an initial public offering. TCG had an unwieldy ownership structure.

The four cable company owners still held all of the capital stock as follows: Tele-Communications Inc., 30%, Cox Communications, 30%, Comcast Corporation, 20%, and Continental Cablevision, Inc., 20%. There were also fourteen partnerships that had been formed beginning in 1993 among the company, affiliates of the owners and certain other cable operators to develop and operate local telecommunications networks. While these local market partnerships had materially aided TCG in its race with MFS to establish a national presence, they now had to be unwound before a public offering was possible. The company was reorganized so that TCG owned 12 of the 14 partnerships outright and controlled the remaining two which had minority ownership by TCI. Reorganization left TCI with the largest ownership share: Tele-Communications Inc., 37% , Cox Communications, 30%, Comcast Corporation, 20%, and Continental Cablevision, Inc., 13%.[28]

TCG went public on June 27, 1996. The company issued 27 million shares of stock, $300 million in Senior Notes and $1,073 million in Senior Discount Notes to raise gross proceeds of $1.3 billion.[29] Not everyone in the financial community thought that placing these dollars in the hands of TCG was a good idea. Editorial comment in Barron's magazine noted, "Instead of approaching break-even as revenues have climbed, Teleport's results have deteriorated... This suggests that Teleport's markets have become far more competitive, with less revenue realized on more intensive effort."[30] The editorial went on to note,

Teleport is not an unproven company. It has proven it can make repeated and rapidly growing losses, accompanied by extremely poor revenue gains per dollar of capital investment. The principal purpose of the offerings, of course, is to further increase Teleport's capital spending, with results we would rather not surmise.[31]

TCG Keeps Swinging

Undeterred by the possibility that one of its major owners might merge with an RBOC, TCG kept up its criticism of RBOC attempts to enter the long distance business within their operating regions. TCG suggested that RBOCs were wasting everyone's time by preparing to submit applications before they had satisfied the "competitive checklist" required by the Telecom Act of 1996 as proof that they had opened their local markets to competition.

TCG again distributed copies of the "Nine Points" and suggested that RBOCs first be certain that they had satisfied these before claiming to have met the more rigorous requirements of the Telecom Act. TCG's Atkinson said,

> The RBOCs are familiar with our checklist exam because we've published our 'Nine Points' and suggested readings for the past five years. There are no surprises or trick questions. The Congressional checklist for local telephone competition tracks TCG's checklist so our exam should be a fair predictor of whether an RBOC can earn a passing grade at the FCC.[32]

> ...Unfortunately, we can't think of one market in the country where any RBOC could check off all nine boxes today. That means that the essential prerequisites for effective local exchange competition are not satisfied in any community, and it would be premature for any RBOC to try to take the FCC's final exam.[33]

TCG "Seizing the Right Opportunities"

For Annunziata the appropriate company focus was on building infrastructure and growing revenue, not worrying about near-term profitability. Investors agreed, and by year end 1996 TCG stock had nearly doubled.

Titling its first annual report as a public company as "Seizing the Right Opportunities," TCG boasted that it had, since its inception, spent one billion dollars to build fiber networks in 65 markets across the United States.[34] Annunziata pointed with pride to corporate developments in 1996 including the opening of the Howard W. Bruhnke Advanced Technology Center, a state-of-the-art central office with voice and data facilities to develop and test sophisticated, new, value-added customer services.[35] He also noted that TCG had acquired a 49.9% ownership of wireless transport provider, BizTel, with an option to remaining shares.[36] BizTel held licenses to serve 160 markets via very high frequency (38 GigaHertz) microwave that could be used to dramatically reduce the "last-mile" cost of expanding TCG's network.

While these short wavelength microwaves are subject to rain attenuation and hence limited to paths of three miles or less, they are quasi-optical and require a dish antenna only 12 to 15 inches in diameter to produce a narrow beam. As a result, by beaming a signal from a hub location connected to the fiber network to small dishes on surrounding rooftops, TCG could extend service to those buildings quickly and inexpensively. By contrast, extending service by the traditional method of constructing a fiber link from the core fiber network in the street to a nearby building often cost $50,000 to $100,000 and months of delay.

Annunziata also indicated that two important acquisitions were in progress that would improve TCG margins and leverage its infrastructure investments. First, TCG, like MFS, would take an active role in the Internet business through the acquisition of a major Internet Service Provider. TCG was acquiring San Diego-based CERFNet, a premier Internet Service Provider with 6,000 business customers. Second, with the pending closure of the Eastern TeleLogic acquisition, TCG would have interconnected networks spanning the Northeast Corridor from Boston to Washington, D.C. As a result, TCG would be able to offer regional long distance service with minimal outlays.

Such aggressive participation in long distance would be a significant strategic change for TCG that had always limited its activity in this area in order to avoid alienating its long distance carrier customers. However, in this post-Telecom Act world the rules had changed. AT&T, lacking local networks of its own, apparently was not only *not* offended but even signed joint marketing and development agreements with TCG and five other CLECs.

IntelCom Group Becomes ICG Communications

Although it was the third largest CLEC behind MFS and TCG in total revenue in 1996, IntelCom was having great financial difficulty. In an effort to address these difficulties, the Company reorganized and refocused during 1996 to emphasize the offering of retail dial-tone service.

IntelCom Group was originally a Canadian company. In the reorganization it became a subsidiary of a new publicly-traded U.S. corporation, ICG Communications, Inc. (ICG). The reasons given for becoming a U.S. corporation rather than a Canadian federal corporation were that nearly all of the Company's operations were in the United States.

In addition, ICG said that it viewed the United States as its primary source for raising capital. It also noted that certain aspects of its operations were regulated by the FCC, whose rules impose some restrictions on the interests a foreign company may hold in telecommunications businesses in the United States.

ICG refocused by selling four of its five teleports and shifting its marketing of switched services away from wholesale carriers and toward retail end user customers, particularly those living in its five major market clusters. ICG particularly targeted the California market, initiating local dial-tone service in December, 1996, and installing six frame relay/ATM switches to provide state-wide data service.[37] As part of its California initiative, ICG acquired a 60% interest in CLEC, Linkatel of San Diego, and negotiated agreements with several utilities—Southern California Edison, the Los Angeles Department of Power and Water and the City of Alemeda Bureau of Electricity—to dramatically increase its network mileage.

By year-end 1996, ICG had quadrupled its fiber network mileage to 2,385 miles and had deployed 14 5ESS central office switches from Lucent Technologies. Switched service revenue tripled; and of the $190 million revenue for the year, $109 million came from telecommunications services. However, ICG remained a company in trouble with increasing losses and a heavy debt load. Its losses increased to $199 million on revenue of $190 million in 1996, and its liabilities by year-end exceeded $800 million.[38]

MCImetro Struggles

MCImetro closely followed ICG in revenue in 1996 but continued to have difficulty developing business other than that of MCI Communications itself. In September 1996, MCI de-emphasized the MCImetro name. Although still retained as the legal entity owning local facilities and filing with state PUCs, the MCImetro designation was no longer used to market local service offerings.[39] MCImetro revenue hit $178 million for 1996, but cash flow was increasingly negative.[40]

MCI did, however, continue a relatively aggressive investment in local facilities. In 1996 MCI spent $390 million on local facilities and ended the year with seventeen switches deployed and networks operating in seventeen major cities.

Some industry observers forecast that, despite being hampered by slow-moving and acrimonious negotiations with RBOCs, MCImetro might yet rival MFS in national local market coverage. RBOCs, observers noted, considered MCI (and Sprint and AT&T) to be more formidable competition than MFS. They feared that MCI would be able to capitalize on the brand strength and market presence of its long distance business.[41]

After 1996, MCI totally re-integrated CLEC marketing operations into the core company and renamed its local service operations, MCI Local Service.[42]

Intermedia's Data Revenue Exceeds Its Local Telecom Revenue

As with all the leading CLECs, Intermedia developed a more diverse business mix that went well beyond basic CAP access services, expanding into long distance as well as growing its data business.[43]

Aided by the acquisition of frame relay provider, EMI, in 1995 Intermedia's data network soared to almost 10,000 nodes in 2,200 cities served by 89 switches by 1996. Intermedia boasted in its 1996 annual report that, "the company currently has more frame relay nodes in place than the combined total of America's top three local telephone companies."[44] With 31% of its $191 million revenue coming from data services, Intermedia now derived more revenue from these services than from local telecommunications services. No other CLEC was so dependent on data services.

McLeodUSA

McLeodUSA appeared among the leading CLECs for the first time in 1996. The company, founded by Cedar Rapids, Iowa entrepreneur, Clark McLeod, in 1991, took an indirect route to become the sixth largest CLEC. McLeod was a veteran of the long distance industry. He had founded Iowa-based long distance company, Teleconnect, in 1980 and served as its Chairman and CEO. Teleconnect had grown to become TelecomUSA, America's fourth largest long distance company. McLeod was President of the 6,000 employee company when it was purchased by MCI for $1.25 billion in August 1990.[45]

McLeod formed McLeod Telecommunications, Inc. in June 1991 and won a contract to provide maintenance services for Iowa's statewide, fiber optic network. The company reincorporated as McLeod Telemanagement and began selling bundled local and long distance service in Iowa and Illinois in 1994.[46]

The local service was provided by reselling U S WEST Centrex service in Iowa and Ameritech Centrex service in Illinois, combined with resold service purchased in bulk from long distance carriers such as AT&T, MCI and Sprint.[47,48] U S WEST opposed McLeod's petition for certification, arguing that companies like his could drain away the business customers and force higher rates for residential customers. The Iowa Utilities Board ruled in McLeod's favor in 1994.[49] Although the margins on resold Centrex service were small, McLeod's intent was to ultimately migrate the traffic to his own AT&T central office switch when the judicial and regulatory proceedings were resolved.[50]

McLeod found enthusiastic financial backers who had made large profits from Teleconnect. McLeod acknowledged that he was out to repeat his success of a decade earlier. He said, "We feel we are going to do what we did before to an even higher level than what we did in the 80s with the Teleconnect Co. This is a much bigger arena."[51]

As Congressional action moved toward passage, McLeod began to position his company to own its own facilities rather than to be a reseller. In April 1995, McLeod acquired competitive access provider MWR from electric utility, MidAmerican. MWR owned and operated a fiber network in Des Moines, Iowa. Following the passage of the Telecom Act, McLeodUSA went public. A public offering in June 1996 raised $259 million.[52] The company did not use these funds to buy or build new networks as did most CLECs. Instead, McLeod acquired two highly profitable telecommunications-related businesses in Cedar Rapids. McLeod purchased a telemarketing company in July 1996 and a directory and yellow pages publishing company in September.[53,54]

Leveraging these assets, McLeod returned to the financial markets with a secondary stock offering in November 1996. Bolstered by its acquisitions, it was now a much more substantial company with an annualized revenue run-rate in excess of $100 million.[55] With the new money gained in the secondary offering, McLeod now pursued the more traditional CLEC strategy of acquiring switches and building fiber networks.

However, Clark McLeod had at least one more unconventional tactic to employ in building his CLEC company. In 1997, he acquired a rural telephone company, Consolidated Communications, Inc., serving customers in 45 cities and towns primarily in Illinois. With the addition of Consolidated Communications' 73,000 local customers, McLeodUSA, Inc., while still deriving significant revenue from resale, had suddenly taken a giant step toward becoming a facilities-based super-regional carrier.[56]

GST Telecommunication

Under founder John Warta's restless leadership, GST Telecommunications expanded into multiple lines of business, participating in nearly every area of communications. GST built local fiber networks in cities across the western United States and Hawaii as well as a long haul fiber network in the Southwestern United States. GST operated a digital microwave network linking the islands of

Hawaii and added a submarine cable network. GST owned several long distance resale companies, shared tenant service and wireless operations and Internet Service Providers. GST even owned a company which manufactured a small telecommunications switch. GST deployed both voice and data switches. In May 1996, GST linked its frame relay network to that of Intermedia to provide seamless nationwide coverage.

Warta's close friend and GST President and COO, Earl Kamsky, once said, "John's a terrific and brilliant guy but I wish someone would slow him down a little. It's difficult to implement as fast as he comes up with new ideas."

Warta's association with GST would ultimately come to an abrupt end. On June 15, 1998, he resigned as CEO and Chairman of the Board and on October 15 as a Director. On October 20, 1998, GST brought suit against Warta and five other former officers and directors of the company, alleging that they had conspired to divert a business opportunity in Mexico from GST to an independently controlled company in Canada.[57] Warta countersued and the parting was acrimonious.

Brooks Fiber Goes Public

In order to fund its intended strategy to have networks operational in fifty small to medium-sized cities within the next three years, Brooks tapped the public equity market. On May 2, 1996, Brooks Fiber Properties went public with a 7.6 million share offering at $27 per share. This brought the number of shares outstanding to 27 million, so that Brooks Fiber had a market capitalization of $730 million. Remarkably, this value had been created in just 49 months from start-up.

Brooks increased its involvement with MCI. On May 30, 1996, its agreement with MCImetro was expanded with MCImetro agreeing to purchase all of its local access for new end-user services in seventeen specific markets from Brooks Fiber. In July, 1996, MCImetro announced that it would make a cash investment in subsidiaries of Brooks Fiber with the option of converting this to common stock.[58] A year later the "preferred provider" agreement would be extended to cover 37 cities.[59] By year-end 1996 Brooks Fiber was operational in 23 cities, had 20 switches in service and revenue of $45.6 million.[60] To fuel its expansion, Brooks Fiber completed a $250 million private placement of senior notes, which closed May 29, 1997, followed by a $250 million credit facility with Goldman Sachs Credit Partners in July.[61],[62]

Brooks continued to acquire as well as build. Among the Brooks Fiber acquisitions in 1997 was Metro Access Networks with networks operating or under development in seven Texas cities.[63] Owned by independent telephone company, Century Telephone Enterprises, Metro Access Networks was the third CLEC started by Intermedia Communications of Florida co-founder, Richard Kolsby.

Electric Lightwave

The other CLEC founded by John Warta, Electric Lighwave, continued to be among the leading CLECs ... the ninth largest in revenue in 1996. Electric Lightwave continued to operate as a subsidiary and receive all of its capital funding from Citizen's Utilities, a Stamford, Connecticut-based utility holding company.

By year-end 1996, Electric Lightwave had deployed five Nortel DMS 500 switches and fifteen frame relay switches in its major markets.[64] Net losses for 1996 were $29 million on revenue of $31 million. Electric Lightwave projected losses to continue for several years as it expanded its fiber networks.[65] By 1997, capital investment was expected to exceed $400 million. In order to avoid carrying all this capital investment load, Citizens Utilities began preparing Electric Lightwave for an Initial Public Stock Offering in 1997 and planned to reduce its ownership below 51%.[66]

NEXTLINK Communications

On July 4, 1996, NEXTLINK Communications became one of the first CLECs to offer facilities-based local dial tone under the Telecommunications Act of 1996.[67] By year-end 1996, NEXTLINK was operating five Nortel DMS-500 switches, serving eight markets.[68] Prior to April 1996, NEXTLINK funded its expenditures with $55 million in equity investments by companies controlled by cellular pioneer and billionaire Craig McCaw. To continue its growth the company then issued a $350 million debt offering of Senior Notes and prepared the company for an IPO in 1997.[69]

Telecom Act Years 2-3: Consolidation Gains Momentum

In 1987 and 1988—Years Two and Three of the Telecom Act—the CLEC industry took on a dramatically different look. By the end of 1988, MFS, Brooks Fiber Properties and MCImetro would all be part of WorldCom; and TCG would be part of AT&T. The line between a CLEC and a long distance carrier would become progressively indistinct. Ranked solely by their CLEC-based revenues, however, MFS and TCG continued to lead the industry in 1997 and 1998.

Leading CLECs Ranked By 1998 Revenue[70] ($millions)

	CLEC	1997 Revenue	1998 Revenue
1.	MFS WorldCom (CLEC revenue only)	$2,250.0	$4,894.0
2.	Teleport Communications Group	494.3	-
	TCG/AT&T(CLEC revenue only)	-	901.0
x.	MCImetro (acquired by MFS)	343.0	-
3.	Intermedia Communications	248.0	712.8
4.	McLeodUSA	267.9	604.1
5.	ICG Communications	245.0	397.6
x.	Brooks Fiber Properties (acqd. by MFS)	128.8	-
6.	RCN	127.3	245.1
7.	GST Telecommunications	119.0	163.3
8.	e.spire Commun. (formerly ACSI)	59.0	156.8
9.	Winstar Communications	79.0	141.5
10.	NEXTLINK Communications	57.6	139.7
	Others	1,190.3	2,264.7
	Industry Total	$5,644.3	$10,620.6

Appearing for the first time among the leading CLECs in 1997 were Kiewit-backed RCN, e.spire Communications founded by former MFS CEO Anthony Pompliano and Manhattan-based Winstar Communications. Winstar, a high-frequency microwave transport company, acquired LOCATE in 1996 and began CLEC operations.

Since the early days of the creation of competitive local carriers, it had generally been assumed that long distance carriers would ultimately absorb them to form miniature versions of the once unified Bell Telephone System. CLECs had generally envisioned the three major long distance companies, AT&T, MCI and Sprint, as the most likely acquirers. But, except for MCI's less than spectacular MCImetro initiative, the major carriers seemed unwilling or unable to move aggressively to build local networks or acquire CLECs. This appeared to be due in part to a fear that aggressive moves into local service would hasten the day when RBOCs would be permitted to enter the long distance business.

However, with the hyperactive WorldCom's acquisition of MFS, Brooks Fiber Properties and MCImetro (along with MCI) many CLECs said privately, and only sometimes in jest, that their business plan consisted of building up their local networks and selling out to WorldCom's Bernie Ebbers.

WorldCom Acquires Brooks Fiber

On the 25th of June 1997, WorldCom President and CEO Bernard J. Ebbers sat in the lobby of a Manhattan hotel waiting his turn to speak to the investment community at the Montgomery Securities' Media and Communications Conference.

There was a high level of excitement in the air. In addition to WorldCom's recent acquisition of MFS, Microsoft had revived the flagging interest in cable as a telecommunications media with a major investment in Comcast; and AT&T and SBC corporation were discussing joining forces to partially recreate the Bell System.

A reporter approached Ebbers. The reporter expressed amazement at the speed with which Andy Lipman and the rest of MFS WorldCom's regulatory staff had won approval to build fiber networks and to open telecom markets in the countries of the European Union. "Sometimes," the reporter offered, "I think Andy Lipman must walk on water." "Wrong religion," Ebbers shot back dryly.

A group of analysts drifted over to the table where Ebbers sat. "Bernie," one asked, "tell us what you're going to buy next." Without hesitation Ebbers replied, "Brooks Fiber." The analysts laughed and moved away.

Ebbers turned to Gary Brandt, his Vice President of Public Relations. "Gary," he said, "do you know (Brooks Fiber Chairman) Bob Brooks and (Brooks Fiber CEO) Jim Allen?" "Yes I do," Brandt replied. "In fact I think they just walked in. They are over there across the lobby." "Introduce me," Ebbers said.

Less than four months later, on October 1, 1997, Brooks Fiber announced that it had entered into a definitive agreement to be acquired by MFS WorldCom in a stock swap valued at $2.9 billion.[71]

By the time the acquisition was completed at year-end, Brooks Fiber was operating 39 networks and 35 switches and had revenue of $129 million. In 47 months Brooks Fiber had gone from a start-up to a company valued at nearly $3 billion.

Brooks Fiber CEO Allen said,

> Our company was the recipient of an offer from the one company that possessed a currency representing the kind of growth potential that was attractive to us. WorldCom is ideally positioned to be the premier telecommunications company in the world by virtue of its substantial long distance business, coupled with a national geographic footprint in first and second-tier cities for local exchange services in the United States and in Europe. In addition, the combination of Brooks Fiber's networks with WorldCom's global leadership position as a provider of Internet services through fiber optic networks creates endless opportunities.[72]

WorldCom Acquires MCI

All during 1997, MCI had struggled to take advantage of the Telecom Act and to enter local telephone markets. MCI President Timothy Price announced that MCI Communications expected to lose $800 million in pursuit of the local service market in 1997 and even more in 1998.[73] There was speculation that MCI might lose $2 billion on local service over two years.

MCI President Price accused the telephone companies of using unfair tactics and bureaucratic delays to frustrate and block competition for local service. He called on the FCC to institute a "Fair Play Test" to ensure that the objectives of the Telecom Act of 1996 were not subverted by the telephone monopolies.[74] Shortly thereafter, FCC Chairman Reed Hundt formed an Enforcement Task Force to "ensure that pro-competitive policies of the Telecom Act and the FCC's local competition rules are being followed."[75]

The RBOCs responded with derision. The CFO of BellSouth, Ron Dykes, accused MCI of purposely building its new local fiber networks only in the high-cost urban centers to serve business customers and of ignoring the needs of its traditional base of residential long distance customers. He said,

> MCI purposely made their problems worse by launching a project to build networks in some of the nation's largest cities, ignoring potential revenue from residential customers along their network grid. They're doing this so they can argue there's no competition in local (and thus keep) the Bells out of long distance. In their typical way, they are using half truths to pervert the political process.[76]

MCI was fighting a multi-front war. In addition to seeking to enter the domestic long distance market, it was also attempting to expand both its domestic and international long distance business. MCI met some of the large capital funding this entailed through an investment by international telecommunications giant, British Telecom, which acquired a 20% share of MCI. In 1997 British Telecom sought to acquire the rest of MCI, putting the company in play.

This attracted the attention of WorldCom's head, Bernie Ebbers. From early on in building his long distance empire, Ebbers had dreamed of the day his company would be among the industry leaders. Although WorldCom was only the fourth-largest long distance carrier, with a meager 5% market share, it owned a powerful currency in the lofty price of its stock.[77] The market had awarded WorldCom's stock a high price to earnings multiple because of the company's prospects for continued rapid growth. At year-end 1996, WorldCom's market capitalization exceeded $20 billion. Ebbers boasted that a $100 investment in his company in 1989 was now worth $2,200 in 1996.[78]

On October 1, 1997, MFS WorldCom announced its intention to acquire MCI, offering to exchange $41.50 worth of WorldCom stock for each share of MCI stock. This transaction, valued at $30 billion, represented a $9 billion increase over an earlier offer by British Telecom. WorldCom ultimately raised its offer to $51, and British Telecom reluctantly allowed its interest to be bought out. Many industry observers were incredulous that an upstart like MFS

WorldCom could acquire MCI, a company almost four times its size in annual revenue. Ebbers joked in response to a reporter's question, "AT&T was our first choice but (AT&T Board member) Walter Elisha didn't know who we were."[79] In fact, an acquisition bid for AT&T had been seriously considered by Ebbers before the MCI offer was made. The bid for MCI was made instead because AT&T's business mix was not as compatible with WorldCom's as was MCI's.[80]

Even though capital expenditures slowed toward the end of 1997, due to MCI's pending acquisition by WorldCom, they totaled $550 million for the year; and MCI was operating 30 local switches and had fiber networks in 40 major cities by year-end. By the time MCI ceased to exist as an independent company, it had invested $1.3 billion in local facilities. These assets became an important addition to the arsenal which WorldCom would employ in its bid to be the leading integrated local/long distance carrier on a global scale.

MFS WorldCom's John Sidgmore said, "(In 1994) no one ever heard of WorldCom; we were just a dorky little company from Mississippi. Maybe we're still dorky (but everyone knows MCI WorldCom now)."[81]

Why Did MFS WorldCom Acquire MCI?

Given the acquisitive track record of Ebbers in rolling-up telecommunications companies, the crowning move of acquiring MCI, the second largest long distance carrier, seemed merely the next logical step. Prominent industry analyst, Jack Grubman, suggested that it was much more than that.[82]

Following its acquisitions of MFS/UUNET and WilTel, WorldCom had assembled a unique set of facilities and was the only carrier able to provide end-to-end, building-to-building connectivity on its own network from major cities in North America to major cities in Europe and the Pacific Rim for any type of voice and data service. The problem was that this capability was a complete mismatch with the existing WorldCom base of long distance customers.

The bulk of WorldCom's customers had been acquired in the LDDS days of the company's creation. These were typically small business operators who used less than $1,500 per month in long distance calling, didn't make international calls and didn't need data services. End-to-end connectivity held no appeal for them. Grubman asserted that to fully leverage the assets that had been assembled, WorldCom needed MCI's more sophisticated base of larger corporate customer, its national account sales force and its technology resources capable of creating advanced product sets.

AT&T Acquires Teleport Communications

Speculation now centered on whether and when TCG would be acquired. As one analyst put it in urging investors to buy TCG stock, "With the WorldCom takeover of MFS Communications affirming the value of the Competitive Local Exchange Companies, why wait?"[83] Although TCG was now a public company, it continued to be controlled by its three remaining cable shareholders: Cox Communications, Comcast and Tele-Communications Inc. These cable shareholders collectively held all of the shares of TCG's Class B stock, representing 66% of the equity and 95% of the voting power.

Investors who expected a bidding war for TCG were disappointed. There was a sudden announcement on January 8, 1998, that TCG had entered into an agreement to merge with AT&T.[84] Since control was in the hands of the three major stockholders, TCG had simply negotiated the deal in private. All that was required was for each of the cable stockholders to execute and deliver a written consent in favor of and approving the merger agreement. It was a *fait accompli,* and no further vote or meeting of the stockholders was required.[85] Public stockholders were irate. The all-stock transaction provided 0.943 shares of AT&T stock for each share of TCG stock, placing an $11.3 billion value on TCG. At the January 8, 1988, stock values, this meant that TCG shares were worth $59. Many analysts who had placed a $65-$70 value on TCG shares now speculated that the cable shareholders had sold out cheap because they were eager to divest themselves of their interests in the contentious local services market.[86]

AT&T Chairman and CEO C. Michael Armstrong said, "Joining forces with TCG will speed AT&T's entry into the local business market, reduce our costs and enable us to provide businesses the any-distance services they want."[87] Annunziata noted that TCG would continue to build local networks. "Right now AT&T spends about $10.7 billion in local-access charges," he said. "So we have about 10.7 billion reasons to build."[88]

For the second time in his career, Annunziata would be an AT&T employee. Armstrong indicated that Annunziata would be named an executive vice president of AT&T and lead a new local service and access management unit built around TCG. Armstrong declared, "Bob Annunziata is an outstanding addition to AT&T's senior management team. His impressive track record and more than a decade of experience in the competitive local exchange carrier business make him ideally suited to head up our new combined local services unit."[89] The merger announcement noted that "to ensure that AT&T will benefit from the experience and expertise of TCG's proven management team, Annunziata and his top managers have signed employment agreements with AT&T that extend into the next century."[90]

However, the announcement also said that Annunziata would not report only to Armstrong but would also jointly report to AT&T President John Zeglis. Adding lamely, "like all of AT&T's most senior officers..."[91] Both CLEC and veteran AT&T watchers read that to mean that Bob Annunziata would be a short-timer at AT&T.

AT&T Seeks Multiple Network Paths For Local Service

While TCG's fiber and microwave network was extensive, it was designed to address the business market. For ubiquitous local telephone coverage, including residential, AT&T need a much greater reach. It proposed to do this by a combination of media including fixed wireless systems and cable television systems.

Rumors had circulated of a secret AT&T project to build a massive fixed wireless system to bypass the residential local loops of the telephone companies. It was alleged that this project was initially started in Craig McCaw's cellular company and continued at AT&T after they acquired the company. Originally called Project Dino for the Flintstones' pet dinosaur, it was renamed Project Angel at AT&T. AT&T spent $2 billion to acquire wireless spectrum licenses covering 93% of the U.S. population.[92] Whatever the wireless strategy might be, AT&T also began acquiring some major cable companies (such as, Tele-Communications, Inc., MediaOne) and negotiating with the others for use of their cable systems including help in upgrading the systems to two-way transmission in order to deliver local telephone services.

A Restructured CLEC Industry

With MFS, MCImetro, Brooks Fiber and TCG now owned by WorldCom and AT&T, the CLEC industry looked radically different. Leading standalone CLECs were now Intermedia, McLeodUSA, ICG and RCN followed by an eclectic collection of smaller companies pursuing a great variety of business strategies.

By year-end 1998, one hundred sixty CLECs were producing total industry revenue of $10.6 billion with only 23% of the revenue coming from the traditional dedicated access and private line services on which the industry was founded.[93]

Switched local services, the largest service category, contributed 33% of CLEC revenue. In pursuit of switched service, CLECs had 579 voice switches in operation and served 5.6 million access lines either on their switches or through resale.[94],[95]

Switched Data Service, The Fastest Growing CLEC Service

Although the explosion of the Internet demand opened the door to successful data-communications-based businesses for the CLECs, it did not turn the industry overnight from a voice to a data dominated entity. Rather, data offerings became an important component and one of the fastest growing segments of nearly every CLEC's revenue mix.

From 1996 onward there was a rapid deployment of frame relay, ATM and multi-functional data switches. A study by International Data Corporation reported that service revenue in the packet/cell switched market in the United States in 1996 went 58% to frame relay, 36% to X.25, 4% to ATM and 2% to SMDS.[96] However, they also predicted that, given the respective growth rates, the market would be five times larger by 2001 and dominated by a combination of frame relay at 73% and ATM at 19%. Their forecast for X.25 and SMDS was that both would fade to niche services.

Throughout the CLEC industry, data switches were installed at a rate that was difficult to follow. By 1997, CLECs reported that more than 400 data switches had been installed in their networks, and by 1998 the number reported was nearly 900.[97] This may be an undercount, since data switches, unlike room-sized voice switches, may merely be one shelf in an equipment rack. Over the same period CLEC voice switches increased from 315 to 579.[98] CLEC revenue from switched data services grew rapidly and became an increasingly larger component of the total CLEC industry revenue, which itself was growing dramatically. From 1996 to 1998, revenue from switched data services grew from 4% of total revenue to over 20% of total revenue.

The Benefits Of Hosting An Internet Service Provider

All facilities-based CLECs were besieged by Internet Service Providers seeking to collocate equipment with them since LEC collocation was more expensive and much less "user friendly." CLECs quickly went into the "Collocation Hotel" business.

As an added bonus for CLECs, collocated Internet Service Providers pulled traffic originating on the local telephone company network to terminate on the CLEC switch, causing the LEC to pay "termination charges" to the CLEC.

When CLECs had first entered the switched services business, they had proposed that CLECs and LECs not exchange payments for traffic originating on one local network and terminating on another local network. The LECs refused this arrangement, assuming that more calls would flow from the small CLEC network to terminate with users on the larger LEC network. However, the presence of the Internet Service Providers reversed this flow and caused a net payment for termination to go to the CLEC. Although it was assumed that this "anomalous" situation would be eventually removed by regulatory action, CLECs enjoyed the bonus in the meantime.

The Local Loop Becomes Selectively Digital

The demand for high-speed access to the Internet also led to the creation of a whole new category of CLECs. By collocating digital electronics in the central office, it was possible to drive high-speed data transmission over the existing copper-wire local loop to the residential or business end user. A family of such electronic devices, operating at different speeds, became known as Digital Subscriber Line (DSL) devices.

Led by Covad Communications of Santa Clara, California, which was initially funded by electronics giant, Intel, companies formed specifically to lease local loops from LECs, install DSL and offer high-speed data access to Internet users.[99] On a user selective basis, these companies were really fulfilling the promise of ISDN to complete the "digitizing" of the telephone network all the way to the end user.

These new competitive companies were labeled by some as DataCLECs or DLECs, a title they disliked as too confining.[100] Just as CLECs had begun as niche-filling CAPs, the new DSL-based companies saw their initial Internet access service as just a market entry point from which to grow. Even as ISDN had intended to deliver both voice and data over a digital local loop, DSL technology was quickly enhanced to do the same. The so-called DataCLECs soon began to integrate multiplexed voice services with their Internet access services and to expand to a broader range of offerings. Ironically, this new breed of competitive company faced exactly the opposite challenge from that of the traditional telecommunications carrier. Starting in the world of data, their challenge was to move into the voice world.

The Impact Of The Internet On The CLEC Industry

CLECs became successful data communications vendors thanks to the demand created by the Internet. Clearly without this demand, only the most determined CLECs were destined to build a data business based on specialized applications like LAN interconnection. Furthermore, nothing in the prior data universe approached the sheer size of the Internet opportunity.

Beyond altering the revenue mix for CLECs, involvement with the Internet changed the character of the CLEC industry. CLECs were launched irrevocably upon a path beyond that of the traditional telecommunications carrier. For some, the fact of their expanding service portfolios drew their attention to bundling services as an integrated communications provider.

But the change was really deeper. Having grown from a narrow niche within the existing telecommunications structure, CLECs now had before them an expanding variety of potential roles as providers of a broad range of information services, uniquely packaged in ways limited only by the creative imagination.

Consolidation Among Local Telephone Companies

Consolidation was not confined to the CLECs and long distance companies, but embraced all parts of the telecommunications industry, including incumbent local telephone companies.

When the Bell System was broken up in 1984, the smallest, in terms of revenue, of the seven RBOCs formed was Southwestern Bell. Southwestern Bell provided local telephone service in Arkansas, Kansas, Missouri, Oklahoma and Texas; but the majority of its revenue came from Texas. Southwestern Bell grew aggressively, renamed itself SBC Communications and moved its headquarters from St. Louis to San Antonio. In 1997, SBC acquired fellow RBOC, Pacific Telesis, and its operating territory in California and Nevada. In 1998, SBC acquired independent telephone company, Southern New England Telephone in Connecticut. In 1998, SBC also announced an agreement to acquire fellow RBOC, Ameritech, and its operating territory in the five Great Lakes states: Ohio, Indiana, Illinois, Michigan and Wisconsin. The merger would have given SBC pro-forma revenue of $46 billion in 1998.[101]

The action didn't stop there. In 1998, RBOC, Bell Atlantic, acquired RBOC, NYNEX, joining its operating territory in New Jersey, Pennsylvania, Delaware, Maryland, the District of Columbia, West Virginia and Virginia with NYNEX's in New York, Maine, Massachusetts, Vermont, Rhode Island and New Hampshire. Bell Atlantic then initiated a merger with GTE, the largest independent telephone company, with mostly rural operating territories in 31 states. Suddenly the seven original RBOCs had become four, and the independent local telephone companies were disappearing. Alarmed that telecommunications companies were merging rather than competing for local telephone service, the FCC imposed thirty conditions on the SBC—Ameritech merger to ensure competition. These conditions were intended to encourage CLEC competitors to operate within the SBC regions and to encourage SBC to conduct CLEC-like operations of its own within the territories of other RBOCs. The agreement specifically called for SBC to enter 30 markets outside its territory in 30 months. SBC Chairman Edward Whitacre commented, "We've got plans to do that and we've had them for a long time. If the process (of FCC approval) hadn't taken so long, we'd already be in (new markets)."[102]

At a New York conference a telecom analyst attempted to get WorldCom's Bernie Ebbers to comment on the charge that SBC was the most resistant to CLEC operations. "We're told by many CLECs," the analyst said, "that those guys in Texas are the meanest, dirtiest competitors that CLECs face. Is SBC the toughest RBOC?" Ebbers grinned and replied, "Maybe. Maybe not. I will say this, SBC is the best run RBOC... by far."

MCI WorldCom Moves To Acquire Sprint

Although the acquisition of MCI appeared to be his crowning achievement, Ebbers was not content to stop there. In September 1999, MCI WorldCom announced that it was in talks to acquire Sprint, the third largest long distance company.[103] Combining MCI WorldCom's 26% of the long distance market with Sprint's 11% would still leave the merged companies short of AT&Ts 43% market share; but, nevertheless, such market power concerned regulators.[104] With a market capitalization of $151 billion MCI WorldCom had a higher valuation than market leader AT&T's $140 billion.

MCI WorldCom won a brief bidding war with RBOC BellSouth with an offer to buy Sprint for $115 billion. By folding Sprint's extensive wireless and Internet assets into his company, Ebbers could create a new entity called simply, WorldCom, which would have the muscle to face AT&T or any combination of RBOC market entrants.

Telecom Act Year-Four Status of Local Competition

Whether the Telecom Act of 1996 was actually working to open markets to competition was a matter for contention. The RBOCs had gone to court numerous times to contest the implementation rules laid down by the FCC and had constantly urged Congress to revisit the legislation. As mergers and growth created larger competitors, the RBOCs complained that they were being unfairly held out of the long distance market by FCC rejections of their applications. Not all of these pleadings were well received in Congress. An exasperated Senator Ernest Hollings wrote to Commerce Committee Chairman John McCain asking that hearings be held to look into the status of local telephone competition. He accused the local telephone companies of a "concerted effort to subvert the (Telecom) Act (through legal challenges). "Now, having failed in the courts, these companies have crawled back to Congress where they are asking that we exempt them from the market-opening requirements of the Act."[105]

Newly installed FCC Chairman William Kennard concurred.

> Unfortunately, the first three years of the implementation of the Telecommunications Act of 1996 were characterized not by cooperation, but by confrontation. Litigation instead of collaboration. What we got was uncertainty, confusion and delay. We lost valuable time. It is time to move on... It is time to take the battles out of the courtroom and into the marketplace.[106]

By year-end 1999 Chairman Kennard was optimistic, saying,

> Multiple networks freely interconnecting is no distant dream. The forces of convergence are beginning to pry open markets that have been closed for decades. After years of monopolies, high prices, and stifled innovation, we are beginning to see the benefits of competition in many areas. We have an opportunity —not unlike the opportunity policy makers had at the turn of the century—to make these markets competitive.[107]... robust competition is within reach. Long distance providers, cable companies, wireless operators, incumbent and competitive local exchange providers: all are beginning to compete with one another. And we must make sure they continue competing.[108]Next year, fifty years, a hundred years from now, we must make sure that people look back on what we have done and say that we had the foresight to abandon the regulatory shibboleths of old and meet the demands of consumers in the Information Age.[109] Our legacy must be that we helped unleash the entrepreneurial energy of the American people ...[110]

Footnotes Chapter 13: Consolidation

[1] "*1997 Annual Report On Local Telecommunications Competition,*" (Chicago, IL: New Paradigm Resources Group, Inc. and Connecticut Research, Inc., 1998, Chapter I, Table 2, 7.

[2] "Teleport Communications Group, Inc.," Donaldson, Lufkin & Jenrette, October 28, 1996, 5.

[3] Sources: Company financial reports, New Paradigm Resources Group, Inc. and Connecticut Research, Inc. estimates.

[4] MFS Communications, Inc. Proxy Statement-Prospectus, July 12, 1996, 38.

[5] Ibid.

[6] Ibid. , 39.

[7] Ibid., 41.

[8] "MFS Communications Completes Merger With UUNET Technologies," MFS Press Release, August 12, 1996.

[9] MFS 1993 Annual Report, 22.

[10] WorldCom Corporate Milestones, www.wcom.com.

[11] Steve Rosenbush, *Telecom Business Opportunities,* (Newport, Rhode Island: Aegis Publishing Group, Inc., 1998) 265.

[12] Ibid.

[13] "WorldCom Has Its Eye on No.1 / Company Started In A Coffee Shop Now Major Player In Industry," *Newsday,* www.newsday.com.

[14] WorldCom Corporate Milestones.

[15] "WorldCom Inc.," *Salomon Smith Barney Research Report*, April 9, 1998, 13.

[16] Ibid.

[17] WorldCom Corporate Milestones.

[18] WorldCom, Inc. and MFS Communications, Inc. Joint Proxy Statement For Special Meetings Of Shareholders, December 20, 1996, 32-33.

[19] Ibid.

[20] Ibid.

[21] "WorldCom, Inc. and MFS Announce Merger To Form Premier Business Communications Company," Press Release, August 26, 1996.

[22] "Analyst Reactions Mixed," *Telecom Monitor,* September 2, 1996, 4.

[23] *Telecom Monitor,* September 2, 1996, 3.

[24] Ibid.

[25] "MFS Communications Reports Third Quarter 1996 Results," MFS Press Release, October 31, 1996.

[26] :Whatever Is To Become Of TCG?," *Local Telecommunications Report,* October 27, 1993.

[27] "Teleport Using IPO Cash To Buy Out Continental," *Multichannel News,* May 13, 1996, 44.

[28] Teleport Communications Group, Inc. Prospectus, Merrill Lynch & Co., Morgan Stanley & Co., Donaldson Lufkin & Jenrette, Lehman Brothers, Deutsche Morgan Grenfell, June 3, 1996, 6.

[29] Teleport Communications Group 1996 Annual Report, 25.

[30] "Offerings In The Offing - Teleport Communications," *Barron's,* June 1996, 48.

[31] Ibid.

[32] "Teleport Communications Group Challenge RBOCs: If You Can't Pass Our 'Nine Points' Test For Effective Local Phone Competition, You Can't Pass Congressional Test, Says TCG In Checklist Distributed Today," TCG Press Release, February 15, 1996.

[33] Ibid.

[34] Teleport Communications Group 1996 Annual Report, 13.

[35] Ibid., 4.

[36] Ibid.

[37] "ICG Communications, Inc. Reports Revenue Increases For Quarter And Fiscal Year End, September 30, 1996," ICG Press Release, December 5, 1996.

[38] ICG Communications 1996 Annual Report, 17-18.

[39] "MCI Reveals Local Market-Entry Plan, Future Arguments For State Commissions," *Telecommunications Reports,* September 2, 1996

[40] MCI Communications Corporation Form 10-K, December 31, 1996.

[41] "MFS WorldCom - A $12 Billion Merger Verifies The Value Of Local Access," The Yankee Group White Paper, August 1996, 2.

[42] "*1998 Annual Report On Local Telecommunications Competition,"* (Chicago, IL: New Paradigm Resources Group, Inc. and Connecticut Research, Inc., 1998, MCI - Pg. 1 of 18.

[43] Intermedia Communications 1996 Annual Report, 21.

[44] Intermedia Communications 1996 Annual Report, 15.

[45] Prospectus for McLeod, Inc., Salomon Brothers Inc., Bear, Stearns & Co. Inc., Morgan Stanley & Co., November 15, 1996, 61.

[46] Ibid. , 35.

[47] Ibid. , 36.

[48] Centrex is a service in which the telephone company partitions, by software, a portion of its central office switch to serve as though it were a single customer's PBX.

[49] "Busy Signals In Iowa's Telephone Wars," *Business Record,* March 28, 1994.

[50] Prospectus for McLeod, Inc., 38.

[51] "Busy Signals In Iowa's Telephone Wars," *Business Record,* March 28, 1994.

[52] "McLeod Inc. Offers 12 Million Shares Of Class A Common Stock At $20 Per Share," McLeod Press Release, June 10, 1996.

[53] "McLeod, Inc. Agrees To Acquire Ruffalo, Cody & Associates, Inc.," McLeod Press Release, July 15, 1996.

[54] "McLeod, Inc. Completes Acquisition of TELECOMUSA Publishing Group, Inc..," McLeod Press Release, September 23, 1996.

[55] Prospectus for McLeod, Inc., 6.

[56] "McLeod USA - Consolidated Communications: Merger Model Or Just A Model Merger?," *Research Report On Competitive Telecommunications,* NPRG, Inc. July 1997.

[57] GST Telecommunications, Inc. Form 10-K, December 31, 1998, F-24 .

[58] "MCImetro Makes Additional Investment In Brooks Fiber, Names Brooks Fiber 'Preferred Provider ' In 17 Markets," Brooks Fiber Press Release, July 9, 1996.

[59] "Brooks Fiber Properties Announces Expanded Agreement With MCI Covering Additional Cities," Brooks Fiber Press Release, July 10, 1997.

[60] 1996 Brooks Fiber Annual Report.

[61] "Brooks Fiber Properties Announces Completion Of $250 Million Private Debt Placement," Brooks Fiber Press Release, May 30, 1997.

[62] "Brooks Fiber Properties Announces Commitment For $250 Million Bank Credit Facility," Brooks Fiber Press Release, July 18, 1997.

[63] "Brooks Fiber Properties Completes Previously Announced Agreement With Century Telephone Enterprises, Inc. To Merge Metro Access Networks, Inc. With Brooks Fiber," Brooks Fiber Press Release, May 6, 1997.

[64] Prospectus For Electric Lightwave, Merrill Lynch & Co., Morgan Stanley Dean Witter, Deutsche Morgan Grenfell, November 24, 1997, 3, 8.

[65] Ibid.

[66] Ibid., 10-11.

[67] NEXTLINK Communications, Inc., 10-KSB For Fiscal Year 1996, 1, 4.

[68] Ibid. , 2.

[69] NEXTLINK Communications, Inc., 10-QSB, September 30, 1997.

[70] Sources: Company financial reports and NPRG, Inc. and Connecticut Research, Inc. estimates. "Named Leading CLECs" defined as companies with primary revenue from local services. Some companies with large total revenues dominated by contributions from non-local service (e.g. long distance) are lumped in "Others" category.

[71] "WorldCom To Acquire Brooks Fiber Properties In $2.9 Billion In Tax-Free Transaction," Brooks Fiber Press Release, October 1, 1997.

[72] Ibid.

[73] "In The Midst Of Chaos, MCI Plans To Stick To Its CLEC Strategy," *Local Competition Report,* July 21. 1997, 1.

[74] "MCI Outlines 'Fair Play Test' For Local-Service Market," *Local Competition Report,* July 21, 1997, 3.

[75] "In The Midst Of Chaos, MCI Plans To Stick To Its CLEC Strategy," *Local Competition Report,* July 21. 1997, 2.

[76] Ibid.

[77] WorldCom, Inc., Joint Proxy Statement/Prospectus, November 14, 1996, 1.

[78] Steve Rosenbush, *Telecom Business Opportunities,* (Newport, Rhode Island: Aegis Publishing Group, Inc., 1998), 263.

[79] "WorldCom Has Its Eye On No.1 / Company Started In Coffee Shop Now Major Player In Industry," *Newsday,* October 1997.

[80] "Charging The 'Net," *Barron's,* September 20, 1999, 20.

[81] Ibid.

[82] "WorldCom Inc.," *Salomon Smith Barney Research Report,* April 9, 1998, 13.

[83] "Teleport Communications Group, Inc.," Donaldson, Lufkin & Jenrette, October 28, 1996, 1.

[84] "AT&T And Teleport Communications Group To Merge; TCG To Become Core Of AT&T's Local Services Unit," TCG Press Release, January 8, 1998.

[85] Teleport Communications Group, Form 8-K, January 8, 1998, Item 5.

[86] "CLEC Landscape Changes As AT&T Acquires Teleport," *Local Competition Report,* January 19, 1988, 2.

[87] "AT&T And Teleport Communications Group To Merge; TCG To Become Core Of AT&T's Local Services Unit," TCG Press Release, January 8, 1998.

[88] Undated AT&T-TCG web posting, "Merger Moves Business Services Into Spotlight,"

[89] Ibid.

[90] Press Release, January 8, 1998.

[91] Ibid.

[92] "How AT&T Lucked Into A Wireless Secret Weapon" *Business Week,* March 10, 1997, 30.

[93] "*1999 CLEC Report,*" (Chicago, IL: New Paradigm Resources Group, Inc., 1999), Chapter 1, Table 3, 11 of 12.

[94] Ibid., Table 6, Chapter 6, 11 of 34.

[95] Ibid., Table 13, Chapter 6, 27 or 34.

[96] "Packets Pack A Punch," *Telephony,* November 24, 1997, 32.

[97] "*1999 CLEC Report,*" (Chicago, IL: New Paradigm Resources Group, Inc., 1999), Chapter 6, Table 8, 15-16.

[98] "*1999 CLEC Report,*" (Chicago, IL: New Paradigm Resources Group, Inc., 1999), Chapter 6, Table 6, 10-11.

[99] "*1999 CLEC Report,*" (Chicago, IL: New Paradigm Resources Group, Inc., 1999), Chapter 9, 2-3.

[100] "Identity Crisis," *Telephony,* October 4, 1999, 6.

[101] 1998 SBC Communications Annual Report, 26-27.

[102] "FCC Clears SBC's Ameritech Purchase, Sets 30 Conditions To Ensure Competition," *The Wall Street Journal,* October 7, 1999, B18.

[103] "MCI WorldCom, Sprint Ponder Merger," *The Wall Street Journal,* September 24, 1999, A3.

[104] "U.S. Hires Axinn To Review MCI-Sprint Deal," *The Wall Street Journal,* December 14, 1999, A3.

[105] "A Fed Up Hollings Asks Senate For Open Market Rules: With Teeth," *TelOSSource Magazine,* Sept/Oct 1999, 6.

[106] "Competition And Deregulation: Striking The Right Balance," Speech by FCC Chairman William Kennard to the United States Telecom Association, San Francisco, October 18, 1999.

[107] "Fostering Competition In A Converging World," Speech by FCC Chairman William Kennard before the Practicing Law Institute/Federal Communications Bar Association Policy and Regulations Conference, Washington, DC, December 9, 1999.

[108] Ibid.

[109] Ibid.

[110] "Blazing A Trail: A Vision For The Twenty-First Century," Speech by FCC Chairman William Kennard to the National Association Of Regulatory Utility Commissioners," San Antonio, Texas, November 10, 1999.

14. REBIRTH

Death By Consolidation

With telecommunications merging into mega-companies on every side, it seemed fair to argue that the era of smaller, innovative, entrepreneurial companies had passed. Such an outcome would be somewhat ironic. As they had contended to penetrate the local telephone markets, CLECs had often referred derisively to the incumbent monopoly companies as dinosaurs whose time was passing. They asserted that these multi-billion dollar giants were bureaucracies that were too big and clumsy to adapt to change and would ultimately perish in a fast-moving competitive telecommunications environment.

RCN's 1997 Annual Report featured this theme, and CEO David McCourt wrote,

> Once they ruled the earth. But a cataclysmic change occurred and the dinosaurs couldn't adapt. They died. An evolutionary dead end. Something similar is under way in the telecommunications industry. A shift as profound and far-reaching as the transformation from horse and buggy to the automobile ... the telegraph to the telephone.[1]

But now it appeared that the world was really evolving into one in which a handful of mega-companies would compete on a global basis with bundles of service spanning the entire spectrum of communications-related services—local and long distance telephone, data, Internet, wireless and cable. Physical and human assets, whether conceived in the womb of competitive or monopoly operations, would ultimately become simply internal cogs and gears within the international megagiants. Innovative entrepreneurs seemed destined to be rewarded and sent home or embraced and suffocated inside new-world bureaucracies.

Breaking Out

Innovative individuals within acquired competitive communications companies found it impossible either to retire to Florida with their winnings or to settle down to routine assignments in the new company. Given the knowledge they had absorbed in building their companies, the continuing elimination of regulatory barriers, the availability of investment capital, the outpouring of new technology tools and explosive growth of new markets—particularly those related to the Internet—the temptation to play again was too great.

By the scores, senior executives, middle managers and creative individuals streamed out of the merged entities and struck out on their own, forming new, start-up companies. These new companies were, in general, not simply knock-offs of old CLEC models, but encompassed new ideas and strategies. They reflected both the experiences of their founders in terms of what did and did not work and creative concepts about how to exploit the rich opportunities of the deregulating world. Therefore, these new competitive telecommunications were not narrowly constrained in their strategies. While the terminology, CLEC, continued to be applied, they did not conveniently fit under any traditional label of LEC, CLEC, long distance carrier, cable company or Internet Service Provider.

Allegiance Telecom

Having served as President, COO, co-founder and highly visible public spokesman for MFS Communications, Royce Holland now found himself in an uncomfortable position following the acquisition of MFS by WorldCom. His job seemed to be redundant, and he felt relegated to the sidelines. Holland charged that pre-merger agreements were not being honored by WorldCom, and he decided to leave to start his own company. "To keep me out of the market, WorldCom tried forcing me to sign some noncompetitive provision in violation of my deal," Holland told a reporter. "It looks to me like it has been an orchestrated campaign to prevent a competitor from trying to enter the market. It is beneath a great company like WorldCom to stoop to that level of anitcompetitiveness."[2]

At an annual meeting of ALTS, the industry association, in Orlando, Florida, Holland met with an old friend, Tom Lord, to brainstorm. Lord, as an investment banker for Bear, Stearns & Co. in 1992, had led the underwriting of the first initial public stock offering for a competitive company, Intermedia Communications of Florida. Seeking privacy for their discussions they held their meeting on the monorail ride at Disney World's Magic Kingdom.

In April 1977, they formed Texas-based Allegiance Telecom with Holland as Chairman and CEO and Lord as Executive Vice President of Corporate Development.[3] Unlike the earlier years of the CLEC industry, investment bankers were eager to back this new company; and by August Allegiance had closed on the largest equity capital raised for such a company to date ... $100 million.

WorldCom did not let go easily. In court papers they claimed that former MFS employees had raided their ranks to staff Allegiance. WorldCom charged that if allowed to continue its "lifeblood will be drained, its ability to service customers and manage its existing operations will be gutted." Allegiance noted that at this point it had 30 employees while WorldCom had almost 14,000.[4]

Holland was eager to put into action the lessons learned from building MFS, the major lesson being the need to create adequate back-office support, software and customer care systems. "At MFS," he said, "we had terrible operations support systems. We waited too late to invest the type of time and effort that are needed ... I'm sure I'll find some new mistakes to make, but I'm not going to make that one again."[5] "I never again want to be in the position of not being able to deliver what I sell."

Allegiance launched a program of becoming a switch-based CLEC in the 24 largest cities in the United States.[6] However, unlike early CLECs, Allegiance adopted a "Smart Build" construction program that concentrated capital spending on key assets such as switches and deferred ownership of many other physical network assets, such as fiber, by leasing until the customer base had been established.[7] Allegiance found fund raising surprisingly easy. The company went public in July 1998, raising $138 million in the IPO and selling $205 million in Senior Notes.[8] A notable director of the new company was Reed E. Hundt, former FCC Chairman.[9] By year-end 1999, Allegiance was operating with a revenue run-rate approaching $200 million.

e.spire Communications, Inc.

Anthony J. Pompliano, the deposed CEO of MFS Communications and CEO of its predecessor, Chicago Fiber Optics, was not ready to hang it up and felt certain that he knew how to build a successful CLEC. Following a pattern that would be repeated many times by

CLEC executives displaced from their positions by merger or reorganization, he started his own CLEC.   Upon the expiration of his non-compete agreement with MFS in 1993, Pompliano formed American Communications Services, Inc.(ACSI), headquartered in Annapolis, Maryland.   American Communications Services' strategy was to develop fiber-based CLEC operations primarily in small cities but also linking them to networks in medium-sized cities across the Southern United States. By March, 1995, American Communications Services was large enough to go public.

As with other CLECs, American Communications Services found Internet access to be the fastest growing part of its business. This growth became so strong that the Company decided to rename itself after its Internet access product which was service-marked as "e.spire." On April 13, 1998, American Communications Services officially changed its name to e.spire Communications, Inc. Pompliano succeeded in growing e.spire Communications into one of the larger CLECs. By year-end 1999 e.spire Communications had an annualized revenue run rate approaching $300 million.

KMC Telecom

Industry pioneer G. Scott Brodey once again tried his hand at creating a competitive telecommunications company. In 1995, with the backing of independent power entrepreneur, Harold Kamine, he started a new CLEC which was eventually named KMC Telecom. The company is headquartered in Bedminster, New Jersey.

The company's strategy is to build fiber networks in Tier III cities (population 100,000 to 750,000) in the south such as Huntsville, Alabama and Baton Rouge, Louisiana and to deploy 5ESS switches. The services include a bundled offering of local, long distance and Internet access in addition to private line and dedicated access transport. The company launched an aggressive multi-city rollout led by Brodey as Executive Vice President of Construction. The formation of KMC Telecom involved several well-known industry players in addition to Brodey. Among these were former Chicago Fiber Optics executive, Tricia Breckenridge, who became KMC's Executive Vice President of Business Development and investment banker, Rod Hackman, who had helped many of the early competitive companies find financing.

KMC Telecom also called upon more industry veterans. Michael Sternberg, former Senior Vice President of Marketing at MFS, became KMC's President and CEO; and Roscoe Young, former MFS Senior Vice President of Network Services became KMC's Chief Operating Officer. Gary E. Lasher, former President and CEO of Eastern TeleLogic, joined the KMC board. The company grew rapidly but, as of March 3,1997, Brodey was no longer part of the team.[10]

KMC Telecom raised $250 million in a January 26, 1998 offering of Senior Notes to fund is expansion. By year-end 1999, KMC was operating thirty-three networks and had deployed thirty-one 5ESS switches. Annualized revenue run rate approached $115 million entering the year 2000.[11]

Level 3

Just three weeks after MFS was acquired by WorldCom, Jim Crowe left his new position as Chairman of MFS WorldCom and returned to the Kiewit company.

Walter Scott, Jr. offered Crowe the leadership of the $3 billion Kiewit Diversified Group. Kiewit Diversified was involved in an eclectic collection of business lines including construction, coal mining, independent power production and computer outsourcing, as well as investments in cable and telephone. The attraction for Crowe was the promise that he could sell or transform these assets into a new enterprise. They would be his seed money to develop his concept of the communications company of the future. There was ample reason for Scott to place such confidence in Crowe. Over the seven years that Crowe was building MFS, the Kiewit company had invested $500 million. In 1995 when Kiewit distributed its shares of MFS to its shareholders, they had a market value of nearly $1.75 billion.[12]

In August 1997, Crowe was named President and CEO of Kiewit Diversified Group. On January 19, 1998, it changed its name to Level 3 Communications.[13] Other former MFS executives, including R. Douglas Bradbury and Kevin O'Hara, left MFS WorldCom and joined Level 3. Bradbury became Executive Vice President of Level 3, and O'Hara became Executive Vice President of Operations. Eventually 18 of the top 20 executives at Level 3 came from MCI WorldCom. Ebbers was reportedly angered by these defections, and there were hard feelings between the two companies. When queried by reporters, Crowe made light of the situation pointing out that the WorldCom mergers had left many executives in redundant positions and underutilized. Crowe said, "So we didn't write letters and make job offers to the 18—that's just taken out of context."[14]

Level 3 announced that it intended to create the first end-to-end network designed and built specifically for Internet Protocol based services. The plans called for the construction of local and long distance networks in the United States and overseas. Crowe said,

> We are building a network from the ground up incorporating Internet technology. We are optimizing the network for (Internet Protocol). As far as I know, we are the only organization with that kind of business plan. So our customers will fully benefit from the many advantages of Internet technology and packet switching.[15]

> ...There is a fundamental shift occurring today—as fundamental as the shift from the telegraph to the telephone or the mainframe computer to the PC—that is the shift to Internet technology and Internet Protocol-based communications. What will continue to drive that shift is economics. These new networks are simply less expensive—a lot less expensive—than traditional hundred-year-old telephone networks.[16]

The name, Level 3, was derived from the open systems network model which describes computer-to-computer data transfer over a communications network in terms of seven layers or levels. At the top, level 7, is the application program on the computer. At the bottom, level 1, is the physical network linking the two computer locations. In the levels in between, information is packaged and unpackaged, error checked, presented for transmission, monitored, controlled, verified and re-transmitted as required. Level 3 intended its business to involve more than simply physical transport of information. It dealt also with some of the "intelligence" functions performed at level 2, the datalink layer, and level 3, the network layer.

The Creation Of Level 3 Communications

Crowe set to work to design his communications company. The construction group was split off and took the name, Peter Kiewit Sons, Inc. The remainder of the company was renamed, Level 3 Communications, Inc. The independent power company, CalEnergy, was sold for $1.16 billion; and the cable interests, Cable Michigan, were sold for $129 million. The coal mining companies were prepared for divestment.

Construction was begun on a 16,000-mile national fiber network. In order to begin business without waiting for the completion of construction in 2001, Level 3 leased 8,300 miles of fiber from Frontier (formerly Rochester Telephone) to link fifteen U.S. cities.[17]

The company revealed that, in addition to the national fiber network, it intended to lease or own local networks in 56 North American markets, to build a 4,750 intercity fiber network in Europe, to lease or own local networks in 23 European and Pacific Rim markets, to lease transoceanic cable capacity and to construct a high-speed transatlantic cable.[18]

To finance these activities Level 3 issued an enormous debt offering in 1998 including $2 billion in senior notes (the largest junk bond offering to that time) and $834 million in senior discount notes. The following year Level 3 issued another $750 million in convertible subordinated notes and $1.5 billion in a secondary stock offering. Level 3 found itself in the unusual position of being a "start-up" with $4 billion in the bank.

Turning The World Upside Down

The true dimensions of Crowe's plans gradually emerged. He asserted, "We're not looking to get just 4% or 5% of the traditional vertically integrated telephony market and be content to live in AT&T's shadow. We think that technological change is in the process of blowing the telecommunications industry apart and that we can be the dominant, low-cost player in the business of transporting data."[19] From the days of building MFS, Crowe had been offended by the concept of granting telephone companies monopoly status. He said, "It was based on the mistaken notion that they needed protection because of the capital intensity of their operations. Yet what

society ended up getting in return for its trouble was waste, ineffi-
ciency and sluggish innovation."[20] "Monopolies offend me," Crowe
said, "they stifle innovation and lead inevitably to waste.
Introducing markets to monopolies is a lot of fun."[21]

Now he was setting out not merely to undermine local telephone
monopolies but to take on the entire world of traditional network
carriers, including AT&T and MCI WorldCom, and to decimate
their businesses in the process.

Crowe felt that he had experienced a kind of epiphany after the Bill
Gates warning in 1995 when he saw a chart in a consulting report.
It showed that a 42-page fax over the phone lines from New York to
Tokyo cost $28.83, and sending the very same document by e-mail
cost 9.5 cents.[22]

When Crowe looked hard at network architecture, he concluded that
he could build a fiber-based, cell-switched network based on the
Internet Protocol for $8 billion to $10 billion. He intended to build
this highly efficient data network and to migrate voice traffic onto it
using voice over Internet Protocol, a newly emerging technology.

The implications of this were far-reaching. Data traffic (primarily
fax and modem transmissions) on the existing circuit-switched networks in 1999 accounted for some 50% of the total traffic but only
10% of the revenue. Voice traffic produced 90% of the revenue.
Migrating voice to the data network would mean that voice bits
would produce fifteen times the revenue of data bits.[23]

While in the near term this would help pay for the new data network, such a pricing disparity would be unsustainable. If a significant portion of the voice traffic migrated to the data network, the
price of voice bits would be driven down toward that of the data
bits. Crowe anticipated that he could initially under price traditional
circuit-switched networks by 20% for voice traffic. However, he
expected this to be only the beginning with rising volumes and "silicon economics" in combination allowing him to drop the prices on
his data network by 50 - 60% per year.[24]

Crowe envisioned soaring traffic volumes as unit costs declined in a
manner analogous to the proliferation of PC applications as the unit
cost of a computer's transactions declined. He foresaw a scenario
of soaring volume and the unit prices for voice crashing down as

phone traffic was siphoned off by Internet-based networks. Crowe saw this cannibalization as ugly but unavoidable and catastrophic for circuit-switched network carriers.[25]

Furthermore, he did not think that traditional carriers could respond to this threat even though they saw it coming. He reasoned that investors in traditional carriers would never allow them to defer earnings while making the multi-billion investments required to rebuild their networks.[26] Level 3, by contrast, was viewed by investors in a manner similar to that held for most Internet companies. Near-term profitability was irrelevant. Even though Level 3's enormous network investments resulted in a business plan which did not turn profitable until 2004, investors were not deterred.[27] They still gave the stock multiples that made it potent acquisition currency.

How Do We Get Unfair Advantage?

While Crowe's network faced significant challenges, including development of seamless movement of traffic between his cell-switched network and the existing circuit-switched networks and the development of Internet Protocol voice traffic of acceptable quality, he did not consider these to be the major barriers to success. He considered the recruiting and retaining of the talented people needed to execute the Level 3 strategy to be the greatest hurdle to cross. "How do we get an unfair advantage in attracting and keeping the right kind of people?", Crowe asked.[28]

Level 3 hired Arthur Anderson Consulting in 1997 to conduct a nationwide study that included surveys of hundreds of high-tech professionals and engineering students. The study analyzed potential locations for a Level 3 headquarters and campus. Silicon Valley, Denver, the Northern Virginia high-tech corridor near Washington, D.C., Boston and North Carolina's Research Triangle areas were considered. When the Denver area ranked near the top with each group and also had the fewest negatives, it was chosen as the location.[29] Level 3, dedicated its 42-acre campus in Broomfield, Colorado on November 1, 1999.

Crowe entered the new millennium well-funded and confident. "At worst," he said, "we'll become part of someone else's strategy. The (telephone) industry spent 100 years building a network which, in effect, extends our ears around the world at a reasonable cost.

We're now at the Model T stage of building a network that can extend your eyes around the world at a reasonable price."[30]

RCN And The Poster Boy For The Residential Market

While Level 3 addressed a global strategy, it also owned nearly half of Dave McCourt's RCN which focused solely on the domestic residential market. Many analysts were convinced that the local residential market was impervious to competitive challenge through any network except the existing one owned by the local telephone company.

Prominent analyst Scott Cleland pointed out that the local loop network is so expensive that, unlike the long distance network, it was not reasonable to create a second or third network. He noted that local telephone companies have networks worth $270 billion, while long distance networks are worth only $40 billion. "Congress got it wrong," Cleland said, "It thought the local loop is like long distance."[31] Many industry observers concluded that there could only be one local network due to the high cost of duplicating it, and, noting the failure of companies that attempted local service resale, asserted that the benefits of competition, as envisioned in the Telecom Act of 1996, would never reach the residential telephone customer.

McCourt did not agree. While isolated locations might be difficult to reach, he saw no reason why networks could not be built to cost-effectively reach customers in high density regions and apartment complexes, particularly if the network delivered not just telephone service but a whole package of services including cable television and long distance service. Cleland conceded that, "The high density (market) allows you to have a pretty good opportunity to be successful at it. I would question how successful you might be in other areas of the country."[32]

Regulators who had shepherded the Telecom Act legislation through a sometimes dubious Congress were, however, delighted to see someone take dead aim at the politically sensitive issue of bringing the benefits of competition to the residential consumer. Reed Hundt, FCC Chairman from 1993 to 1998, began referring to McCourt as "the Poster Boy for Residential Competition.".

Creating The Residential Network

McCourt was not the first to conceive of a single pipe delivering telephone and cable service to the home. This was long-time dream of cable companies and motivated their involvement in the CAP/ CLEC business from its very earliest beginnings.

However, while playing a significant role in the competitive industry through ownership of CLECs like Teleport Communications, cable companies made very little progress in converting their cable infrastructure to support telephone service and other services requiring two-way traffic on their systems.

McCourt was contemptuous of their efforts. He regarded the cable companies as monopolies cut of the same cloth as the RBOCs. He saw them as culturally unable to convert themselves into providers of innovative and competitive services. "It wasn't the oil lamp guy that got into the light bulb business," he said. "It wasn't the horse and buggy guy that got into the automobile business."[33]

McCourt did not originally plan for RCN to build its own networks but intended to leverage the fiber networks of MFS through his partnership with Kiewit by leasing excess capacity. However, traffic on the MFS network was surging; and when RCN needed capacity in 1995, MFS had none to spare. "My first reaction was to panic," McCourt recalled, "but then I said, maybe our premise that we couldn't afford to build our network was faulty. We were lucky the MFS deal didn't work out."[34]

To promote the development of the RCN network, McCourt entered into partnerships with electric utilities, Boston Edison in Boston and Potomac Electric in the greater Washington, D.C. area. In Boston, McCourt again clashed with Cablevision which accused RCN of illegally delivering cable service without a license. This Massachusetts Cable Television Commission issued a show-cause order asking RCN to prove it was operating legally. RCN argued that it was an Open Video System provider, a new category of cable transport service provider defined by the Telecom Act of 1996.[35]

Cablevision also charged that Boston Edison had diverted fiber assets to the partnership with RCN without proper compensation of the utility rate payers who had paid for the fiber network. RCN beat back these and other challenges; and their lead attorney, Andy

Lipman, exalted, "We have been extremely successful bringing choice to residential consumers of communications services—over the frequent and strenuous objections of incumbent phone and cable providers."[36]

RCN focused its network development on the densely populated Washington, D.C.-to-Boston corridor on the East coast and the San Diego-Los Angeles corridor on the West coast. To finance these build-outs RCN raised over $2 billion in stock and debt financing in 1998-99. The original RCN business plan did not envision the Internet; but recognizing its rise, RCN acquired four Internet Service Providers and became a major industry player. In 1998, RCN went from no Internet service subscribers to over 500,000. McCourt said, "With the addition of Internet access, the RCN business plan went from a good plan to a phenomenal plan."

Sleeping With The Enemy

In 1999, the value of cable as the potential "second wire" to the home began to receive new appreciation as AT&T:acquires: cable companies initiated its program of buying up cable companies. The added potential of two-way cable to support high-speed Internet access as well received a shot in the arm when Microsoft made a $1 billion dollar investment in Comcast.

This was followed by a sustained roll-up of cable companies by Microsoft co-founder and billionaire, Paul Allen. Proclaiming a vision of "wired world" with all American homes having access to interactive video services, Allen spent over $20 billion to acquire seven cable companies and create Charter Communications, which suddenly was one of the country's largest cable companies. On November 11, 1999, Allen startled the cable industry by announcing that he was investing $1.65 billion in RCN. The industry was aghast.[37] RCN's aggressive CEO, McCourt, was one of the most vilified personalities among cable system operators.[38] McCourt vowed that his network would "...knock $20 billion off the market cap" of existing cable companies, and it seemed impossible that RCN and a cable company would ever cooperate.[39]

McCourt was as brash as ever. Of the outcry from the cable industry he said, "What a bunch of crybabies."[40] The cable companies retorted that RCN was far more talk than action and claimed that the company was an also-ran that would not amount to much with or without Allen's money. McCourt answered, "My vision, my work ethic, my passion, combined with Paul Allen's financial backing—it scares them."[41]

Winstar And Wireless

While most competitive companies continued to emphasize fiber networks, a few incorporated a strong dependence on very short wavelength microwave. TCG had begun to employ this technology to speed its network expansion shortly before it was acquired by AT&T. The strongest advocate of this technology was Winstar Communications which referred to it as "wireless fiber."

The combination of wireless technology with more conventional fiber networks and central office switches allowed New York City-based Winstar to grow very rapidly into a leading CLEC. By year-end 1999, its annualized run rate was approaching $500 million. As the largest holder of wireless spectrum rights in the United States, Winstar held licenses covering markets encompassing more than 200 million people and more than 80% of the business market in the United States.

The importance of these wireless assets in the facile delivery of high-speed Internet access was underscored in December 1999 when Winstar announced an agreement with Microsoft to deliver broadband applications and an investment by Microsoft and several leading investment firms of $900 million in Winstar for network expansion.[42]

Convergent Communications[43]

In the wave of emerging companies which spun out of the CLEC tradition were some so novel as to be difficult to classify. One such company, Denver-based Convergent Communications, was founded by three former executives of ICG Communications: John Evans, Keith Burge and Phil Allen in 1995. Based on their experiences as part of a traditional CLEC operation at ICG, they conceived of a business which would be more customer-oriented and less capital intensive.

Convergent bundles communications and data equipment with services and offers to act as the out-sourced resource for the small and medium-sized business office. Convergent takes responsibility for provisioning, installing and servicing the information resources on the customer's premise as well as providing the external network services. Convergent calls this "inside-out" since they attempt to position themselves inside the customer's company looking out at the world of LECs, CLECs, DLECs, long distance carriers and Internet Service Providers. The fastest growing portion of Convergent's business is e-business in which it provides combined packages of equipment, service, network and applications for small to medium business e-commerce.

Convergent raised $160 million with a high-yield offering in March 1998. In 1998, they gained a national presence through the purchase of TIE Communications. Convergent Communications went public with an initial public stock offering on July 20, 1999. By year-end 1999, Convergent had installed Cisco switching platforms in sixteen cities to provide IP and ATM services over a leased fiber network. Entering the year 2000, Convergent had operations in 35 cities, 1,550 employees, 33,000 customers and an annualized revenue run rate of $200 million.

Global Crossing

AT&Tcompleted its acquisition of Teleport Communications in July 1998. In September 1998 Bob Annunziata was appointed President of AT&T's $22 billion business services group, responsible for AT&T's global network and for providing voice, data and Internet services to eight million business customers worldwide.[44] Five months later Annunziata was gone. On February 24, 1999, two-year old upstart, Global Crossing Ltd., announced that Annunziata would become its CEO.[45] Annunziata said,

> I have enjoyed my second stint at AT&T and working with Mike Armstrong, but running Global Crossing is the single most exciting opportunity in telecommunications today. Global Crossing is leading the industry in building a seamless worldwide network designed to meet the exploding demand for bandwidth to handle Internet, voice, video and data services. Without the burden of legacy equipment, we have a unique opportunity to become the global telecom operator of choice for the new millennium.[46]

Hamilton, Bermuda-based Global crossing was founded by financier Gary Winnick to fill the missing link of adequate undersea fiber cables. The venture was a stunning success. Global Crossing began construction of a transatlantic link between Europe and the United States in 1997 and completed it in 1998. By year-end the company had contract sales of $1 billion and, amazingly, showed a positive net income of $72 million (before dividends and non-recurring items) and had begun three more undersea and two terrestrial (Europe and Japan) network projects.

Forbes editors noted, "If Andrew Carnegie were alive today, he'd be laying cable and J.P. Morgan would be financing it. And they would be making money faster than they did in steel. Photons move faster than atoms."[47] Money flowed to Global Crossing. The company went public in August 1998 with a $400 million initial stock offering followed by a $483 million preferred stock offering in December. By the time Annunziata took the helm as CEO in February 1999, Global Crossing had raised $4 billion for network construction.

A Bid To Swallow An RBOC

On March 17, 1999, Global Crossing made an $11.2 billion bid for Frontier Corporation. Frontier, the former upstate New York independent telephone company Rochester Telephone, was one of the first telephone companies to open its local market and expand into other lines of business including national fiber transport, long distance service and Internet Web hosting. Annunziata said, "We will now have a strong U.S. infrastructure to complement the IP (Internet Protocol)—based fiber network we are building in Europe, Japan, Mexico and Central and South America."[48]

Two months later, with the Frontier merger still pending, Global Crossing announced an even bigger surprise. On May 17, 1999, they revealed a definitive agreement to merge with RBOC, U S WEST, to form a seamless end-to-end local-to-global high speed network. Annunziata commented, "A decade and a half after the break-up of AT&T, competition in the telecommunications industry has spread around the world. Today we are joining forces with a former regional Bell operating company that knows how to compete and offers customers a compelling array of integrated voice and data services."[49]

Not Without A Fight You Don't!

Global Crossing was not permitted to complete these deals in peace. On June 13, 1999, long distance fiber company, Qwest Communications International, made a competing $55 billion bid for U S WEST and Frontier. Denver-based Qwest was founded by billionaire railroad magnate Philip Anschutz, and its CEO Joseph Nacchio had once been one of the top three executives at AT&T.[50]

Reporters tried to characterize the struggle between Annunziata and Nacchio as a brawl between two in-your-face street fighters from New York City.[51] However, Annunziata said, "I think it is fair to say that I am a competitive person by most people's standards. Joe and I have been friends for 25 years. We are on the opposite side here, but it is nothing personal."[52]

After a brief bidding war, a compromise was reached allowing Global Crossing to proceed with the acquisition of Frontier, while U S WEST disappeared into a "merger of equals" called Qwest.

After the dust had settled Annunziata noted that,

> Coming from nowhere, we have launched several acquisition efforts in an attempt to rapidly take advantage of an emerging market opportunity—the opportunity to become the first global telecommunications carrier and service provider ... One of our competitors was quoted in the press, incredulous that a company with "a couple of cables under the ocean" was even in this game ... The truth is, Global Crossing ... is a very substantial and asset-rich company.[53]

The Competitive Industry Entering The Year 2000

The waves of consolidation and the melding of the CLEC industry into the broader telecommunications industry following the passage of the Telecom Act of 1996 produced multiple effects. One of the most far-reaching and least anticipated was the redistribution and relocation of key personnel and their intellectual assets among companies and agencies. The individual instances are far too many to enumerate, but a few examples serve to illustrate. As detailed in this chapter former CLEC senior executives such as Jim Crowe, Royce

Holland, Tony Pompliano, and others formed or staffed new companies. There was also a significant redistribution and infusion of talent into regulatory and advocacy organizations. After years of leading the regulatory fight from his post at Teleport, Bob Atkinson left the company to become the Deputy Chief of the Federal Communications Commission's Common Carrier Bureau on January 4, 1999, to oversee the Bureau's Enforcement and Policy and Program Planning Divisions. FCC Common Carrier Chief, Lawrence Strickling, himself former General Counsel at Ameritech, said "Bob is one of the country's foremost experts on local competition issues. He will bring his considerable experience and knowledge of the CLEC industry to bear in his new role, and we are fortunate to have him join us."[54]

The Senior Legal Counsel and advisor to the Democratic Senators, including the influential Senators Hollings and Inouye, during the formulation of the Telecom Act of 1996, John D. Windhausen, Jr., became the President of ALTS. Windhausen greatly increased the strength and influence of ALTS and its staff both inside and outside the "Beltway."

This great stirring and mixing radically altered and generally elevated the level of skill and competence in every aspect of the telecommunications industry from government agencies to corporate operations. Scores of new competitive companies were created on every hand, their number entering the year 2000 being estimated as high as several thousand. The core of the competitive industry, companies with physical facilities and substantial revenues, reached 190 companies with 828 central office switches, 1,416 data switches and combined revenues of $26 billion in 1999.[55]

Although people outside the telecommunications industry worried that serial consolidations might lead to a new monolithic structure or, at least an oligarchy, insiders saw a different end result. They saw that each new merger or acquisition which produced a larger competitive entity, also produced a steady stream of seasoned industry veterans who struck out on their own to form new enterprises.
Armed with experience and inspired with new ideas for formulating creative services, they sought the psychic and financial rewards of creating and nurturing their own companies. Rather than consolidating into a massive reincarnation of the AT&T Bell System, the competitive telecommunications industry evolved into an engine of constant rebirth.

Footnotes Chapter 14: Rebirth

[1] 1997 Annual Report Of The RCN Corporation, Cover.

[2] "Mr. Holland's Next Opus," *tele.com,* December 1997.

[3] "He's Back ... Royce Holland Is Out To Show The CLEC Industry How It's Done," *America's Network,* February 1, 1998, 29.

[4] "Mr. Holland's Next Opus,"

[5] Ibid.

[6] Amendment to Allegiance Telecom's S-1 Registration, March 1, 1999, 4.

[7] "Mr. Holland's Next Opus,"

[8] Amendment to Allegiance Telecom's S-1 Registration, March 1, 1999, 20.

[9] Ibid. 67.

[10] Prospectus For Senior Notes, KMC Telecom, Morgan Stanley Dean Witter, January 26, 1998, 60.

[11] "*CLEC Report 2000,*" (Chicago, IL: New Paradigm Resources Group, Inc. 2000), vol. II, Chapter 8.

[12] Preliminary Prospectus Supplement For Level 3 Communications, Inc., Salomon Smith Barney, Goldman, Sachs, Credit Suisse First Boston, Merrill Lynch, J.P. Morgan, Morgan Stanley Dean Witter, February 18, 1999, S-33.

[13] "Kiewit Diversified to Focus On Business Information and Communications Services, Company Changes Name to Level 3 Communications," Level 3 Press Release, January 19, 1998.

[14] "Crowe's Feat," *tele.com,* September 1998.

[15] Ibid.

[16] Ibid.

[17] Offering Memorandum of Level 3 Communications Senior Notes Due 2008, Salomon Smith Barney, Goldman, Sachs, Chase Securities, J.P. Morgan, UBS Securities, April 23, 1998,13.

[18] Prospectus Supplement to Level 3 Communications Prospectus for Convertible Subordinated Notes due 2009, Goldman, Sachs, Salomon Smith Barney, Chase Securities, Credit Suisse First Boston, J.P. Morgan, Morgan Stanley Dean Witter, September 7, 1999, S-2.

[19] "No Mercy, Jim Crowe Wants To Crush His Foes In The Fiberoptic Wars," *Barron's,* June 14, 1999, 32.

[20] Ibid.

[21] "Bell Buster," *Forbes,* August 25, 1998.

[22] Ibid.

[23] Ibid. , 33.

[24] Ibid., 34.

[25] Ibid. , 33.

[26] Ibid. , 34.

[27] Ibid., 32.

[28] "Crowe Taking Telecom To Next Level," *Denver Post,* August 29, 199.

29 "Level 3 Communications Opens World Headquarters In Colorado," Level 3 Press Release, November 1, 1999.

30 "Bell Buster, "Forbes, August 25, 1998.

31 "C-Tec Surges Ahead In Phone, Cable Markets," *USA Today,* September 15, 1997.

32 "Telecom's Live Wire," *Boston Herald,* May 4, 1998.

33 Ibid.

34 "C-Tec Surges Ahead In Phone, Cable Markets,"

35 "RCN Ramps Up In Boston With Win In Hand," *Multichannel News,* August 19, 1996.

36 "RCN Continues To Blaze Competitive Trail In Local Phone, Cable Markets ... Competitive Provider Of Phone, Cable and Internet Service Testifies Before FCC, On Heels Of Legal Victory Over Rival Cablevision," RCN Press Release, December 17, 1998.

37 "Is Allen The Bogeyman?," *Cable World,* October 18, 1999, 4.

38 "RCN Investment Casts Paul Allen As Industry Turncoat... Charter Communications' Owner Jars Cable-TV With Stake In 'Overbuilder'," *Wall Street Journal,* November 11, 1999, B4.

39 Ibid.

40 Ibid.

41 Ibid.

42 "Microsoft And Winstar Announce Agreement To Deliver Broadband Applications," Winstar Press Release, December 15, 1999.

43 Authors Note: The author serves as a Director of Convergent Communications.

44 "Global Crossing Names Robert Annunziata Chief Executive Officer," Global Crossing Press Release, February 24, 1999.

45 Ibid.

46 Ibid.

47 *Forbes Magazine,* April 19, 1999.

48 "Global Crossing And Frontier Announce $11.2 Billion Merger," Global Crossing Press Release, March 17, 1999.

49 "Global Crossing And US West To Merge," Global Crossing Press Release, May 17, 1999.

50 "Two Fighters Square Off In A Showdown For U S West," *The Wall Street Journal,* June 15, 1999, B1, B4.

51 Ibid.

52 Ibid.

53 "Remarks Of Robert Annunziata - Telecom Business Keynote," Global Crossing Press Release, August 23, 1999.

54 "Robert C. Atkinson To Be Named Deputy Chief, Common Carrier Bureau; Valerie Yates To Be Named Assistant Chief Of The Bureau," *FCC Press Release, December 10, 1999.*

55 "*CLEC Report 2000,*" (Chicago, IL: New Paradigm Resources Group, Inc. 2000), Chapter 1, Table 2.

EPILOGUE

The spectacle of previously unknown companies like WorldCom, Level 3, Global Crossing and Qwest growing almost overnight into multi-billion dollar giants, and rolling-up traditional telecommunications companies that had seemed impregnable only a few years ago, illustrates how far the revolution has come.

The successes of mega-companies in creating fiber networks of global reach show that there is really nothing local about telecommunications. The bifurcation of telephone service into local and long distance has become an artificial distinction that is passing.

But to those alarmed by the fear that consolidation might ultimately result in an oligarchy of a handful of international giants, there is another observation to be made.

The genie is out of the bottle. Talented and innovative people have been energized by the opportunities unfolding in a deregulating world. They now know that with their knowledge and drive they can launch new enterprises and find significant financial backing. Technology continues to pour out new tools which redefine the possible. Opportunities are expanding, not contracting.

Today, even modestly successful competitive telecommunications ventures often produce revenue streams greater than $100 million within a few years of start-up. Risk takers have a reasonable expectation of being significantly rewarded in public stock offerings of their companies. Not only are public equity and debt markets receptive to entrepreneurial efforts, private investment capital in the billions of dollars is not-infrequently available to create new competitive companies on a scale to challenge established incumbents overnight.

The telecommunications revolution did not simply free markets.

It empowered creativity.

SOURCES

This book had its origin on a very memorable day, October 19, 1987. On that day the stock market dropped 23%, its largest plunge since the Crash of 1929.

I was in Chicago meeting with the management of a fledgling company, Chicago Fiber Optics. Emerging from a brief tour of the network facilities and of the fiber optic cables housed in abandoned freight tunnels under the Loop business district, I found a world in momentary panic. Groups of stunned people formed in front of every building with an electronic stock ticker display and stared in disbelief. Pawnshops near the Board of Trade actually experienced the normally mythological event of brokers leaving the floor of the exchange to hock their expensive watches. At public phones, there were lines of people trying unsuccessfully to contact their brokers who had stopped answering their phones.

Although the slightly surreal disorder and confusion around me were unrelated to developments in the telecommunications world, it served to underscore the moment. In a flash I could envision how momentous a change in telecommunications might be pending and what an extensive disruption of the status quo it might produce. I was seized by the conviction that the fiber-based technology I had just witnessed foreordained a revolution.

Nothing dramatic occurred immediately in either the financial or telecommunications spheres. Financial markets quickly recovered from their attack of "the vapors." The telecommunications world continued to function serenely, firmly in the grasp of the incumbent franchise holders.

One might suppose that the idea that a few skimpy competitive networks seriously threatened the massive, established local telephone industry required exotic logic. For those familiar with the history of the industry, it did not. The situation was not the equivalent of witnessing the brief, awkward flight of the Wright brothers' primitive airplane and envisioning the Boeing 747. For many of us, however, it was crystal clear that the embryonic, technology-enabled competition would not be a transient phenomenon. The patient was infected, and the competitive fever would run its course.

Would-be entrants to local telecommunications competition had before them the example of competition in the long distance market. MCI had blazed the trail by forcing open that market. It had demonstrated that a tiny start-up company with ludicrously meager assets could successfully challenge even the mighty AT&T. In addition, competitive companies now benefited from the general mood in the country that favored competition over monopoly wherever feasible. With appropriate technology to enable it, the attempted extension of competition into the once sacrosanct local telephone markets was predictable. What was in question was: Who would do it? How would they do it? How successful would they be? When the smoke cleared, what would telecommunications in the United States look like?

This publication seeks to provide some of the answers.

After the 1987 epiphany, I continued to closely follow the development of the competitive local telecommunications companies—then called Alternate Local Transport Companies or ALTs. In 1989, my company, Connecticut Research, published a 64-page report titled, *"The ALTs ... An Emerging Industry."* To call the handful of tiny companies then in the business "an industry" was a bit of an exaggeration. Their collective revenues for the year barely amounted to $30 million.

In subsequent years Connecticut Research's annual overviews of the growing competitive local telecommunications industry became well established and were frequently referenced as authoritative sources both within and outside the industry. The publications contained data and descriptions of industry statistics, technology, major developments, market trends, revenue forecasts and company profiles. Profiles were included for every company, public or private, known to be active in competitive local telecommunications. Information was collected through personal interviews, telephone interviews and mail surveys. As a result of these activities, I became acquainted not only with the companies in the competitive industry but also with most of the major players who created and drove the growth of the industry.

The annual Connecticut Research report grew along with industry. Beginning in 1993, it was entitled the *"Local Telecommunications Report."* In 1997, the publication was acquired by the New Paradigm Resources Group of Chicago, Illinois and is now published in multiple volumes as *"The CLEC Report*™*."* Information on the latest edition can be found at www.nprg.com.

In preparing the "Tele-Revolution," I drew upon multiple sources. These included the material developed over the years for the publication of the annual reports, the extensive files of Connecticut Research including the press releases and collateral material of competitive companies, archived news, newsletter and industry press references, legal and regulatory filings, personal experience and interviews of industry participants.

Recent interviews, specifically for the purpose of compiling this book, were conducted with Michael Aldridge, Cliff Arellano, Robert Atkinson, Terrence Barnich, Scott Bonney, Tricia Breckenridge, Roger Cawley, John Evans, Rhodric Hackman, Royce Holland, Richard Kolsby, Andrew Lipman, David McCourt, Rod Resky, David Ruberg, John Shapleigh, Ron Vidal, Michael Viren and Scott Williamson, among many others. Interviewees were not given the opportunity to review the draft prior to publication and therefore errors of attribution or interpretation are solely my responsibility. Conflicts of recollection were resolved based on my understanding of events and of the historical framework.

The interviews conducted during the preparation of this book were used primarily to provide context and understanding and are seldom quoted directly. Wherever possible I have attempted to provide quotations from sources published at or near the time of the event. There are two reasons for this. The first is to provide a guide to public records for those who seek independent documentation or more extensive background. The second is to counter any tendency of the recollections of participants to become shaped by the passage of years and the knowledge of subsequent events.

Quotations that appear without reference are from statements made to or witnessed by me.

I am particularly grateful for the aid given by Roger Cawley and Laura Sheridan of the Teleport Communications Group in providing material from the files of TCG and for arranging requested interviews. I would also like to acknowledge the material provided by Ron Vidal on the early days of MFS Communications. Acknowledgment is also due to Royce Holland formerly of MFS Communications and Bob Atkinson formerly of Teleport

Communications whose openness, encouragement and cooperation over the years materially aided Connecticut Research's efforts to cover the industry.

The author thanks Terrence Barnich and Craig Clausen of New Paradigm Resources Group, Inc. for both sharing material, reading the manuscript and offering editorial comment on the original draft. Thanks also to J. Thomas Markley of JTM, Inc. for his editorial comments and helpful suggestions.

☎

INDEX